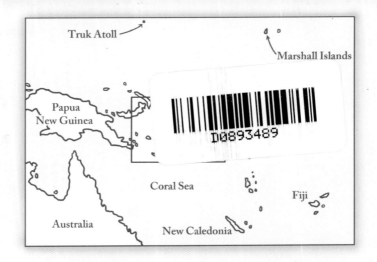

Truk Atoll

Marshall Islands

Papua
New Guinea

Coral Sea

Fiji

Australia

New Caledonia

SOUTH PACIFIC

Choiseul

Vella La Vella

Barakoma

Kolombangara

Munda

Santa Isabel

The Slot

Rendova

New Georgia

Tulagi

Guadalcanal

Henderson
Airfield

Espiritu Santo

Efate, New Hebrides

100 miles

CORSAIR
DOWN!

TALES OF RESCUE AND SURVIVAL
DURING WORLD WAR II

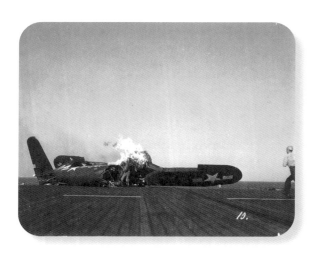

MARTIN IRONS

SCHIFFER MILITARY

4880 Lower Valley Road   Atglen, PA 19310

Designed by Jack Chappell
Cover design by Jack Chappell
Type set in Labor Union/Agency/Montserrat/Minion

ISBN: 978-0-7643-6224-8
Printed in China

Published by Schiffer Publishing, Ltd.
4880 Lower Valley Road
Atglen, PA 19310
Phone: (610) 593-1777; Fax: (610) 593-2002
E-mail: Info@schifferbooks.com
Web: www.schifferbooks.com

For our complete selection of fine books on this and related subjects, please visit our website at www.schifferbooks.com. You may also write for a free catalog.

Schiffer Publishing's titles are available at special discounts for bulk purchases for sales promotions or premiums. Special editions, including personalized covers, corporate imprints, and excerpts, can be created in large quantities for special needs. For more information, contact the publisher.

We are always looking for people to write books on new and related subjects. If you have an idea for a book, please contact us at proposals@schifferbooks.com.

Dedicated to 1Lt. Philip S. Wilmot, USMCR
VMF-451, "The Blue Devils"
Carrier Air Group 84, USS *Bunker Hill* (CV-17)

CAVU (ceiling and visibility unlimited)

CONTENTS

ACKNOWLEDGMENTS

IF IT TAKES A VILLAGE TO RAISE A CHILD, then I'd argue it takes a US Navy or Marine Corps air station to write a book about World War II Corsair pilots. A project of this scope has required the assistance of many. They have given freely of their time, knowledge, and materials.

Thank you to the surviving pilots who provided firsthand accounts of their adventures. Many also shared generously from their own memoirs and collections: 1Lt. Philip S. Wilmot, USMCR VMF-451; F/Sgt. Bryan Cox, RNZAF; 1Lt. Richard Steele, USMC VMSB-245; Lt. j.g. Ed Pappert, VBF-83; Col. Dean Caswell, USMC VMF-221; Capt. Nicholas Mainiero,* USMCR VMF-441; 1Lt. Ralph O Glendinning,* VMF-221; Col. Wm. Nowadnick,* USMC VMF-217; Ens. Bill Redmon,* VBF-85; Lt. John E. Freemann Jr. and Rob Molleston, ARM3c of VB-6; Ens. Leon Devereaux, VF-85*; and Sgt. Harry J. Leam,* USAAF.

Numerous pathfinders unhesitatingly shared their knowledge. I am indebted to Barrett Tillman; Bruce Gamble; Jenny Scott; Douglas E. Campbell, PhD; Mark Carlson; Gregory Pons; Robin Rielly; Jeff Veesenmeyer; Dana Bell; Bryan Bender; Eric Hammel; Brent Jones; Stan Wolcott; Tom Phillips; and Terry Dodge Jr.

The author and my friend, the late Henry Sakaida, dubbed me a "forensic historian." It is a title I wear with pride.

Several flight engineers and plane captains let me crawl all over their Corsairs and ask a thousand questions: Ed McGuiness, Mark Corvino and the volunteers of the Connecticut Air and Space Center, Dave Santos of the New England Air Museum, and Dave Prescott and Laura DiRado of the Warbird Factory

Without the yeomen, history would be lost to time. "Job well done" is in order to Russ Fahey; Guy Robbins, Accident-Report.com; Benjamin Kristy, aviation curator, National Museum of the Marine Corps; Chuck Meadows of the Flying Leatherneck Historical Association and Leon Simon and Linda Apodaca (formerly) of the Flying Leatherneck Aviation Museum; Don Moore; researchers at the National Naval Aviation Museum Emil Buehler Library; Annette Amerman, branch head and historian, Historic Reference Branch, Marine Corps History Division; Mary Ames Booker, curator, Battleship *North Carolina*; Pat Tillery, editor of Kilroy Was Here: Remembering the War Years website; Colby Burl; Justin Taylan of *Pacific Wrecks*; Eric S. Van Slander, Holly Reed, and the many other researchers at the National Archives at College Park, Maryland; Jack Cook; Carvon Hudson; Kirk Sinn; Joe Ditler; Jack Fellows; Regan Grau of the National Museum of the Pacific; Michael P. Hernandez; Matt Virta and Layesanna Rivera (formerly) of the National Park Service; Tim Rizzuto of the USS *Slater*; Alex Glidden from Wellington Warbird Research; Chris Fahey, Planes of Fame; and Carol Scott, who made our little village public library the equivalent of the Library of Congress during my research.

Special thanks to Martin Mickelsen, who opened his vast research files to help fill in the gaps for the chapter "Escape and Evasion." He also should be credited for determining that "Gunther," a legionnaire who appeared several times through accounts written by the Saigon Six, was Adjutant Chief Augusté Andérés.

Many navigators flew with me during various parts of this mission: Nelson Jaquay, Dave Homewood, Mark Herber, Ray Marr, Jeff Joyce, Hank Ottinger, and Morris Gillett,* CRT, USNR.

Mission support came from numerous families of the brave Corsair pilots: Richard M. Boyle and Pat Crunkleton; Sheila Lynch McCallum and the Lynch family; Richard D. Fetzer; the Lambros family; Capt. Mark Moranville USN (Ret.); the Santopadre family; John Swickle and Gloria Lints; Chris Dixon; Larry and David Enders; David Hiser; Graciela Strandtman; the family of Lt. j.g. Vernon T. Coumbe; Bill Snider Jr.; Tom Morris; Greg "Komo" Komisarek; Rob C. Mears; Susan Stith; the Beha family; Larry Rowley and the Tomlinson family; Stephanie Kaneb; Steve Sagers and Lisa Sagers Chadwick; Peggy Bottorf; Nicky Auld; Rod Dixon; Elizabeth Dowdle; Craig J. Vittitoe; Pamela W. Palmer; Linda Landreth Phelps; the Smunk family; Viola Simkunas Stanny;* the Rinabarger family; Joseph A. Syslo Jr.; Anne Styles Overbeck; the De Mott family; and Lea Carpenter. I appreciate the photo loaned by Carroll M. Carpenter and family.

Joshua DeJong of the Rigger Depot served as the parachute rigger. Cartographers Tom Houlihan and Rhy Davies helped bring complicated rescue missions to life.

The Rev. Thomas Papazoglakis served as the Air Group chaplain, travel companion, and friend.

With gratitude, I thank the quartermasters who provided bunks and rations: Leslie Trulove, Cameron and Linda LiDestri, and Lt. Col. John and Clare Neal.

And finally, my wife and family, who have offered support and love as I spent time divided between World War II and present time.

* Deceased.

FOREWORD

I FEEL VERY HONORED AND PRIVILEGED to be asked to write the foreword to this extremely interesting account of the survival and rescue of World War II pilots who flew the amazing Corsair aircraft, mainly in the Pacific region. The bent-wing bird was flown by pilots of the US Marine Corps, US Navy, and British Fleet Air Arm, and also by our Royal New Zealand Air Force, who operated 424 of them in thirteen squadrons.

I say privileged, since I found the Corsair to be a magnificent aircraft, with immense power from its 2,200 hp Pratt & Whitney R-2800 engine, easy to fly when treated with respect, and very maneuverable. It had a long range, simple systems, and a beautifully laid-out cockpit with everything where a pilot would expect it to be.

The Corsair was the first single-engined fighter to exceed 400 mph, on its maiden flight in May 1940. It had few vices and could be pulled so tightly in a turn that it just buffeted without any tendency to spin, whereas an Australian P-51D I had a turning duel with in Japan was constantly "flicking" due to its slender laminar-flow wing design. On another occasion with an Australian P-51D, we had a race in tight formation at a low altitude, and when the P-51D reached full throttle, I still had water injection available, which required breaking a wire in the throttle control.

Due to its MAUW (maximum all-up weight) of 14,000 pounds fully loaded, spinning the Corsair was prohibited, which probably wouldn't occur from a gentle stall at lighter weights, but one of my friends had to bail out from one when he hit the slipstream of another in a friendly dogfight during a very tight turn at 11,000 feet, managing to vacate his aircraft at only 1,000 feet! The P-40s we flew in training prior to the Corsair were more prone to flicking from tight maneuvers—as I found out!

Prior to turning eighteen, I was a cadet in the Air Training Corps in New Zealand for twenty-one months. I entered the RNZAF at age eighteen in May 1943 and was only nineteen when conducting operational flying training at Henderson Field, Guadalcanal, in November 1944, followed by operations over Rabaul from Green Island in No. 16 Squadron RNZAF. During two and a half years between September 1944 and March 1947, I was fortunate to fly 113 different Corsairs in New Zealand, the South Pacific, and finally Japan for a year as a pilot in No. 14 Occupational Squadron, based at Iwakuni, close to Hiroshima.

In fact, for me the Corsair was such an easy aircraft to fly that I did a few gentle aerobatics on my first flight, with less than 200 hours' pilot-in-command time in my logbook, at the tender age of only nineteen years. On only my fifth flight in a Corsair, we were sent up to 35,000 feet to check the oxygen system and superchargers, but we all kept going higher until, at 39,500 feet, I decided it prudent not to risk a stall/spin situation in that rarified atmosphere so returned to our base at Ardmore airfield near Auckland. Our transition from Tiger Moths to Corsairs, via Harvards and P-40s, took only seven months.

Unfortunately, the Corsair was not without its problems as a shipborne fighter when introduced to the US Navy in late 1941. They soon discovered that it had a tendency to bounce on landings, creating difficulty in contacting the arrester wires on the carrier decks with its tailhook. Forward visibility both on takeoff and landing was also a problem with its long nose in front of the cockpit. In the event of a stall on a carrier approach, it would viciously drop the left wing—recovery from which was a vertical dive! I personally always made the stalled three-point landings with never a problem.

With the Japanese rapidly advancing southward immediately after Pearl Harbor, the US Navy had no option but to adopt the Grumman Hellcat for its carriers, which had a top speed about 20 knots slower than the Corsair. The Corsair was also offered to the British Fleet Air Arm, which sent a small evaluation team across to the US to assess its usage on British carriers. They made many recommendations, all of which were adopted by the Vought-Sikorsky Company, which included redesigning the undercarriage oleo system, which cured that problem. To improve forward visibility both on takeoff and landing, they heightened the tailwheel assembly by about a foot and also developed a bubble canopy, allowing for the seat to be able to be raised by several inches.

To improve the wing-drop stall characteristic, they attached a small "spoiler" to the leading edge of the starboard (right) wing to make it stall earlier, virtually curing that problem. So by the time the British Fleet Air Arm and also the Royal New Zealand Air Force received their Corsairs, the problems that had plagued the US Navy were virtually all cured, and they were a delight to fly. Another technique adopted by the British Fleet Air Arm during landings was to make a turning approach, keeping the carrier deck in view throughout the approach, which we also adopted with our land-based Corsairs in New Zealand and operationally in the Solomons.

The US Marines received the newer, improved Corsair model, resulting in a very high success rate of approximately 11:1 against the previously invincible Japanese Zeros!

By the time we received our Corsairs in 1944, our P-40s had destroyed ninety-nine Japanese aircraft in the Solomons/Rabaul areas. When we converted into the Corsairs in late 1944, we retrained as dive-bomber pilots, with our main task being to prevent the Japanese from using their five airfields at Rabaul, plus close support bombing for the Australian army on Bougainville.

Prior to my first tour based on Green Island in January 1945, our No. 16 Squadron had been based on Bougainville, where one of our young sergeant pilots, "Rip" Reiper, had experienced a horrific accident in the air when, after flying into bad weather while approaching his home base, he was the only pilot of his section of four Corsairs to land safely. Flying blind in rain, pilots Ellison and Maclean collided, their explosion causing their leader, F/Lt Keith Starnes, to also crash, leaving "Rip" Reiper the only one to land safely at Torokina airstrip. He was still in the squadron when I joined on my first tour at Green Island, and I recall that he had developed what we commonly called "the tatas," causing his hands to shake!

In my own case, I can thank Corsair NZ5261 for "getting me home" on the night of January 15, 1945, my twentieth birthday, after flying into a tropical storm in darkness while returning from Rabaul after an unsuccessful attempt to rescue another of our pilots shot down over Rabaul earlier in the day. Only eight of us reached Green Island out of a flight of fifteen Corsairs.

Despite the attributes of the Corsair and the skills of her pilots, men and machines were lost during the conflict with the Japanese. Many were friends; others were pilots I knew. Some survived, and some did not. For those of us in combat, often there was no corpse to bury or time for reflection after the loss of a comrade.

From visiting World War II cemeteries postwar, it is apparent that the average age of Air Force casualties worldwide was twenty-two years of age, with many twenty-year-olds serving in our squadrons. Aged twenty-six, our CO squadron leader, Paul Green, was considered very old! Today my twenty-year-old grandson doesn't even have his driving license—whereas I learned to drive our family Model A Ford at age sixteen.

Survival and rescue relied on a variety of methods: coast watchers, Navy ships and submarines, amphibious airplanes (including our own No. 6 Squadron of PBY Catalinas), and various combinations of craft. But luck was often the foremost reason pilots survived in the battles against men, machines, and the elements.

I highly commend Martin Irons in his endeavor to preserve the events and personal stories of those fateful days, and also the history of such magnificent aircraft as the Corsair in particular. Therefore, I strongly recommend his commendable efforts to all readers.

Bryan Cox
Warrant officer, RNZAF, NZ437270, 1943–1946
Tauranga, New Zealand, 2016

INTRODUCTION

WHAT GOES UP,
MUST COME DOWN.

NEWTON'S THIRD LAW OF MOTION

DANGER ACCOMPANIED EVERY FLIGHT.
EVERY PILOT HAD CLOSE CALLS.
RESCUE WAS NEVER GUARANTEED.
SURVIVAL EVEN LESS SO.

By the time the first experimental Corsair took to the air in 1940, Messerschmitt Bf 109s and Mitsubishi Zeroes dominated the storm clouds in Europe and the Pacific. The US Navy sought a fast fighter that would still be able to fly slow enough to land on its carriers. The transition from short-ranged biplanes to a fighter that could match the potential of the planned Essex-class carriers was essential.

With a 13-foot, 4-inch, three-blade prop bolted to the strongest Pratt & Whitney engine available, Vought's Corsair was the first single-engine plane to crack 400 mph in level flight. Its top speed was 70 miles an hour faster than the Wildcats already in service! The Navy saw the potential and initially ordered nearly six hundred Corsairs. Additional contracts were awarded to Vought. As the need for more Corsairs exceeded the capabilities of Vought to manufacture them, the Navy awarded contracts to Goodyear to build the FG-1 and to the Brewster Aeronautical Corp. for the F3A versions. The former was every bit as successful as its Vought twin. The latter had a tarnished reputation for quality and was never used in combat by American air forces.

Development

Though its inverted gull-wing profile did not change dramatically during the war, the Corsair was continually improved. The F4U-1s that entered combat in 1943 were distinguishable from later variants by their "birdcage" canopies. The F4U-1A model made its combat debut in the second half of 1943. It featured a larger canopy with just two horizontal braces. The seat was raised for greater vantage. Engines with emergency water injection were developed to provide a temporary power boost. A new propeller blade design provided greater acceleration and rate of climb over the dash-ones.

The development of the F4U-1D marked the next major evolution. Up top, it wore a fully blown canopy with no metal bracing to obstruct the view. Underneath it left the factory with pylons for fuel tanks and bombs. Wing-mounted rails were added for 5-inch, high-velocity aerial rockets (HVAR). Internally, an upgraded R-2800 Double Wasp engine provided up to 2,200 horsepower.

Small batches of the F4U-2 were produced. Distinguished by the radar dome mounted on the right wing, this birdcage night fighter saw limited service during the war. Another limited production run was of the F4U-1C. Four 20 mm cannons increased the lethality of the plane in ground support roles. But in aerial combat, the weapons were unreliable. Many a pilot pulled the trigger only to have just three, two, one, or none of the Hispano-Suiza autocannons fire. They made their debut in the spring of 1945 in the air over Okinawa with land- and carrier-based squadrons.

The ultimate variant of the Corsair in World War II was the F4U-4. A more powerful Pratt & Whitney R-2800 engine was mounted. It further increased top speed and rate of climb. A four-blade Hamilton prop was featured, while a ventral air intake was incorporated into the nacelle. Several subtypes were built from this version.

With its unique gull-wing profile and the sound created by air passing through the inlets in the wing anhedral, the Corsair had a unique persona among fighters. An enthusiastic wartime press suggested that the Japanese gave her the moniker "Whistling Death."

Among the golden-wing graduates of Pensacola and Corpus Christi flight training, it had another nickname: "the Ensign Eliminator." The Corsair was temperamental. It stalled easily and was nearly impossible to recover from a spin. With its cockpit set behind the wings, its blind spots were huge, especially when landing on carriers. The original framed "birdcage" canopy, common to planes of that period, did little to aid the pilot's vision. The Vought had no guidance system other than the navigational chart each pilot brought aboard. There was no ejection seat, nor was it flown by wire. She was built in the methods of her time: steel, aluminum skin, cloth and dope, hydraulics and cables, analog gauges.

Operational losses for the Navy and Marine Corsairs totaled 922 Voughts, Goodyears, and Brewsters.[1] "That damn plane was more of a threat to us pilots than the Japanese," groused one old Marine aviator long after the war. "You could make a mistake in a Hellcat, spin it, whatever; you'd survive. You make a mistake in a Corsair, you're dead."[2]

But Corsairs were rugged and lethal in combat: they were built to withstand the punishment of carrier landings. That strength allowed Corsairs to shoulder a ton of bombs with ease. They could give a licking and take one too. The six .50-caliber Browning machine guns, three to a wing, made the bent-wing bird deadly at close range. Pilots benefited from the power of the Pratt & Whitney R-2800 Double Wasp engine through its speed, rate of climb, and ability to dive away from danger. The plane was exceptionally maneuverable for what was considered to be a large fighter plane. The cockpit was roomy. Its layout was straight forward. Most importantly, Corsairs carried armor and self-sealing fuel tanks, unlike their Japanese adversaries. Many a Marine and Navy pilot survived due to these plane features.

Adm. William Halsey praised radar as the second-most-important weapon of World War II. Serving with the fast carriers in 1945, radar-picket destroyers with fighter-director teams provided pilots with advanced warning of incoming bogies, thus providing pilots the upper hand in air-to-air combat. By the end of the war, American Corsair pilots claimed 2,140 kills against the Japanese, with just 189 aerial-combat losses, an incredible 11:1 kill ratio, and almost twice the kill ratio of the Wildcats they replaced.

First Lieutenant Jimmy Johnson VMF-112 points to the damage Zeroes inflicted on June 7, 1943. Despite losing half his rudder, the hydraulics, and a tire, he landed safely. Bureau Number 02245 was just the eighty-seventh Corsair accepted by the Navy.

As the war progressed, especially after the conquering of Okinawa in June 1945, Corsair pilots saw few Japanese planes. But losses due to antiaircraft fire were a constant threat, from the first combat flights in 1943 until the final days over the Japanese home islands two and a half years later. The waters surrounding both Rabaul and Kikai Jima (a small island north of Okinawa) became Corsair graveyards as the enemy gunners had almost daily opportunities to refine their skills. All totaled, 349 US Corsairs were lost to enemy antiaircraft fire.[3]

THE STONE THE BUILDERS REJECTED HAS BECOME THE CORNERSTONE.

MATTHEW 21:42

Deployment

At the time of the attack at Pearl Harbor, the Navy and Marines had more trainers and transport planes than combat aircraft. Marine aviation comprised just thirteen squadrons, only one of which was a frontline fighter squadron. They entered the war saddled with Brewster Buffalos. They transitioned to the tough Grumman Iron Works F4F Wildcat. Though the barrel-chested fighter could not dogfight the highly maneuverable Mitsubishi A6M Zero, they proved their mettle at Guadalcanal. Capt. Joe Foss racked up twenty-six kills while flying Wildcats to become the top Marine ace.

The US Navy decided in 1942 not to assign Corsairs to its carriers, due to a combination of poor landing characteristics and carrier-supply logistic issues. Instead, Vought's best was sent to Marine squadrons fighting in the Solomon Islands in early 1943. However, one Navy squadron, VF-17, did retain its Corsairs as a land-based squadron. Tailhooks were unbolted and tossed aside.

The Marines turned the F4U into legend. America was hungry for victory, and the silhouette of the Corsair was instantly recognizable in print and newsreel. With exceptional speed, maneuverability, and range compared to the Wildcat, the Corsair wrestled the advantage from the Zero. Marine Fighting Squadron 124 (VMF-124) led the charge during the spring of 1943. Second Lieutenant Ken Walsh blazed into glory as he racked up twenty kills. Other aces followed as more Marine Corsair squadrons entered combat: Archie Donahue, Trigger Long, Jim Swett, Gus Thomas, Don Aldrich, and the missionary's son, 2Lt. Bob Hanson, were but a few. The Navy's VF-17 had no fewer than fifteen aces.

But no Corsair ace was better known than Maj. Gregory "Pappy" Boyington of VMF-214, "the Black Sheep Squadron." The former "Flying Tiger" commanded a re-formed squadron that was followed daily in the American press as it battled Japanese planes over the Solomon Islands and Rabaul. His reputation as a fighting marine grew with each enemy kill. Boyington's disappearance near Rabaul after tying Foss's record furthered the legend. It was cemented when the most famous Corsair pilot of World War II emerged as a freed prisoner of war in Japan twenty months later.

A pair of planes were associated with Boyington: number 86, "Lucybelle," which was used in publicity photos showing the ace and the Rising Sun kill flags temporarily affixed to the fuselage. Newsreel cameras caught Pappy flying no. 883 during one of his final attempts to break Eddie Rickenbacker's and Joe Foss's all-time American kill record. But Bureau Number (BuNo) 17883 could be found in the logbooks of many other pilots during the same period. Pilots did not have their own planes, with the exception of VF-17. Early in the war, the highly complex Corsairs were often downtimed due to repairs. Frequently up to a third of Corsairs had to turn back from missions due to mechanical difficulties. The reality was that the Marine pilots flew what was available. The same situation would later hold true when Corsairs were finally deployed on carriers: pilots ran to a Corsair at a specific spot on the deck. The air group commander might have been the only pilot with his own personal Corsair.

The Marine squadrons typically flew three six-week combat tours, with breaks in between to rest and recuperate, absorb new pilots, and retrain for the next tour. When a tour was finished, the squadron left the theater, but their planes stayed with the service squadron for reissue to other Marine squadrons.

As the Japanese defensive perimeter began to collapse, Marine Corsair squadrons moved forward: the Marshall Islands, the Ellice Islands, Peleliu, and the Philippines. There was little chance of becoming an ace, but the duty was no less dangerous.

Corsairs were exported to two Allied countries. The Royal Navy purchased nearly two thousand. All three manufacturers were represented in their batches of -1, -1A, and -1D versions. Because Corsairs were stowed on carriers with their wings folded up, the Fleet Aviation Arm's carrier-borne Corsairs had wings 8 inches shorter than their American cousins due to lower hangar height. The British distinguished their variants as Mk. I–IV.

The Royal New Zealand Air Force flew 364 Vought Corsairs during the war. The planes were virtually identical to the American models -1, -1A, and -1D. Unlike the British Fleet Air Arm, the Kiwi squadrons were land based. Thirteen RNZAF Corsair squadrons saw combat during 1944–45, primarily in areas that had become backwaters: Guadalcanal, Bougainville, Green, and Emirau Islands, as well as Jacquinot Bay, New Britain.

Carrier Duty

Nearly a year after they entered combat in the Solomons, Corsairs finally flew from American flattops when VF(N)-101 went to sea for six months during the first half of 1944 with their F4U-2 night fighters. Their British cousins of the Royal Navy's Fleet Air Arm began carrier operations during the summer of 1944 in the Atlantic. By then, design changes had worked out the problems necessary to make the Corsair a suitable carrier plane.

With the advent of organized kamikaze attacks in October 1944, the American Fast Carrier Task Force needed more and faster interceptors than the Grumman F6F Hellcat. Marine Fighting Squadrons 124 and 213 were hurriedly deployed onto the USS *Essex* at the end of that year.

The first squadrons of Marine Corsair pilots in 1943 fought over the chain of islands that stretched from Espiritu Santo to Rabaul. Navigation was simple for the pilots flying up and down "the Slot." Airborne on carriers in 1945, the battlefield was large, open stretches of the unforgiving Pacific as the attacks moved toward the Japanese home islands.

The Marines' debut in January 1945 with the Fast Carrier Task Force 38/58 was not auspicious. They were tasked with flying mostly combat air patrols (CAPs). A combination of poor weather, inexperience with navigation and carrier operations, and a lack of opportunity to engage enemy aircraft led to many losses with little to show initially for their deployment.

With the high tempo of carrier operations in 1945, replacement Corsairs were available from escort carriers (CVE) that steamed with the replenishment oilers. In exchange, flyable duds (planes needing major servicing or repair) were sent to the CVEs. Heavily damaged Corsairs were often stripped and jettisoned over the side. They were expendable. Replacement pilots were also carried by the CVEs. Expendable they were not.

When the fast carriers headed to Tokyo during February, ten Navy and Marine Corsair squadrons were found in the hangars of Task Force 58. To make space for the Corsairs, fewer

Avengers and Helldivers were carried. In their place, Marine and Navy Corsairs capably filled the void as fighter-bombers. The invasions of Iwo Jima and Okinawa followed. The British Pacific Fleet, Task Force 37/57, arrived on station with their clipped-wing Mark IV Corsairs.

The pilots flew various CAPs, ground support missions for the soldiers and marines fighting on the island, fighter sweeps against enemy airfields, and as escorts on strike missions. Marine Corsair squadrons based on Okinawa added to the punch.

Nosed over, Corsairs served admirably as dive-bombers. In a glide, it served as a bomber or a platform for rockets. Cmdr. H. L. Miller, USN, commander Air Group Six, offered praise of its capabilities: "The finest airplane in the Carrier Navy, the F4U-4, has performed beyond any pilot's expectations." He went on to say, "It is a beautiful dive-bomber and tops as a fighter."[4]

Starting on April 6, 1945, Operation Kikusui was started against the Fifth Fleet and the British Pacific Fleet in the waters surrounding Okinawa. The Japanese launched ten massed attacks. In all, nearly two thousand kamikaze missions were initiated. The Fast Carrier Task Force, which previously had been known for its stealth and speed, was tethered to operations supporting the invasion of Okinawa. Corsairs were used as kamikaze hunters to great effect in the role that the Navy envisioned when VMF-124 and -213 came aboard the *Essex* earlier in the year.

After Okinawa was declared secure in June, the Marine fighting squadrons were released from their service with the fleet carriers, replaced by Navy Corsairs. Other VMF and RNZAF squadrons were stationed in the North Solomons, in the Philippines, and on remote island bases tasked with crippling and suppressing Japanese forces. By 1945, they rarely encountered Japanese planes.

Four Marine Corsair squadrons flew briefly from escort carriers (CVE). VMF-511, the first, saw action in May 1945. The jeep carriers and their Corsair squadrons entered combat independently, participating in Okinawan operations, the invasion of Borneo, or attacks against Rota and Pagan Islands in the Marianas. They, too, had few opportunities to mix it up with enemy planes.

The Fast Carrier Task Force and the British Pacific Fleet moved their operations from Okinawa to the Japanese home islands for the duration of the war in July 1945. A dozen bent-wing bird pilots became prisoners of war, though another pilot was fortunate enough to be recovered from northern Honshu in a daring rescue mission.

At the conclusion of the war, Navy Corsairs were part of the air force used to scour the Japanese home islands for prisoner-of-war camps. Pilots dropped what they could as they buzzed the camps. Morale soared when "PAPPY BOYINGTON HERE" was spotted on the roof of a POW barracks near Tokyo.

Rescue

Rescuing pilots was given the highest priority by the Navy and Marines. Though replacement pilots were available, squadron commanders wanted to keep their teams together both for tactical and morale purposes.

After Corsairs went to war in the South Pacific in 1943, local assets were used to recover pilots: Grumman J2F Ducks and the "crash boat" were utilized for accidents close to base. There were no dedicated rescue assets for open-sea rescues, though Consolidated PBY Catalinas, commonly referred to as "dumbos," often trailed the fighter sweeps and the bomber strikes as the hunt moved north to Rabaul. Coast watchers aided pilots who came ashore or parachuted into enemy-held islands. With the help of friendly natives and clandestine radios, the silent watch of the Solomons saved hundreds of allied aviators and sailors.

Serving with the Fast Carrier Task Force, little Vought Kingfishers, usually tasked with gun-spotting or antisubmarine patrols from cruisers and battleships, occasionally were able to retrieve downed pilots. These seaplanes were not well suited for open-water rescues.

Destroyers served "plane guard" duty with the carriers for airmen whose plane never caught air when taking off or had missed the cut to land and ditched in the drink. Destroyers on picket duty ahead of the carriers often became de facto ditching points. The destroyers might spend hours combing the seas back and forth for pilots, even for those with a low chance of survival. Lt. Armistead Dennett USN of the USS *Haynsworth* (DD-700) noted that "Only about 50 percent of those that went in the water were we able to actually recover."[5]

As the war progressed, "lifeguard" submarines were pre-positioned on days of carrier attacks against enemy territory. By the invasion of Okinawa, dedicated air-sea rescue squadrons with specially equipped Martin Mariner PBMs stood by for the dumbo calls.

Rescue occurring postditching wasn't limited to tin cans and subs. Pilots didn't hesitate to land on the seas near any manner of Allied vessel. Rescuers ranged from yard tugs to Navy blimps.

Pilots

Training taught the pilots to survive. The lessons learned were incorporated into the training syllabus both in the classroom and up in the air. Grampaw Pettibone, an ancient cartoon aviator, gave examples of young hotshots who bucked the flying rules and didn't live to tell about it. *Naval Aviation News Magazine* gave further examples of flights gone wrong. Navy Bureau of Aviation (BuAer) books, manuals, and comics filled with lessons of safety and survival could be found in squadron offices and classrooms. Survival-training films were shown in the classrooms. Swimming and vigorous physical training were part of the ground syllabus. Canopies were always locked back in the event of a disaster when taking off and landing from the carriers. Trips down the "Dilbert Dunker," an SNJ cockpit on rails, into a pool prepared them for the shock of hitting the water.

Survival training continued as squadrons prepared for deployment. When Air Group 4 pilots attacked targets in the South China Sea during January 1945, they carried Chinese money, silk maps, and chits written in many languages asking for assistance evading capture. After 2Lt. Joseph O. Lynch returned to Hawaii after a harrowing escape with the French Foreign Legion in Indochina, he was immediately pressed into service delivering survival lectures for squadrons headed to combat.

Though pilots trained how to escape from the cockpit, pull the ripcord, and land on the ground or in the water, most pilots preferred to ditch their wounded Corsairs on the seas than take to the silk. The inverted gull wing lent itself to excellent landing characteristics. But the nose-heavy fighter had no floor beneath the pilot. Buoyancy was poor. Corsairs sank in as little as thirty seconds. For a pilot struggling to unplug himself and escape the sinking plane, frequently there was not enough time to retrieve the raft pack before the planes descended to the ocean floor.

The things they carried were meant to save them: a Goodyear rubber raft, "Mae West" life vest, and emergency supplies. Their flight suits were further burdened with canteens, pistols, extra rounds, knives, whistles, flashlights, and other gear. Lucky items or mementos were stashed in their pockets. One young Marine pilot kept his wife's Chanel No. 5–infused garter wrapped around his flight helmet headset. He cheated death on numerous occasions.

Enough. Let's climb up on the wing, insert a toe into the footholds, grasp the cockpit edge with our hands, swing our legs inside, strap in, push the throttle forward, and go flying.

CHAPTER 1

TRAINING FOR THE FIGHT!

A NAVY FLYER'S CREED

I am a United States Navy flyer.
My countrymen built the best airplane in the world and entrusted it to me. They trained me to fly it. I will use it to the absolute limit of my power.
With my fellow pilots, air crews, and deck crews, my plane and I will do anything necessary to carry out our tremendous responsibilities. I will always remember we are part of an unbeatable combat team—the United States Navy.
When the going is fast and rough, I will not falter. I will be uncompromising in every blow I strike. I will be humble in victory. I am a United States Navy flyer. I have dedicated myself to my country, with its many millions of all races, colors, and creeds. They and their way of life are worthy of my greatest protective effort.
I ask the help of God in making that effort great enough.

It Became Par for the Course

During a test of the first Corsair, the XF4U-1, test pilot Boone Guyton was low on fuel in the skies over eastern Connecticut when a summer storm came in behind him on July 11, 1940. The ceiling closed on him, the sky darkened, the low-fuel light lit up on the dash. Guyton searched for a place to put the handbuilt plane down. Spotting a golf course, the former Navy carrier pilot brought the Corsair down to land as the rain poured.

There was no landing-signal officer to guide his approach, or the firmness of a spruce deck. No arrestor wires lay in place to snag the tail. The pastoral setting turned out to be a hot and fast runway. The brakes on the first Corsair did not slow the bird down on the slickened green. The big bird slid out of control until the trees that lined the fairway acted as a barrier. The XF finally came to a halt, but not before the wooded gauntlet took its toll. "Half covered with broken branches, its wheels sticking straight up, stiff and gaunt like a dead bird, lay XF4U-1 Serial 2443. One wing was missing, the stub of the center section showing an ugly gap where it once was attached," wrote Guyton.[1] The force of the sudden stoppage was mostly absorbed by the tail empennage and wing. Over the course of World War II, pilots discovered that the Vought could and would shed its wings and tail during crash landings.

The XF4U-1 became a phoenix. The critical structures (center wing section, landing gear, engine accessory section, and the massive propeller) had survived the crash mostly intact. Vought rebuilt it and had it airborne within three months. Deliveries to the Navy of the F4U-1 began in the fall of 1942.

Left: XF4U-1
Right: Bureau Number 02601. *Courtesy of Dana Bell*

Topless

Young pilots, on average twenty-one years old, had to be taught to fly the most powerful naval plane in the world in short order. They called the bent-wing bird "the ensign eliminator," but it was Marine second lieutenants who suffered the most during the plane's early years.

The area behind the pilot, the turtle deck, was an aluminum structure. Without a steel roll bar, when the hognoses flipped over, the surviving lieutenants learned that the birdcage canopies would collapse.

Second Lieutenant Paul K. McKinney of VMF-321 discovered this fact for himself the hard way. With just a few F4U flights signed in his logbook, he took to the skies on June 11, 1943. The flight was uneventful but the landing was not. McKinney applied both brakes with sufficient force to stop the F4U and tilt it up on its nose before it fell over onto its back. The birdcage and turtle deck were pushed into the cockpit and fuselage as the tail gave way. Amazingly, McKinney escaped serious injury. Old 02601 was righted and towed back to the barn, another major overhaul to be completed to a plane flown by a fighter rookie.

McKinney eventually made it into combat with VMF-115. He was shot down flying 49820 off the coast of New Ireland on September 29, 1944. A VP-52 PBY-5 from Green Island affected the rescue while his -115 buddies above provided fighter cover. He flew with the squadron through January 1945.

Streaking Comet

Flat-Hatting Sense, Training Division, Bureau of Aeronautics, US Navy

They Had Been Warned

No flat-hatting. But with a powerful fighter under their control, pilots enjoyed showing off their skills to themselves, their buddies, or a pretty girl.

Ray Swalley of VMF-451 took an opportunity to try to impress his gal ahead of their date. Breaking away from his flight, he leveled off and came in low for a mile toward her parents' lakeside home. "My girlfriend ran out onto the dock to wave at me. I thought, I'll go down in front of her. So I kicked it over and down I went, right in front of the dock, and back up over the trees." He continued on to land at a nearby airport. When he called her from the field, asking that she come pick him up, she refused. "I spent all morning getting my hair fixed and getting ready for us to go out tonight. I ran out to the dock to wave at you. You came by and made a wave and washed me off the dock and into the lake!" She continued, "Not only that, but you capsized my parents out on the lake in a canoe with the wake!"[2]

Sometimes Punishment Came by Other Means

A pilot flying recklessly faced being placed in hack if caught. If they were lucky, they brought their bent-wing bird back in one piece. Bill Reynolds of VMF-124 recalled the time that 1Lt. Roy Wallace Huston threw caution to the wind: "Hots Huston flew through a power line. His flight was flat-hatting [*sic*] down the east slopes of the San Gabriel Mountains. Tore a big gash in the wing, and the wing tank gasoline streamed out. There was a comet of burning 130 octane chasing his plane until the tank was empty. Controls were okay and he made normal approach and landing back at the base. It caused a big power outage in San Bernardino County."[3]

Swalley survived his girlfriend's rejection and the kamikaze attack against the USS Bunker Hill. *He is one of the last two surviving pilots of the "Blue Devils" squadron. Huston deployed with VMF-124, one of the first two Marine Corsair squadrons to fly from Navy carriers. During 1945, he participated in attacks against Formosa, Indochina, Hong Kong, Tokyo, and Iwo Jima. Huston earned the DFC for flying combat missions north of the 38th Parallel during the Korean War. He passed away in 2006.*

Props into Plowshares

With a bent prop and the tail empennage torn away, this Corsair is done. *Courtesy of Thomas C. Crouson*

FORCED LANDINGS: "Pilots should remember that ground which appears smooth and level from the air frequently turns out to be rough, crossed with ditches, soft, or full of obstructions when the actual landing is made." — Corsair Pilot's Handbook of Flight Operating Instructions

The big bird won praise from the pilots who flew it in combat, but for the squadrons still in training, it could be a handful. As the pilots gained hours in the bent-wing bird, their confidence rose, but at the end of the day it was still a machine, and machines sometimes break unexpectedly.

Returning from a gunnery practice mission, VMF-323's 2Lt. Del Davis was in the landing pattern awaiting his moment to land at MCAS El Centro. But as he descended to less than 500 feet, the Pratt & Whitney quit. Too low to bail and with just a few seconds to find a landing spot, Davis turned his steed toward a farm as he tightened his flight harness and switched off the battery, generator, ignition, and fuel selectors. The 4-ton fighter slammed into the furrowed earth, splitting into two just behind the cockpit. Davis suffered a cut over his eyes when his forehead struck the gunsight. The "Death Rattler" joined the fraternity of saved *Corsair* pilots who wore the common "forehead badge of courage."

Davis deployed with VMF-323 to Okinawa in April 1945. He shared a Betty kill with two other pilots and also claimed a shared Zeke kill.

Dueling Birds of Prey

During squadron training, the danger of collision between the bent-wing birds was ever present. The young fliers of VMF-312, "Day's Knights," practiced section and division flying in the skies over their nest, Cherry Point, North Carolina. The division flew in the familiar "finger-four formation," a combination of two two-plane sections flying in a formation that were spaced like the fingertips of the right hand's fingers. Each section/element had a leader, and each leader had a wingman. The first element leader, flying in the middle-finger position, was also the division leader.

During a familiarization flight on October 5, 1943, 2Lt. Buell T. Reynolds jousted with a buzzard. The pilot won the duel, but both birds lost. As the canopy shattered, the young pilot was blinded. Reynolds extricated himself from his dash-one, dived below the tail, and pulled his chute's handle. Both the metal and feathered birds of prey fell to the earth. Despite his eye injuries, Reynolds eventually returned to duty with a new squadron, VMF-514.[4]

THEY ALWAYS THINK THEY'RE HOT UNTIL THEY START CLIPPING THE PALMETTOS!

Warning not to drink and fly

His Own Worst Enemy

The pilots were warned in a comic brochure produced by the Navy Bureau of Aeronautics that "It should not be necessary to remind anyone that flying is a poor chaser for alcohol. Alcohol and gasoline have never mixed, and never will."[5]

The young studs. Marine officer's uniforms, wings of gold upon their chest, wallets flush with cash. Flying went hand in hand during training with carousing in their downtime. Alcohol was not a stranger to the majority of pilots. All had known friends who had died, all were serving under the stresses of flying a demanding plane, and all were young. It should not have been a surprise to -114's flight officer that pilots returning from liberty Sunday night would report to the Ewa flight line hung over on a Monday morning. Faced with an early-morning high-altitude gunnery flight, a young lieutenant requested that he be taken off the mission roster. The combination of sleep deprivation and recent intoxication did not enhance 1Lt. Robert G. Smith's aviation skills. Nonetheless, he was told to grab his gear and get to his mount.[6]

A common treatment for a hangover was deep breaths from the ship's oxygen. On another day, he might have survived. On February 27, 1944, his number was up. "Lt. Smith was the fifth and last plane in a tail chase led by Capt. Jack E. Conger, USMCR. After completing an Immelman, his plane went into a spin. After attempting vainly to recover, he went into a steep dive from which he never pulled out. All routine reports and an inventory of his personal effects were accomplished."[7] The former All American basketball star Rags Smith was no more.

Liquor Is Quicker

Capt. Lou Smunk was no rookie. He was part of the first team of Marine pilots that introduced the bent-wing bird to the Japanese. The Guadalcanal vet had taken to the air for the VMF-212 and -124 when the Corsair was new to the battle. A year later he was flying from the Marine base at Mojave. Assigned a familiarization flight on April 11, 1944, Smunk took to the air after midnight. Playing on the gridiron for Fordham, he had taken many hard hits as a running back. None of those compared to the hit he took on that flight.

As his bird became airborne, the Pratt & Whitney began to cough and lose power as one of the magnetos failed. The twenty-four-year-old airedale was faced with ditching his plane in the desert on a particularly dark night. He kept the wheels up, lowered the flaps, tightened his harness, and locked the canopy open. The dash-one slammed onto the baked desert soil. A railroad bed acted as the barrier before the Corsair came to rest on the tracks.

The Springfield, Massachusetts, native sat stunned in the Vought corpse. Moments later, a rescuer arrived on the scene. Walking the line that evening, a hobo heard the unholy sound of a metal bird colliding with the earth. Mounting the Corsair, the bum helped extricate the marine from his steed. Smunk, who had been scared to death, collapsed against the wrinkled skin of the old bird. Turning to his rescuer in the dark, the pilot said, "I sure could use a drink." The vagabond was of similar mind: "That scared me too. Let's both have a drink."[8] He produced a bottle of wine for them to share. By the time the air-base's search-and-rescue team arrived on scene, the anesthesia was taking effect as the drifter's empty bottle lay at the pilot's side.

Smunk earned two Distinguished Flying Crosses, one for his efforts in World War II and another for action in Korea. In August 1944, as a major with VMF-124, he was rescued from the Pacific when, during a carrier qualification landing aboard the USS Makassar Strait *(CVE-91), the tailwheel assembly broke off, causing the arresting hook to break free. Smunk's Brewster Corsair F3A 19601 bounced over the barriers before crashing into the ocean. The plane guard destroyer plucked him from the seas. Capt. Smunk retired as Lt. Col. Smunk in 1961. He passed away in 1990.*

Lost off Hawaii

VF-12, 1943

The "ensign eliminator" moniker came about after the Navy's first Corsair squadron, VF-12, got its birds in October 1942. Stationed at NAS San Diego, they suffered through slow delivery of their planes and the usual teething problems of the early birds. Just weeks after receiving their Corsairs, Lt. Walter Burkhart Bayless, USN, was forced to crash-land 02167, just the fifteenth dash-one built. With a thousand hours of flying time in his logbook, the Annapolis man put his bird down on a mesa near La Jolla. After tearing through wire fencing and colliding with fence posts, Bayless was able to stop his bird just short of a 300-foot cliff. Both man and machine would eventually return to the air on another day.

Attrition was high for the Fighting Twelve, with fourteen pilots lost through mid-1943. From San Diego, the squadron moved to Pearl Harbor in the spring as preparation for eventual carrier-based missions aboard the USS *Saratoga*.

On the fourth of May, Lt. Cmdr. Bayless led a predawn flight of four birdcages from Maui. The division was last seen entering a storm front. They never returned. Subsequent searches for the lost division found just oil slicks and flotsam riding the waves. Whether the birds were lost to structural failure in the heavy winds, a loss of control in the storm, or a midair collision was never determined. The twenty-nine-year-old Bayless and his charges were listed as "missing." Eventually the Navy recategorized them as "dead."

Fighting Squadron 12 traded their Voughts for Grumman Hellcats when they ventured east for the fight. They flew F6Fs for the rest of the war. It would be left to VF-17 to debut a Navy Corsair squadron in combat.

CHAPTER 2

COMBAT

First Loss

Second Lieutenant Ken Walsh

Walsh was part of the "Old Breed," an interwar marine who earned his wings of gold at Pensacola as a young enlisted man. By the time the VMF-124, the first Marine Corsair squadron, deployed in February 1943, Walsh had over 1,600 hours of flight time. He almost didn't make it.

After arriving in the South Pacific theater (SoPac), Walsh took BuNo 02172 up for an altitude check. It was a handbuilt bird, just the fourteenth Corsair to be accepted by the Navy when it came off the line in September 1943. It was also the first Corsair to be "ditched," a landing on the water. The high humidity over Noumea, New Caledonia, caused the magnetos to fail at 30,000 feet. The spark plugs failed with the magnetos.[1]

As every pilot who ever had to ditch a Corsair would learn, Walsh's bird was not seaworthy. It sank immediately. Walsh struggled to clear the cockpit, but his harness and parachute fouled his attempts. "I couldn't get out. I don't know how deep I was, but when I finally struggled out, my last view of the plane was like it was one big gray whale, vanishing."[2]

Struggling beneath the surface, Walsh found the toggles for the two compressed gas bottles on his life vest. His "Mae West" became buxom. An exhausted Walsh broke the surface. He inaugurated a scenario repeated up until the last hours of World War II, when Lt. j.g. John Clifford Dunn ditched in a Japanese lake and was briefly taken prisoner.

After Walsh's rescue, VMF-124 flew its F4Us into combat two weeks later. Walsh would lose two more Corsairs in combat but racked up an incredible score: twenty kills between April and August 1943. He earned the Medal of Honor. His final kill came with VMF-222 flying from Okinawa in 1945. Walsh ranks officially as the third-greatest Corsair ace of all time. Doubts over Maj. Greg Boyington's final two kills leave Walsh unofficially as the second-highest-scoring Corsair ace. He served in the Marine Corps until his retirement in 1962. Walsh passed away in 1998.

Into the Combat Grinder: VMF-222 Strikes Kahili

The First Week in Combat Could Be the Cruelest

For its inaugural combat mission on August 9, 1943, VMF-222 sent sixteen Corsairs to cover B-24 bombers attacking the Kahili Airdrome on Bougainville. The "Flying Deuces" were jumped by Zeroes. Lt. Joe Craig was forced to bail out after his engine was hit. His wingman, "Benjo" Williams, flew top cover before attracting the attention of a Navy landing craft. He led the boat to Craig before ditching himself, his fuel tank almost empty. Aboard the boat, the two air marines joined their brother mud marines who were about to come ashore on Vella Lavella. "Every Marine is a rifleman" is the Corps' motto. Williams and Craig were no different. They were issued rifles. Both pilots put the weaponry to good use as they came ashore under fire.[3] With the belief that they were more valuable to the Corps with six Browning machine guns rather than a single Garand, the pilots stayed on the beachhead and awaited rescue.

Two other "Deuces" returned to Munda, but both were flying on fumes. They lined up on the runway from opposite ends, causing an inadvertent aerial duel. "Pappy" Reid quit the game of chicken but used the last of his petrol to get out over the water before ditching. The crash boat was his savior. The other Corsair landed safely.

First Lieutenant Johnny Morris was forced to go around for a second approach when one of his flaps collapsed. At low altitude, his bird began to fall and rotate over on its back. At the last moment, Morris was able to bring the plane back to level. It hit the water with wheels down. Squadron mate John Foster described what happened next: "When Morris felt the plane going over, he unsnapped the safety belt and was catapulted completely out of the cockpit with his parachute. He hit the water, and a couple of seconds later the tail of his plane smacked beside him with a great splash—missing his head by inches."[4] Field personnel dove into the surf to save Morris.

Things didn't improve during the next four days. On the tenth, 1Lt. John C. Thornton was assigned a tired old bird. When he took to the air, it had been flying the length of the "Slot" for eight months. War weary and mechanically exhausted, the Double Wasp in Lt. John Thornton's old birdcage, BuNo 02211, began to vibrate excessively. With oil and smoke belching from the engine, Thornton bailed out. A Navy crash boat hauled him in.

Three days later, two divisions of "Deuces" were on patrol when they made contact with a large group of enemy fighters and bombers. Capt. Willie Moore was last seen in a dogfight. He never returned. Maj. Pierre Carnagey's bird was shot up. He nursed it back to base but was forced to bail out since his hydraulics were gone and the backup CO_2 system failed. Lt. Johnny Morris limped back to base. Major Anderson, the operations officer for VMF-213, described the sight in the skies:

In the late afternoon an F4U circled high over the field a couple of times and attracted the attention of those on the ground when the cockpit hood was jettisoned. The plane went into a loop. The pilot bailed out and the plane crashed into the water and exploded about 500 yards off shore. The pilot, swinging in the air as he slowly descended, presented a spectacle rarely seen. The spectators on shore were similar to the audience of a boat race, urging a barge and crash-boat on to the rescue. The barge won out.[5]

Morris was uninjured, but the "Flying Deuces" had lost eight valuable planes in just four days. All pilots were safe but one.

None by Air, Two by Sea

August 18, 1943. Flying from Munda, a division of -123 birds were vectored to intercept bogies heading toward an American naval task force. Pouring on the coals at just 1,500 feet, the "Eight Balls" arrived on station before the enemy. The greetings from the fleet and land-based batteries on Vella Lavella was not a friendly salute of thanks. As the sky filled with tracers and black smoke, 2Lt. Foster Jessup's birdcage rattled from the impact of rounds hitting home. Jessup leapt from the burning plane, pulled the D-ring handle of the parachute, and floated into the seas off the island. A 36-foot Higgins landing craft pulled the twenty-two-year-old California native aboard.

Safety was fleeting. As the LCVP got underway, explosive geysers erupted all around. Under air attack by a gaggle of Aichi D3A "Val" dive-bombers, Jessup, who was no stranger to tracking aircraft, grabbed one of the machine guns. At the end of the fight, Jessup, who had no aerial victories, was credited with two probables after his ship-based actions.[6]

Jessup returned to VMF-123. On a test hop in mid-September, his engine failed. Russell Island natives rescued the young Marine aviator.

Nowhere Is Safe

VMF-312 F4U after a Japanese howitzer round, Okinawa, April 1945. *Courtesy of the National Archives, photo 80-G-373370*

Even a year after the American invasion of Guadalcanal, "Cactus" was still a hotspot. A division of VMF-215 F4Us landed on the island on September 5, 1943, after a flight from their base at Munda:

We found our old quarters just as we left them. At approximately 1330 the Japanese and American ammunition dump close to our quarters burst into flame and started exploding. It burned and exploded into the night. In the afternoon a five inch shell, which luckily was not fused, was projected into our quarters. It tore a hole six or seven feet in diameter in the roof of one of our huts. Needless to say we were all in our dugouts by this time as the shell fragments and shells themselves were flying hot and heavy in our direction. We all agreed, however, that it was much safer at Munda![7]

Native Riches

The greatest advantage you can have in hunting is to see your quarry before it sees you.

—*"How to Survive on Land and Sea"*[8]

First Lieutenant George Sanders, USMCR. *Official USMC Photo*

It was mid-August 1943 when a section of VMF-215 birds were sent on a mission against enemy targets at Rekata Bay. Flying from the Munda field on the west coast of New Georgia, the pair crossed the Slot to the east coast of Santa Isabel Island. As they zoomed down to the deck, they spied a taxiing float Zero. After completing a first strafing attack, they came back for another turn. This time the antiaircraft gunners were ready for them. Rounds punctured the engine of 1Lt. George Sanders's bird. Very quickly the Pratt & Whitney's oil pressure dropped to zero. At low altitude, his only chance was to ditch.

The young Oklahoman reached for the cabin emergency release handles' safety pins to jettison the hood. But they were stuck fast. He pulled the birdcage canopy back and braced it with his arm hung over the side. As quickly as he ditched, so did the plane sink from under him. Sanders cleared the cockpit, but his pistol and jungle pack went down with his bird. Despite the fear of being seen, the marine inflated his Mae West. Though within sight of shore of the Japanese-held Santa Isabel Island, Sanders was more afraid of sharks than the enemy. He inflated his dinghy and used his sea anchor to keep away from Santa Isabel's coast. As the sun gave way to night, he paddled his way to the island, finally making land hours after midnight.

Sanders stayed out of sight until light broke. Spotting a fisherman in a canoe, he broke his cover and called to the "friendly native." The sounds of the sea smothered the salutation, but for Sanders it was just as well. As he approached, Sanders realized the native was not native at all, but a Japanese soldier! He hadn't been spotted, so he headed back into the fauna for cover, only to cross paths with a large crocodile that had been nesting in a sandy patch. The scaled beast fled. After dark fell, the marine used the spot to camp for the night.

After drifting off to sleep, a crunching sound startled the airedale. Suddenly awake, Sanders found himself facing the gaping jaws of the crocodile! He fled the nest with the reptile running alongside. Sanders took to the safety of a tree, the croc to sea.

It was several days before Sanders made contact with a friendly native. Until that time, he moved south daily, surviving on coconuts, green crabs, and oysters. At night he slept with his raft as cover. "It was in the morning of August 24 that I came upon my first native. I had traveled about a mile and was resting up when I heard somebody coming and saw the native. I stepped out and said, 'Me friend, me American.' I smiled as big a smile as I could. He answered me in good English, 'Yes, I know.'"[9]

Alan, the native, brought Sanders to his village, Baolo. Now in the sixth day of his adventure, the marine was treated to a feast of roasted potatoes, nuts, pineapple, and boiled pig. A coast watcher was notified by messenger that the young leatherneck was in the protection of the local village. The evacuation was about to begin.

The first leg was a 45-mile journey in a 30-foot war canoe to rendezvous with the coast watcher. Two days later, Capt. Michael Forster, the British district officer, arrived. Though the coast watcher failed to contact Guadalcanal on his captured Japanese radio transmitter, he did have his cook provide a roast pig dinner. Sanders was given new clothes and the opportunity to bathe. Two more days of evacuation by canoe followed. Along the way, the pilot was lavished with gifts, banquets, and songs sung by children during rest periods in local villages. In return, Sanders taught his serenaders "The Eyes of Texas."[10]

It was the tenth day of his adventure before they arrived at Forster's plantation. Sanders spent another week enjoying breakfast in bed, hot baths, target shooting, sunbathing, and time spent in the company of the locals while the details of his rescue were planned. Finally, on the seventeenth day of his "ordeal," a PBY landed near the plantation. The dumbo flew the young marine to Tulagi. From there he hitched a ride on a boat that brought him to Guadalcanal.

For Sanders, being reunited with his buddies was almost embarrassing. While they had been flying from the squalid conditions of the Munda airfield, Sanders reappeared like a vacationer returned home from holiday: He was rested and had gained weight. The Sooner sported a native walking stick, a collection of beautiful seashells, a war canoe paddle, and a .38 pistol recovered from the corpse of a Japanese pilot!

We Are Poor Little Black Sheep That Have Gone Astray, Baa! Baa! Baa!

The coughing engine spat oil through its cowling, fouling the windscreen. Lead rain tore holes through the bird's metal and canvas skin. The 20 mm incendiary round that had lit up the cockpit was burning its way back out of the bent-wing bird's thin metal skin. Over a hundred miles from his base, the Zeroes continued to nip at the Black Sheep. As the life blood seeped out of both the mount and its jockey, hiding in the cumulus cover would be his only chance for survival.

Storm clouds blanketed Europe during the late 1930s. The United States Civil Aeronautics Authority (CAA) created the Civilian Pilot Training Program (CPTP) in the waning days of 1938. They were late to the game. The Nazi Party had already replaced their interwar Deutscher Luftsportverband, a Hermann Göring–led front for training military pilots surreptitiously, with its paramilitary wing, the Nationalsozialistisches Fliegerkorps. With the advent of the Luftwaffe, a ready corps of pilots were available to fill its ranks, including a pilot who would become the greatest ace of all time, Erich Hartmann.

The British initially were no more prepared than the United States. In December 1939, the Plan—the British Commonwealth Air Training Plan—was launched. Since the sun never set on the empire of King George VI, greater numbers of pilots and aircrew would be needed by the Royal Air Force, Royal Navy Fleet Air Arm, Royal New Zealand Air Force, Royal Australian Air Force, and Royal Canadian Air Force. The goal was to train 50,000 aircrew annually.

The American CPTP was designed to stimulate the light aviation industry, increase interest in aviation, and create a pool of pilots that could be drawn upon by the military in the event of an emergency. At its outset, America had just 7,400 civilian and commercial pilots. The goals were more modest than its European cousins: 20,000 pilots would be trained each year, culled from the ranks of volunteer college students. Male or female, each trainee had to be a US citizen between the ages of eighteen and twenty-five with at least two years of college and no prior flight experience. As a condition requested by the military, Congress legislated that each trainee had to pass a military physical, though no requirement was set in place that graduates had to join the military's air services.

After an adolescence consumed with tales of the Red Baron, Eddie Rickenbacker, Lucky Lindbergh, and the daring barnstormers of the roaring 1920s, Rolland Rinabarger chased his dream. The lanky Oregon State Beaver—a junior studying mechanical engineering and a lettered member of the college boxing team—entered the Civilian Pilot Training Program in January 1941, just a couple of months past his twentieth birthday.

Flying from the nearby Albany airfield, Rinabarger spent much of 1941 aloft in a successive group of trainers: a lithe Rearwin Sportster, the biwing open-cockpit Waco UPF-7, and the roomy Fairchild F-24G with its powerful 145 hp Warner Super Scarab radial engine. His flight experience was enhanced with coursework in aerology, navigation, engines, airframes, and the theory of flight and flying. After fifty hours of stick time, he earned his license. More training and an additional fifty hours' flight time followed while he was enrolled in an acrobatic course at South Oregon College of Education.

Left to right: "Boo" Bourgeois, Virgil Ray, Boyington, Rinabarger, and Bill Case. *Courtesy of the National Archives, photo 80-G-54302*

Of the nearly fifty-eight thousand pilots trained by the CPTP in 1941, the majority chose to remain civilians. But after nine months behind the stick, it was time for action for Rinabarger. Along with three other CPTP pals, he headed north to Seattle and enlisted in the Navy's V-5 Aviation Cadet Program ten weeks before the Japanese came roaring into Pearl Harbor's airspace. "There was a war brewing. It was a good place to be."[11]

The United States was transformed after the first Sunday of December 1941. The CPTP became the War Training Service five days after the attack. The program remained under civilian control, but from that point on, it was devoted to training future military pilots. Female pilots were dropped from the ranks, but African Americans and other minorities stayed in the program. With the expansion of the air branches of the military, so did the WTS grow its training capacities.

By January 1942, Rinabarger had completed elimination flight training at Seattle Naval Reserve Aviation Base. From there it was on to NRAB Dallas. In February, his enlistment was terminated and he officially became an aviation cadet, with a winged gold-metal V-5 badge adorning his blouse and $125 monthly filling his wallet.

Before the next phase of training began, a decision was made. "They asked you what you would like to do, but what you wanted wasn't necessarily what you got."[12] While other pilots from Dallas went on to fly bombers or patrol planes, for Rinabarger it would be fighters. The Navy transferred him to Pensacola for primary training. There he mastered the N3N-3 biplane. Advanced training was conducted at Ocala, with time spent behind the stick of Grumman's F3F and the Brewster F2A Buffalo.

By June, Rollie had earned his instrument rating in the SNJ and the coveted "Wings of Gold," the Navy's aviation pilot badge, for his uniform. He was assigned instructor duty as the ranks of the Navy's pilot corps continued to expand with CPTP/WTS graduates. Capt. Arthur Radford, director of the Bureau of Aeronautics, commented, "Without question, the Navy is profiting greatly from the CPT Program; it saves time in planes, saves time for instructors, and prevents loss of wastage by reducing the number of students eliminated."[13]

The Navy kept Rollie as an instructor pilot for the balance of 1942. His logbook filled with hours as he took to the air in N3Ns and SNJs in the skies over Florida. He traded his US Navy khakis for Marine greens when the opportunity arose to take a US Marine commission. And so, he began his fighter pilot training in early 1943 at Jacksonville, flying the barrel-chested Grumman F4F Wildcat, the defender of Wake Island.

As the ice broke up on the Great Lakes, Rinabarger spent just enough time at NAS Chicago to become carrier qualified, landing on one of the Navy's two side-wheel carriers, *Sable* and *Wolverine*. From there, it was off to San Diego and then to the South Pacific. VMF-124 had debuted the Corsair in combat just a few months earlier. Older squadrons were swapping out their Wildcats for the hot fighter from Connecticut. Rinabarger was eager to join them.

Transit was not of the fast aeronautical variety. Instead it was a plodding 10-knot journey on a zigzag track aboard the USS *Rochambeau* (AP-63) to New Caledonia and Espiritu Santo. Packed aboard were troops, other replacement pilots, and a young Navy lieutenant junior grade from Massachusetts who was on his way to command PT-109 in the Solomons.

The *Rochambeau* finally dropped anchor at the US Navy anchorage Button—code for Espiritu Santo—by mid-May. Button and the other New Hebrides islands served as the staging area for the Allies' advance in the South Pacific. Rollie was assigned to the replacement pool of pilots. As Marine Fighting Squadron 112's front line echelon took their rest and rehabilitation leave, he was transferred to their rear echelon. The "Wolfpack" had been duking it out with the Japanese since November of the previous year as they flew from the precariously held Henderson Field on Guadalcanal. Flying the stubby Grumman for seven months before transitioning to the bent-wing bird, a group of pilots became aces during the air battles over the Slot. Capt. Archie Donahue would eventually nab nine, while 2Lt. Jefferson DeBlanc ran his total to eight. A Medal of Honor would await DeBlanc postwar for his heroics.

When the "Wolfpack" returned, Rollie was reassigned to another squadron's rear echelon. The transfers continued through the summer, but all the while he was adding hours to his logbooks during training flights, first in Wildcats and then later in Corsairs. He was a skilled pilot in need of a permanent home.

The elder pilot had been transferred from ground assignment to ground assignment since his return to the Pacific theater in January. Despite his claimed six victories with the "Flying Tigers," he struggled to be assigned to a fighter squadron. Having abruptly quit the American Volunteer Group, his reputation as a broke hothead with a drinking problem preceded him. Grace and absolution that would not have been forthcoming in a peacetime Marine Corps was awarded to him after much effort and politicking as the Corps expanded their flying ranks. He was granted his request, and a permanent squadron command landed in his lap. His four-and-a-half-month escape from purgatory would become the stuff of legends.

In late August, with a borrowed squadron number, Maj. Gregory Boyington established the first Marine fighting squadron born outside the United States. Long months of maturation were the norm for new fighter squadrons, but Boyington did not have the luxury of time. The former flight instructor collected a talented group of fliers. Many had combat experience; several already had kills notched. Others, such as Rollie, were offspring of the CPTP and former flight instructors who had more stick hours than many combat pilots. There were a few green pilots from the repo pool, but VMF-214 was born of pilot strength. The squadron nickname "Swashbucklers" was swapped out for "Black Sheep." And legends followed.

The squadron was stood up on September 7, 1943, after a week of gunnery and tactics flying. Five days later they were on the move as they took their Corsairs from Espiritu Santo to Guadalcanal. Rinabarger had been assigned to 6th Division as wingman to 1Lt. William N. Case, a combat-bloodied pilot with one kill already to his credit and seven more to come as a "Black Sheep."

With their twenty Corsairs (and a few borrowed from -123), two dozen "Black Sheep" took to the air on the fourteenth for their first combat mission. They escorted a dozen lumbering B-24s for their bombing mission against the airfield at Kahili. More fish than enemy were killed as the bombs fell wide from 22,000 feet. Light ack-ack greeted the "Black Sheep" as the few enemy fighters in the air stayed away.

The fifteenth proved to be a milk run as they escorted a photoreconnaissance mission over Choiseul Island. But "Boyington's Bastards" drew blood the next day. As the high cover escorting TBFs and SBDs targeting Ballale, they were greeted by a swarm of thirty to forty Zeroes erupting from the clouds. It became a wild melee of dogfights that spread over an area of 150 to 200 square miles, from nearly 22,000 feet all the way down to the deck. For thirty minutes the "Black Sheep" fought their battles in a sky whose palette was colored with blue Navy and Marine planes, brown Army fighters, and a mixture of black and mottled brownish-green/greenish-brown fighters of the British Empire. Golden tracers filled the air; black plumes trailed across the skies.

Rollie Rinabarger. *Courtesy of the Rinabarger family*

After losing their second section after a series of attacks against the enemy, Case and Rinabarger discovered four Zeroes taking runs on a pair of Corsairs. Diving against one of the Zeroes, Case's rounds found their mark. A trail of black smoke across the sky charted the Zero's demise.

The action wasn't over. Mistakenly, Rollie joined up on another Corsair under the impression it was his section leader, but Case was already headed home with a Hellcat. Rollie's adopted section came across a "daisy chain"—a string of planes both foreign and domestic—each on the tail of the next. Seeking to smoke the last Zero in line, he dived but the conga line dissolved before he had range enough to engage.

Exhausted and exhilarated, the sheep returned to Munda in ones and twos over a twenty-five-minute period, a sign to the ground echelon that their pilots had engaged the enemy in combat. By 1630, twenty-two of the twenty-four were on the ground and taxiing their birds to their revetments. An hour and a half later, Pappy returned after refueling on Munda. He was an "ace in the day," with five kills added to his tally. The ground attendants there noted his bird was almost dry, its ammo pans nearly empty.

It had been a good day of hunting. The final tally was eleven kills and eight probables for the reconfigured squadron. Though Rollie penned "no luck" in his logbook, the "Black Sheep" had proven themselves to be proficient warriors in their first aerial combat. The sole casualty was Captain Bob Ewing, who failed to return.

There followed a week of routine patrols and escorts that were broken up on the eighteenth. As cover during a shipping patrol over Barakoma, Case's division was at 23,000 feet when Rollie sighted a swarm of thirty Zeroes circling below them. Tally ho! After the initial overhead pass, Case—separated from his division at this point—joined some other F4Us and followed them down on another pass. Score another kill for Case, but Boyington suffered through his flight. Minutes after taking off, both his radio and Double Wasp went bad but he stayed on station. Lt. Ed Harper's Wasp quit as he was taking off for a final late patrol. He almost had to put it down in the water but was able get his bird down with a dead-stick landing.

The Solomons were at the end of a very long supply line back to America. Spare parts and spare planes trickled up to the frontline squadrons. As a result, maintenance on the complicated birds suffered in the primitive forward area, but every last flight had to be wrenched and wrung from the birds. Another Marine squadron complained about the flock:

The planes assigned to VMF-221 are definitely not suitable for combat due to excessively hard usage and poor upkeep. The majority need major overhauls. The guns have not been kept up properly. Some of the wing tanks do not draw, so that they are impossible to empty. The blowers do not function properly. Apparently the newest planes in this area are used for training in the rear areas and the oldest ones are left in the combat area.[14]

The "Black Sheep's" planes were no different. Soon after taking off on the twentieth for an escort mission to Parapatu Point on Kolombangara, Tom Emrich's R-2800 shut down. He got his bird back on the ground safely. After taking off for a strafing mission the next day, Walter Harris brought his bird back when it was apparent the gas gauge was kaput. He was followed by another "Black Sheep," future ace Don Fisher, whose landing gear wouldn't nest in their compartments.

After the attack against a 70-foot Chinese junk and a Japanese bivouac area, Chris Magee showed off his flying skills when he found that he had the same problem as Emrich and the opposite situation of Harris: "He made a figure 8 to lose altitude, dropped wheels, was undershooting, brought up wheels, dead sticked and put wheels down when thirty feet off ground by cracking CO_2 tank." Scored Lt. Frank Walton, "Nice landing."[15]

The Gremlins' Efforts Continued Unabated

On the twenty-second, a quarter of the twenty-bird flock missed the mission due to mechanical maladies. Don Fisher's and Bob McClurg's birds couldn't get off the ground. Burney Tucker's cockpit had more gas fumes than breathable air, forcing him to go on oxygen and return. Ed Olander's guns refused to fire while the oxygen failed to flow from its tank. Rollie's bird had a checklist of malfunctions: "Temperature down, motor rough, no radio receiver, generator quit out, and according to fuel gauge had used 110 gallons of gas in fifteen minutes at low power."[16] Groused the intelligence officer Walton, "Another example of the maintenance work being done on our planes here."[17] Plane trouble reports arrived on Walton's desk at a regular basis.

While the birds were returned to their plane captains for additional repairs, the fifteen who had made it aloft found themselves in encore performance of the sixteenth. Teamed with Army P-38s, P-39s, and P-40s, they escorted groups of SBDs, TBFs, and B-24s to Kahili when another large group of Zeroes rose to hunt the Consolidated bombers. The "Black Sheep" intercepted the enemy at 24,000 feet. Boyington's boys scored four times, but Denmark Groover's Vought was chewed up by twenties and seven-point-sevens. Wounded, Groover would be evacuated out of the theater. Moon Mullen discovered a souvenir 7.7 mm round in his parachute pack after investigating a left shoulder wound. Major Bailey, while protecting a P-40 pilot who had taken to the silk, was caught in the crosshairs of several enemy planes. He escaped but landed with thirty-four holes in his bird.

The twin-radial on Bob Alexander's Vought ran rough during a mission on the twenty-fourth as the "Black Sheep" tore into a swarm of Zeroes attacking Army B-24s returning from bombing Kahili on the southern coast of Bougainville. Major Bailey ordered Alexander back to base, but the wingman stayed with his division leader as protection. Soon, Alexander was the target. He turned south as his engine belched and coughed. Fearing it would quit altogether, Alexander pancaked at Vella Lavella. The runway was a work in progress, with heavy equipment and trucks as obstacles to landing. He pinballed down the side of the runway, but a ditch proved to be more dangerous than the seven-point-seven slugs aimed at him minutes earlier. The wheels dropped into the trench, the Hamilton chewed into the ground, and the bird's tail completed a 180-degree arc. Stunned but unhurt, Alexander staggered free of the aluminum corpse. A Duck brought him home a couple of days later.

Several days of escorts and patrols followed for the "Black Sheep." The gremlins tailed Harris and Mad Man Magee again on the twenty-fifth. Magee's bird had various mechanical difficulties, while Harris's brakes gave out when he landed. A ditch brought his flight to a close. Some days the planes themselves were greater threats to the pilots than the Japanese.

Twelve "Black Sheep" Corsairs taxied from their revetments midday on the twenty-sixth. Major Bailey, Moon Mullen, and Hank McCartney led their divisions as high cover for an SBD and TBF strike against AA positions at Kangu Hill near the Kahili airfield. Rollie—flying in Mullen's division—had drawn BuNo 55876. She was a new bird, a dash-one-A, with the improved canopy, fresh factory paint on her skin, and only a few hours on her airframe.

The "Black Sheep" were joined by another Corsair division from VMF-213. Navy Hellcats, Army P-39s, and New Zealand P-40s covered the other approaches. At the same time, Army B-24's—with P-38s as high cover—were to target the Japanese airfield at Kahili

The flying circus had already begun when the "Black Sheep" encountered the B-24s near the Shortland Islands, south of Bougainville. After completing their bombing run, thirty Zeroes were hot on the twin-tailed Liberators. Bailey led his birds up to angels 20 (a measure of relative altitude) for the interception. The gun chargers were turned on, the gun switches were flipped up, and the CO_2 vapor dilution system was activated to ensure that the atmosphere in the 62-gallon wing tanks was inert.

While Bailey's and McCartney's divisions scissored over the brawny bombers, Mullen's boys turned to engage the bandits. Rollie was at the end of the whip. Four left hands in four Corsairs pushed the throttles forward past the "Military Power" stop to the "War Emergency Power" setting. And then Rollie was betrayed.

Combat Was a Fickle Mistress

Favor that was awarded one moment vanished the next. The "War Emergency Power" setting, designed to give pilots extra horsepower and the opportunity to gain advantage against the enemy, failed to engage. As the last plane in the turn, Rollie was left behind as his three mates powered away. Advantage was now disadvantage. Lagging behind, his lone Corsair filled the sights of a diving Mitsubishi.

The Zero's presence was punctuated by the rounds that punctured Rollie's bird. A hailstorm of 20 mm cannon and 7.7 mm machine gun fire raked his bird from tail to cowl, tearing at his right stabilizer and entering his left wing tank. Piercing the turtle deck behind his seat, a round entered the cockpit and struck the Ka-Bar knife sitting against Rollie's left hip. The knife shielded the full impact of the round, but the deflection caused the projectile to shatter and enter his leg like buckshot. At that moment, Rollie and BuNo 55876 became wounded prey.

Vought's birds were tough, especially compared to their Japanese counterparts. The original design had incorporated the newly developed self-sealing fuel tanks. Armor plate protected its pilots. Though its wingspan was just 2 feet wider than the Zero, the Corsair weighed nearly twice as much when fully loaded. The pugilist's plane could take a beating.

The hawks came back for another pass at Rollie as his own division maneuvered to counter the attack. "A second 20 mm shell exploded in his left wing; a third struck the right side of his cowl, breaking his oil line and putting one cylinder out of commission; another entered his fuselage and exploded back of his cockpit, starting a fire; still another hit his left wing, bursting his tire and destroying his flap control on that side, while machine gun bullets raked him fore and aft."[18]

The explosive round that penetrated the cockpit blazed bright before eventually burning its way back out the thin aluminum skin. Engine blood seeped through the cowl and coated the windscreen. The starboard horizontal stabilizer was nearly shot off. Many of the instruments were shattered including the air speed indicator. Rollie pushed the stick forward to dive clear of the attack, a trail of smoke emanating from the nose marking his path. He was still 140 miles from Munda and burning gas fast.

The former collegiate boxer fought to keep his bird in the air, ducking and weaving through the cover of clouds where they could be found, while his teammates maneuvered to keep the vultures at bay. All the way, the left flank of his flight suit turned crimson. Blood filled his left boondocker; the overflow greased the pedal channel and dripped into the bilge of the floorless fighter plane. At high rpm with the throttle set at "Auto Rich," the gas gauge continued to drop. His was a race against time.

As his life's blood flowed away, the former flight instructor relied on his inherent piloting skills honed from his years of experience. Fly the plane. Keep it straight and level. Stick and rudder. Watch the gas. Keep the rpm up. Check the engine temperature. It was an unconscious checklist to bring it home in one piece, the most basic of skills from his days as a CPTP trainee.

Above him, the other "Black Sheep" kept the attackers at bay. Mullen scored one kill and damaged a second Zero before the enemy retreated from the fight after 40 miles of dueling.

As New Georgia came into view, Rollie banked his plane to port slightly, just enough to get a view of Kokenggolo Hill to his left. Banking back to starboard, he was pointed due east, as Rendova appeared ahead to his right. Below, the seas turned from sapphire to turquoise as he crossed over the reef. Munda airfield lay straight ahead, but he still had to get his bird on the ground.

Rollie came in hot and blind. "The plane was smoking; the radio and most instruments were out, wing flaps were gone and the tires shot up."[19] Battle-denuded palm trees denoted his descent. Tail high, he careened down the short fighter strip.

Despite being in shock, his forward vision impaired, and the bird having lost both its virginity and some of its mechanicals, Rollie kept her on the strip. Running past the Martson mats, he entered the construction zone of airstrip expansion as the Seabees labored to lengthen the runway. "I hit one of their graders, tearing a wing off my plane."[20] The Vought pivoted against the grader before it rolled over. When the freshly manufactured bird finally came to rest, it lay shattered.

Rollie emerged from the carnage just long enough to show his rescuers he had survived before crumpling aside his shattered steed. The squadron surgeon, Doc Reames, and other rescuers gathered up the unconscious twenty-two-year-old "Black Sheep." The Vought was bulldozed to the boneyard.

After Rollie was evacuated to the hospital tent, Reames and his medics cut away the flight suit, tended to the pilot's burns and wounds, and stemmed the blood loss. Under a damp canvas roof, shrapnel was extracted, antibiotics applied, painkillers administered, sutures sewn, wounds bandaged, and fluids replaced in the primitive field hospital.

Boyington and squadron intelligence officer Frank Walton came to see him as soon as possible. Walton remembered, "He lay on a canvas cot in the hospital, a long tent with open sides and a bare, muddy coral floor. His face was pale, and we could see that his wound was painful."[21]

Mindful of the loss of the squadron's fresh bird, 55876, Rollie apologized to his squadron commander: "Gee, skipper, I'm sorry I wrecked the plane."[22]

After stabilization, air evacuation was to be Rollie's next flight. But the Japanese weren't through that afternoon.

The wail of the air raid sirens belatedly joined the cacophony of enemy bombs raining on Munda. Caught flatfooted, the medics struggled to evacuate the wounded from the hospital tent: "Bombs started coming down and two guys picked me up on the stretcher that I was lying on and headed for a dugout not very far away."[23] Self-preservation caused the lead stretcher bearer to drop the litter as he disappeared into the safety of the dugout without his patient. As adrenaline surged through his veins again, Rollie found himself temporarily abandoned in the open until salvation appeared: "Hell, the guy on the rear . . . he deserved a medal. He ran back into the tent and got a mattress and threw himself on top of the mattress.[24] Sandwiched between the canvas litter and medic-weighted mattress, Rollie survived the latent raid.

Reames ordered Rollie evacuated to Cactus the next day. From Henderson Field at Guadalcanal, he was medevaced to a hospital in New Zealand. The fighter had fought his last round against the Japanese, but he was not down for the final count. Rinabarger would indeed return to the air.

Rollie rejoined the "Black Sheep" in late November 1943. After several days of local flights, he collapsed at Guadalcanal, having not fully recovered from his wounds and the malarial parasites migrating through his blood. He was evacuated two days ahead of his twenty-third birthday. While the "Black Sheep" and Boyington continued to rack up a storied score, Rinabarger was transferred to the US Army Schumacher Hospital in Oakland. The surgeons were still "pulling pieces of metal out of me nine months later."[25]

Rollie was finally released from Schumacher in July 1944. He married and then brought his wife, Becky, to El Toro and then Santa Barbara, where he served as an instructor with several Marine fighting squadrons. By this time, the last of the WTS graduates had joined the ranks of the military as the program wound down.

After the war ended, Rollie was reunited with his wartime commander, Lt. Col. Greg Boyington, when the "Black Sheep" gathered at NAS Alameda to greet the returned warrior. Rollie flew in a –ID marked to represent Boyington's bird to the Black Sheep reunion.

Postwar, Rollie continued to fly in the United States Marine Corps Reserve. Before his retirement, he was the commander of VMF-216. He retired as a colonel in 1961. Though he owned an electrical contracting business postwar, he continued to fly as a crop duster. The "Black Sheep" passed away in 1987.

The Civilian Pilot Training Program / War Training Service trained over four hundred thousand Americans to fly before the program was phased out. It was responsible for the creation of an entire generation of fliers. About 88 percent of the CPTP/WTS pilots who entered the Navy earned their wings of gold. The majority of Marine fighter pilots also came from these ranks.

Rest and Relaxation (If You Make It That Far)

Pilots Don't Like to Be Passengers

"All fighter pilots think that only God can fly as good as they can," recalled 1Lt. Phil Wilmot. "But God has to sit in the right [copilot] seat!"[26]

Battle-Hardened Veterans Entered the Belly of the Beast

VMF-321 had completed their first tour at the end of January 1944. They had flown during the peak season of aerial attacks against Rabaul, a time when aces were made and others perished. After a night spent at the "Hotel de Gink" on Guadalcanal, half the squadron boarded a PBM Mariner at Efate, New Hebrides, for the long flight to Sydney, Australia. Being a pilot was one thing; being a passenger, another. After just a few hours in the bowels of the seaplane, nearly all the Corsair pilots were airsick. As the stench of vomitus filled the air, 2Lt. John Stith testified, "Boy, those transport drivers thought it was the funniest thing they'd ever seen!"[27]

If You Survive

After VMF-215 completed their second six-week tour at Munda, groups from the "Fighting Corsairs" boarded R4Ds. Headed to Espiritu Santo on their way to a week of R&R in Australia, a dozen of the combat pilots almost didn't make it. First Lieutenant Richard G. Newhall reported the following:

> An hour after takeoff, we ran into a very severe weather "front." We entered this "front," which was very dark and turbulent with rain, at about 10,000 feet. We encountered a gust of extreme violence which forced the nose up in spite of the efforts of both pilots. The plane was inverted. The twelve of us in the cabin found ourselves suddenly hurled to the roof[,] where we remained for several seconds. The pilot recovered by pulling through the rest of the loop until nearly vertical then rolling out. He told us, afterward, that his speed was about 250 mph. Recovery was finally completed at 4- to 5,000 feet.[28]

Newhall and his "Fighting Corsairs" comrades eventually arrived safe but shaken at Espiritu Santo.

"Unfriendly" Fire: Baa Baa "Black Sheep"

The Corsair carried six of John M. Browning's famed .50 cals. With the cooling provided by flight, the AN/M2 aviation version was a lighter, shorter-barrel version of the Browning standard HB/M2. Its cyclic rate was 750–800 rounds per minute, substantially higher than the standard ground-bound HB model. With all guns charged on the Vought, a second on the trigger put eighty rounds in the air at 2,910 ft./sec. A pilot could burn through his ammo load in just thirty seconds. Many pilots flew with the two outer guns turned off to maintain an emergency supply of ammunition.

It was late in September 1943 when three gull-wing birds of Pappy's squadron left Munda for a morning patrol. Flying near Kolombangara, the group spotted a group of ships below. Diving from out of the sun, they came in from the stern at just 300 feet. The "Black Sheep" startled a group of American patrol torpedo boats. Recognizing the Corsairs as friendlies, the PT boats went to full speed, turned the rudder hard over right, and waved the American flag. The flight leader, Major Stan Bailey, called to his pilots that the boats were friendly,

First Lieutenant Robert Alexander's grave. *Courtesy of the National Archives, photo 127-N-70711*

and to hold their fire. Two F4Us passed over without incident, but 1Lt. Robert A. Alexander let loose with his .50s. The rounds walked up the water into PT-126's bow, splintering wood, knocking out an engine, and starting a fire. A sailor and an officer were killed.

A PT boat carried more firepower than a Corsair. One of the Elco boat gunners unleashed a short fusillade of lead from his twin .50s. He found his mark. Alexander's bird veered off, crashed, and exploded in the Kolombangara jungle.

Two months later on December 5, Pappy Boyington led a group of "Black Sheep" to Kolombangara. The eight marines eventually discovered the shattered remains of Alexander and his steed. They gathered up what little they could find of him, dug a grave, oriented it toward Tokyo,[29] and buried the remains. His name inscribed on one of the propeller blades served as the Hawkeye's headstone.

In his memoir, Boyington noted that the burial of Alexander was the only time a missing "Black Sheep" was found, yet Boyington would eventually emerge as an enigma after twenty months as a prisoner of the Japanese.

From Rookie to Veteran in a Hurry: Bob Hanson

Second Lieutenant Robert Hanson, VMF-214, after his first mission, August 4, 1943. Though he scored a victory, his enemy scored hits too. *Courtesy of Bruce Gamble*

His Path to Combat Was Long

The son of Methodist missionaries, Robert Hanson lived most of his youth in eastern India before bicycling across Europe. His college wrestling days in Minnesota ended when the Japanese attacked Pearl Harbor. The twenty-two-year-old was accepted in naval flight training in the spring of 1942. By the fall of 1943, he was in the starting lineup for the VMF-214. Flying from Efate on August 4, two divisions of "Swashbucklers" were directed to Munda, where they encountered a dozen enemy fighters. In a wild melee, three of the young lieutenants claimed a Zero. Bullet and cannon rounds punctured the skin of several of the bent-wing birds. By the time Hanson disengaged, his right wing was showing daylight through the skin. He landed safely at what was the start to a brilliant but short six-month career.

When the "Swashbucklers" finished their tour, the longtimer was transferred to VMF-215. With two kills already to his credit, Hanson's tally was on a meteoric trajectory after the move. His inaugural mission with his new partners was more dramatic than his introduction to combat with the -214.

After a year of chasing and fighting enemy birds from Rabaul, the Allies were moving up the Slot. The American Navy and Marine fighter planes did not have the long legs of the lighter Japanese aircraft. The decision was made to invade Bougainville so an airbase could be established closer to the fortress Rabaul. The invasion landings commenced early on the November 1.

Gathered off the west coast of the island was US Navy Task Group 31.5. Fourteen thousand marines of the reinforced US 3rd Marine Division embarked from a dozen combat-loaded attack transport and attack cargo ships. These mother ships were protected by eleven destroyers and a school of destroyer-minesweepers, minelayers, and small minesweepers. By dawn's early light, 3- and 5-inch shells began to rain down on Cape Torokina. Northern and southern Bougainville were reinforced with large garrisons of Japanese troops, but just a small contingent was on hand to repel the invasion on the central west coast. Though the meticulously planned invasion went smoothly, it was just a matter of time before the emperor sent his regards from Rabaul by air and sea.

American planes attacked targets ashore as the marine attack echelon prepared to hit the beach. On schedule, the landing craft crossed Empress Augusta Bay at 0730 to commence the invasion. From the north, nine Val dive-bombers protected by forty-four Zekes were the first appearance of enemy birds. Army P-38s and P-40s plus Marine Corsairs tangled with the flock sent to destroy the invasion forces. Only a handful of enemy planes were able to evade the screen and close the landing force. For their efforts, little damage was inflicted on the ships.

Midday, a second wave of one hundred enemy birds targeted the American invaders. They were countered again by fighters from AirSols, the joint Allied air force command of the Solomon Islands. The Allies earned a good accounting for themselves. Targets were ripe for the plucking for the defenders. The only loss to the invasion fleet was time unloading materiel for the marines on the beach.

Part of the defense was Hanson's division. On patrol over western Bougainville, Hanson's dash-one was haunted by gremlins. After his radio failed, he ran out of oxygen. Motioning to his division leader by hand that his Vought had problems, the group descended to 13,000 feet. Below them were six Zeroes followed by thirty more planes heading southeast. Each of the Americans closed on the tail of an enemy plane. The ensuing maelstrom dissolved into a series of individual dogfights. Capt. Arthur Warner nailed a Zero, as did 1Lt. Lloyd Cox. The division broke off when 2Lt. Samuel Sampler radioed that he was having engine trouble. At 1500, three Corsairs pancaked at Vella Lavella. Hanson was not with them, nor had he been seen since the battle commenced. He was declared missing in action.

But Hanson was not lost. His first rounds hit the mark. Scratch one Zero. Setting his sights on a second Mitsubishi, the lead hail spouting from his Brownings hit the gas tank. An angry roiling orange-and-black cloud filled the sky where the Zero had been. With a quick adjustment, Hanson made a lowside approach on a group of Kate torpedo bombers. One got away, but the next Kate in his gunsight was not as lucky. It nosed over and crashed into the Augusta Bay. With this score, the twenty-three-year-old marine had joined the elite fraternity of pilots, the aces.

Earning the Title "Ace" Did Not Guarantee That a Pilot Would Land Safely

The most famous rookie Marine pilot was then 2Lt. James Swett of VMF-221. Seven months earlier, during his first combat mission, he had led his division against a gaggle of Vals flying near the Russell Islands. Swett finished off seven of the dive-bombers before he ran out of ammunition. The back-seaters in the Aichis scored some hits, though, as did some friendly fire from Allied AA gunners. When the Wildcat's engine seized, Swett ditched the Grumman in the seas. As the plane sank into the waves, the wounded Swett finally broke free and surfaced. He was rescued from Tulagi Harbor. It was the start of a brilliant fighter career that lasted through the fighting in 1945. The instant ace earned the Medal of Honor for his score on April 7, 1943.

Exiting the Aerial Melee, Hanson's Pratt & Whitney Quit

Hanson turned his dying steed back toward the task force, making a dead-stick ditching 6 miles south of the invasion caravan. The Corsair remained above the seas for just thirty seconds before beginning the descent to the seafloor. Hanson escaped the plane but found that his life vest would not stay inflated. His raft, however, functioned as expected. He climbed aboard, dropped some dye markers, and began to paddle the 6 miles north toward some destroyers he had spotted during his ditching.

With the transport and cargo ships west of the beach, three destroyers protected the southern flank of the invasion. *Sigourney*, *Anthony*, and *Wadsworth* provided close-in fire support to the beach with their 5-inch guns. It was early afternoon. Hanson was aware that the vanguard would head to deeper waters before dark. "I paddled with considerable effort because I knew they were to leave soon. I was also singing 'You'd Be So Nice to Come Home To.'"[30] He was seen before he was heard. After four and half hours of paddling, Hanson was rescued by a tin can.

By the end of the afternoon, all the invading Marines had been sent ashore, and unlike the debacle at Guadalcanal fifteen months earlier, most of the combat-loaded gear, supplies, and food made it to the beach before Task Force 31 retired for the night. With the report of an armada of Japanese surface ships en route from Rabaul, the collection of transports and small combat vessels steamed south to safety.

Hanson spent two days aboard the USS *Sigourney* (DD-643). Life aboard ship in the black-shoe navy was in direct contrast to the primitive conditions the boondocker-wearing marine flier had experienced living on land. "I had some very welcome meals, noting the conspicuous absence of Spam. The eggs, steak, and ice cream were a real treat. I went ashore at Tulagi, caught the ferry to Guadalcanal, and reported to ComAirGuadal. I was treated very well and drew some gear which I had lost. After receiving proper permission, I ferried an F4U back to Vella LaVella."[31]

Hanson Returned to the Air Soon After

During the squadron's third tour starting in January 1944, Hanson turned in the most prolific score in American flying history. Over a period of seventeen days, the ace among a squadron of aces brought down twenty enemy aircraft. His career came to an end as a quintuple ace. On the day before his twenty-fourth birthday, the aggressive "one-man air force" strafed a lighthouse at the tip of southern New Ireland. In response, a flak battery turned its guns at the marine's bird. The enemy rounds punctured the Vought plane. Hanson, like in November, turned his wounded steed seaward. One wing tipped into the water, sending the fighter cartwheeling across the waves. The F4U-1 disappeared beneath the seas, thus entombing Hanson, the greatest Corsair ace to ever fly.

First Lieutenant Robert Hanson was posthumously awarded the Medal of Honor. He was the third and last Corsair jockey to earn this distinction. Hanson also was awarded the Navy Cross and the Air Medal. The Navy commissioned the USS Hanson *(DD-832) in his honor on May 11, 1945.*

Bird of the Aces: 17883

The great hunter was running out of time. In just a few days, VMF-214 "Black Sheep" would finish their third tour and rotate home. The all-time kill record was within sight for Maj. Gregory Boyington. His eighteen kills in the South Pacific, combined with his six claimed kills with the "Flying Tigers," left him two shy of tying Eddie Rickenbacker and Joe Foss.

On December 27, 1943, Boyington mounted Bureau Number 17883. It was a newer F4U-1A Corsair. It had been ferried into theater from the West Coast in November 1943. A bubble canopy with two dorsal frame rails made it distinguishable from the earlier F4U-1, which had "birdcage" canopies. The pilot's seat was raised 7 inches over the old model to provide better vision. The "dash-one A" models had largely replaced the birdcages in combat.

From Vella Lavella, Boyington led a force of fifty-nine Marine Corsairs and Navy Hellcats on a fighter sweep over Rabaul. Flying in a huge Lufbery circle undulating over 6,000 feet, Boyington initiated diving passes against a pack of thirty to forty enemy planes. Five "Black Sheep" scored kills. Pappy notched his twenty-fifth kill as he sprayed lead from 150 yards while pursuing a mottled brown Zeke.

Pappy's return to the Barokoma airstrip did not go unnoticed. With him closing in on Rickenbacker and Foss, the Marines' publicity machine was in high rev. The squadron intelligence officer, Frank Walton, had worked since the early days of the "Black Sheep" to garner as much press for the squadron and their flamboyant CO as he could. Waiting for Boyington were cameras and reporters. Boyington held up one finger after moving 17883 into its revetment. Breaking the record would have to wait for another day.

Left: Maj. Boyington holds up one finger for one kill after flying BuNo 17883 on December 27, 1943.

Right: Bureau Number 17883 after its final flight

Though their Corsairs were assigned to the squadron, none were assigned to a specific pilot. With most missions, a different Bureau Number (BuNo) was added to the pilot logbooks. Capt. Chris Magee, a "Black Sheep" ace with nine kills to his credit, took '883 up for a hop on New Year's Day. Boyington flew it again the next day without success on a fighter sweep to Rabaul.

"Gramps" Boyington tied the kill record on January 3, 1944, while flying BuNo 17915. He was taken prisoner while flying this last combat mission. The "Black Sheep" folded their tent several days later after concluding their second combat tour. VMF-214 had flown three tours (one as the "Swashbucklers") and so rotated back to America to re-form. Their birds stayed behind.

Two weeks after the start of their tour, Two Fifteen was racking up the kills. Previous aces added to their scores while others achieved the elite status. By January 28, the aces 1Lt. Robert Hanson (a former VMF-214 "Swashbuckler") and Capt. Don Aldrich led the way with twenty-one and thirteen kills, respectively.

The twenty-eighth was another maximum effort by AirSols. Two divisions of "Flying Corsairs" were assigned to the mission. Aldrich drew BuNo 17883. Though it had appeared in numerous photographs and movie reels with Boyington flying it on December 27, 1945, it was just another of the forty-four *Corsairs* flown by -215, -211, and VF-17 on January 28.

Five dozen SBDs and TBFs attacked Rabaul. The escorting Army, Navy, Marine, and RNZAF fighters were attacked as they crossed the New Britain coastline. VMF-215 was flying behind the TBFs. Aldrich reported: "I did not have contact with the Zeroes until we had crossed the field and were out over the water headed for the rally point, that a Zeke made runs on some F4Us beside but ahead of me and turned into me almost head-on. I got a good burst into him, and there was a large flash of fire as he slid under me. This was at 5,000 [feet]."[32] Aldrich climbed and then dove on another Zeke before flaming it. "Then I swung to the right, still behind the bombers, and saw a Zero attacking some F4Us below me. I dove on him, but the Zero saw me and tried to pull up into a head-on run. I fired from 20 [degrees] from ahead and dove, and the Zero burst into flame around his engine and wingroots."[33] The fighting wasn't finished: "Then I got a Zero on my tail and pulled through some violent maneuvers to get rid of him, but not before he had gotten some shots into my left wing and gas tank."[34] Aldrich pushed 17883's stick forward and dove to safety. Opportunity presented itself again: "Then I dove down onto the tail of a Zero at 500 feet and gave him a long burst."[35] The score for Aldrich had climbed from thirteen to seventeen in just a few minutes.

Battles raged across the skies. In fifteen minutes, VF-17 scored seventeen kills. P-38s from the 347th Fighter Group flying top cover scored five more kills. VMF-211 scored seven victories. Two other VMF-215 pilots scored one each to bring the squadron's total to six. Even a TBF from VMTB-143 scored.

Finally clear of the enemy, Aldrich turned his attention both to body and machine. Shrapnel had pierced his shoulder and thigh. His plane had been struck multiple times by enemy guns. Despite the pain from wounds, he brought the shot-up 17883 back to the Piva airstrip. The flaps could not be lowered. Bullets had flattened one of the tires. Despite the damage, Aldrich brought her in for her final landing.

Aldrich sought medical help for his wounds. He returned to the fight within twelve days. The same could not be said for 17883. It was too badly damaged for the mechanics to waste time repairing. The demand to keep other Corsairs flying was too great. 17883 was towed to the boneyard, its parts used to keep other Corsairs flying. The bird of the aces was officially stricken later that spring.

Aldrich scored three more kills before VMF-215 finished its final tour. His twenty kills ranked him as the fifth-greatest Marine ace of all time. Aldrich was killed in 1947 when his Corsair crash-landed on a muddy airstrip.

Bureau Number 17883 became forever associated with Pappy Boyington, though it is extremely likely that it was flown by some of the eighteen other aces of VMF-214 and VMF-215. The bird of the aces is attributed to at least five kills. Postwar, it has become the most portrayed Corsair by illustrators and painters.

Island Girl

For three weeks the Marine pilots of VMF-122 had been transitioning to Corsairs before they flew their first combat mission in bent-wings on June 20, 1943. Two divisions were scrambled toward Rendova. Flying through rain under a low ceiling, Lt. Hank "Boo"

Bourgeois's wingman radioed he was turning back due to engine problems. By the time Bourgeois had turned around, he had lost sight of 1Lt. David M. Brennan. He continued the search in vain. During the hunt, Bourgeois chased a Betty bomber and shot it from the skies.

Lost

Bourgeois joined up on nine VMSB-132 SBDs. Their situation was no better. Five SBDs peeled off, but Bourgeois stuck with the others. Low on fuel, they all ended up ditching in a lagoon at Rennell Island. The Dauntlesses stayed afloat for nearly four minutes, but Bourgeois's birdcage went nose down and sank almost immediately. His raft went down with the plane. Struggling to stay afloat, natives paddled out and rescued Boo before saving the other airmen.

Bourgeois was fed canned corn beef and rice before being taken to meet the village chief. Speaking decent English, the leader asked Boo if he was "number one?"[36] The marine agreed that he was indeed "number one!" The reward was an evening spent in the chief's hut with his daughter.

As a fighter pilot, Bourgeois was in a profession that took lives (though the pilots counted only planes downed). It was a rare occasion for a pilot to save a life other than a fellow pilot. The morning after his rescue, Boo was brought to an island where a pregnant native was in distress. From his medical pouch, the pilot produced aspirin and gestured that it should be given to the woman. When a PBY arrived to rescue the marine aviators, Bourgeois sent the corpsman to check on the expectant mother. The situation seemed dire, so a radio call went out to fly doctors to the island. Bourgeois flew back to Espiritu Santo.

The next day, a carved gift arrived from the chief for Boo. The medical attendants told him that a baby boy was born. He was named "BOO-zher-rah!"[37]

Bourgeois later flew with VMF-214 Black Sheep, where he earned a DFC with two Gold Stars. He stayed in the Marine Corps postwar. Bourgeois passed away in 2009. Decades after the war, Bourgeois's Corsair Bureau Number 02524 was discovered by a diver on the bottom of the Rennell lagoon. Two SBDs lay nearby.

To Live and Drown in LA (Vella)

First Lieutenant Bob Wilson's Corsair inverted, BuNo 17884. *Gary Wilson Collection, courtesy of Gregory Pons*

Submarines, Radar, Planes, and Bulldozers Won the War

That was the assessment of Adm. William "Bull" Halsey. Asked the same question regarding the battles of the Solomons, Gen. Alexander Vandegrift, USMC, might have put a greater emphasis on the bulldozers and planes than did his navy counterpart. For it was the Navy's own construction battalions (abbreviated as "CBs" but known affectionately as the "Sea Bees" by those who saw them at work) that created airfields out of tropical jungles in mere weeks. Runways were constructed on sand, coral, and volcanic ash.

To keep terra firma in place in the tropical environments of the Solomons (and later across Allied airfields as the battles moved closer to the Japanese Empire), a new construction aid was incorporated. Simple perforated steel planks were interconnected atop the fields. A Marston mat (also referred to as "Marsden") was a 10-foot-by-15-inch sheet of steel with three columns of twenty-nine 3-inch holes. The mats could be quickly assembled to create temporary landing strips, runways, and taxi ways for the warbirds. The holes and interlocking channels allowed drainage from the daily deluge. Most importantly, a small team of men could lay an entire runway in just several days.

Surrounding these steel fields could be found construction debris, plane revetments, and drainage ditches. It was in one of the ditches that a young marine aviator almost gave his life for his country.

A pair of "Flying Deuces" divisions were sent aloft from Barakoma airfield (Vella Lavella) for a routine patrol over Torokina the morning of December 14, 1943. It was here that the 3rd Marine Division had come ashore just six weeks earlier during the invasion of Bougainville. CBs started hacking an airfield out of the thick jungle almost immediately.

The patrol was canceled early on, and the -222 pilots were ordered to set down at Torokina. The strip had been open just four days when the "Deuces" landed. Seven had smooth landings, but 1Lt. Bob Wilson's left brake failed. His bird veered to the right and left the steel matting just before the wheels dug into the soft sand. It was enough to flip the 9,000-pound bird up and over. Now inverted in the channel between the runway and the taxiway, Wilson was 3 feet underwater and strapped into his bird:

The prop hit the ground and over I went, landing upside down on my neck with all the weight of my body, my parachute, a one-man rubber life raft[,] and the backpack we wore with all kinds of survival equipment in it—water, some food, fishing gear—so there was probably about 100 pounds of gear holding me down, plus my body. Then, I found out the canopy had closed, so there I am upside down in water, can't breathe. You can only hold your breath just so long.[38]

When the dash-one begun to flip, Wilson had accidentally discharged his Brownings. The sudden seizing of the Double Wasp combined with the racket of the .50s caught the attention of those nearby. Racing to the scene, they labored to lift the Vought high enough to open the canopy.

I don't know if I passed out or not. . . . They later described it as a "Keystone Cop" operation. They would get the tail up but didn't have enough people to hold it up for very long, so they would drop it back down in the water. Of course I didn't know what was going on, but eventually enough people were there to hold it up, and someone got the canopy open and dragged me out. My sinuses were full of black volcanic water. It was weeks afterwards before my sinuses were clear.[39]

For their time and trouble, Wilson's rescue party stripped the pilot of his gear as rewards for their efforts

Wilson flew three combat tours with the "Deuces." He was credited with two kills during his time in the Solomons.

Back to Your (Wing) Roots

Left: Center spars with cockpits attached at the factory
Above: Lesley Strandtman

Every ship has a keel. For the Corsair, with its mighty reciprocating engine and massive propeller, the center spar gave the plane its distinctive bent-wing profile and was the starting point for assembly. Everything emanated from the 17-foot-wide section: the engine was mounted forward, the cockpit above it, and the main fuselage with tail empennage behind it. The folding points for the wings were found at either end of the spar.

The Rising Sun's Rays Lit Up the Cockpits

On an early-morning mission, a division of VMF-114 "Death Dealers" flew north from Green Island to New Ireland. Mission for the day: barge sweep and plane counts at the Kavieng and Panapai airfields. But the mission for the Japanese there was simple: shoot down planes.

They almost got one. A 40 mm round tore through the right wing root, emerged through the top, and shattered 1Lt. Lesley Valentine Strandtman's canopy. Shards from the green house wounded the twenty-four-year-old pilot in the neck. The right wheel, housed in the center spar, was punctured, and the aerial was shot away. Counting on the strength of his bird, the Texan nursed his bird back to the nest.

Bill Cantrell of VMF-114 witnessed the landing: "The tower had been alerted and crash crews and an ambulance were standing by. Val greased it on, and, at first, all seemed well. Then the right landing[-]gear strut collapsed and the right wing went down."[40]

The F4U-1A flipped and tumbled down the runway. Sparks flew as the 2,500-pound engine broke off. The plane bled out as gas and oil. Hydraulic fluid spewed. The heavy center pin at the wing folds gave way, causing both wings to tear free. The fuselage behind the cockpit ripped away. "Val was left sitting in the center section of a Corsair without wings, an engine, or a tail."[41]

Amazingly, the lanky lieutenant survived his bird's acrobatics. Despite bleeding from numerous cuts and lacerations, he was initially reluctant to be saved: "When the corpsmen pulled him from the crash, he insisted they not cut his leather flight jacket—it was a new one!"[42]

Strandtman made a career of the Marines. He earned the DFC in World War II and flew night fighters during the Korean War.

The Main Man: 2Lt. Nick Mainiero

The ground crew strained their eyes for the damaged plane and wounded pilot coming in for an emergency landing. After medical personnel rushed to the Corsair to extract the bloody pilot, the marines crawled onto the wings. Looking at the pools of blood in the torn-up cockpit, they marveled how the pilot got his plane home.

It had been nearly a year since he had set foot on American soil. But as he stood behind the sailors manning the rails as San Diego came into view, 2Lt. Nicholas J. Mainiero's service in combat had come to an end. He was now one of hundreds of Marine patients evacuated to the states aboard the attack transport USS *Mendocino* (APA-100). They all had suffered, some physically, some psychologically. There were the expected cases of gunshot wounds and combat fatigue, but maladies spanned the medical horizon: jungle rot, tuberculosis, pustular acne, hookworm, malaria, duodenal ulcers, narcolepsy, hepatitis, brain abscess, sexual psychopathy, and traumatic psychoneurosis, to name but a few.

Waiting for Mainiero in his native Bridgeport, Connecticut, was his young bride and a newborn daughter he had never held. His family was anticipating his arrival. For his father, Tony, a machinist for Vought building Corsairs, Nick would bring thanks from his golden-winged brothers flying in the central Pacific. Mainiero was happy to be home. He almost hadn't made it.

When the Empire of the Sun attacked Pearl Harbor, Mainiero was a student at Manhattan College. He had grown up in the heart of American aviation production. Vought was building OS2U Kingfishers and F4U Corsairs in Stratford. Sikorsky and United Aircraft Corporation factories were nearby. Lindbergh and Earhart had flown from the nearby Curtiss Hangar. Across Long Island Sound, Grumman and Brewster were also building warplanes.

Having already earned a civilian pilot license, Mainiero had the choice of flying for the Navy or Army. After signing with the Navy in 1942, he earned his Golden Wings in Pensacola. Marine commissions were available as the Corps expanded their aviation capabilities. The idea of joining the fliers who were battling the Japanese in the skies over Guadalcanal suited him fine, and Mainiero volunteered again. He opted for Marine olive drab over Navy whites.

Mainiero wanted to fly fighter planes. From Pensacola he was transferred to Jacksonville, and it was here he learned to fly the planes his father and friends' fathers were building back home in Connecticut. It was big, well armed, aggressive looking, and the hottest American fighter plane. That suited him fine too.

Mainiero began his yearlong odyssey as a combat fighter pilot when he was assigned to Marine Fighting Squadron 441. It was a trek west from California that took him to the central Pacific and then back again.

VMF-441 (the "Black Jacks") was formed overseas and had been flying against the empire since March 1943. They started combat in the squat Wildcats but began the transition to the Vought Corsairs at the end of 1943.

By early 1944, they were slated to nest at the newly conquered Roi airbase in the Marshalls. A core group of pilots had remained with the squadron, but Marine Air Group 31 had reclaimed a few of the experienced pros. To fill out the roster, many rookie pilots arrived in March. Mainiero, having accumulated fifty hours behind the stick of an F4U, was a top draft pick for the squadron.

In late January and early February 1944, the Kwajalein Atoll had been conquered as part of Operation Flintlock, the first penetration of the empire's farthest outer concentric rings of defense. From here, the island-hopping campaign began. With Kwajalein and Eniwetok under Allied control, various enemy-held islands would be held captive by airpower, thus negating the need for invasion.

To the east of the Marshalls was Wotje Island. Just a speck of an island at only 3.1 square miles, it was from Wotje in March 1942 that the second attack on Pearl Harbor emanated. A pair of long-legged flying boats, Kawanishi H8K Emilys, left the seaplane base with the ultimate mission of flying nearly 2,500 miles to reconnoiter the harbor and drop just 2 tons of bombs on the battleship drydock. Arriving after midnight, the pilots found the islands blacked out. They scattered their bombs on the sea, the side of an extinct volcano, and near a high school. The pests turned tail and then returned to the Marshalls.

A year later, the Olympian and US Army Air Corps bombardier 1Lt. Louis Zamperini was brought ashore by a Japanese patrol boat after being adrift for forty-seven days. He and 1Lt. Russell Phillips were evacuated the next day, July 15, 1943. They were possibly the last Americans to leave Wotje alive, but the hell of Ōfuna and other Japanese prison camps awaited them.

March 26, 1944

The "Black Jacks" entered the game with runs at Ormed and Wotje Islands. Marine SBDs sent bombs away against targets while the Corsairs covered them. Following the bomb runs, the Voughts broke away to strafe.

And thus began a regular routine of forcing the isolated Japanese garrisons to keep their heads down and antiaircraft guns loaded. VMF-441's game partners were Dauntlesses, Venturas, and the other Marine Air Group 31 fighter squadrons, VMF-311 and VMF-422, at Roi and Engebi Islands, respectively. As the Black Jacks gained experience, the missions changed from fighter escort to bomber strikes.

The Black Jacks carried the entire inventory from the ammunition dump: napalm tanks, 100-pound fragmentation cluster bombs, and general-purpose bombs ranging from 250 to 1,000 pounds. On occasion, when the supplies of the dumb iron bombs ran low, they dropped depth charges.

Some squadrons, such as the famous VMF-214 and VF-17, were posted where active aerial combat was commonplace. With the dogfighting came newsmen. Wotje, however, was a desolate atoll, a tiny cog in a large war machine. There were no cameraman capturing their glory.

Danger still accompanied the flights. Roi to Wotje was a 340-mile round-trip hop, just three hours in the air, but the flights were not milk runs. Though only one enemy plane was ever seen in the air (a Betty bomber that was quickly shot down), the emperor's land forces never capitulated. Mainiero and his comrades were still in a shooting war. Though AA was considered "meager" on most missions, it still could ensnare a bird occasionally.

Other planes were lost when the Pratt & Whitneys experienced a loss of power during takeoff. Napalm cannisters that were hung up on the shackles forced the pilots to bail out after returning to Roi. Not every pilot survived these plane losses.

During a strafing run against Wotje in May, Mainiero nosed over from 8,000 feet with his sights on the coral airport. Mainiero's steed exceeded 350 knots as he unleashed his Brownings. The speed was beyond the strength of the rudder. The dark-blue canvas and dope gave way. By the time the lieutenant returned to Roi, all that was attached to the tail fin were a few ribs of the rudder.

Bryan Cox RNZAF explained diving in a Corsair:

We were trained for dive bombing as soon as we were posted to squadrons, but it depended on the CO of the squadron as to whether we used the dive brake function, which only extended the main wheels, or dived clean. One problem of using dive brakes was that if you were hit by ground fire, your glide capability would be much less than if you were "clean"—affecting your ability to glide clear of the enemy! When dive brakes were selected, the tailwheel assembly didn't extend, as it wasn't strengthened to cope with the aerodynamic forces of a very high-speed dive, so only the main wheels extended.

We also had one pilot who dived his Corsair so fast that he shredded the elevators. It was when we were sent up to 35,000 feet on only our fifth flight to check oxygen and superchargers—with just over 200 hours' pilot in command time in the logbook. We all kept climbing, in my case to 39,500 feet, when I "chickened out," scared that it may stall and spin. On my way down I controlled my airspeed, which was massively underreading at that altitude, but another pilot, Miles King, decided to descend in a steep dive, with an airspeed reading of 360 knots passing through 26,000 feet—but that would compute to a terminal airspeed of 530 knots—or 610 mph! He did tend to experience a reversal of controls, indicating that he was experiencing what we called "compressibility" or what we now know as the speed of sound![43]

Second Lieutenant Nick Mainiero's birdcage lost most of its rudder during a dive in the spring of 1944. *Photo courtesy of the Connecticut Air & Space Center*

They Were Days of Déjà Vu

With the sameness of constant temperatures, old magazines in the ready room, and being surrounded by the sea on the tiny twin islands of Roi-Numar, the days took on a sameness. The conditions were initially primitive. Pilots lived in tents, did their own washing, and were fed powdered eggs, Spam, meals from cans, and rehydrated foods. It was almost a private war.

For nine months, -441 flew almost daily poundings against Wotje, the Marshalls, Enybor Island, and the Jaluit Atoll, but it was Wotje and its large garrison that felt the tip of the arrow the most. There were CAPs to be flown, standby alerts to be endured, and regular missions against the cutoff Japanese forces on other nearby islands. "It was a job," recalled Mainiero. "We did it every day."[44]

Occasionally the monotony was broken. The flight surgeon, Lt. Raymond T. Anderson, regularly rotated pairs of pilots to Hawaii for a short period of R&R to keep morale up. In May, Cmdr. Eddie Peabody played banjo with his troupe of performers for an hour during a break in their travels to Eniwetok. A few weeks later, jazz pianist Claude Thornhill visited the atoll. Surrounded by palm trees and suntanned marines, he brought down the house when he played his 1941 hit, "Snowfall." But, for these men stranded in the central Pacific, it was the all-too-brief visit ashore by a group of nurses from the hospital ship USS *Solace* that brightened morale.

Several celebrities visited Roi in early September: Jack Benny brought his troop and the pinup Carol Landis to the island, but it was the arrival of the greatest aviator that caught the pilots' attention. Vought Factory representative Charles A. Lindbergh demonstrated that the Corsair was capable of shouldering heavier bombloads. On his first mission against Wotje, Lindbergh dropped a 1-ton bomb. Five days later he dropped a 1-ton bomb plus two 1,000-pound bombs. No other fighter had ever carried such tonnage before.

His Ticket Was Punched to Go Home

December 14, 1944. After nine months in combat, Mainiero's bags were already packed in anticipation of meeting his new baby daughter. He didn't have to fly his last mission. Forty-nine missions were penned in his logbook, but his CO asked him to lead a division of new pilots on an early-morning raid against Wotje. Twenty-two -1Ds took to the air in an attack against personnel shelters on the island. Some planes, such as Mainiero's division, carried 500-pounders while others carried the full-tonners under the fuselage, like Lindbergh had demonstrated in September. After dropping their ordnance, the planes rendezvoused over a nearby island before circling back to Wotje for strafing attacks. By this time, the gunners on the ground were ready when the dark-blue Voughts came screaming in for the second attack. "Light and medium AA fire was observed emanating from positions located in the areas assigned as strafing targets. It was intense and accurate."[45]

On the island, a gun team manning a Japanese type 98 20 mm machine cannon was ready. Tracking a group of the "whistling death birds," they opened fire when the flock came within range. One round hit home, puncturing the cowling of Mainiero's bird, before passing through the canopy, gunsight, and the instrument panel while another 20 mm round took out a piece of the left horizontal stabilizer.

As the canopy exploded inward, Mainiero's hand instinctively pulled the stick back as his head jerked against the headrest. Shrapnel punctured his flight suit, tore into his flesh, and pierced his goggles. The vision in his right eye went black. Warm blood streamed down his cheek and throat, while the well-worn flight suit turned crimson across his right arm. Mainiero was in trouble.

Strapped into his bird, Mainiero was faced with a life-or-death decision: ditch, bail, or try to make the hour-long 170 mile flight back to Roi. Ditching meant escaping from a sinking plane, inflating his raft, and then climbing aboard while seriously wounded. The young pilot didn't think he could do that, and that the odds against recovery were against him. Pinpointing a pilot in his Mae West floating in the ocean could be akin to finding a needle in a haystack if his escort had to leave before the dumbo could arrive.

To Mainiero, a rescue mission on June 8, 1944, represented the highs and lows of attempted rescues at sea. Second Lieutenant Joe Mortimer Glover was picked off by the enemy gunners on Wotje. He disappeared beneath the waves. As the call went out for a destroyer to come to the rescue, 2Lt. Theodore Wyatt's Corsair was hit. He ditched. Ninety minutes later a PBY arrived. It struck a wave violently and lost both propellers. Now ten airmen were in the water. The shore batteries concentrated on them. Finally they were rescued by the destroyer as its 5-inch guns dueled with the shore batteries. Marine VMSB-231 Dauntlesses dived through the darkening skies to finally silence the Japanese guns.

Bleeding profusely, Mainiero chose to be his own savior and attempted to land at Roi. He keyed his microphone, "I want to go home—fast."[46] Any thoughts of him ditching were evaporated when he turned his Corsair west.

Though it was damaged, Lt. Mainiero's F4U-1D was still flyable, still responded to his input. Mainiero had gone to college on a football scholarship. The pilot and the plane from Stratford were equally tough. Reflex and experience took over. He fashioned a tourniquet to stem the profuse bleeding from his arm. He intended to get back to Roi. He was determined to someday be reunited with his family.

News of the wounded pilot reached Roi. Crowds gathered to see Mainiero's return. Wounded pilots or those in an emergency usually skipped the landing pattern and came straight in to land. With Mainiero's depth perception lost, the landing would be even trickier. "Over the home base, his amazed comrades circled slowly and watched in amazement as he brought his ship into the traffic pattern, peeled off, and made a perfect landing. He taxied to the edge of the runway, cut his motor, and collapsed."[47] Ground crew climbed onto the plane to witness the gore for themselves.

The wounds to Mainiero's face, neck, and arm could all be treated locally, but the damage to his eye required an immediate evacuation. The flight surgeon, Lt. Raymond T. Anderson, accompanied him on the long journey to Pearl Harbor. After initial treatment there, he was evacuated to the United States for an additional operation in the hopes of fully restoring his vision.

Despite having no recollection of the return flight from Wotje, Nick Mainiero had brought his bird home. His service earned him a Purple Heart, a Distinguished Flying Cross, and an Air Medal.

Second Lieutenant Nick and Shirley Mainiero. *Photo courtesy of the Connecticut Air & Space Center*

Stratford, Connecticut, 1969

Mainiero brought another wounded Corsair home. On a mission to find a gate guard for the Stratford Sikorsky Memorial Airport he managed, Mainiero flew to El Salvador. In their boneyard was a triumvirate of weary gull wings. All had landed wheels up; all had been pushed to the side. Mainiero picked one and arranged to have it sent back to the States. The mission was accomplished with the aid of friends who donated their services. He erected the Corsair Monument to honor the people who designed, built, tested, and flew his beloved Corsair. For four decades, Mainiero's bird sat high on a pedestal overlooking the Housatonic River and Long Island Sound, where thousands of factory-new Vought Corsairs were first flown and first checked out during World War II.

The Corsair was brought down from its post in 2008. Time and salt air had taken its toll on the metal. It is currently being restored in the old Vought Corsair factory in Stratford by the Connecticut Air & Space Center. Nick Mainiero continued to supervise the restoration of the Goodyear Corsair FG-1D BuNo 92460 until his death in October 2016. He was ninety-four. Like the spirit of the Corsairs that flew from Stratford, Mainiero's spirit continues to be felt in the hangars and the hallways of CASC.

Will It Come Down?

What goes up, must come down. —Newton's third law of motion

All the birds of the flock came off the lines at the Stratford, Warminster, and Akron assembly plants with essentially the same parts, the same construction, the same design. There were variances from build series to build series, but a Corsair built in 1945 looked remarkably similar to its older brothers of 1942 vintage.

Several weeks into their third tour, VMF-114 was flying short-range missions against dug-in targets on Peleliu, Yap, and Ngeregong in the Palau Islands. During mid-October, they got their first chance to drop tanks of napalm, jellied gasoline, against entrenched targets. But the release speed of the newly built weapons racks were not to the pilots' liking. Overnight the mechanics worked with the release mechanisms to improve their efficiency.

The next day, twenty birds took to the air with napalm. Nineteen toggled their ordnance. One egg refused to let go. First Lieutenant Nick Virgets tried various airborne maneuvers to shake the bomb free, but to no avail. He was ordered to bail rather than bring the bird back to the field.

Two destroyers and the dumbo were on standby for the rescue. Maj. Jack Conger, already a double ace, sought to make lemonade of the situation: he asked his junior pilot to trim his plane so that the senior airman could shoot it down. There were no Japanese planes in the area, nor had they had any aerial duels in their previous two tours. This was an opportunity to get some gunnery practice against a flying plane.

Virgets struggled to get out but eventually got over the side, pulled the steel D ring, and floated down to the water. There was no need to inflate his raft. The rescue tin can was upon him quickly. But as the thin-skinned vessel approached the aviator, it was buzzed several times by a Corsair flying lazy chandelles. After completing several passes, and looking every bit like a haphazard kamikaze, it dove from the sky and crashed near the destroyer. A roaring fire on the seas marked its grave. For the officers and blue jackets of the tin can, the burning wake was a bit too close for comfort. The twenty-five-year-old Virgets immediately recognized the plane that almost bombed them: it was his own Corsair!

Thanksgiving

"STREAMS AND VALLEYS: Following a stream generally requires much fording, detouring, and penetration of thick vegetation. In mountain country there will be falls, cliffs, and side canyons. In flat country, the stream will meander, the vegetation will be dense, outlooks will be rare, and swamps common. Even so, it presents many advantages in strange country. It gives you a definite course which may lead to inhabited areas, and will also be a source of food, water, and a means of travel by boat or raft." —from *How to Survive on Land and Sea,* Aviation Training Division, United States Navy, 1943

Thanksgiving Came Early to Okinawa

After nearly three months of close-quarters ground combat, enough of the southern end of the island was under American control that on June 26, a Catholic chaplain celebrated a "Thanksgiving" mass. American forces had suffered over eighty-two thousand casualties. Pockets of resistance still remained.

Air battles were no less contentious. VMF-322 nested at Okinawa during the height of kamikaze season. Launched from the USS *White Plains* forty-eight hours after the most devastating kamikaze attack of the war, Kikusui No. 1, they took roost at the Kadena airfield on April 9, 1945. The captured air base was the new home to several Marine Corsair squadrons. Over the next ten weeks, the Japanese Empire launched nine additional mass *kikusui*s before the island was declared secured on June 22. The mission for the "Cannonballs" had metamorphosed from ground attacks to combat air patrols to prevent enemy birds from the home islands and the northern Amami Gunto island group from attacking the Allied fleets.

Early on June 26, a division of bent-wing birds took flight for their CAP mission. They flew north of the east coast before heading west at Oura Wan to cross the island. At just angels 2, 2Lt. Gordon Duffin's bird began to cough. The power loss was felt immediately. As the pilot attempted to adjust the mixture, he passed through a cloud. His instruments began swinging as the plane entered a spin. As he attempted to recover, the wings "popped." Now in a stall, Duffin's steed had dropped to 1,500 feet, just a few hundred feet higher than the mountains of the region. To survive, the Utah native had to take action immediately.

After locking the canopy back, Duffin took to the silk. No sooner had the parachute blossomed than Duffin was on the ground. To speed his escape, the twenty-two-year-old pilot abandoned his parachute and the survival gear. Duffin was now an army of one, armed with just a Ka-Bar knife and his Colt .45 in hostile territory.

Duffin's first encounter with an enemy came in the form of an Okinawan native . . . a large, venomous habu snake. Rather than engaging the viper, he advanced in reverse and headed southeast for the coast. Duffin forded a creek before advancing on several grass huts and four enemy personnel. He abandoned the creek, doubled back north, and took to the ridges. After fighting his way through the brush most of the morning, the exhausted aviator finally took to a trail. He came across a native foraging roots. With pistol drawn, the lieutenant mimicked swimming motions. The pantomime was understood, and soon Duffin was led down the ridge to a local village. Wary of a trap, Duffin released his guide and made his way around the settlement. It wasn't long before he was discovered.

Weary but on guard, the dogfaces marched down the trail, burdened by their dusty boots, weapons, magazines, and canteens. "There is a Jap pilot!"[48] Startled by an army patrol, Duffin yelled back that he was an American. M1 carbines and Garands were pointed toward Duffin. "Take off your helmet!" came the challenge. Duffin complied. Despite the filthy flight suit, the soldiers decided that Duffin was friendly, and lowered their weapons.

The patrol led the young pilot back to their command post. The marine lunched with an army colonel and then was taken by jeep to a small landing strip. An artillery spotting plane returned Duffin to Kadena in time for evening chow. For Duffin, it was a chance to offer his own "thanksgiving." He was able to track down his brother, Leland, a soldier fighting on the big island. They swapped mail from their mother and apple pie from home for some of the squadron's medicinal brandy.

Duffin survived the war and was awarded three Air Medals. He passed away in 2011.

CHAPTER 3

THE CATERPILLAR CLUB

The Vought test pilot was in trouble. High in the Connecticut skies, his F4U-1A's engine was on fire. Bill Boothby jumped from the Corsair. His chute opened prematurely. Boothby was flung into the plane's tail. His last words before he jumped were "I always did want one of those little pins . . ."¹

Just a few pounds of silk or nylon were all that prevented death for thousands of airmen in the Pacific. By the Second World War, no fighter pilot went into the air without a parachute. Though parachutes were in use by balloonists in the late eighteenth century, it wasn't until 1912 that an Army captain safely parachuted from a fixed-wing plane. Their use proliferated during the golden age of aviation after a civilian, Leslie Irvin, formed the first parachute company. To meet the needs of the military during the Second World War, multiple companies produced parachutes. Even the American Corset Company shifted its focus from girdles to chutes.

Caterpillar Club pin

Irvin recognized the survivors who successfully used his parachutes with a gold pin. The Caterpillar Club was born in 1922. During the war, the club was supported by a dozen parachute manufacturers. Their ranks expanded exponentially during the conflict.

US Navy and Marine fighter pilots wore the Quick Attachable Seat (QAS) harness over their life vest. The AN-6510 seat parachute and the raft packs clipped to the rear of the QAS. Pilots sat on the stacked seat cushion, parachute, and raft. Depending on the emergency, pilots could detach themselves from the parachute or raft pack. Evacuating the plane was not always easy.

Textbook

First Lieutenant Frederick Edison provided an example of a textbook bailout when his F4U-1C began leaking gas while on a combat air patrol north of Okinawa:

> I realized almost immediately that I wasn't going to be able to make the field. As I had long since made up my mind that if I ever found myself in such a predicament over water I would bail out, I had one less problem to worry about. I always figured it would be easier to land 160 pounds than seven tons. I increased speed at once to get as near to the base as possible, unfastened my oxygen mask, checked my chute and seat pack, and then sat back to wait. About ten miles northeast of the field at 6,000 feet, my engine quit and I notified my division that I was bailing out. I then unfastened my shoulder straps, pulled out the radio receiver cord, dropped full flaps, trimmed the plane for straight flight[,] and slowed to 80 knots. With these details attended to, I crouched in the seat, laid [*sic*] over the starboard side, and, pushing off with my feet, cleared the tail comfortably by eight or ten feet. I delayed opening my chute for a few seconds until I was sure my plane was continuing on course according to plan, then pulled the rip cord. About 1,000 feet above the water I unfastened my leg straps and at 200 feet unhooked the chest buckle and pushed my canteen, knife[,] and pistol outside the hardness to avoid fouling on releasing the chute. The moment my feet touched the water I raised my arms, slid easily out of the chute, and then inflated my Mae West. I then broke out the life raft, inflated it only part way[,] which makes it easier to crawl into. As soon as I had myself and

my gear aboard I inflated the raft the rest of the way, broke out some dye marker, waved to my pals and[,] after bailing out the boat, began looking around for Dumbo. In about fifteen minutes it appeared on the scene[,] and I fired a smoke shell just to be sure they had the word.[2]

A Martin PBM Mariner rescued Edison. Once airborne, Edison requested they land in the water near Chima airfield on Okinawa rather than return to the PBM base at Kerama Rhetto: "Of course I offered to swim ashore[,] but they said all specimens had to be exhibited at their base."[3]

Second Lieutenant John E. Dixon, VMF-115. *Courtesy of the Dixon family*

In Combat It Often Came Down to Seconds

Few pilots had the luxury of time as Edison did. Second Lieutenant John E. Dixon of VMF-115 was flying a short hop near Cebu City, Mindanao, to bomb Japanese reinforcements who threatened a ridge held by guerrillas on February 24, 1945. Coming in low over the enemy, Dixon's Goodyear FG-1 was touched by fire:

When advised by a wingman that my Corsair was smoking, I looked at my oil pressure. It read "zero." The plane began to stall. I suppose I had been hit by somewhere by Jap 12.7's. I ascertained that all switches were on so that the plane would blow up on crashing, and promptly prepared to bail out. To prevent banging my leg on the tail assembly, I grasped the trailing edge of my right wing, suspended myself from there by my hands, and from the cockpit by my toes, and pushed myself down. The tail assembly went a good six feet over my head. I bailed at 1,200 feet and the chute opened at 500 feet.[4]

Three other Corsairs strafed the enemy to keep them suppressed while Dixon struggled to free himself from his harness as he hung from the bamboo trees, trapped 12 feet up in the air. The guerrillas Dixon had been trying to protect from the air rescued him on the ground. Sore but relatively uninjured, Dixon eventually made it back to VMF-115 after four days.

Quick Attachment, Quick Detachment

VMF-214 was in its third configuration by the spring of 1944. As the "Swashbucklers" in 1943, they flew stubby Wildcats against Japan's first team in the Solomons. Before their second tour, they traded the Grumman Iron Works fighters for the mighty pursuit planes built across the Long Island Sound in Stratford, Connecticut. Following the second tour, Major Boyington led the reformed squadron as the "Black Sheep" for the rest of 1943. After its time in the Pacific, -214 returned to the US to re-form at MCAS Santa Barbara in January 1944.

As the rookies with golden wings gained expertise and confidence behind the sticks of their fighters, the time was not without tragedy. On the afternoon of April 14, 2Lt. John Boland Collins approached his Goodyear FG-1 from the right side, mounted the wing, and, using the integrated foot- and handholds in the skin of the Corsair, climbed into his steed. Inside he found the parachute and pararaft kit already on the aluminum seat of the Corsair, left there after earlier flights in the day. The twenty-two-year-old pilot clipped his flight harness onto the rings of the quick-attachment system that held a cushion, the raft, and his chute together.

Above Carrington Point on Santa Rosa Island, Collins prepared for his run against a towed target sleeve. Bruce Gamble, in his book *The Black Sheep*, described the catastrophe that ensued:

> He began climbing and was passing through five thousand feet when his Corsair suddenly pitched over. Out shot Collins with no parachute; he fell to his death while the life raft fluttered down behind. It was later determined that he released his harness, which allowed the expanding raft to shove the stick forward; the sudden onset of negative g's ejected him.[5]

News of Collins's tragic death traveled through channels to the Marine air stations on the West Coast. "They issued us Marine Ka-Bar knives in case the same thing happened to us when we were flying,"[6] recalled 2Lt. Philip Wilmot, USMCR, whose squadron was flying out of El Toro during that period.

No Guarantee of Survival Came with the Parachute Pack

For two months after invasion day, Navy and Marine birds pounded the hell that was Peleliu. As marines and soldiers fought for inches against an entrenched enemy under a blazing equatorial sun, Corsairs delivered lead, iron, and napalm against targets on the wasteland. By November 1944, Japanese gunners had ceased to use tracer rounds in their guns. It only worked against them. With the bent-wing birds flying low-level support missions, the avenues of approach had been identified. Golden tracer rounds served only to give away the Japanese positions.

A dozen VMF-114 Corsairs, each racked with a 500-pound general-purpose bomb, took to the air on November 22 for a bombing and strafing run against targets on nearby Yap Island. The "Death Dealers" pushed over from 8,000 feet, screamed toward the target, and toggled their ordnance release at 1,800 feet before pulling back up and heading out to sea. No resistance was seen to come from the ground, but 1Lt. Robert Spain's bird did not regain air.

No ack-ack was visible to the pilots in the skies, but splashes from 20 mm and 40 mm fire ripped across the waves. Spain called his division leader and alerted the dumbo that he was in trouble. The Pratt & Whitney was in its death throes. Maj. George Bastian queried whether Spain was going to put his plane down or take to the silk. There was no response.

Just 200 feet above the water, Spain jumped. His parachute didn't blossom until he hit the water. He was spotted initially but disappeared beneath the waves as the chute became an anchor. Spain was not seen again. After several minutes without a pilot, Spain's Vought finally crashed just yards from where the marine had submerged. Neither was saved.

There Were Also No Guarantees That the Parachute Would Open

VMF-112's 1Lt. James Percy was jumped by six Zeroes on June 7, 1943, after earning his sixth kill. He stayed in the fight until the controls were shot away. The ace bailed, but the parachute never blossomed. Both BuNo 02331 and Percy hit the seas hard. In spite of a broken pelvis and two sprained ankles, Percy managed to swim for seven hours before he was rescued by natives. Survival was Percy's reward. No Caterpillar Club pin was awarded.

Maybe it was his time with VMF-122 during 1943 that caused Maj. Emerson Dedrick to try to ditch his Corsair on March 24, 1945. Flying with VMF-451 during an attack against the Yontan airfield on Okinawa, his hydraulics were shot away. Most of the electronics failed. Yet, Dedrick did not want to bail out. He radioed 1Lt. D. Wambsganss, "I'm gonna land it in the water, Dewey." His wingman radioed back, "God be with you, fella."[7]

The destroyer USS Waldron was on hand when Dedrick ditched. The tail empennage broke away when he hit the waves. The forward portion submarined down. Despite the destroyer crisscrossing the area for hours, Dedrick was never recovered.

Valentine's Day Present

Before he was based with the VMF-223 on Samar Island, 1Lt. James T. Sykes had received his final training as part of the replacement pool at Efate. There, pilots in flight gear jumped off a ramp into a pool of water. After inflating their Mae Wests, they pulled their rafts from the boat pack and practiced climbing aboard. For those who heeded the lessons, the practice would serve them well.

February 14, 1945, was supposed to be a day for maintenance, a day off from their combat missions supporting the Army's efforts on Samar Island, but instead two last-minute strafing missions were assigned. Sykes led his division from the Guinan strip to strafe airfields on western Negros. After a low pass over Talisay, Sykes's section strafed a supply building before spotting their next target: "As I came around I saw the Betty bomber that had been interrupting our sleep[,] so here I came around again with guns blazing and got a big hit in my left wing. I nearly hit the ground!"[8] But it wasn't Cupid's arrow that had holed his wing: a 40 mm antiaircraft gun had found its mark. Sykes and his wingman turned back to Guinan as Sykes's bird slowly gained altitude.

As he approached the airfield, it was apparent that his FG-1A was not responding correctly to the controls at low speeds with the wheels extended. Sykes's training paid off: "I knew that I could not land the plane and had to jump—which I did. Thanks to the parachute riggers, it worked beautifully."[9] The drogue canopy pulled the chute from the AN-6510 parachute seat pack. Overhead, the twenty-four-panel parachute blossomed into a perfect 24-foot canopy.

Sykes slipped from his chute as he entered the sea, inflated his life vest, and took to his Goodyear boat before an LCM came to his rescue. He was returned to the squadron before Valentine's Day was over.

Sykes kept his parachute as a souvenir. "Four years later, my fiancée, Margie, had her wedding dress made from that beautiful piece of silk."[10]

The Last of the Early Birds

First Lieutenant Bill Nowadnick *(left)* on F4U-1A BuNo 17913, Guam, 1944. *Courtesy of Col. Bill Nowadnick, USMC, Ret.*

The young aviators had been warned in the Pilot's Handbook of Flight Operating Instructions, Navy Model F4U-1 Airplane: "No intentional spinning is permitted."

At an Espiritu Santo airstrip, war-weary Corsairs were revetted behind dirt berms. Marine Fighting Squadron 217's commander had complained to the higher-ups that the birds they had inherited upon the squadron's arrival were in very poor condition. But since Marine fliers had been waging battle over the skies of the South Pacific since August 1942, the new Marine squadrons would take what they could get. Among the veteran birds, one stood out: Bureau Number 02185. She was a very old Corsair.

Built in October 1942, 02185 had been just the thirty-third bent-wing bird to come down the line at the Vought factory in Stratford, Connecticut. Vought had kept six of the earliest planes for their own testing after they were built. A few of the early birds were damaged or lost in training stateside as the Navy and Marines adjusted to flying them. Twenty-four of the summer-of-1942 Corsairs arrived in the Pacific in January 1943. VMF-124 flew the Corsairs into the war, but before they even got into combat with them, the future Marine ace 2Lt. Ken Walsh lost 02172 during a training flight when his magnetos failed. He survived, but it was not an auspicious start for the F4U-1.

In the rush to get the F4U-1s into combat, they had been released from the factory and accepted by the Navy despite the need for critical changes to be implemented. Correction kits and modifications in the field would have to be completed, since Vought could not stop the production line. Their test pilots and engineers worked continually to improve the planes. Changes to the pilot's seat position, modifications to the canopy and master brake cylinders, strengthening of the tail's horizontal stabilizer, improving the belt feed of the machine guns, replacing the ignition harness, ensuring that the fuselage fuel tank would remain attached to the bulkheads, and dozens of other fixes were completed both stateside and in the primitive conditions of the South Pacific.

Bureau Number 02185 was a survivor. Ten of her sisters had been lost in flight during the first four months VMF-124 flew them. Others were taken off flight status when they were no longer airworthy. Pushed aside, they became steel-and-aluminum organ donors to keep other Corsairs in the fight against the Japanese over the Slot and Rabaul. But 02185 was still capable of taking to the skies. She had been the ride for numerous squadrons by 1944. After arriving with -124, she eventually was transferred to VMF-222 for their first tour. From there she was flown by VMF-211. The "Wake Avengers" transferred her back to the "Deuces" in September 1943. When the "Deuces" completed their second tour, 02185 was assigned to VMF-217. By January 1944, 02185 was the oldest Corsair in the Pacific. No pilot would eagerly take her on a long mission, but she could still fly, and so towing the target sleeve while divisions of newer Corsairs ran gunnery missions would be her role as VMF-217 readied for combat.

Not scheduled to fly on January 26, 1944, 1Lt. Bill Nowadnick was fooling around near the flight line when a call went out for a pilot to tow the target sleeve for division gunnery practice. The twenty-two-year-old pilot didn't bother to change out of his moccasins as he grabbed his gear and headed toward his steed for the day, 02185. It was to be her last chance to soar, the last time she took to the air, but the Washington native could not have known that her time was limited when he climbed on the right wing, pulled himself over the side, and strapped himself into her immense cockpit.

02185 wore the early-style birdcage canopy. Oil stains streaked back from her cowl to the front of the canopy. Her paint was scraped and scuffed across her leading edges and was worn thin on the wings, where mechanics had labored for months to keep her airworthy. Her dark-blue finish and black propeller had been sandblasted and salt-blasted over the course of the previous year. She had the original low-style tailwheel assembly, and so her nose pointed higher toward the sky than did her newer sisters on the flight line. Her seat was stuck in the highest position.

Nowadnick taxied the Corsair out of her revetment and brought her onto the steel Marsden mat runway. The big Hamilton propeller grabbed the air as she left the earth and took to the sky. Though she was tired, she was still a superior fighter compared to the little Grumman Wildcats the squadron had first flown while training at the Marine Corps Air Station in El Centro, California.

The VMF-217 division flew their four Corsairs to a position 2,000 feet above Nowadnick to dive and fire against the target. Below, the young marine took evasive maneuvers to challenge the attacking fighters. Minutes into the gunnery practice, the plane jumped and dipped one wing as a metallic thud shook the bird. Trying to correct the sudden spin, Nowadnick discovered that the tow cable had become tangled in the elevator.

Nowadnick tried to release the cable, but with his seat stuck at its highest position and himself strapped in, he could not reach the handle on the floor behind his left foot. Without use of the elevators, Nowadnick's bird began an inverted spin. Knowing that he would be unable to recover, Nowadnick's survival tottered on just a few seconds. There was no chance to call for help, no choice but to bail out.

Locking the canopy back, Nowadnick jumped. His feet caught the windshield, his moccasins staying with the plane. As he fell out, his focus was on clearing the tail as the two cables whipped back and forth behind the fighter. But it was Nowadnick's own microphone cable that wrapped around his throat. For a dangerous moment, he was strangled before his weight ripped the cable free of the dash. The marine hurtled toward the sea, stunned momentarily by the wire's brief hold on his neck. Nowadnick reached across his chest with his right hand to pull the parachute handle. The canopy shot up, bloomed, and then jerked him again.

The white chute was silhouetted against the blue South Pacific sky. The VMF-217 flight leader spiraled around Nowadnick as he floated to the sea. Nowadnick was seen to safely hit the water and climb into his raft; 02185 was done, though. Her spin increased as she screamed unmanned toward the sea. After eighteen months of service, she was gone, a watery grave to receive her remains.

While awaiting rescue, Nowadnick spread shark repellent, put out a dye marker, took inventory of his supplies, and waited. The rocking motion of the little Goodyear raft left the pilot seasick. But before the day was out, a Grumman J2F arrived on scene to save the Washington State native. After circling him for ten minutes, the Duck departed, the sea too rough for the amphibious biplane to set down. Injured but safe, Nowadnick was finally rescued when the crash boat arrived on scene within an hour.

For shoeless Bill Nowadnick, his souvenir of the action was the ripcord handle of his parachute, a stay in sick bay for two weeks, and eventually a "caterpillar" pin for a successful bailout.

The destruction of 02185 was just about the end of an era. The first batch of Vought F4U-1s sent to the Pacific was almost extinct by January 1944. Newer -1As had been arriving in theater since mid-1943. A few of the handbuilt early birds flew deep into the war years stateside, providing pilot training.

Caterpillar Club Members

Textbook
First Lieutenant Frederick W. Edison earned his only kill, a Zeke, on July 2, 1945, during a sweep and strike against Ronchi airfield, Kyushu. He passed away on June 24, 2007.

Came Down to Seconds
Second Lieutenant John E. Dixon of VMF-115 stayed in the USMCR postwar. He flew an additional one hundred missions in Korea to add to the 86.5 missions he flew in World War II. Dixon passed away in 2011.

No Guarantees
VMF-112's 1Lt. James Percy, whose parachute did not open, spent more than a year recovering from his fall. He later flew in the Korean War. His final tally was 135 combat missions. Percy was not awarded a Caterpillar Club pin for his World War II bailout.

Valentine Present
First Lieutenant James Sykes's silk parachute ended up becoming the wedding dress for his wife. Decades later, his daughter was married in the same dress!

Early-Bird Bailout

First Lieutenant Bill Nowadnick shot down a Zeke on February 17, 1944. He retired as a colonel in 1973 after flying in World War II, Korea, and Vietnam. He flew nearly 5,000 hours in thirty different planes. Twelve different carriers provided a roost for him. Nowadnick took to the silk again in 2011, when at age ninety he went skydiving, nearly seventy years after bailing out of his Corsair. On his career in the skies? "It was all fun." Nowadnick passed away in 2020.

CHAPTER 4

WEATHER YOU SURVIVE

An unexpected image emerged: a lone F4U-1D descended over the runway, having escaped the storm clouds to the north. By the time the pilot was debriefed, it became apparent a major calamity was unfolding.

VMF-422 at MCAS Santa Barbara, Goleta, California, 1944

It Was a Disaster That Never Should Have Occurred

Common sense at upper echelons had been sacrificed for field expedience. The material cost was twenty-two new Corsairs lost. The human cost was six Marine pilot lives.

VMF-422 was headed toward its baptism of fire in advance of the invasion of the Marshall Islands, Operation Flintlock. They had departed Marine Corps Air Station Santa Barbara in the fall of 1943. They hopscotched from California to Oahu and then onto Midway Island. They returned to MCAS Ewa in preparation for combat deployment. Twenty-four new Corsairs were loaded onto the USS *Kalinin Bay* (CVE-68). On January 24, 1944, they were catapulted to Tarawa.

After arrival on the tiny island in the Betio Atoll, the VMF-422 commanding officer, Maj. John S. MacLaughlin Jr., was notified that the squadron would transfer to Funafuti by way of Nanumea in the Ellice Islands. He requested an escort, a common practice when single-engine planes had to travel great distances overwater. MacLaughlin's request was taken up the chain of command but denied.

The "Flying Buccaneers" stayed overnight before departing the next morning for Nanumea. The weather report stated there would be favorable flying weather. Unbeknown to MacLaughlin, the forecast was outdated. In retrospect, Lt. Robert Scott, whose Corsair had starter trouble, may have been the luckiest pilot in the squadron. Twenty-three birds departed the sun-drenched Hawkins Field without him.

The planes traveled in three flights. As they headed southeast, they passed over numerous islands that served as checkpoints. VMF-422 was just minutes from arrival at Nanumea when a Navy R4D passed them heading north. The Navy pilots were the last people to see all twenty-three Marine pilots alive. At that point in the flight, the Marines were on time, were on track, and had plenty of gas still in reserve.

The path to Nanumea became blocked as a cyclone rose across the horizon. The torrential rain made it impossible to see through the front windscreen. Keeping position by glances through the side of the canopy, they finally broke through the front. Five of their planes did not emerge into the eye of the storm with them, but radio contact was maintained with the errant fliers.

Minutes later, they exited the eye and entered the storm again. Since they were close to Nanumea, they assumed they were over the island. Flying through the cyclone, many pilots were forced to fly at full throttle to stick with their leaders. Several pilots reported that their fuel levels were getting low.

The storm took its first victim: Lt. Christian Lauesen ditched after reporting engine trouble. He escaped his sinking plane but lost his raft. Afloat just by the buoyancy of his life vest, Lauesen was seen by the flight floating on the stormy seas before they continued on. In a selfless act, Lt. Curly Lehnert stayed overhead of Lauesen until he ran out of fuel. Lehnert bailed out near where he thought Lauesen was. Lehnert managed to inflate his raft but was not able to find Lauesen.

In the belief that they had overflown Nanumea, MacLaughlin initiated several course changes. The storm continued to worsen. As they searched in vain, Capt. Rex Jeans tried to contact MacLaughlin by radio. Failing to do so, Jeans flew his Corsair across the CO's horizon to get his attention. MacLaughlin transferred the flight lead to Jeans, who would try to bring them back to Nui, an island between Nanumea and Funafuti. MacLaughlin then flew by himself away from the other sections. His two wingmen attempted to stay with him. All three disappeared into the storm.

The flight of twenty-three planes was now down to fifteen planes. Lt. Robert Moran was able to serve as a radio relay between Jeans and Nanumea. Now two hours past their ETA, Moran radioed Jeans that he was out of fuel. Despite being advised to ditch by Jeans, Moran bailed out. He failed to clear his harness as he entered the water. Moran drowned in the storm.

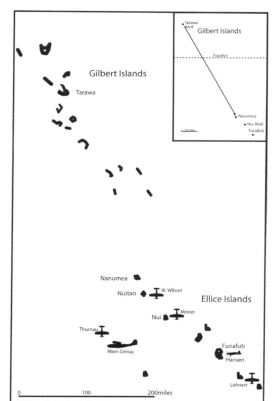

Map of "Lost Squadron" flight

Funafuti

One pilot made it through. Lt. John Hansen was with two other pilots who had become separated from their flight. Flying on instruments, he attempted to climb through the storm. Hansen found himself alone but still with plenty of gas. He made the decision to try to find Funafuti.

Hansen finally broke through the storm and saw what he thought was Nanumea. MacLaughlin and Jeans were still attempting to find the beam to Funafuti. Reaching Captain Jeans by radio, Hansen asked how to find the beam. Jeans relayed the question to MacLaughlin. When the info came back, Hansen was able to get his bearing: "At what I estimated to be thirty to forty miles from Funafuti my engine began to miss and sputter badly, although my instrument readings were normal."[1] He nursed the bird down. Beneath him in the atoll was moored a small American armada. The runway ran the length of Fongafale Island, a coral strip just above sea level.

The blue bent-wing bird came to a stop at 1415. Soon the authorities learned that somewhere to the north, twenty-two other Corsairs were missing.

Lost in the storm, it was not long before other pilots were forced to ditch due to low fuel. Lt. William Aycrigg and 1Lt. Ted Thurnau ditched 7 miles apart. Even though some pilots reported having more than an hour of fuel left, the hour was late. Jeans decided that the remaining thirteen pilots should ditch together. "We formed a traffic circle and tried to land [as] near each other as possible. We jettisoned hoods, dropped full flaps[,] and floated in."[2]

As Lt. Robert Wilson mentally ran through the ditching checklist, his focus was also on his log and pay account in his flight suit. Lt. Mark Syrkin went through a mental rehearsal, too, and took steps for ditching: "I took off my shoes and tied them around my neck. I threw my chart board over the side because it was loose and I was afraid it might have injured me when I landed. I then fired my guns[,] as I had previously read that it would lighten the plane considerably."[3]

All safely escaped their planes, though one pilot lost both his raft and his flight suit in the attempt. Jeans continued, "We tried joining up on Lts. Thurnau and Aycrigg[,] but the sea was so rough it was impossible to spot them."[4]

The twelve rafts held thirteen pilots on the stormy seas. Said Jeans, "We were jostled around so much that it was difficult to remain in the raft."[5] The marines had become mariners.

1800 Hours

Within two hours of Hansen's appearance at Funafuti, air and sea rescue missions were initiated. Patrol Squadron 53 immediately put all available PBY Catalinas into the air. Twelve days of searching began. The tin cans of Destroyer Division 38 brought all their boilers on line as they left their moorings at the atoll. The USS *Hobby* (DD-610) led the USS *Welles* (DD-628), USS *Gillespie* (DD-609), and USS *Kalk* (DD-611) from the lagoon. In a column bound for the vicinity of Nui Island, the eight stacks trailed black smoke. Minutes later the sun disappeared on the western horizon.

Wednesday, January 26: First Light

Patrol planes flew their search routes. DesDiv 38 continued to search the seas around the Ellice Islands. The first break came when a PBY sighted a beached plane on Niutao Island. The *Hobby* rescued Lt. Walt "Jake" Wilson from a bevy of potential native brides. He was the only pilot saved that day.

The convoy of Goodyear rafts floated undetected by air. By sea, a group of sharks developed an interest in the thirteen marines. Sizing up their prey, the predators made repeated passes against the group. They scraped against the sea anchor and the rubber boats. When their aggression grew too great, Capt. Charlie Hughes drew his sidearm and shot one of the sharks. That ended their curiosity, and they swam off.

The day continued without salvation. As the wave height increased, the moorings for the ropes began to break. To stay together, the pilots had to hold on to the other rafts by hand, further taxing their strength. Dark came early in the equatorial skies. "Frequent 'prayer meetings' and songfests led by Lt. Don Walker helped to bolster morale."[6]

Court of Inquiry, USS *Curtiss* (AV-4), Tarawa

Whereas the search would continue for eleven more days, the commander of Air Central Pacific, Adm. John Hoover, convened a board of inquiry immediately after the disaster was discovered.

Thursday, January 27

It was a morning of frustration for the destroyers and patrol planes. Despite nearly two days of air and sea searches, no further sightings of the marines were reported. The first bit of luck came early in the afternoon. Braving 10-to-12-foot swells, Lt. j.g. Herb Shively put his Catalina PBY-5A down in the chop to rescue Lt. "Curly" Lehnert west of Funafuti. Including Hansen, who had landed at Funafuti, only three of twenty-three marine pilots were accounted for after forty-eight hours.

When word was received in Funafuti of Shively's rescue, Ens. George Davidson was ordered to fly his Catalina to search the same area. After he failed to find anyone, Davidson turned west to search an adjoining search area. His intuition saved thirteen marines. Chartreuse dye staining the ocean was spotted.

The Marine armada was ready: "We had all rehearsed what we were going to do when anyone sighted a boat or plane. One was to release three dye markers, another was to fire a Very pistol, someone else was to shoot tracers, one was to wave a canvas—and the rest of us were to pray," reported Lt. Mark Breeze.[7]

With the waves running high, Davidson was faced with the same challenge Shively had experienced, but with one major difference: even in the unlikely event he could land safely, the extra weight of the Marine pilots aboard the Catalina would further reduce Davidson's ability to get the flying boat airborne again. That scenario would put his own crew at risk.

Davidson reported his situation to Funafuti. The choice became his: to land at sea or not. The hour was late. A storm was brewing in the skies. Davidson chose selflessly—he landed the PBY. The marines celebrated by consuming the rest of their rations.

Battling 12-foot swells and a 16-knot wind, Davidson taxied to the group. Eight marines from seven rafts were rescued, but five other rafts had broken free of the main group. Davidson's flying boat acted as a surface craft as the ensign steered from raft to raft, marine to marine. As darkness enveloped them, all thirteen marines were safely aboard. At that point, it was too late to attempt a takeoff.

When word reached Destroyer Division 38 of Davidson's sighting, three of the tin cans steamed at flank speed to the reported position. They arrived after dark. Brother Catalinas dropped flares and landing lights to guide them to Davidson.

The *Hobby* closed Davidson's Catalina while the other destroyers searched independently for further survivors. After the *Hobby* transferred the marines aboard, the plane was taken under tow. Shortly after midnight, Davidson and his crew transferred to the tin can.

Friday, January 28

Another marine was saved from the seas. The *Welles* located 1Lt. Ted Thurnau just a few miles from where the main group was discovered. The destroyers searched for the rest of the day, but neither Aycrigg nor any of the other pilots were found.

Still under tow by the *Hobby*, Davidson's plane was taking on water. The Catalina could not be saved, so it was decided to cut the plane loose. Gunner's mates on the *Hobby*'s 20 mm and 40 mm guns sank her.

Saturday, January 29

Overnight, Destroyer Division 38 returned to Funafuti. The fourteen marines came ashore. They were treated for the usual maladies that came with spending two days on the water: nausea, immersion, general weakness, sunburn, bruises, and lacerations. The rescue search continued for nine more days, but no more "Flying Buccaneers" were recovered.

The surviving pilots were ordered to return to Tarawa to testify as witnesses for the Board of Inquiry.

After the butcher's bill was totaled, twenty-two of twenty-three planes had been lost. The CO was among five missing pilots who would never be discovered. A sixth pilot had drowned when he became entangled in his parachute. The "Lost Squadron" suffered the single greatest loss of airborne Corsairs in one day by a squadron. Later known as "the Flintlock Tragedy," it was the worst accident in naval aviation history. And the "Buccaneers" had yet to enter combat.

Like many large tragedies during World War II, the story of the Lost Squadron was not well known. Adm. Nimitz released a press release three days after the pilots arrived at Funafuti, but it did not identify the squadron. The VMF-422 ground echelon and its other pilots did not learn of the losses until coming ashore several weeks later.

The Court of Inquiry released its initial findings in February. The Fourth Marine Base Defense Air Wing commander at Hawkins Field was given a letter of censure for not providing an escort for the Buccaneers. The board recommended that appropriate escort planes be provided whenever single-engine planes or air units were flying long distances overwater. This recommendation was adopted by the Navy.

After the rescue, the squadron drew replacement planes from other units. The Flying Buccaneers entered combat on April 1, 1944. Two of the survivors of the January 25 flight later perished that spring. In 1945, during a mission to Japan, the hard-luck VMF-422 ignobly suffered the greatest loss of Marine Corsair fighter pilots during World War II in which weather and enemy fire were not the cause, when bombs carried by three of their planes exploded spontaneously. Four more Flying Buccaneers were killed in the latter tragedy.

I like to think that you winged your way
Up through the dusk of that deep darkening day
That God leaned down and took you by the hand
And led your soul into that other land.
Because He saw, engraved across the sky,
The paths you made where others dared not fly;
And saw you dim the distance of the West
A little nearer Heaven than the rest.

—Unknown[8]

Black Monday: January, 15, 1945

Fl. Sgt. Bryan Cox with his Black Monday steed, F4U-1 NZ5261, BuNo 49771.
Courtesy of Bryan Cox

By mid-February 1944, the airspace above Rabaul had been cleared of enemy aircraft. Though Japanese birds did not rise to tangle with Allied fliers, ack-ack did. And as it was across the crumbling empire, areas that were subject to relentless attacks from the air were protected by very experienced crews on the antiaircraft guns. Rabaul was no different.

Simpson Harbor could have been called "aluminum bottom sound" for the collection of broken Allied planes lying on its bottom. It was a sunken volcanic caldera on the northeastern end of New Britain. It was enveloped by mountains, and planes that dared enter the airspace were subject to overlapping fields of fire. To keep the fortress neutralized, regular attacks were sent against the cutoff Japanese garrison.

On the morning of January 15, 1945, three dozen New Zealand dash-one and dash-one Ds took off from Green Island and Bougainville to strike the Toboi Wharf in Simpson Harbor. The Nos. 14, 16, and 24 Squadron pilots faced exploding black clouds as they attacked the target. One gun crew found their mark. No. 14 Squadron flight lieutenant Francis G. Keefe's bird shuddered from the impact. With a wing on fire, black smoke emanating from the engine, and his plane hurtling toward the harbor, the twenty-eight-year-old pilot bailed.

Witnessing Keefe's dire straits, another pilot followed him down to ensure he survived. Keefe escaped from his parachute. He didn't dare inflate his raft at this point, since the yellow Goodyear would have served to highlight him to the gunners on the mountains ringing the harbor. Instead, Keefe decided to swim for it and reach the open water of St. George's Channel, where potentially a dumbo could set down. His Nos. 14 and 16 teammates stayed on station to strafe enemy gun positions and any potential "rescue" boats sent by the Japanese.

Back on Green Island, a rescue package was hurriedly assembled to bring the Auckland native back to safety. Sixteen gull wings from Nos. 14 and 16 Squadrons (one turned back with mechanical difficulties) were joined by a No. 2 Bomber Reconnaissance Squadron Ventura. Its goal was to drop two hurriedly constructed native rafts to Keefe. The rescue vessel would be a PBY-5A. Based at Green Island, VPB-44 routinely kept one of its "Black Cat" night raiders on standby, the plane and its crew ready for immediate take off for dumbo missions.

It was a 150-mile flight for the group. Arriving on scene, Keefe was still attempting to swim to safer waters. The "Black Cat" circled nearby out of harm's way. Capt. Lee Dobberstein's requests to effect a rescue were denied twice.

W/O Ron Lindsey RNZAF brought his Ventura low over the scene in an attempt to drop the pair of rafts near Keefe. He was escorted by a pair of F4Us flown by Squadron Leader Paul Green and Flight Sergeant Bryan Cox while Flying Officer Grev Randell orbited at 10,000 feet to provide a VHF link with the home airfield.

Cox reported, "I flew close behind the Ventura for the raft drop, and Paul flew in front, indicating Frank's position by firing his guns in the water. Ron Lindsey dropped the rafts right on target."[9]

Twelve Corsairs were sent to strafe the Simpson Harbor waterfront during the raft drop, aiming to keep the enemy's heads low and their fingers off the triggers of their guns.

For Keefe, exhaustion overcame hours of adrenaline-fueled efforts. He hung limply over a log as the tide and wind turned against him, slowly pushing him back toward Rabaul. He did not take advantage of the nearby rafts. Finally, the rescue team was forced to turn back due to the late hour. Keefe would survive for a time, but his rescuers could not have foreseen the disaster that was about to occur.

A Black Curtain Developed across the Horizon

As the fifteen Corsairs returned to their island nest, a tropical front rose from the sea to the heavens. Its depth was unknown. After passing the southern end of New Ireland, the group turned northeast in an attempt to circumvent the storm. When they were due north of Green Island, they were vectored south for the short flight to return to base.

Hell poured from the heavens. Corsairs were not nocturnal; no landing lights were installed. Despite the hour, the storm turned the day into night as the planes flew through the driving rain. Pilots struggled to stay with their sections as they flew in pitch-black conditions through a torrent of rain. Recalled Cox, "Its unusual 'inverted gull-wing' design gave it more lateral stability and therefore held a heading better than other fighter aircraft."[10] Enveloped in black ink, pilots had to rely on their instruments since there were no visual cues outside of the canopies. The weight of the last gallons of fuel being consumed were offset by the volume of water making its way past the seals of the canopy.

After just several moments in the storm front, two -1Ds collided. Flt. Sgt. John S. McArthur and Flt. Lt. Bruce Hay were gone. Moments later, Flying Officer Albert Saward was seen to disappear from the sky. Whether from a lack of fuel or disorientation in the storm, the fate of the twenty-two-year-old pilot was not determined. No. 16's flight lieutenant Thomas Johnson and flight sergeant Ronald Albrecht did not escape the storm's rapture. Their bent-wing birds crashed into the seas.

Several of the Kiwi birds were able to land safely, but not all did. As they approached Green Island, Flight Sergeant Ian Munro was seen entering the landing pattern. But before he could put his plane down, the twenty-year-old pilot pulled his stick back and flew back up into the storm. He was never seen again. At low altitude, Flying Officer Greville Randell missed the runway, crossed the lagoon, and crashed into the jungle on the opposite shore. The twenty-four-year-old pilot did not survive the impact.

With fuel running low, No. 14 Squadron's Bryan Cox faced death on his twentieth birthday. Flying in tight formation with Squadron Leader Paul Green on entering the front, it was still daylight, so Cox failed to switch on either cockpit or external lighting. However, dusk occurred very rapidly with the storm. Following his attempts to find the cockpit-lighting switch in the dark, as well as hold close formation, he inadvertently turned off his battery switch with his right hand while feeling among the switches on the starboard electrical panel. For the rest of the flight he had neither lights nor radio, instead having to rely on the luminosity of his artificial-horizon instrument and the glowing markings on his altimeter.

Continuing to fly level at 1,000 feet[,] I tried to decide whether to wait for the engine to stop and then ditch in the sea, which was somewhere in the black void below, or bail out before it stopped[,] and land in the water with my parachute on top of me, to no doubt become enveloped in the darkness and drown, or at best be devoured by sharks during the night. Not having a landing light, the ditching didn't seem too practical[,] as I wouldn't know where the water was in the complete darkness.[11]

The storm provided his savior:

When I had a flash of lightning[,] I didn't see the airstrip and flare path, but only the atoll directly below me for half a second. I had a brief glimpse of trees directly below me[,] so had to guess where the airstrip would be and turned towards it. I know there was another flash of lightning[,] as I got a brief glimpse of my airspeed indicator[,] which showed me where the 100-knot mark was, so reduced power to keep the ASI needle pointing in that direction whilst commencing my approach to where the flare path should be! Between the lightning flashes[,] none of the instruments were visible—just the needles![12]

Cox had never completed a night landing in a Corsair, but he had no choice. He lowered the wheels, dropped the flaps, and kept an eye on his airspeed. As he lined up with the runway, he realized that he was approaching from the wrong direction. The runway lights and a searchlight were barely visible, but he stayed airborne, turned his steed out to the sea, and came back for another attempt. He had lost sight of the field's lights but managed to find them at the end of his turn. Praying that no birds were taxiing in the almost complete darkness, he set his mount, NZ5261, down.

Cox was one of just eight pilots who safely returned to earth of the fifteen that set out to aid in the rescue of their mate in Simpson Harbor. Half a mug of rum and a shot of morphine were administered to calm his nerves. "Although I was now aware of the tragic events involving many of my friends, I developed an uncontrollable feeling of elation and relief at the realization that my parents would be spared the terrible shock of my death, which I had fully accepted only a short time before."[13]

A "Black Cat" was sent aloft in an attempt to find the missing pilots. It continued the search until dawn. Cox returned to the air the next morning. Despite his search of the waters around Green Island, no flotsam from the bent-wing birds floated on the waves, and no survivors were ever found.

January 15, Black Monday, was the single greatest loss of Royal New Zealand Air Force pilots during World War II. Flying Officer Grev Randell's remains were interred two days later. In Simpson Harbor, it is believed that Flight Lieutenant Francis Keefe made his way to a pair of rocks that jutted from the water of Simpson Harbor. He was captured by the Japanese but died two weeks later of "blood poisoning." Only a handful of fliers and aircrew captured at Rabaul survived the war.

CHAPTER 5

LUCK, DUMB LUCK, GREMLINS, AND OTHERWISE

"A[n] F4U pilot on a ferry mission experienced engine failure mid-flight. As he brought his bird down for a wheels[-]up landing in a field, he took all the correct steps except one[,] hours earlier. In attempt to save time, he had removed his seat to stow his bags in the fuselage. Carelessly, he did not fully reset the locking pins that held the seat in place. As the prop and wings contacted the ground, the seat pins sheared. The plane deacellerated [sic] but the pilot did not. His injuries were fatal."

—*Naval Aviation News*[1]

Slow-Motion Rescue: Capt. Frank B. Baldwin

Off the coast of Santa Barbara, a pair of fighting falcons dove on their prey when one bird clipped the tail of the other.

VMF-221 had already earned an enviable record and a proud combat history by the spring of 1944. They had defended Midway in the spring of 1942 as best they could with their tired Grumman Wildcats and Brewster Buffaloes before re-forming at Ewa. The spring of 1943 found them flying their Wildcats from Guadalcanal. Between Solomon tours, they transitioned to Vought's mighty fighter. The Fighting Falcons' third tour ended in November with several aces on the roster, including the Medal of Honor winner James Swett. From SoPac, it was back to California to re-form the squadron in the spring of 1944, along with -214 "Black Sheep" and -115 "Joe's Jokers."

Capt. Frank Baldwin led his wingman, 1Lt. Ewell Harold Haynes Jr., from MCAS Santa Barbara on a gunnery mission during the morning of May 13, 1944. As they dove, their focus was on the target sleeve. The rookie Haynes was perhaps too focused. His Goodyear FG-1 dropped onto Baldwin's Brewster F3A. The 13-foot Hamilton Standard prop almost became the executioner's sword as it sliced through the four longerons, several frames, and the thin aluminum skin that composed the monocoque fuselage. The severed birdcage Corsair's tail spiraled slowly to the seas while the nose tipped down, the forward portion of the fighter careening out of control.

Haynes ditched his wounded bird in the heavy seas off the California coast, 25 miles west of Point Conception. Though Haynes cleared his sinking plane, he was unable to extract his raft pack. He inflated his vest but never released the attached dye packet after he entered the water.

Baldwin struggled to push the birdcage canopy back before escaping his own plane and taking to the silk. The canopy blossomed. The section leader floated down to the Pacific. Baldwin was able to shed the parachute, inflate his Mae West, and get into his yellow boat.

Rescue boats were launched and air-sea rescue planes were sent aloft. Spotter planes from MCAS Santa Barbara and NAS San Pedro participated in the search. The sub chaser USS *SC-758*, on patrol south of Point Conception, joined the effort as well. Coming upon the scene, the rescue dumbo found just Baldwin. With heavy seas running, the PBY pilot decided he could not put his plane down safely. Just two days earlier, a PBY was swamped during an attempted rescue and had to be sunk by gunfire. Meanwhile, the twenty-four-year-old Baldwin was nearing exhaustion as he was buffeted by the strong waves. It was likely that it would be several hours before surface craft could arrive on the scene. It was also likely Baldwin would succumb to the seas if a rescue did not emerge in the short term.

On routine antisubmarine patrol, Lt. j.g. Peter Culbertson piloted K-95, a Goodyear blimp, from its base at Santa Ana. Directed to the scene, he found Baldwin's own Goodyear, a tiny one-man raft, bouncing on the seas. Blimp Squadron 31 had experimented with the air-sea rescue of a dummy pilot in a raft by a blimp. The idea was abandoned: "The conclusion was thus drawn that rescue from the sea by an airship is almost impossible or too dangerous to a survivor."[2]

But without another vessel capable of performing the rescue in the area, Culbertson piloted his craft down in an attempt to save the marine pilot. Almost as long as a football field and as tall as a five-story building, the nonrigid airship flew to just 15 feet above the waves as the twenty-five-year-old pilot managed the twin R-1340 Pratt & Whitney engines.

A rope was lowered to Baldwin, but the marine was too exhausted to hold on when it was raised. After several tries, the rope was pulled back aboard the blimp. A crewman tied a harness to the end, and it was lowered again for another rescue attempt. That did the trick. With Baldwin secured to the harness, he was hauled aboard.

In a war that spanned almost all points of the earth and a majority of the world's population, at times the conflict seemed very small. Once aboard the blimp's tiny control car, Baldwin went forward to offer thanks to the craft's pilot. Rather than greetings punctuated with military rank, to their surprise it was simple salutations of first names. Before the war, Baldwin had wrestled against Culbertson in the college ranks, Waynesboro Teacher's College wrestling team versus the matmen of the University of Minnesota, Frank against Pete.

Back at the home of Blimp Squadron 31, Santa Ana station, Baldwin praised his rescuers, since "if he hadn't been pulled aboard at that time, he could not have lasted much longer." He later went on to tell an Associated Press reporter that "one of the happiest moments of my life was when I saw that airship approaching."[3]

Two other blimps continued the search for Haynes, but the Athens, Georgia, native was never recovered.

The "Fighting Falcons" got back into the shooting war in February 1945, aboard the USS Bunker Hill. Baldwin added two kills to his previous three collected in the Solomons. The ace finished the war with two Distinguished Flying Crosses and Seven Air Medals.

Lt. j.g. Culbertson was awarded his own DFC following a daring rescue in the desert in July 1944. He passed away in 2000.

Sleight of Hand

Side by side sat two tanks in the cockpit. One could save the plane during combat. The other could save it during landing. Mixing them up could prove to be fatal. That juxtaposition, a design flaw, eliminated an ensign over enemy territory.

On February 4, 1944, VF-17 Corsairs escorted lumbering B-24s on a mission to Rabaul. Each of the Liberators carried ten souls. The bombers were heavily armed but still relied on fighter escort to get safely to and from the targets. When a large group of enemy fighters appeared, Ens. Percy Divenney reached down to open the yellow handle of the CO_2 tank that would purge gas fumes from his wing tanks as a safety precaution. Instead he turned the red handle on the other CO_2 tank. Down came the landing gear. Once forced down, the wheels could not be retracted.

Immediately Divenney became a target. The squadron commanding officer, Lt. Cmdr. Tom Blackburn, ordered Divenney to bring his Corsair within the protective range of the Liberators' guns. The young pilot did not obey the order. Blackburn recounted in his memoir, "Our job was to protect the B-24s, and we all had our hands full doing that, so I made the brutal decision to withhold cover for Divenney."[4]

Divenney continued to fall back. With enemy fighters after him, Divenney's section leader, "Chico" Freeman, and two other pilots broke from the ranks. They tried to save Divenney. Though "Beads" Popp nailed one enemy plane, their effort was for naught. Divenney's Corsair began to smoke before it spun down to the ocean.

The fallout was immediate, both in the air and across the world. The cause of Divenney's loss went up both the chain of command and through the Vought reporting channels. In the Solomons, locking pins were installed over the top of red-handled tanks. At the factory, the tank positions were changed, but it was too late to save Ensign Divenney.

Frequent Flier

While VMF-114's pilots were known as the "Death Dealers," there were many Japanese gunners in the Palau Islands also striving to earn that epithet. And so the battles of opposing forces struggling against each other on a regular basis took on a familiar, but still deadly, feel. First Lieutenant William Sonnenberg, USMC, was part of a barge sweep mission on November 28, 1944. After months of being cut off from resupply, targets along the coastline of Babelthuap Island were scarce. Targets for enemy guns were not.

Ack-ack racked the Sonnenberg's dash-one Goodyear. With flames pouring out of the engine, he turned his bird out to sea before pushing back the canopy and bailing out. He swam across the channel before making landfall on a reef just a half mile offshore. In short time, the dumbo was on the scene. Lt. j.g. K. F. Brissette dropped a raft to Sonnenberg, marked the rescue point with smoke bombs, and then set his VPB-54 Catalina down when the Marine pilot was in position. Sonnenberg was back with his buddies in no time.

Four weeks later, Sonnenberg's division set out for another barge sweep of Babelthuap. The enemy gunner's aim was true again. The ordnance found purchase in the vital guts of the eighteen-cylinder engine. Fatally wounded, the Pratt & Whitney quit. Dropping too quickly to bail out, the young lieutenant ditched in the Pacific, inflated his raft, and paddled to the reef 2 miles offshore. While he awaited his dumbo ride, a nest of coral snakes kept his attention. Danger was always nearby for pilots.

VPB-54 sent Lt. j.g. John Love, who had already rescued two other aviators in the previous weeks. Sonnenberg, who was already rehearsed in the procedure of a Catalina rescue, was ready and so was on board soon enough. Two close calls were enough for the twenty-one-year-old Marine pilot. Medicating himself liberally with medicinal brandy kept aboard the big cat, Sonnenberg staggered from intoxication when he finally set foot on Peleliu again.

The "Death Dealers'" war diary noted, "Score for Sonnenberg 28 Nov. to date: 1 jump, 1 dead stick water landing, no errors. Plenty of skill, quick thinking and a fair amount of good luck."[5]

Sonnenberg was later awarded the DFC for "extraordinary achievement while participating in aerial flight, in action against enemy Japanese forces in the Pacific Theater of Operations during World War II."

Wakeman's Walkabout

No-Man's Land

Bougainville had been a tug-of-war between the Japanese and the Allies since November 1943. Though the Americans had established airfields on the island, the Japanese had not been conquered. Attacks and counterattacks of low and high intensity continued. By December 1944, the American army troops had been relieved by Australians. Fighting continued until war's end.

January 29, 1945, started with a dawn patrol for the RNZAF No. 21 Squadron. Taking off early from the Piva North airfield, Flight Sergeant Keith Wakeman joined his section leader in the skies over Bougainville. The two engaged in a mock dogfight under the low rising sun. As the twenty-year-old Wakeman slipped in behind his partner, Fl. Lt. Keith Dockery, his Corsair was violently buffeted by the slipstream before stalling and entering a spin. Fighting the controls, the effusive Kiwi knew he had to bail out immediately. There was no recovering from a spin in the Vought bird.

Wakeman reached forward to free the red safety pins on the canopy, then grabbed the safety handles, pushing upward and forward, against the strain of the spin. The canopy was carried away by the slipstream. For his own evacuation, he tried to exit over the side, but centripetal force kept him in the bird. He took the path of least resistance and fled the plane from the other side, clipping the tail with his back. The spin had started at angels 11, but by the time he exited and pulled his parachute ring, he was under 1,000 feet. Underneath his dangling feet was the no-man's land between Allied and Japanese lines, an impenetrable jungle.

The flight sergeant's partner had not seen Wakeman's dash-one spin into the jungle, nor the silk dropping into the sea of green. Wakeman's chute snagged several branches, so for a period he was caught in the jungle canopy. He eventually was able to cut himself free of the chute but took the time to stash the beacon of his arrival. Capture meant certain death. Though the sun was rising higher in the sky, the jungle remained dark and the air steamy in the equatorial climate. Mosquitoes and other insects arrived to greet the airman. Artillery barked in the background. Though planes could be heard overhead, Wakeman had no way to signal them. To survive, Wakeman would have to keep on the move despite injuring his back.

Raised in the tough Depression era, Wakeman slogged through school, but dyslexia held back his grades. He survived by his wits instead. Outgoing, highly intelligent, and calculating about any situation he engaged, the New Zealander looked for a stream as he fought his way through thick underbrush. He followed a stream downhill until it was large enough that he could float downriver. With his air vest inflated and his boots tied around his neck, Wakeman became a human raft. He wasn't alone. Crocodiles on the riverbank saw a potential feast moving by. Not of a mind to wrestle crocs, the pilot flapped his arms vigorously, screaming and yelling to scare the carnivores away. He broke a cardinal rule of survival: always keep your footgear, but when a 7-footer approached and another croc entered the water within yards of him, he hurled his leather boots at the beasts to keep them at bay.

Wakeman finally came to a bridge, but, unsure of whether it was controlled by the empire or the Crown, he hid himself in the jungle nearby, afraid of any enemy patrols. He finally thought it was safe to come out when two Allied bridge guards appeared. Injured, bitten up, dripping wet, exhausted, filthy, and shoeless, he presented himself for inspection after thirty-eight hours in the jungle. His trip back to the Piva North airfield took an easier route.

Wakeman arrived back at his hut to learn his mates were ready to go on with life without him! "His bailout not being observed, he was reported 'missing believed killed.'" His bunk was ready to be assigned to another flier, his personal effects to be sent back to his parents were sequestered, and his private canteen of alcohol and cigarettes had already been divided among the other fliers! Luck was still on Wakeman's side: he had emerged from his walkabout before his father had told his mother that he was missing!

Flight Sergeant Wakeman collapsed the next time he tried to mount his Corsair. He was evacuated to New Zealand suffering with dengue fever but eventually returned to fly with his squadron. Wakeman stayed with the bent-wing birds as a member of No. 14 Squadron, New Zealand's only postwar Corsair squadron in occupied Japan. Eventually, he became a champion glider pilot, winning numerous awards and setting many records. Postwar, Wakeman owned his own air charter business. Two bank robbers once used his plane for their getaway! Wakeman tipped off the police. He passed away in 2004.

A Shot in the Dark

Gen. Douglas MacArthur had set his sights on his returning to the Philippines. But for that to happen, control of the Dampier and Vitiaz Straits west of New Britain and the air rights above the Bismarck Archipelago had to be wrestled from the empire. The string of islands was dominated by New Britain and New Ireland. They sat at the top of the infamous "Slot," the ladder of parallel islands from Guadalcanal to Bougainville. The battle had started at the 'canal in August 1942. Corsairs entered the fray in February 1943 with Marine Fighting Squadron 124. With the decision to capture the Green Islands, north of Bougainville and east of Fortress Rabaul, troops were embarked for the invasion in January 1944.

After transport to Espiritu Santo in early January 1944, VMF-217 prepared to do battle. "Max's Wild Hares," nicknamed for their CO, Maj. Max Read, moved to the Piva Yoke field on Bougainville on January 29. Less than twenty-four hours after their arrival, the squadron took to the air for its first mission. Two divisions escorted Army B-24 bombers on their mission to rain iron on the Vunakanau airfield south of Rabaul. Two of the hognosed fighters had to turn back due to mechanical problems. Another failed to make the rendezvous, leaving just five -217 birds as part of the cover for their larger army brothers. On the return flight, a third bird lost power. Second Lieutenant Robert M. Ranagan's first mission ended as he ditched his plane 60 miles west of Bougainville. His wingman witnessed Ranagan emerge from the cockpit and get into his life raft.

After the remaining "Hares" returned to base, another division was sent aloft to escort a dumbo plane in search of the missing junior pilot. Results were negative. But floating on the seas below was Ranagan, a "Black Irishman" counting on the cultural luck of his clan. After the water landing, his dash-one stayed afloat for several minutes, more than enough time to climb out on the wing and inflate both his Mae West and his raft. He was already aboard the Goodyear when the Corsair nosed downward into the seas, its tail finally disappearing below the waves. Though he had hurt his wrist, it was only midday, and his wingman had circled him before heading off to base to report his position. The chance of recovery seemed strong.

It would be four hours before two more Corsairs did a low pass nearly overhead. Lady Luck seemed to be smiling on the effusive Ranagan, who could not know that his brothers had not seen him in his yellow dinghy or the dye surrounding it. Convinced that help was on the way, the New Yorker drank all his water, shot his .45 at some low-flying birds, and paddled occasionally to keep within the dye ring. An hour later, a Dauntless circled him but departed with the daylight. Surely, Ranagan thought, it was just a matter of time before the crash boat would arrive. After a few hours, it seemed appropriate to fire some flares into the dark night skies to aid in his rescue.

Rather than the airfield's 80-foot crash boat arriving in response to Ranagan's glowing stars, out of the darkness the prow of a 2,000-ton American destroyer bore down on the pilot. Escorting three hundred New Zealanders on their way to raid Green Island, the USS *Guest* (DD-472) happened upon Ranagan. He was aboard in just seven minutes. The twenty-two-year-old pilot remained as a guest of the *Guest* for two days before *PT-167* brought the lucky Irish American back to base.

First Lieutenant Robert Ranagan was back in the cockpit two days later. He was later awarded the Distinguished Flying Cross for extraordinary achievement while participating in air attacks against the Japanese Empire's forces during World War II.

25-Meter Dash

RNZAF Corsair racked with a 1,000-pound "daisy cutter" bomb

By late spring of 1945, for the Kiwi squadrons flying from the islands of the South Pacific, the sighting of a Japanese plane rising to do battle was akin to a vision of a mermaid. Rabaul and the Slot had become backwater battles, but missions continued against the emperor's ground forces. Though the Japanese air force was not ready to mix it up with the bent-wing birds, the gunners on the ground had years of experience against attackers from on high.

The morning of May 11, Squadron Leader Gordon Delves mounted his bird. Slung below were two "daisy cutters," 1,000-pound general-purpose bombs with long pipe-nose extensions designed to clear the thick jungle foliage and devastate ground troops. As he taxied his dash-one onto the Marsden matting of the Piva North (Uncle) airfield on Bougainville, his No. 26 Squadron team pulled in behind him, each with one of the antipersonnel bombs. Delves, aware of the additional weight of the bomb racked below, brought his engine up to 54 pounds of manifold pressure. As he released his brakes, he began the shortest flight of his career.

After gaining air, Delves pushed the landing-gear lever up with his left hand, retracting his oleos and wheels. At the same moment, the Pratt & Whitney began to cut out, vibrating strongly in its engine brace. Despite his opening the throttle, the engine failed. Delves had no choice but to return to the earth. The Stratford bird fell back to the runway as Delves rapidly switched off the battery, generator, ignition, and fuel. With a thunderous collision, Delve's plane skidded down the metal-plated runway. The large bombs acted as skis. Metal screeched and sparks flew. The other squadron planes managed to take off over their commander's broken gull while ground personnel fled for cover.

When his wounded plane finally came to a rest, the squadron leader emerged from the cockpit. Despite his flight suit, Mae West vest, pistol, headset, harness, parachute pack, and raft, plus his survival gear, Delves may have set a 25-meter dash record for a fully dressed pilot as he bolted into the jungle.

NZ5331 / BuNo 48892 was eventually repaired and brought back to service. Squadron Leader Delves continued to lead the squadron through war's end.

Blown to Hell

Second Lieutenant Hugh Irwin's Corsair, BuNo 57518. *VMF-251 Aircraft Action Report No. 169*

The squadron insignia for VMF-251, "Lucifer's Messengers," was a bomb with bent wings being flown to hell by the devil. One of their pilots nearly took such a ride.

Dumb luck was a constant companion of the aviators. Consider the tale of 2Lt. Hugh Emmett Irwin. After the invasion of the Philippines, VMF-251 provided close air support to the Army troops. On April 8, 1945, Emmet and his wingman took off from a strip on Samar Island, each with a pair of 500-pounders strapped beneath the cockpit. Their mission: blast targets as the 23rd US Army Infantry fought to retake Cebu City. Irwin described the action years later: "I was in touch with the forward air controller and made my run[-] in with my wingman. On the first pass, we each dropped one bomb. On our second pass, my wingman dropped his[,] but I couldn't get mine off. I tried the manual release[,] and that was no luck either."[6]

After it became apparent that the bomb was hung up on the rack, the second lewey employed violent maneuvers to shake it loose over the seas. The Corsair was too valuable to discard, and Irwin was confident he could bring it back in safely: "I had no qualms about such procedure since several months earlier when landing at Green Island after a strike on Rabaul, a 1,000-pounder dropped from my plane and rolled harmlessly onto the runway."[7]

That's when dumb luck took a joyride in the "Lucifer's Messengers" Corsair. After radioing his request to make a straight-in approach to the field, Irwin brought her down the strip. He "felt the bomb hit twice against the plane, then it exploded, blowing off the entire fuselage aft of the cockpit."[8] Suddenly airborne again, the bird came back to earth, its tail clinging to the shattered fuselage by just a pair of longerons. The bird was blown to hell, but its rider had dumb luck with him. Amazingly, Irwin suffered just minor injuries: scratches about the face, and a wound to his shoulder. The same could not be said of the dash-one D! BuNo 57518 was stricken from the inventory.

Thinking the pilot was dead, the base ambulance ignored the plane's jockey and turned its attention to three wounded ground personnel!

It took several months before Irwin was able to return to flight status. Squadron ordnance men and a bomb disposal technician of MAG 14 determined later that the bomb broke loose on landing, thus shearing away the arming vane and nose of the fuse. In an armed condition, the bomb detonated.

Irwin was later awarded the Distinguished Flying Cross.

No Escape: Tale of the Locking Pin

VMF-422's 1Lt. Theodore Thurnau escaped death on January 25, 1944, during the Flintlock tragedy, but his luck ran out just a month later. As he became airborne from the O'Hare airfield on Abemama in the Gilberts, the left-wing locking pin worked out of the locked position. A little red tab lifted on the wing to indicate the failure of the wing to lock. Whether it had been a mechanical failure in the locking pin, a failure to ensure the wings were locked before takeoff by Thurnau, or just a gremlin, the result was the same: the left wing folded up while in flight. The birdcage stalled. As BuNo 03826 struck the ground, the left wing was torn from the center spar. The fuselage snapped in half at the cockpit. The Westwood, New Jersey, native perished in the crash.

Thine Own Worst Enemy

Violence rocked the formation. Where there had been a Corsair was now an orange-and-black cloud raining debris over the Pacific. Another Corsair was spewing oil and losing altitude. Its aluminum hide was perforated by shrapnel from its brother. The flight leader ordered the remaining birds to toggle their bombs immediately, despite the fact they were still minutes from the target. Some pilots did not acknowledge the order. The clock was ticking and they would pay the price.

Secret weapons are created in the never-ending chess match of gaining tactical and strategic advantages against an enemy. They are effective only if their use, design, or actions are unknown and thus cannot be countered. Yet, one of the most effective secret weapons of World War II passed through the hands of tens of thousands of soldiers and sailors, but its development and manufacture were held to a level of secrecy almost rivaling that of the atomic bombs.

The "variable time" fuze was born of a collaboration between the US and Britain. Scientists across the pond created a fuze like no other. Instead of causing an explosion on impact or detonation after a certain time had passed, this new fuze exploded only when it was close to its target. Inside the warhead, a small Doppler radar triggered the detonation. And so, no longer did a shell have to strike a target to cause its destruction. And thus, the "proximity" fuze had been created.

British scientists began the research, but Britain lacked the capacity to bring the weapon to full maturation. Its development and production were shifted to America, where scientists at Johns Hopkins University Applied Physics Lab were able to solve the problem of miniaturization while building it strong enough to withstand use in cannon. Its application in combat changed warfare and saved untold thousands of civilians and military personnel alike.

It was known as the "VT" fuze, but its moniker belied its actual mechanics. It was exceedingly complex: tubes, condensers, resistors, oscillator coils, mercury switches, and a battery were components. These were sourced from over two thousand suppliers and then assembled in secrecy in several manufacturing plants.

The US Navy tested them initially against target drones. It took only a few rounds from 5-inch/.38 guns using the VT fuzes to bring them down. Widely successful, they produced similar results after their introduction to combat. The USS *Helena* brought down an Aichi 99 Val dive-bomber with just two salvos from her 5-inch guns in January 1943. Capt. Charles P. Cecil praised the new weapon: "The value of the Mk. 32 fuzed projectile cannot be too highly stressed[,] particularly against formation attacks."[9]

The VT fuze was a force multiplier: For a warship such as the *Helena*, her eight 5-inch/.38 guns had the lethality of forty of the same weapons when using the VT fuze versus ordinary fuzes. Fewer rounds of ammunition needed to be produced after its introduction, but its value was complicated by its secrecy. To prevent the enemy from reverse-engineering their own proximity fuze if a dud was recovered, or creating countermeasures to offset it, the fuze was used only on weapons pointing seaward.

The proximity fuzes continued to prove their worth in battle after VT-fuzed artillery rounds were added to the defenses against German V-1 rockets. The kill ratio quadrupled. The same was true shipboard. For enemy planes that tried to penetrate the outer defenses of the US Navy task groups, it became nearly suicidal to venture within range of the 5-inch/.38 guns. Adm. Arleigh Burke commented, "When I went as chief of staff to Adm. Mitscher[,] who commanded the Fast Carrier Task Force, all the 5-inch/.38 and 5-inch/.25 ammunition was fitted with VT fuzes[,] and as you well know, those fuzes knocked down enemy planes by the dozens. Had it not been for those fuzes, our ship losses and casualties in the Fast Carriers in the last half of the war would have been enormously larger than they were. That fuze was a magnificent help!"[10]

The VT fuze was finally turned landward at the Bulge. American forces pinned down in Ardennes put the fuzes to effective use against the marauding German foot and armored forces. Exploding in the air over the enemy, the VT-fuzed bombs became antipersonnel weapons, a means of harassment, a more effective way to destroy enemy supply dumps, and a new method to interrupt enemy communication lines. German morale sagged in their wake during the bitter winter fighting.

As the war progressed, VT fuzes were developed for the bombs carried by fighters and bombers.

After three months of battle, Okinawa was declared conquered on June 22, 1945. The enemy had been defeated inch by inch. The Japanese death toll, both military and local citizens, is unknown but estimated to be in the range of 117,000 and a quarter million fatalities. Nearly 1,800 kamikazes were sent against the ships of the 5th Fleet during ten major attacks, *kikisuis*. On the ground, over twelve thousand Americans gave their lives. Seven earned the Medal of Honor, including an army medic named Desmond Doss. For the Americans, more blood stained the earth on Okinawa than on any other island in the Pacific.

With Okinawa vanquished, the focus remained on the upcoming invasion of Japan. The approaches to Okinawa, soon to be the staging area for the invasion, had to remain neutralized. Across the Ryukyu Islands chain, enemy airfields continued to be regularly attacked to prevent use by enemy planes from Formosa, Korea, or the home islands.

Dawn Attack

Friday, June 29, 1945. With the sun at their back, ten VMF-422 Corsairs led by Capt. Jefferson DeBlanc took off from Ie Shima as part of an early-morning strike package of Marine Air Groups 2 and 22 birds against targets on Miyako Shima, an island halfway between Formosa and Okinawa. DeBlanc had come to prominence after becoming the Marines' first "ace in a day" during an air battle in the Solomons on January 31, 1943. In an action that spanned but a few minutes, his Wildcat tore five enemy planes from the sky. It was not a one-way action. An enemy fighter had DeBlanc in his sights. Rounds ripped through the Grumman, wounding the pilot and destroying the engine. The Cajun bailed out over enemy territory. It would take twelve days for friendly natives, a missionary, two coast watchers, and a PBY to rescue him.

DeBlanc eventually returned to combat when VMF-422 was re-formed in early 1945. His wingman was twenty-six-year-old 1Lt. Donald A. Beha, who was a prewar marine who had traded stripes for bars as an enlisted pilot and was eventually granted a commission.

The Avengers carried small 100-pound fragmentation bombs, while the Corsairs were each railed and racked with four 5-inch HVAR rockets and two 500-pound general-purpose bombs. VT fuzes tipped the bombs, and contact fuzes were attached to the bomb tails should the proximity fuze fail. Arming wires were attached to the fuze vanes. Following the release of the bombs, the wires would be pulled from the fuzes, thus activating the sequence that initiated the arming process. If they were lucky, the Americans would find enemy planes parked in revetments ripe for destruction. But good luck was not on the flight manifest for the "Flying Buccaneers."

As the flight approached the target, the bent-wings birds weaved lazily over the slower pregnant turkeys. Without warning, 2Lt. Edward McCoy's Corsair was vaporized in a flaming black cloud that rained metal and organic debris. The bird of his wingman, 1Lt. Richard Hale, smoked and lost altitude after the detonation, its skin perforated from cowl to tail. Oil stained the hood and fuselage. Two other Corsairs joined on Hale as he turned his plane back toward Okinawa, but after several minutes his plane slipped off to the right before plunging 4,000 feet into the Pacific. He did not emerge from the wreckage.

The first warning that there may have been problems with the VT fuzes occurred forty-eight hours earlier. A flight of brother MAG 22 VMF-314 Corsairs were sent to bomb targets on Ishigaki Shima. "Some of the VT[-]fuzed bombs exploded 3,000 to 4,000 feet above ground[,] causing one pilot a few uncomfortable seconds as he was violently jostled about."[11]

Capt. DeBlanc immediately ordered the remaining pilots under his charge to toggle their bombs. Another division of four pilots complied, but the three pilots of his own division did not. Repeated hand gestures by DeBlanc went unheeded. He wrote of the experience that he "dropped below and flew under Lt. Landsberg's flight and looked at the VT fuze linkage. All seemed okay. I flew under Lt. Stevenson's plane[,] and again all seemed in order."[12]

1st Lieutenant Donald A. Beha, center plane. *Courtesy of the Beha family*

By the time DeBlanc finished his quick inspection, they were closing Miyako Shima. At best, it had been a cursory glance of the arming wires from at least 20 feet away. But as he formed up on Beha in preparation for the attack, disaster was poised to strike again.

The attack commenced as they pushed over from 12,000 feet. Diving out of the sun, their airspeed increased to 380 knots. Landsberg and Stevenson followed DeBlanc and Beha. As a result of the increased speed, the airstream pulled against the wires that had been incorrectly anchored. Their vibration pulled the safety pins free on the T50E1 fuze ring enclosure surrounding the arming vanes. As the Double Wasp pumped several thousand times per minute and the big Hamilton Standard prop turned in kind, unbeknown to the pilots, small arming vanes on the bomb fuzes began to rotate prematurely. With each revolution, the wind-driven detonator rotor brought the weapon closer to being armed. The fuzes needed just 3,600 feet to arm the weapons.

Beha, who was still carrying his bomb, released it safely from 4,500 feet. He and DeBlanc pulled out of their dives after launching their rockets. But behind them, disaster struck. As 2Lt. John Stevenson passed 7,000 feet, one of his bombs exploded while still racked on the center spar. As the detritus rained from the sky, 2Lt. John Landsberg suffered the same fate seconds later, when one of the VT fuzes initiated his execution.

DeBlanc was initially unaware of the tragedy: "I failed to see my second section during the rendezvous. Lt. Beha was already locked in on my wing, but Lt. Landsberg and Lt. Stevenson were absent from the second[-]section slot. I called for them during the join[-]up period, but failed to get an answer. I realized what might have happened."[13]

Of the ten VMF-422 birds that took off that morning, only six returned to Ie Shima. Three were lost due to the premature arming of the proximity fuzes, while a fourth was a collateral casualty. While six pilots survived the tragedy, only one Buccaneer, 1Lt. Beha, dropped his bomb on the target and lived to tell about it. The mission of June 29, 1945, would remain the deadliest day in combat for a Marine Corsair squadron in World War II where no aerial attacks, antiaircraft fire, or weather figured in the losses.

Just two days after the mission, the United States Navy Bomb Disposal School published a warning about VT-fuzed bombs that might be brought back from aborted missions still in their racks but missing their arming wires: "These fuzes will be armed and should be destroyed or dropped in deep water."[14]

All three Corsairs that were destroyed by their own bombs had been built at the Vought Stratford plant. The VT fuzes may have been assembled at the GE factory in nearby Bridgeport, just 2.5 miles away. It was one of three GE factories that assembled them for the military.

VMF-422 lost no more pilots after the June 29 debacle. After Japan's capitulation, the hard-luck squadron was stationed in Japan.

Donald Beha returned to his native Utica, New York, postwar to raise his family, and he worked for Sears Roebuck for thirty years. He was recalled during the Korean War to help train pilots at Marine Corps Air Station Cherry Point. He retired from the USMCR as a major. Beha passed away in 1999.

Beha's machine on the June 29 mission was Bureau Number 82537. Postwar it was transferred to the Japan Air Self Defense Force. It was written off in 1959.

Capt. Jeff DeBlanc finished the war with nine kills. He was awarded the Medal of Honor by President Harry S. Truman in December 1946. Highly decorated, Col. DeBlanc retired from the United States Marine Corps Reserve in 1972. Long after the war was over, he remained in contact with his wingman, Donald Beha. In the civilian world, he taught middle and high school postwar. DeBlanc passed away in 2007, at the age of eighty-six.

CHAPTER 6

PROP CHOP

That the Corsair had bent wings to accommodate the massive propeller that protruded from its cowling was one of the myths that followed the revolutionary fighter after it entered production. Rather, the Hamilton Standard Hydromatic Prop was designed to be the largest possible propeller that would fit the Vought. Each blade was 75½ inches long. The arc measured over 13 feet across. In his memoir, "Black Sheep" 2Lt. Robert McClurg wrote, "The propeller was gargantuan when compared to any other fighter I could think of at the time. We joked about the intimidation factor that must have represented by itself; could you imagine being a Jap pilot and seeing something with a huge propeller arc like that coming at you?"[1]

Shave and a Haircut

The massive prop bearing down on 1Lt. Russell Hunchar VMF-113 must have been very disconcerting on Independence Day 1945. Second Lieutenant Martin W. Harke followed Hunchar down as they ferried planes to Ie Shima from Okinawa. Harke came in too fast and misjudged the distance between his Goodyear and Hunchar's FG-1D. Harke's Hamilton prop chewed its way across the left side of Hunchar's plane. The aluminum skin of the fuselage was just 0.062 inches thick, hardly enough to stop the prop. Both Goodyears were surveyed. Remarkably, both pilots escaped without injury!

VMF-113 FG-1D 88441 after 88399 crossed paths on the runway. First Lieutenant Russell Hunchar survived.

Danger in the Air

Second Lieutenant Robert A. Enders was airborne when another pilot's Hamilton Standard Hydromatic chewed through his F4U-1:

On 19 January, 1944, I was one of four (4) planes in a column. We were in a fairly steep dive, and I was slightly to the right and behind the number two man. We made a right turn[,] and I began to rapidly advance on the man ahead. I contemplated sliding under him and once more got on his tail; therefore they met[,] chewing off the whole tail assembly. There wasn't much of a shock to my plane. Immediately it nosed down and was out of control. I found the rip cord handle in my right hand and opened the hood in a normal manner. I felt I was hanging on my belt[,] so I unfastened it and fell free of the aircraft. This was approximately four thousand

(4,000) feet. I waited a short time and fell about fifteen hundred (1,500) feet, according to others who observed. I pulled the cord and the chute opened quite rapidly. There was a jerk, but not enough to bother me. When I came to the deck I judged the approximate spot I would land. There were trees all around, and I was quite fortunate in hitting the ground unhurt.[2]

Enders was able to enlist the help of friendly natives. They led him to a local plantation owner but kept his parachute for themselves. Soon the crash boat arrived on scene to bring Enders back to his squadron. After arriving, he discovered that the second pilot had been able to land safely after the midair evisceration.

Just five weeks earlier, two VMF-222 pilots had gotten crossed up in the landing pattern over Barakoma. As a division of gull wings were given the green light by the tower to enter the traffic circle, 1Lt. Martin "Smitty" Smith Jr.'s birdcage weaved in front of 1Lt. John Witt's dash-one. In an instant, Smith's plane was filleted into three parts. The engine, wing assembly, and aft section of the fuselage crashed to the ground. Smith did not survive.

Witt had survived the initial collision but was still in danger. First Lieutenant Bob Wilson was a witness:

Second Lieutenant Robert Enders.
Courtesy of the Enders family

Jack Witt's plane went into a flat spin[,] which made it come down more slowly. Standing there on "Vulture Hill" watching this episode, we saw Jack's canopy open[,] and he crawled out and stood on the wing. We were hollering "Jump, jump" as though he could hear us. He finally got off the wing and pulled his ripcord. The parachute blossomed, stopped his rapid fall, and simultaneously, his feet hit the runway. It was very dramatic.[3]

Mere feet away, Witt's plane struck the earth. He was unconscious and bleeding, and his parachute served as fuel for the fire consuming his birdcage. The ground crew grabbed hold of him and pulled Witt away from the conflagration. He was lifted into a jeep and whisked away for treatment at the "Acorn 10" hospital. Diagnosis: skull fracture, lacerations, and contusions.

What was left of Smith's remains were collected on a stretcher. The squadron assembled at the base cemetery four hours later. Smith was buried simply in a small grave dug in the sand and the coral. Palm leaves sufficed as its cover. The national ensign served as his pall. Taps sent Smith on his final journey.

Witt eventually returned to the air with the "Flying Deuces" in 1944. The badger finished his third tour in early April. Two and a half victories were credited in his logbook; on his tunic he wore a Distinguished Flying Cross and an Air Medal.

Weapon in the Air

Flying from Kadena airfield, Okinawa, VMF-312 Corsairs were on combat air patrol on May 10, 1945, when at 10,000 feet they spotted vapor trails at 35,000 feet. Two of the CAP managed to crawl to 38,000 feet before beginning a 150-mile chase of two Nick fighters. Beyond the usual range, the Americans fired their Brownings, hoping to slow down the faster Japanese planes. Capt. Ken Reusser finally managed to strike one plane before running out of ammunition. As 1Lt. Robert Klingman closed to finish off the wounded prey, he discovered his .50s had frozen up in the rare air. The only other weapon at hand was the Corsair itself.

Klingman made three runs on the enemy's tail, each time chewing away more of the rudder and right stabilizer with the tip of his Hamilton Standard. He battled both prop wash and enemy rounds with each approach against the twin-engine fighter. Its tail gunner sprayed 7.7 mm rounds at the F4U-1D. Klingman won the duel as the enemy plane spun into the ocean.

With the two bent blades, the third blade shortened by 6 inches, the gas tank almost empty, debris from the enemy plane embedded in the Corsair's cowling and propeller, and bullet holes in the engine and wing, Klingman rolled the dice that he could land back at Kadena. Despite losing 300 feet of altitude per minute with the damaged prop, Klingman won again. He brought the wounded fighter in for a dead-stick landing. The Hamilton Standard prop windmilled as Klingman safely put the plane down.

Lt. Robert
Klingman

Klingman was awarded the Navy Cross for his victory. He served in the Korean War and retired from the Corps as a lieutenant colonel in 1966. Klingman passed away in 2004.

Two Can Play That Game

It was one of those days early in the Corsair's combat career that the plane became legend. One of its pilots did too. The call came midmorning on June 7, 1943, to scramble all available aircraft to intercept a large enemy formation. Over one hundred Kate torpedo-bombers and Zero fighters were just 150 miles away and headed down the "slot." Four air forces answered the call: the army sent P-38s and P-40s; the RNZAF sent forth their own P-40s; the navy answered with Wildcats; the marines scrambled a dozen VMF-112 Corsairs.

During a running forty-five-minute air battle, two -112 pilots became aces (including the CO, Maj. Robert Fraser). Capt. Archie Donahue brought his personal tally to nine with two more kills.

Second Lieutenant Sam Logan came to the aid of an RNZAF P-40 being chased by a Zero. After driving off the enemy, Johnson's birdcage was rattled by enemy rounds. The Corsair no longer responded to the controls. Logan cleared the bird and jumped at 10,000 feet. As his parachute blossomed, there lay 2 miles between him and the sea. The enemy pilot, intent on finishing off his adversary, strafed Logan twice. Logan responded by trying to collapse the parachute to increase his rate of descent. That threw off the enemy pilot. As he dove on Logan a third time, an aluminum propeller blade sliced through Logan's right boot. Half of his foot was cut away. An RNZAF P-40 came to the rescue and forced the butcher away. Logan inflated his life vest and passed out.

Logan regained consciousness upon entering the sea. Though seriously wounded, he managed to unhook the parachute, inflate his raft, and climb aboard. The partially amputated foot continued to squirt blood. He fashioned a tourniquet over the wound. Sulfa tablets warded off infection. Morphine tablets numbed the pain. Despite it all, Logan was determined to survive. He started to row his little craft.

Soon a Grumman Duck set down near Logan. He was hauled aboard. Surgeons at a field hospital completed the amputation the Mitsubishi's propeller had begun. After a long stateside hospital convalescence, Logan received an artificial foot. Eventually he returned to flight status flying multiengine aircraft stateside, performing transport duties. During a chance encounter with a former AirSols pilot, Maj. Bruce Porter, Logan reflected on his second chance in life: "It's not like flying fighters, Bruce. But it is flying."[4]

CHAPTER 7

ESCAPE FROM RABAUL: THE ROOKIE AND THE ACE

Fifty Baker Twenty-Eight[1]
By an anonymous pilot
USS Coos Bay (AVP-25)
March 25, 1944

He was over Rabaul bombing
When some flak got in his way
And his engine coughed and spluttered
And then called it a day
He was gliding down the channel
And was cursing at his fate
When suddenly he remembered
Fifty Baker twenty-eight.

He opened up his R.T.
And he broadcast loud and clear
This plane of mine has had it
And the water's getting near
I'm fifteen south of Cape Gazelle
So please don't make me wait
Just send me out the Dumbo
Fifty Baker twenty-eight.

So that PBY came quickly
And its fighter escort too
Till they saw the PVs circling
As the PVs always do
They took one look and landed
And I'm happy to relate
They got them all home safely
Fifty Baker twenty-eight.

Now remember this you fighters
And bombers large and small
If you ever get shot up
While bombing old Rabaul
Just head down the channel
And get some other crate
To yell like hell for Dumbo
Fifty Baker twenty-eight.

Left: 2Lt. Jack G. Morris, VMF-218. *Courtesy of Tom K. Morris*

Right: Maj. Gregory Boyington, VMF-214

New Britain, Rabaul

The head of the snake. The bastion of the Japanese air forces that controlled the Solomon Islands.

Japanese forces had defeated Australian forces at Rabaul on New Britain in early 1942, as the ramparts of Allied control of the Pacific continued to crumble. With New Britain in hand, the Japanese Empire had taken a deepwater port that supported the major Imperial Japanese Navy (IJN) base at Truk Island, which lay 800 miles north. Multiple airfields were improved or built in the vicinity of Rabaul.

Almost just as quickly as it fell to Japan, Rabaul was under attack by Allied forces. Initially, US Army Air Force multiengine bombers targeted Rabaul, Simpson Harbor, and the airfields. But as American forces hopscotched up the Solomons, the advantage began to teeter toward the Allies. With the construction of airstrips on Bougainville, single-engine Marine and Navy planes could take the fight to the enemy's home starting in December 1943. They were joined by RNZAF P-40s.

Fearless. Aggressive. Talented. Flawed but idolized by his men: Maj. Greg "Pappy" Boyington of the VMF-214 "Black Sheep" led the initial sweep against the stronghold on December 17. Nearly eighty Allied fighters tangled both with skilled enemy pilots and deadly accurate ack-ack. Six days later, Pappy led forty-eight fighters back to Rabaul. The bait had been the B-24 bombers that had preceded the sweep. It paid dividends as the Allied pilots claimed thirty kills, including four by Boyington. He even strafed a Japanese sub before it submerged.

Boyington's tally had risen to twenty-four kills, just two shy of the American record held by World War I ace Eddie Rickenbacker and tied by fellow Marine captain Joe Foss. Boyington inched forward with another kill on December 27, when he led another fighter sweep against Rabaul.

America was watching. "Record-Seeking Pappy Gets 25th Jap" was the byline two days later in the *New York Daily News*. In a United Press article carried in newspapers around the country, Boyington admitted that "he planned to exercise his privilege as squadron commander to go up every day in an attempt to break Foss' record established over Guadalcanal."[2]

On the twenty-eighth, in a fighter sweep against Rabaul, Pappy scored a "probable" against a Tojo, but that did not add to his official kills. The scoring was not one sided: three *"Black Sheep"* did not return. This loss was in addition to three other "Black Sheep" who disappeared on the December 23 mission.

VMF-214 was scheduled to finish their combat tour in early January. The calendar was working against Boyington. War correspondents wanted to know when he would break the record. He admitted to them that he wished he had gotten three kills instead of just one on the twenty-seventh, so the pressure could be taken off his back. The marines on the ground were anxious to see him tie or even break the record. The weather didn't help his score either. His scheduled fighter sweep was canceled on the thirtieth. Boyington wasn't scheduled to fly on New Year's Eve, but it made no difference since the weather forced the mission to be scrubbed again.

New Year's Day 1944: A World at War

Americans learned about a huge American heavy-bomber raid against targets near Paris. Russian troops had the German army on the run in the Ukraine. German authorities had begun evacuating French from the coastal region south of Belgium as a precaution against an Allied invasion. A small article in the *New York Daily News* warned that atomic bombs—weapons based on splitting atoms—were Germany's long-vaunted secret weapon. But in the southern Pacific, Rabaul remained the bull's-eye.

Two divisions of "Black Sheep" escorted Liberators in an attack against the Lakunai airfield. Boyington didn't fly but led the hunting on January 2 in a large fighter sweep against Rabaul. His mount (he had traded an old birdcage that morning) betrayed him as oil wicked past the cowling and filmed over his windscreen. As dozens of Japanese airplanes were mounting a counterattack, Boyington was flying blind. Straddling the fine line between bravery and stupidity, Boyington trimmed the Vought, unstrapped himself from his parachute harness, rolled back the canopy, and climbed up on the seat. With his toes on the edge, he leaned forward valiantly. One hand braced him on the windscreen, while the other tried to clean it. AirSols fighters scored nine victories. Pappy was lucky just to return to base.

His weariness had only increased by the time he pancaked at Vella Lavella. With no kills, Boyington returned to Torokina in anticipation of returning to Rabaul the next day.

Monday, January 3, 1944: New Britain

The sun was already rising when Maj. Boyington led a large fighter sweep from Torokina back to Rabaul. It was just the composite of planes Boyington preferred: mostly Marine Corsairs and sixteen Navy Hellcats. Exhaustion forced him to put small pieces of tobacco in the corners of his eyes to keep him alert.

The flight followed the west coast of Bougainville before arriving at Cape St. George. They continued north up St. George's Channel. As 0800 showed on their watches, Boyington turned the sweep toward Rabaul and Simpson Harbor. The fighters were stacked over the harbor between 20,000 and 24,000 feet when a dozen enemy fighters climbed to engage. Boyington and his wingman, Captain George Ashmun, dove steeply. The tails of a pair of Zekes filled their gunsights. Their Brownings erupted after the red trigger buttons on the control stick were squeezed. Both pilots flamed their targets.

Boyington's kill was witnessed by another "Black Sheep." In the melee, though, sight of Boyington and Ashmun was lost. After the fighters landed midmorning, the squadron intelligence officers awarded seven more kills to various pilots. But the excitement of Boyington tying the record quickly evaporated when both their leader and his wingman failed to return from the mission. Dane Base on Bougainville had received a radio transmission from a pilot who said he had to ditch, but that was the last message received. First Lieutenant Wally Thompson of VMF-211 had been on the sweep: "When we got back[,] we were shocked that he was lost."[3]

War correspondent Fred Hampson reported, "The news spread like the chill wind from revetment to the 'ready room' to the tent camp on the hill. The war stood still for a hundred pilots and 500 ground crewmen."[4] The response to the loss of their beloved Pappy was immediate. Capt. Ryan McCown of VMF-321 (who had also flown in the morning's fighter sweep) led eight "Hell Angels" to escort a VP-14 PBY Catalina on a dumbo mission to Cape St. George. The morning's clear weather had given way to rain squalls. A report of a pilot afloat on a raft was not borne out. Dejected, the rescue team returned to base when fuel got low for the short-legged fighters.

The hunt continued the next day. Before a late-morning fighter sweep against Rabaul, seven "Black Sheep" set off on their own search for Boyington. From Cape St. George they flew up the west coast of New Ireland before circling the islands between New Ireland and New Britain. Flying at low level, they strafed several Japanese barges they encountered. No sign of Boyington or Ashmun was discovered then or in their final two days of combat.

On January 8, the war-weary "Black Sheep" left the Corsairs behind and flew to Espiritu Santo. Their third war tour was over. They claimed ninety-three kills. Their feats were already legendary in the theater and at home in America. Numerous pilots had become aces. But their greatest ace did not return with them.

Saturday, January 8: America

Newspapers across the country carried headlines of the disappearance of the legendary Marine fighter pilot Major Greg Boyington. Just the day before, they had lauded his tying the record of Rickenbacker and Foss.

January 6–8: Espiritu Santo, New Hebrides Islands

The "Black Sheep" returned to Espiritu Santo. Some pilots were on their path back to America. Most were on their way to Sydney for needed R&R. VMF-214 had finished its tours, so the remaining pilots were absorbed into other Marine squadrons to fight again.

The island was a major staging base for the Allied attacks from the Solomon Islands. An escort carrier in the harbor was discharging Corsairs. Two fresh squadrons were disembarked, VMF-217 and VMF-218. Second Lieutenant Jack G. Morris entered a warehouse to store his pilot dress uniforms: "I stumbled over a dark[-]green duffle bag as I rounded the corner. . . . The name stenciled in black stood out vividly: MAJOR GREGORY BOYINGTON. They were his personal effects. We all knew about his exploits as commander of VMF-214, the famous *Black Sheep* squadron, and were saddened by the loss."[5] The bag served as a stark reminder of a pilot's mortality.

January 1944: Rabaul

In the weeks following the disappearance of Boyington, pressure on Rabaul and nearby targets remained intense. More Corsair pilots were reported missing in the daily duels in the skies over Rabaul. Others were seen to be shot down. Nearly eighty Corsairs were lost during this period. But a toll was exacted on the Japanese as more American pilots became aces.

Thursday, January 20: Rabaul

B-25 Mitchells targeted Vunakanau Airdrome, antiaircraft positions, and fuel dumps. Seventy fighters escorted the medium bombers. One division of VMF-321 Corsairs was especially hard-hit after forty enemy fighters pounced. Capt. Ryan McCown (who had led the search for Boyington the day he was lost) suffered numerous hits. His division leader, newly made ace Lt. Robert See, shot down the Zeke, but he lost sight of McCown. In the other section, 1Lt. Robert W. Marshall was hit by 20 mm fire. Oil sprayed into the cockpit. He ditched in St. George Channel. His Corsair split in two. His wingman, 1Lt. Roger Brindos, did not return from the mission, nor did McCown.

Goodyear experienced its first combat loss in the Bismarck Archipelago two days later. The FG-1 Corsair was the twin brother of a different factory mother. In a footnote to fighter history, VMF-321 1Lt. Eugene V. Smith was piloting Bureau Number 14212 when he was shot down. A rescue call went out for one of the rescue PV-1 Venturas, call sign "Two Baker Thirty" (2B30). Smith was rescued the next day, January 23, by a VP-14 PBY, dumbo call sign "Fifty Baker Twenty-Eight" (50B28).

Sunday, January 23: New Britain

A maximum effort by AirSols sent 140 SBDs, TBFs, and fighters to attack Rabaul, the Lakunai Airdrome, and coastal targets. The raid caught the Japanese flat-footed. Flak guns did not open until after the bombers had begun plastering their targets. No enemy airplanes interrupted the attacks. It was during the exit that enemy fighters finally intercepted the retiring strike over Matupi Harbor. The maelstrom continued until the formations crossed the St. George Channel.

In less than twenty minutes the Americans laid waste to the enemy: thirty-two kills were claimed, including one by a Marine Dauntless gunner. Only one bomber was lost, but three Corsairs and a P-38 did not come home.

During an afternoon B-25 strike against Rabaul, 1Lt. Bob Keim of VMF-321 circled a downed pilot before climbing to 10,000 feet to activate his IFF. He continued to circle until a rescue PV-1 (call sign "One Baker Thirty") came upon the scene. The guardian also witnessed an F4U go down in flames. First Lieutenant Richard Marsh, another VMF-321 pilot, parachuted from his Vought. A call for "Two Baker Thirty" brought a second rescue PV-1. Marsh was eventually picked up by the VP-14 PBY that had saved 1Lt. Smith.

Farther up the St. George Channel, a third pilot ditched after his Corsair was jumped by Zekes. Maj. Donald W. Boyle from VMF-212 was reported as "missing in action."

Bailing out or ditching near Rabaul, Allied airmen had little chance of survival. If captured by the Japanese, no mercy was given. The Red Cross was not notified of their capture. Japan had not signed the Geneva Convention.

The pilots and aircrew lived in primitive conditions at forward air bases. The mental strain from combat added to the tropical ulcers, skin infections, malaria, dysentery, and weight loss suffered by the men. If taken prisoner, they were subject to random beatings, medical experiments, and starvation. One horrific experiment involved injecting the blood of guards with malaria into the prisoners in an attempt to create immunity to the disease. Wounds, infections, and diseases were not treated. Their food was not adequate either in quantity or quality.

Thursday, February 3, 1944: New Britain

The attacks against Rabaul continued unabated through the early part of the month. As squadrons completed their tour of duty, new squadrons moved up from Espiritu Santo to replace them. VMF-218 had arrived in theater as the VMF-214 were departing the previous month. After several weeks of training, the "Hellions" made their combat debut on February 3 in raids against the Tobera and Lakunai Airdromes. Two members of another squadron, VMF-215, went missing. The greatest Corsair ace of World War II, 1Lt. Robert Hanson, was shot down by antiaircraft fire over Cape St. George. He did not survive after his Corsair hit the water. Hanson, with twenty-five kills to his credit, was posthumously awarded the Medal of Honor.

Thursday, February 10: Piva Yoke Air Strip, Bougainville

VMF-218, which had arrived at Espiritu Santo in early January just before VMF-214 departed, had spent the month training for combat missions. The "Hellions" were scheduled to fly escort for bombers targeting two of the airdromes at Rabaul. When the squadron came ashore in early January, all of their fighters were brand-new 55-series Corsairs. However, since some of these planes had already been lost, 2Lt. Jack Morris (who had been startled by the sight of Boyington's duffle bag at Espiritu) was assigned an old birdcage (02566) from the pool.

Even with mechanics working around the clock, typically only two-thirds of the Corsairs were mission ready on any given day. And so the older 02-series birdcage Corsairs that were retained in the rear for overhaul and training flights for new squadrons were reissued to frontline squadrons. The CO of VMF-215 complained after a ferry mission on February 4, "The boys who were sent to ferry back 'new' ships got in this afternoon. 'New' ships were old rebuilt crates of the '02' series."[6]

Morris's 02566 was long in the tooth. It had landed in the theater back in June 1943. Since then, it had been transferred from squadron to squadron as combat tours were completed. During October it was damaged during a landing at Espiritu Santo by a pilot from Service Squadron 11. It was repaired and put back into service. "Black Sheep" Ed Harper had flown it in late December 1943 before it was sent back to Espiritu Santo.

Morris had flown the old bird ten days earlier. It was not a flight he cared to repeat:

I remember that plane and the landing. It had made me nervous. Something was not right; I had just flown it six hundred miles over water[,] and the engine made little popping sounds every time I lowered speed. As I entered the traffic pattern at Henderson it really popped when I throttled back; it backfired. I was relieved to get down on the mat. . . . I taxied to the flight line and turned the snorting beast over to a plane captain at the fighter pool. This plane was not one of our squadron planes. It had been at the Turtle Bay Fighter Strip in the New Hebrides for overhaul. It needed more work before its return to combat. Happy to be out of its birdcage cockpit, I wrote it up on the flight report.[7]

Behind the stick on the tenth, the strike package approached Vunakunau. Antiaircraft fire rose to challenge them. As the shepherds flew cover, ten enemy fighters appeared above Morris and his section leader. The enemy had the tactical advantage: "We could turn toward them and take them on or try to out run them or dive out and rejoin the formation later on. The split-second was all we had[,] and before I could warn my leader, it was gone. We both had full throttle but he started to pull away. He had a new plane, I an older re-hab. I hit the mike button and started to speak when a black explosion and a feeling of doom enveloped me."[8]

Cannon fire raked the old birdcage Corsair. As it spun toward the jungle below, a blinded Morris fought to jettison the canopy. He passed out in the efforts. When he came to, Morris was hanging upside down as the Corsair plummeted to earth. He released his straps and fell out. Morris instinctively pulled the parachute handle as the Vought screamed to its demise.

The jungle canopy snagged Morris's parachute. His vision temporarily lost, he feared of being caught or seen as the battle was waged in the air above him. He struggled to free himself and the parachute from the trees. After hitting the ground, he took stock of the situation: Morris was wounded, blind in one eye, and lost in enemy territory. He still had his raft pack and survival kit. Morris would have to rely on his wits and training if he had any chance of escape from this hostile land.

Kempeitai Prison, Rabaul

About 20 miles north, Pappy Boyington was imprisoned in a naval jail at Rabaul. After scoring his twenty-sixth kill on January 3 (he claimed two others postwar), his luck ran out. Twenty enemy fighters pounced on Boyington and his wingman, George Ashmun. Despite the Corsair's superiority over the Zekes, there were too many of the maneuverable enemy planes. Boyington and Ashmun weaved in mutual defense, but the 20 mm cannon fire took its toll: Ashmun's Vought began to smoke before its burst into flames. It crashed into St. George's Channel. Ashmun was gone.

Cannon and 7.7 mm fire had raked Bureau Number 17915 too. The main tank, situated just ahead of the cockpit, was ignited. Boyington's bird turned into a furnace. Exploding rounds sent shrapnel into his legs, wrist, neck, and ear. Pilot and plane were at the end of their combat days.

As the Vought descended to the sea, Boyington clutched his parachute handle and safety belt. His foot pushed the stick down, and he was ejected. He immediately pulled the D handle. It was none too soon. His chute blossomed in the seconds before he hit the water. The impact crushed his canteen and destroyed his Navy wristwatch.

As would remain a recurrent pattern in Boyington's career, the Japanese were not through with him. The parachute's white blossom made him the target after his Corsair hit the water. In wave after wave, the Zeroes attempted to strafe Boyington. He could not trigger his Mae West or his raft. Instead, Boyington, a former college swimmer and wrestler, relied on his innate athletic strength to save him as he repeatedly dived under the water to seek relief from the lead storm. He was burdened not just with a flight suit, but the canteen, pistol and rounds, flight helmet, boots, and other gear, so he began to shed the weight.

Finally the enemy gave up on him. Boyington was left to tread water. His life vest had been holed and so was useless. He had kept hold of his survival and raft packs. The survival or "jungle pack" contained the items he'd need to survive if he made it ashore. His raft was still intact. Pappy inflated it and pulled himself aboard. Naked, he began the naval command portion of his marine career.

Exhausted. Wounded. Lost without his "Black Sheep." Pappy had managed to get off a distress call in the fleeting seconds before he left the cockpit. He hoped that Dumbo was on the way. At the mouth of St. George's Channel, the volcanoes of New Britain were off to his west. New Ireland's shore lay to his east. He was a small target on a choppy sea. He opened his survival pack to tend to his wounds while awaiting rescue.

Like other pilots shot down on Rabaul raids, Boyington had time to contemplate the ditty written by a fellow "Black Sheep":

If the engine conks out now,
We'll come down from forty-thou'
And we'll end up in a rowboat at Rabaul
In a rowboat at Rabaul.

We'll be throwing in the towel,
'Cause they'll never send a Dumbo 'way out here.
We'll be prisoners of war
And we'll stay through forty-four
Getting drunk on sake and New Britain Beer.[9]

By late afternoon, no dumbo had arrived; no Venturas circled overhead. Instead, the conning tower of a Japanese sub broke the surface nearby. Boyington was captured. He described the treatment he received—cigarettes and food—as the best that would be bestowed upon him for the next twenty months. Two hours later the harsh reality of becoming a prisoner of the Imperial Japanese Navy became apparent.

IJN submarine 181 completed its supply run from New Guinea in early evening. After mooring, Boyington was brought to shore. Sailors blindfolded and marched him through Rabaul. Hobbling unsteadily on a wounded leg, rifle butts prompted the naked Boyington to keep moving. Eventually he was placed on a truck, which brought him to the prison compound of the 81st Naval Guard Unit.

Though Boyington's survival kit included antibiotic sulfa powder and sulfa pills, it was taken from him. No antibiotics were given at the jail. The multiple wounds began to fester. In the tropical heat, the smell from the infection was stronger than his unwashed body.

In a former clothing store converted into a jail, the prisoners were held in six cells on the lower level. The upper level housed the high-ranking members of the guard unit as well as the interpreters.

During the day the prisoners were forced to remain in a sitting position. A waste bucket—the "benjo bucket"—served as their latrine. The food rations of mildewed rice topped with food scraps from the officer's mess were meager and contained few calories. Boyington was incarcerated with a TBF pilot, 1Lt. Edward A. Croker, he had seen shot down in September 1943.

After his capture Boyington was regularly interrogated. He suffered beatings. The ropes binding his hands were tightened to cut off circulation. Lit cigarettes were stubbed out on his neck and shoulders. Sometimes the questioning sought military intelligence; other times the questioning was inane.

Boyington could not hide his identity: When rescued, his survival backpack had his name stenciled across it. It may have saved his life in an alternate fashion.

One constant through it all was Edward Chikaki Honda. An American-born and American-raised Nisei, he had moved to Japan to further his education. After the war started he renounced his American citizenship. Sent to Rabaul, he worked as an interpreter/ interrogator. Though stern when other military personnel were present, Honda was less formal when left alone with Boyington. His role was of the "good cop." Honda advised the marine pilot to tell consistent answers when interrogated.

The Bismarck Archipelago was under constant attacks by the Allies. Though Boyington was beaten, his wounds were left untended, and he was deprived of proper nutrition, he was allowed to enter bomb shelters when Rabaul was attacked. But as bombs rained down, Boyington felt that "It was a mixed blessing. On the one hand[,] you knew that it had to happen if you were ever going to get out of this place[,] but at the same time you're hoping to God that one of those bombs didn't have your name on it."[10]

Three weeks into his imprisonment, Boyington was joined by another Corsair pilot, Maj. Donald W. Boyle. During the strike on January 23, 1944, Boyle led his VMF-212 division in an attack against a Zeke. Diving down from 7,000 feet in a stern attack, his .50s found their mark. When it was last seen, smoke was pouring from the Mitsubishi over Matupi Harbor.

Boyle didn't realize that he was in the gunsight of an enemy plane himself. Rounds hit home. He was last seen flying east, low and slowly over St. George's Channel.

When his Double Wasp expired, Boyle ditched. He escaped unscathed from the sinking Corsair with his raft pack. Adrift, Boyle witnessed the afternoon strike. Being so far north in the channel, he was not seen. The PV-1 Venturas that searched for Japanese shipping did not routinely search St. George's Channel as far north as Rabaul.

Barracudas and sharks periodically brushed against his little raft. Day transitioned into night. It was cold and damp, and the overcast skies did not offer stars or moon for navigation. His survival pack had water, rations, and a compass. For the time being he was okay, though he fought exhaustion.

Boyle had renewed hope when he came ashore on Utuan in the Duke of York Islands. After making contact with the natives, he tried to enlist their help. Instead, fear of retaliation by the Japanese caused them to turn Boyle over to the enemy. Just a few days shy of his twenty-seventh birthday, Boyle joined Boyington as a prisoner at Rabaul. He had yet to hold his newborn daughter home in Brooklyn.

Thursday, February 10, 1944: Jungle, New Britain

Out of the trees and his parachute, Morris's immediate thought was "How close is the enemy?"[11] Blinded, Morris took off running. He had left his gear behind. It was not long before he fell. As some of his vision returned, Morris took stock of his wounds: partial blindness in his left eye, a gaping wound across the left side of his nose, a cut across his forehead, and a bruised left side and wrist.

The rookie pilot decided if he were to survive, he would have to work his way east to St. George's Channel. From there, he could inflate his raft and hope to attract the attention of an Allied plane. Unsure of his exact whereabouts, Morris might have been up to 80 miles from the channel. He would have to hike undetected through a sweltering jungle in enemy territory.

But to be rescued, Morris needed his gear. He returned to where he had landed. Morris kept a piece of his parachute. He still had his life vest, Colt .45 and ammunition, dye markers, canteen, utility belt, issue knife, and personal jackknife along with his raft pack and jungle kit.

The jungle kit officially was the USN M-592 Back Pad Survival Kit. It was strapped to the pilot's parachute harness for all combat missions. The kit was a military general store of necessary items for survival in the theme of "If we don't have it, you don't need it." Wounded and lost, Morris needed it all. He grabbed the gear and began his escape.

Morris did not get far. First aid was the first order of business. From his jungle kit, he used bandages to keep his damaged eye (which was out of its socket) protected. After he had applied sulfa powder, another bandage kept his nose together. Sulfa pills were taken to ward off infection, but that required drinking some of his limited water supply. He squeezed a wound on his left arm. A small piece of shrapnel emerged.

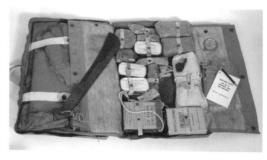

M-592 Survival Back Pad Kit. *Gregory Pons collection, Arnaud Valz-Blin photo*

After resting, it was time to move on. He sought higher ground. "Again I started up the slope. Away from the distant sounds of battle. The jungle tree canopy was dense overhead; the undergrowth about chest high and not too thick, easy to walk through[,] but the incline drained my energy again. Above, there was still the diminishing sounds of aerial combat: bomb bursts, anti-aircraft ack ack, and machine gun fire aloft."[12]

Morris, in pain and exhausted, eventually ceased climbing. He used a morphine syrette from the jungle kit to ease the pain and rest. It had its intended effect but brought forth vivid hallucinations.

The next morning Morris restarted his trek. Hallucinations were his marching companions. A truck and a hut he spied turned out not to be there at all. Helmeted Japanese soldiers approaching him were just branches and leaves blowing in the breeze. He continued on, wary of human contact either real or imagined.

The sounds of the air attacks against the Tobera and Vunakanau airfields, as well as the duels between fighters, reached Morris. Though Morris could not see the air combat, another Corsair pilot was shot down. About 5 miles away, 1Lt. Allan S. Harrison III of VMF-212 lost his battle with a Zeke. The Vought plummeted to earth from 20,000 feet. A fiery black cloud emerged from the jungle canopy to the north.

Morris's goal was to find a stream flowing east that would lead him to the sea. He took stock of the jungle pack's inventory: the compass, matches, signal mirror, and fishing gear would be essential. He followed streams where he could. As he descended down the slope, the underbrush grew thicker. Mosquitoes dogged him. From his survival kit came a mosquito head net.

During the days he nibbled on his rations and took his medicine. "We learned in Survival School that if we cut the vines trailing down from the tree canopy, clean filtered water would drip from them. I tried it and it worked surprisingly well."[13] The portion of the parachute he retained served as a blanket but was useless when tropical rain soaked him. Periodically he would strip down and bathe in pools of water. The sun dried his drenched gear as he rested naked on sandy beaches.

Monday, February 14: Jungle, Gazelle Peninsula, New Britain

After four days battling the jungle, Morris was very hungry. With the jungle pack on his back, raft pack in hand, and all the military gear attached to his flight suit, he was burdened by considerable weight. At the sight of a wild pig, Morris instinctively pulled out his Colt and fired off a round. Only after he missed his shot did he realize he risked discovery. It was foolish, he decided. He didn't have time to roast a pig anyway. Later Morris started fishing in a stream but gave up for the same reason. Time was of the essence.

Morris was wary of discovery: each step closer to the sea also brought him closer to human contact. As he rounded a bend in the river, he spied a native hut. Dried bones hung from the grass roof. As quickly as possible, Morris moved past. The sound of the water covered his steps. As he approached another bend, smoke appeared on the horizon. Trying to bypass the bend, he hacked his way through the jungle: "In the gloom of the thick overhead canopy, and profuse undergrowth, I could neither see the vines tangling my feet nor stinging nettles reaching out for bare skin."[14] He tripped across deadfalls. Flies buzzed his exposed skin. When he broke through, the smoke turned out to be just vapor.

Four days earlier, Morris had set out for the sea but found himself still in the jungle. He returned to his footslog but was discouraged by his perceived lack of progress, the failure to find food, and the harsh tropical conditions. He wondered, "Will I get out of here alive?"[15]

After making camp for the night, the young pilot tried cooking taro roots wrapped in broad leaves, as taught in survival school: "My mouth was watering, readying itself for a small tasty meal, anticipating a warm succulent morsel. But, ugh, it was like a mouthful of pins!"[16] The fire provided some comfort though. Visions of his fiancée rallied his spirits. He struggled on.

Wednesday, February 16: Gazelle Peninsula, New Britain

The day before, at long last, the river broadened and deepened enough that Morris could take advantage of his raft. He floated when he could and waded where necessary. As Morris navigated the snaking river, he could not see around the endless bends but, for the first time, could smell the salt air of the sea.

Coconuts provided sustenance after Morris finished the last of his rations. His weight had dropped noticeably.

Wednesday, February 16: Kempeitai Prison, Rabaul

Evacuation. It was apparent to the interpreter, "Chicky" Honda, that not only were no Allied pilots going to survive being imprisoned at Rabaul, the Japanese stationed there were also on the wrong side of the calendar. The war was going poorly. The angry swarms over eastern New Britain and the interrogations of the pilots confirmed his assessment of the war. Eager to escape himself, Honda suggested to higher authorities that several of the high-value prisoners be sent to the home islands for additional interrogation.

Honda's recommendation for prisoner evacuation was accepted.

Majors Boyington and Boyle along with four other captured aviators were brought out to the flight line. With Honda, they boarded a Mitsubishi G4M Betty bomber. Ahead was a long trip to Japan and long months of confinement.

They almost didn't make it as far as the first leg. The mission had been attempted and aborted the day prior. Soon after becoming airborne, the "Flying Zippo'" encountered the daily "flying circus." Army P-38 Lightnings with Navy and Marine Corsairs escorted B-24s in an attack over the Vunakunau Airdrome. Overcast weather forced the Liberators to drop their bombs blindly. In response, return antiaircraft fire was heavy but inaccurate.

In his biography, Boyington claimed that they heard air fire coming at them. The Betty pilot aborted the flight and sought safety on the ground. The prisoners were led into the woods.

On the sixteenth, the six blindfolded Allied fliers were led back to the Betty. They escaped Rabaul before the daily Allied strikes and sweeps arrived. The bomber flew 800 miles north to Truk, away from the volcano- and ordnance-ringed Fortress Rabaul.

Wednesday, February 16: Truk Atoll

They had flown into the hornet's nest. Truk Lagoon was Japan's largest forward naval base, and home to the IJN 4th Fleet. Hundreds of aircraft were stationed there. As the Betty bomber from Rabaul began its descent to land, Truk was also the target of Operation Hailstone.

As a prelude to the invasion of the Marshall Islands, the US Navy's Fast Carrier Task Force 58 targeted the airfields, support facilities, and ships in the lagoon for neutralization. Before dawn, the first of numerous strikes was sent forth by the nine fast carriers. It was a reversal of the Pearl Harbor defeat, since the Japanese had little warning of the attack. American Dauntlesses and Avengers bracketed targets with near impunity. Hellcats cleared the air of Zeroes. Roughly 70 percent of the Japanese air strength was destroyed.

The bomber carrying Boyington, Boyle, and the other four prisoners managed to land despite the aerial opposition. Boyington described it as "the roughest, shortest of landings, intentionally I know now, I have ever experienced or hope to."[17]

The prisoners hurriedly evacuated the Betty and were pushed into a pit. A Hellcat dived from the sky, its .50s alight as it strafed the bomber. The Mitsubishi was reduced to a burning hulk. The prisoners watched as the devastation continued. Bombs fell around them, shrapnel filled the air, and ammunition cooked off in the destroyed enemy planes. They had a ringside seat to the deadliest show on earth.

Boyington and Boyle had always been on the reverse end of these air attacks. As they cowered alongside the runway, a Zero landed nearby. As the pilot ran for safety, he discovered the Allied prisoners. In English he threatened to kill them as revenge for the attack against Truk. Boyington, frustrated but amused by the threat in the midst of an aerial bombardment, elbowed Boyle in the ribs as he vented to the enemy pilot: "With all the God damn trouble we got, ain't you the cheerful son of a bitch though."[18] Another Hellcat strafing run put an end to the standoff. The Japanese pilot fled as rows of bullets stitched the runway.

Abandoned by their guards, Boyington and the others stayed put as the raids continued into the afternoon.

Wednesday Evening, February 16: Gazelle Peninsula, New Britain

A shout in Japanese broke the silence. With the river mouth in sight, Morris had passed underneath a bridge that spanned the river. "One shout was all I heard. No searchlights. The bridge faded out of sight behind. The waves got higher as I reached farther into the bay. A nice tailwind joined the river current to hasten my escape. The dark unknown ahead felt better than what I knew lurked behind. Morning would tell how well my escape has succeeded, how far from shore I had drifted. I was pretty much at the mercy of nature's forces here."[19] It would not be Morris's last encounter with the enemy.

VF(N)-101 F4U-2s on USS *Intrepid* warming up for February 16, 1944, Truk raid. *National Naval Aviation Museum, photo 1996.488.210.193*

Wednesday Evening, February 16: Truk

While the stronghold had been reduced to smoldering ruins, the Rabaul Six had survived unscathed. After the attacks had ceased, they were moved by a guard and their interpreter to the ruins of an airfield building for the remainder of the day.

When night came, the Rabaul Six were moved again. Without their blindfolds, they witnessed the devastation across the airfield as well as in the lagoon. After crossing the atoll by boat, they eventually were transferred to a jail near the seaplane base. There were just three cramped cells. Boyington, Boyle, and a PBY pilot, Lt. John Arbuckle, were crammed into a cell built to hold just one prisoner, the space so small so that they could not lie down.

Their safety was temporary. Around 90 miles eastward, the Fast Carrier Task Force prepared strikes and sweeps for a second day of attacks against Truk.

Thursday Morning, February 17: Truk Atoll, Dublon Seaplane Base

With several freighters moored nearby, the airspace over the seaplane base was very crowded. The familiar engine sounds of the Hellcats, Dauntlesses, and Avengers reached the Rabaul Six, as did the screams of bombs diving toward their targets. Shrapnel rained on the jail as the prisoners tried to press themselves into the floorboards. Smoke from the freighters and three burning oil storage tanks filled the sky and fouled the air. The attacks continued until midafternoon.

Thursday Morning, February 17: St. George's Channel, New Britain

As daylight relieved night, Morris found the silhouette of New Ireland to his left and the sun-illuminated New Britain to his right. He was still in the channel, but the breeze pushed him on a path toward the open sea. Ahead, an unexpected figure came over the horizon in his direction. Black smoke trailed behind.

Morris pulled his poncho over his raft. With the blue side facing out, he was camouflaged as a Japanese submarine continued its journey up the channel. Undetected, Morris continued drifting silently toward the open sea. Morris prepared himself for the ritual attacks against Fortress Rabaul. On cue, it arrived: "I heard the distant drone of many aircraft in formation."[20]

Seventy Avengers and Dauntlesses attacked shipping at Keravia Bay. The forty AirSols fighters were challenged by an equal amount of enemy fighters. Ens. Clyde Dunn of VF-17 was shot down over the target. Though the heavy antiaircraft fire was described as meager and inaccurate, one round found its mark. About 5 feet of the right wing of Lt. j.g. Jamey Miller's F4U was blown off. The "Skull & Crossbones" bird spun from 10,000 down to 5,000 feet before Miller escaped the cockpit. Squadron member Lt. j.g. Wilbert "Beads" Popp reported, "I watched him come down in a parachute. We strafed the ground. Troops were trying to shoot him while he was dangling in his parachute. We saw him land safely on the runway off the field adjoining Simpson Harbor. He waved at us."[21] The "Jolly Rogers" were under no illusion that they would ever see Miller again.

With the signal mirror from the survival pack in hand, Morris reminded himself, "I must be alert and continue to search the skies, look for that twin-engine, twin-finned Vega Ventura, the PV-1 that skims the channel surface in search of downed fliers and enemy submarines."[22]

Two VB-138 Venturas, "One Baker Thirty" and "Two Baker Thirty," appeared: "Shortly after the second wave of our planes had passed over, I saw it: the dark, side profile of the Ventura I'd been waiting for, way off in the distance, silhouetted against the light[-]blue hills of New Ireland. I pulled out the signal device. Through the hole in the middle of the round mirror[,] I could see the side of my target. I struck it with slashes of sunbeams. Almost at once it changed direction and headed directly toward me; then the small speck of a target started to grow and grow."[23]

Morris's survival training at Espiritu paid dividends. The flashing reflections caught the attention of Lt. William E. Lohse, who was flying "One Baker Thirty." He turned his bird toward Morris, who was now 8 miles south of Cape Gazelle: "Quickly it was upon me, off to my left as it flew over," recalled Morris. "I got a glimpse of the airman in the nose bubble. I saw a waving hand. I felt joyful, grateful, and confident that I would soon be in safe hands."[24]

Lohse came in low on the deck. A canteen was dropped downwind of Morris, who quickly retrieved it. Another go-around brought a ration bundle. While Morris's spirits were rising, so was Lohse's frustration. He was unable to raise the dumbo PBY, "Fifty Baker Twenty-Eight." With "Two Baker Thirty" now on station, Lohse flew to Torokina to refuel.

Eventually, low fuel levels forced Lt. j.g. Leonard A. Dobler's "Two Baker Thirty" to also depart. Once again, Morris was on his own, but there were still several hours of daylight remaining. He hoped dumbo was on its way. But poor weather north of Bougainville had forced the return of afternoon airstrikes. "Warm rays of the mid-afternoon sun along with the rhythmic motion of my boat put me in a sleepy stupor, but my drooping eyelids snapped open and my head came up when the distant hum of a single engine aircraft reached my ears."[25]

Dumbo it was not. About 500 feet above the water and closing fast was a Japanese fighter plane. Responding too late, Morris reached for the sail cloth as he saw the "red meatballs" on the wings pass overhead. It continued on. Unseen or lost in the sparkle of the waves, Morris escaped.

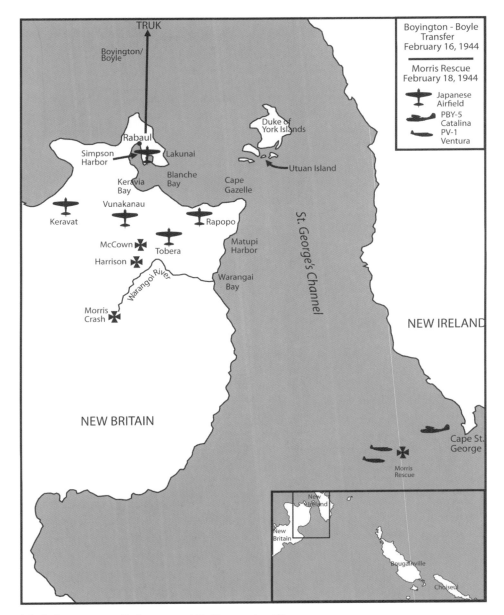

Midafternoon, February 17: Bougainville

Landing at Torokina, Lohse reported his sighting. He refueled and set out to try to find the raft again. A Dumbo mission was initiated. Flying north from the Treasury Islands, a New Zealand Catalina left its tender, the USS *Coos Bay* (AVP-25), and rendezvoused with its fighter escort (four Army P-39s and four VMF-216 Corsairs) west of Torokina. Lohse reported to "Fifty Baker Twenty-Eight" that he was searching for the downed pilot 25 miles due west of Cape St. George.

"Just before sundown, I spotted another plane coming toward me from the southeast." Morris aligned the twin-engine, twin-tailed Ventura flown by Lt. Lohse in the crosshairs of the signal mirror:

> He came roaring in at top speed, went right over the top of me[,] and kept on going toward Cape Gazelle, at the northeast tip of New Britain, then made a broad, sweeping right turn that took him south of me. He straightened up and headed toward the bay I had left the night before. I saw geysers of seawater rise up in his wake, followed a few seconds later by a rumble in the water below. The plane must have dropped a depth charge on a submarine that started early on its nightly mission, or the pilot may have feinted an attack to draw attention away from me.[26]

In fact, neither Lohse nor the dumbo had been able to spot Morris. The search was abandoned due to the late hour and an approaching storm front from the west.

Morris resigned himself to spending the night at sea. His spirits were brightened by the fact he had been discovered twice that day. He had water and food. Though injured and wet from the choppy sea, Morris believed he was close to rescue. Salvation would depend on the rising sun.

Friday, February 18: New Britain

There was no reprieve for the Japanese. XIII Bomber Command B-24s and B-25s attacked Vunakanau and Tobera Airdromes. The Venturas trailed the attacking force. It was a bright, sunny morning. Morris was ready: "First I heard the familiar drones of planes in formation, and I saw the specks that were our fighters and bombers high overhead." Thirty minutes after the first wave came through, providence arrived with the second wave: "There appeared the two low-flying patrol planes over the horizon."[27]

He thought, "There they are! My mirror is at the ready; the flare gun and the dye marker are close by; this has to be my day." In response to the PV-1, "I flashed a sunbeam at the nearest plane[,] and it immediately vectored toward me. I dumped the dye marker liquid overboard to make a bigger target. The PV-1 circled around my raft at once[,] and I waved furiously to him in gratitude and joy."[28]

Lt. Guy Howard of VB-138 had taken up the search for Morris. He turned "One Baker Thirty" toward the source of the light. Spotting Morris at the entrance to St. George's Channel, Howard came in on the deck and dropped a dye marker over Morris. A radio call went out for "Fifty Baker Twenty-Eight."

This time the request got through. An RNZAF PBY Catalina from No. 6 Squadron was sent north. VMF-217 Corsairs flew top cover. The dumbo arrived on scene in little more than an hour. Lt. Howard circled Morris.

After nine days defined by pain, hunger, injury, exposure, and fear of being captured, Morris's mood turned to elation at the sight of his savior. Rescue seemed all but certain: "Then came the sounds of the nearby Ventura[,] and from the distant formations came the familiar, shrill whistle of a Corsair."[29] Its pilot throttled back, pushed back the canopy, and came in for a pass over Morris. A welcoming wave encouraged Morris.

In preparation for the rescue, the dumbo pilot, Flight Lieutenant J. McGrane, swooped in low, dropped a smoke bomb to gauge the wind, and then steered toward Morris.

The Consolidated PBY-5 Catalinas flown by No. 6 Squadron were amphibious birds capable of landing at sea or on airstrips. The wing was mounted on a pylon over the fuselage. Retractable stabilizing floats extended from the ends of the parasol wing. The hull had a two-step design for sea landings and takeoffs. It was a big bird, nearly the size of Boeing's mighty B-17 Flying Fortress. Two Pratt & Whitney R-1830 Twin Wasp engines kept her in the air.

Though considered obsolescent, Cats served in every theater throughout the war. Their range and flexibility proved them adept at numerous roles: transport, antishipping patrols, night bombing, and rescue missions.

For McGrane, an open-water landing was an act accompanied with great risk. The current of St. George's Channel was typically 10 knots, but white caps were on the waves. A hard landing could damage an engine (it was not unheard of for engines to be ripped from their mounts), rivets could pop in the hull, or takeoff could be difficult. Rough seas caused the wing floats to act as a drag if they submerged. Getting proper airspeed was made difficult by the waves, and flying boats would often porpoise on the seas. Many Catalinas saved pilots adrift but then later needed rescue themselves when they could not take off due to damage sustained in landing.

Morris had witnessed the terrific air traffic in the area, both friend and foe. Despite the top cover of a low-altitude division of P-39s and a high-cover division of F4Us, it would be an easy trick for a Japanese fighter to dive through the angels and burn the Cat in a single pass as it floated on the seas. Takeoff was just as risky.

Guided by the smoke bomb, McGrane landed the bird. "The sea was not calm[,] and a stiff breeze was blowing," reported Warrant Officer Bill Leadley. "On landing we came off the crest of a wave[,] then hit the sea with a mighty thump." The hard landing popped rivets throughout the hull: "What a sight, about fifty water spouts between me and the cockpit."[30] Crewmen scrambled to plug the holes in the deck with the navigator's pencils.

We approached the dinghy cross wind, the strong breeze brought him into us[,] and [Flight Sergeant A.] Ormsby arrived in the blister to help. I grabbed ahold of the dinghy and trouble. As it fell away, I managed by good luck to grab a line and held on. One glance at the pilot's face told me he was in a very weak condition, with his right eye out of the socket and his nose split from the nostril to the bridge. How the hell we were going to get him in[side] in that pitching sea[,] I don't know.[31]

McGrane kept the Twin Wasps turning. Without an anchor, the Consolidated seaplane continued to drift in the channel. The crew struggled to bring Morris aboard through the side 0.50 gun blister. Second Pilot Flight Sergeant Harry Farmiloe left the cockpit to see what was taking so long to rescue the American pilot. "I could understand Harry's concern, water was pissing into the aircraft. Time was running out."[32]

Leadley exited the PBY: "I shot out of the blister and climbed topside, hanging on like grim death. As the dinghy rose on the crest of a wave, Harry reached out with both arms wrapped around the guy and then stepped backwards. In he came." Morris turned to his rescuers: "Am I glad to see you!"[33]

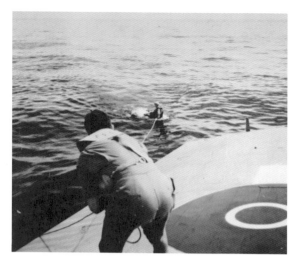

No. 6 Squadron PBY rescue of Maj. Horace Pehl, VMF-218, on February 21, 1944, three days after 2Lt. Jack Morris VMF-218 was rescued

Becoming airborne was the next challenge: "We started riding a wave[,] then as speed increased we ploughed through them, losing revs as the propellers chopped water. The revs picked up again and again. At last we were hitting the top of the waves. It was like riding a mad bucking horse. Then it suddenly stopped and we were airborne."[34]

Dirty, injured, and fatigued, Morris needed attention. "The effort of getting him in had started his face bleeding again. I guess the salt water had stopped infection." Eight days after he was shot down, Morris's wounds were finally treated by Leadley: "Getting the medical kit down[,] I started on his face, putting some tape over his nose. The partially congealed blood I scooped gently out of his eye socket with my little finger. I eased the eye back into the socket[,] putting a dressing over the eye, made sure he was comfortable, and left him with a cup of water."[35] Morris shed his wet coveralls. Hot tomato soup, a warm blanket, and bunk completed the aid.

As they flew south, the deadly verdant jungle of New Britain disappeared from sight. The rookie Morris had begun his long journey home to America.

Saturday, February 19, 1944: New Britain

The air war over Rabaul had been a battle of attrition. A large group of Japanese fighters challenged the Americans on the nineteenth. It was their last gasp. The Japanese high command ordered the evacuation of all flyable planes to Truk. The regular duels that had commenced over Guadalcanal in August 1942 and then climbed the Solomons to Fortress Rabaul were done. The period where the Vought F4U Corsair had first become legend had come to an end.

Truk Atoll, Dublon Seaplane Base

Sweltering in dimly lit cells, the Rabaul Six endured another two weeks before their transfer to Japan. Eighteen months of hell waited for them there. *To be continued . . .*

Five days after Boyington and Boyle were evacuated to Truk, 1Lt. Edward A. Croker—who had shared a cell with Boyington at Rabaul—was executed. Less than two weeks later, thirty-one Allied prisoners held at the Tunnel Hill prison camp near Rabaul were executed. Among the group were two VMF-321 pilots, First Lieutenants Roger H. Brindos and Robert W. Marshall. VMF-214 "Black Sheep" Charles Lanphier would later starve to death in May 1944. Of the nearly 100 Allied aviators held as prisoners at Rabaul, only seven survived until the end of the war.

Jack Morris returned to Gazelle Peninsula in 1991 on a quest to find his old birdcage, BuNo 02566. It turned out easier than expected: the wreckage had already been recovered and lay on the grounds of the Kokopo War Museum. Morris wrote of his war experience and subsequent life in his book, One Angel Left. *He passed away in 2006. The remains of Lt. Allan S. Harrison III and Capt. Marion R. McCown were recovered in the jungle south of Rabaul by the US Department of Defense Joint POW/MIA Accounting Command in 2008.*

CHAPTER 8

QUALIFICATIONS

Steel Nests

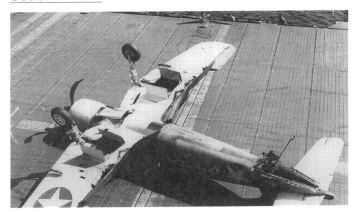

Ens. Fred D. Henderson escaped serious injury when his VF-17 Corsair crashed into the barriers on July 22, 1943.

The gun club had to find new berthing. Pearl Harbor forced a revolution in US Navy tactics. With the loss or damage to most of the Pacific Fleet's battleships, the carriers became the stars. Japan proved the concept at Oahu that a concentrated aerial attack from carrier-borne aircraft could be more devastating than a traditional battle-line versus battle-line bombardment of the admirals' prized battleships. For the cost of five minisubs and twenty-nine planes, the Imperial Japanese Navy sank six ships and damaged thirteen other vessels. They also permanently changed naval warfare.

The future for the US Navy lay in shipyards at Newport News, Virginia; Brooklyn, New York; and Quincy, Massachusetts. Before the first torpedo was dropped at Pearl, eleven Essex-class fleet carriers were either under construction or had been ordered. More orders were placed after the surprise attack.

The Essex-class carriers were the most modern in the world at the time of their construction. Larger than the prewar Yorktown carriers, the Essex class was designed to carry upward of one hundred fighters, dive-bombers, and torpedo planes. The vaunted Vought-Sikorsky's Corsairs were expected to serve from their decks. It didn't turn out that way.

Early Corsairs were plagued by a number of design deficiencies that made landings difficult. Coupled with a critical lack of spare parts and other logistic considerations, Corsair squadrons were not deployed on carriers until 1944. Instead, the bent-wing bird was cast off. It became the Marines' dream fighter in the South Pacific.

To become carrier qualified, pilots initially flew field carrier landing practice, a simulated form of touch-and-go landings on a carrier flight deck outline on a land runway. After these attempts, pilots attempted landings at sea. Eight successful landings typically was the requirement for carrier qualification. Though some squadrons had the advantage of qualifying on the large fleet carriers, often it was done on smaller escort carriers or on a pair of auxiliary ships stationed near Chicago.

Though he had held a civilian pilot's license since 1941, 2Lt. Philip Wilmot was scared as he turned into his base leg. He glanced at the USS *Ranger* over his left shoulder before beginning final approach. He had flown parallel to the carrier's starboard side when he entered the upwind leg to begin the landing procedure, a counterclockwise flight path that descended with the turns. Wilmot had turned left into the crosswind leg ahead of the *Ranger* before turning left again into the downwind leg and left again into the base leg.

VMF-451 had received orders in December 1944 to join Carrier Air Group 84 aboard the USS *Bunker Hill*. The Navy needed Marine Corsairs to act as kamikaze killers for their carriers. Their Navy Corsair squadrons weren't ready yet. The Marine Corsair squadrons, which had flown from the islands of the Pacific, were hurriedly being trained to join the ranks of the carrier-qualified flocks.

Wilmot was moments from his first carrier landing, the culmination of over a year's worth of military flight training. At 100 miles from the California coast, Wilmot's division leader radioed to the twenty-one-year-old that his arresting hook was in the down position. From the base leg into his final turn, "Pots" focused on the landing signal officer.

Air Group 4 Corsair takes a wave off, January 1945. *Courtesy of the National Archives, photo 80-G-258980*

Positioned at the port stern corner of the flight deck, the landing signal officer (LSO) on a carrier functioned as a cross between a traffic cop and St. Peter at the pearly gates. With a pair of paddles in hand, he helped the pilots bring their planes aboard ship. Wilmot recalled:

> If you wiggle your wings on "base leg," it tells him you can only make one approach. The LSO will do everything he can to get you back aboard. If he's there with his arms wide, you're doing fine. If he tips an arm, it's to indicate which way to turn, usually to the left. He's a pilot himself, a good one. He'll start trying to fly the plane for you. He knows you're distracted, you're scared, and he's got to make up the difference. After you get back aboard, the LSO might chew you out for a bad landing, but he knew what you were going through.[1]

Wilmot corrected his approach in response to the paddles. The Pratt & Whitney was nearly at full power. As he approached the stern hanging on the prop and just above stalling speed, the LSO slapped the right paddle to his left shoulder. Nerves aside, Wilmot took the cut signal and, to his surprise, pranged safely aboard.

Right behind him was the squadron CO, Maj. Henry Ellis. He was from the first team of Marine aviators, having commanded VMF-214 before Boyington absconded with the squadron. Ellis took his cues from the LSO. Unlike the rookie, the major received crossed paddles above the LSO's head. Ellis took the wave off, increased his speed, and rejoined the landing pattern.

Pots Wilmot had sixty-seven carrier takeoffs during World War II. He completed sixty-six carrier landings, having to ditch on his second combat mission of the war when he ran out of gas in the landing pattern. Two kamikazes on May 11, 1945, took away his chance for any more landings aboard the USS Bunker Hill.

Lake Michigan Cruise

A Corsair prepares to launch ahead of an F4F Wildcat and a pair of TBF Avengers from the USS *Sable* in 1943.

Ahead of the rookie pilot steamed a vessel born from the needs of war. The USS *Wolverine* (IX-64) was classified as a miscellaneous auxiliary training vessel. Though she looked like an escort carrier, she was an old side-wheel steamer of another era. Her sister was the USS *Sable* (IX-81). The pair had cruised the Great Lakes entertaining tourists before the Navy acquired them in 1942. In just four months their superstructures were removed and replaced with flight decks. Though they were slow, they served their purpose. In 1943, they began qualifying pilots for carrier flights.

On June 12 of that year, Ens. Carl Johnson was flying BuNo 02465, a recently built birdcage Corsair. His approach appeared normal, but like many pilots learning to land the long-nosed fighter on a carrier, Johnson lost sight of the LSO. Johnson missed the cut signal. He pushed the throttle forward to go around again, but his bird was already on the deck. His tailhook snagged one cable. As it caught the next cable, the tailhook assembly broke free. The Corsair went over the port side into Lake Michigan.

Johnson was able to clear the Vought before it settled into the deep, cold water of the lake. The crash boat recovered the pilot; he suffered only minor cuts. The birdcage settled in 200 fathoms of water.

The Navy's determination was that the cause of the plane loss was 100 percent pilot error, equally split between poor judgment and technique. Under the "Remarks" section of the report, it noted, "Aircraft and engine lost in Lake Michigan. Not recovered to date."[2]

Ens. Johnson was killed five months later in a midair collision between two Hellcats over Maui. Sixty-seven years later, 02465 was pulled up from the floor of Lake Michigan. It is currently being restored at the National Naval Aviation Museum in Pensacola, Florida.

How Fast Can They Build Them?

At peak production, the workers in the Stratford Sikorsky plant were completing a Corsair every eighty-four minutes. Each was towed from the factory down Sniffens Lane and across Main Street to two sets of large hangars. Each plane was taken for test flights. Minor issues that were discovered by Vought's pilots during the hops were addressed by mechanics in the hangar near the flight line before the planes were turned over to the Navy. Major flaws were repaired at Building 6, Vought's spot for research and development as well as experimental work.

The bad landing habits of the Corsairs on flattops had been corrected: the landing-gear oleos were less prone to cause bounce when hitting the decks. A change to the tailhook system kept the iron in the down position, thereby eliminating "hook skip." The post-birdcage models had higher seats that allowed for a better vantage by the pilot. And the infamous left-wing stall was solved by the simple edition of a small spoiler added to the leading edge of the left wing.

Vought F4U final assembly, Stratford Factory

The dramatic expansion of the Navy and Marine air forces during the first years of the war forced changes in pilot training. The need was pressing for airmen, especially as the new Essex-class carriers began to come on line in 1943. The training was tougher. The pilots were younger. And the time for Corsairs to serve on the flattops had arrived with the kamikazes in the fall of 1944.

The original Marine F4U squadrons in the Solomon Islands, VMF-124 and -213, were destined to join Adm. Halsey's Fast Carrier Task Force aboard the USS *Essex*. Their forward echelons were already carrier qualified and on the way to join Task Force 38. The VMF-213 rear echelon flew their own carrier-qualification flights during that period. Many of those pilots were bound to fly as replacements for other carrier squadrons in the spring of 1945. British test pilot Capt. Eric Brown warned, "Oh yes, the Corsair could be landed on a flight deck without undue difficulty by an experienced pilot in ideal conditions, but with pilots of average capability, really pitching decks and marginal weather conditions, attrition simply had to be of serious proportions."[3]

Brown's prophecy was proven over two days aboard the USS *Makassar Strait* (CVE-91). Steaming 100 miles west of Oahu on December 17 and 18, 1944, they were busy days on deck. Thirty pilots each made eight successful landings to earn their carrier qualifications. Many pilots, though, did not. There were so many poor landings it turned out to be the worst day of qualification attempts by Corsair pilots during World War II.

The escort carrier's flight deck, at 512 by 65 feet, looked like a short driveway to pilots flying Corsairs with 41-foot wingspans. Making the transition from field landings to deck landings caused many to try to fly onto the deck rather than following the guidance of the landing signal officer and float in.

Nine Corsairs landed with such force that they had to be written off. Six more bent-wing birds suffered structural damage. Barrier crashes, buckled skin, broken tails, and bent props were the calling cards for the two days. The six damaged planes required major overhaul to become airworthy again.

There were days when the squadron commanders and all those topside on the carrier must have wondered, "How fast can they build them?"

Flaps and hook down, canopy locked back: with a slash of the right arm to the left shoulder, the LSO gives an F4U the "cut."

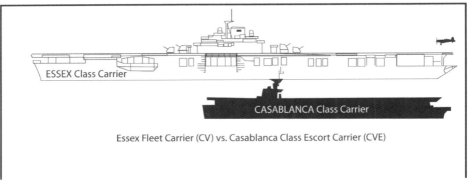

ESSEX Class Carrier

CASABLANCA Class Carrier

Essex Fleet Carrier (CV) vs. Casablanca Class Escort Carrier (CVE)

The Replacements

The VMF-213 Rear Echelon pilots were used as replacements or transferred into other squadrons. Most made it into squadrons on the Essex carriers. Adventures after carrier qualification continued for some of those who had damaged or destroyed Corsairs on the USS *Makassar Straits*. Second Lieutenant Warren E. Vaughn (VMF-123, USS *Bennington*) was captured on February 23, 1945. He was later beheaded and cannibalized by the Japanese on Chi Chi Jima. Second Lieutenant Franklin Kurchinski (VMF-123) was shot down by antiaircraft fire and killed on April 12, 1945, off Kikai Jima, Ryukyu Islands.

Second Lieutenant "Mo" Sagers (VBF-83, USS *Essex*) ran out of fuel during the battleship *Yamato* search-and-destroy mission of April 7, 1945. He was rescued several days later by pure chance, when an American sub surfaced at night to charge its batteries. It was one of the luckiest rescues of the war.

First Lieutenant Robert J. McInnis (VMF-123) was shot down off the coast of Kyushu on May 24, 1945. A daring rescue by a Martin PBM Mariner saved him.

Some Disassembly Required

After departing NAAS Mayport, Florida, en route to Guantanamo Bay on April 5, 1945, carrier qualification for young pilots began aboard the USS *Guadalcanal*. Ens. R. D. Nelson experienced a landing similar to test pilot Boone Guyton's golf course crash. After his Corsair caught the wire, the plane pulled to port and crashed onto the deck and the catwalk. The plane snapped in half just behind the center spar assembly. The cockpit and nose broke free. Nelson emerged from the cockpit under his own power, with just a minor abrasion of his nose. The deck crew arrived immediately to assist before the plane became engulfed in flame. There were ninety-seven landings that day. Only eight pilots qualified.

Planes, Cranes, and the Fire Crew

Lt. j.g. John H. Laney's F4U-1 (BuNo 57693) crashes into the bridge of the USS *Prince William*.

With the war in the Pacific heading toward its cataclysmic finish, Corsairs, originally rejected for service on the fleet carriers, were required in ever-growing numbers. Not only were they destined to serve as kamikaze killers, they were also needed as bomber-fighters to make up for the reduced number of Avengers and Helldivers carried by the ever-increasing numbers of Essex-class carriers.

Fighting Squadron 94 was split into two squadrons: VF-94 and VBF-94. Bomber-Fighting Squadron 94 made its final preparations before deployment. Pilot training continued with a special emphasis on honing bombing, strafing, and rocket-launching skills. Night field landings were followed by the most-difficult landings: carrier day and night landing qualifications.

VBF-94 traveled from Quonset Point to Boca Chima, Florida, to qualify its pilots aboard the USS *Prince William* (CVE-31). February 1945 was a busy period for the baby flattop. As the demand for carrier-based Corsair squadrons increased, so did the daily number of landing attempts. At one point, *Prince William* held the record for the most carrier landings in a twenty-four-hour period, at 370. Not all days were easy days aboard as the young twenty-something-year-old ensigns and junior lieutenants practiced this new skill.

Cruising north of Vardero, Cuba, VBF-94 began two days of qualifying attempts. Collisions with the barrier or the port catwalk were commonplace.

As the hour grew late on February 24, Lt. j.g. John H. Laney prepared to bring his eliminator back aboard the carrier. After flying down the starboard side of the ship, he made his crosswind turn ahead of its bow to enter the downwind leg of his approach. As he flew in the opposite direction of the ship, he went down the checklist for approach and landing. With his shoulder harness locked, he unlocked his tailwheel and adjusted the fuel tank selector, transfer pump, and booster fuel pump. His left hand slid the mixture control forward to the "auto rich" setting, and the supercharger control to "neutral," before moving the cowl flap lever to "closed." His hand pulled the landing-gear lever all the way down before setting his flaps at 50 degrees and releasing the arresting hook from its compartment aft of the tailwheel. Reaching up, Laney turned the master armament switch to "off" and then reached down to set the gun-charging knobs to "safe." After completing the approach-and-landing checklist, he reached over to open the cockpit by shifting the handle on the right away from him, sliding the canopy back. All the while he descended until his airspeed had dropped to 95 knots, just above stalling. The Pratt & Whitney was at full throttle, full rpm, the Hamilton Standard prop at no pitch, the long nose of the Corsair pointed high. His left hand worked the trim tabs on final approach. The pressure was on. The carrier awaited for the young pilot to prang.

With his eyes focused on the batsmen's paddles, Laney took the "cut" signal from the LSO. He landed his bent-wing bird aboard the escort carrier successfully, but rather than killing the throttle, Laney opened it up. His mount leaped forward, hit the barrier, and was thrown up against the bridge, the metal bird shedding its wings. As the wheels hung up on the steel island's observation walk, the Double Wasp broke free of its mount as the Hamilton Standard blades were bent back like wilted stalks. The 237-gallon fuel tank, forward of the cockpit, was punctured as the metal concussion raced down the Vought corpse. A plume of gasoline geysered above the bird for an instant before contact with the hot engine and flying sparks ignited an iridescent fireball that descended on the Corsair. With his plane impaled on the island, its broken nose pointed up and burning, Laney was in trouble. Strapped into the plane and heavily burdened by gear, the wounded pilot struggled as the fire entered the cockpit.

Quick action by bridge personnel saved the pilot. Spraying CO_2 toward the cockpit gave the deck-force crew time enough to attack the fire from below. Firemen extricated the Steelton, Pennsylvania, native from his mount. While several of the ship's complement were injured, Laney suffered just a cut on his face and third-degree burns on his right arm and leg. His flying career with the Navy had come to an abrupt end. The shattered remains of the dash-one were jettisoned over the side. Laney had joined the fraternity of fliers saved by the deck force.

CHAPTER 9

DECK TALES

The Cans Can

Rescue swimmer Henry Michalak, S1c, of the USS *Haynsworth* saving a pilot. *Photo courtesy of Capt. Hank Domeracki, USN*

The young marine flier felt the engine of his mighty Corsair sputtering. He had just taken a wave-off from a light carrier. His own ship, the USS *Bunker Hill*, was unable to take him aboard. A day after scoring an aerial victory in his first combat mission, 1Lt. Philip Wilmot had run out of gas after returning from Tokyo. He retracted the main landing gear, pointed the plane's nose up, locked the canopy back, and dragged the tailhook through the water. The F4U-1D plowed through the first swell before going nose down in the second swell. The Marine Fighting Squadron 451 pilot evacuated the sinking plane. As he held on to the side of the cockpit, he came up empty as he reached for his raft. The Vought plane sank in less than twenty seconds.

Wilmot managed to inflate his Mae West. He pulled a dye marker off the vest and sprinkled it into the seas. A strong swimmer, Wilmot was able to see the various carriers, battleships, cruisers, and destroyers when he crested the waves. Before long, he was encircled in a chartreuse-colored sea as the task group steamed by.

Destroyer Squadron 62 was composed of nine sister Sumner-class destroyers that came off the ways in Kearney, New Jersey, in 1944. Tin cans 696–704 were assigned to guard the carriers of the famed Fast Carrier Task Force 38/58.

Saving wayward pilots from the unforgiving Pacific was a morale booster not just for the tin can sailors; for those who went in the water, there were often rewards to be had. Chief Radio Technician Morris Gillett of the USS *John W. Weeks* (DD-701) was given Lt. Darrell Way's flight helmet after pulling the VF-83 pilot from the Pacific.

Twenty-six-year-old fire controlman second class Robert Plum was rescued by the USS *Haynsworth* (DD-700) after being washed overboard during a storm hammering the fleet in the South China Sea. Plum, who had donned a rescued pilot's Mae West when he went up on deck, opened the dye pack. Tossed about by the surging waves, it took forty-five minutes for the *Haynsworth* to spot the sailor. "It was subsequently reported that twelve men were washed overboard that day from different ships. Only two were rescued. [Cmdr. Stephen Tackney] later acknowledged that it was this dye marker that made all the difference in seeing me at all."[1]

Lt. Joseph Perry, MD, described pilot rescues during his service with the USS *Waldron* (DD-699): "The swimmer, with a small nylon line hooked to a harness type of arrangement, would swim out to the man in the water. Then the crew on deck would pull both men back to the ship[,] where several men clinging to a cargo net over the side would pass the man up to the deck. Then he would be taken to sick bay and I would check him over."[2]

The destroyer USS *Charles S. Sperry* (DD-697) had the plane guard duty. Its captain brought the tin can right alongside the twenty-one-year-old Wilmot. A strong hand was extended by a blonde sailor hanging from the cargo net. Wilmot was aboard the dry steel deck in no time.

Dr. Perry explained, "The swimmer and those on the cargo net who had gotten wet during the procedure were always given a shot of medical brandy, according to Navy custom[,] to prevent pneumonia from being exposed to the elements. This procedure would involve one aviator, one swimmer, and at most three men on the cargo net. I never understood why, when brandy time came, there were ten or more soaking wet in line for the brandy."[3]

Wilmot was taken to the *Sperry*'s cramped sick bay along with his rescuer. The doctor offered both men small bottles of the alcohol to help warm them up after exposure in the cold Pacific Ocean. "Lieutenant, are you going to drink your whiskey?" asked the sailor. Wilmot declined and passed the bottle to his rescuer. The sailor revealed he would later retire to a private part of the warship to get drunk with his booty.[4]

Wilmot remained a guest of the destroyer for two days before he was transferred back to the *Bunker Hill*. A barrel of ice cream served as the ransom. He was one of eleven Corsair pilots rescued by DesRon 62 during its first one hundred days in combat. Another sixty-four pilots and aircrew were saved from the seas during the same period.

But, by war's end, five of the nine destroyers had been hit by kamikazes.

The Dilbert Dunker

"2Lt. William H. Rutledge, pilot of a Corsair (FG-1A) (13908), crashed into ocean two miles offshore from base while rendezvousing after takeoff. Although slightly injured[,] he was able to extract himself from the sinking plane in the pitch-black darkness. He inflated his raft and paddled to shore[,] where he telephoned for the base ambulance. His injuries included a smashed nose, lacerations of the left eye[,] and deep cut in his right leg. The plane was lost. He said the dunking practice of the month previous saved his life."[5]

Steaming from Leyte, the USS *Shangri La* (CV-38) was headed back to the Fast Carrier Task Force's hunting grounds east of Okinawa. She had arrived in these waters in mid-April 1945 for her combat debut. After six weeks on station, the hunters had left for several weeks of replenishment, repair, and relaxation in the Philippines. With Task Force 38 commander VAdm. John McCain aboard her, the carrier was on its way back for missions against the Japanese home islands.

On their second day at sea, Monday, July 2, it was time for Bomber Fighter Squadron 85 to stretch their wings. "We have a squadron refresher flight today," recorded Lt. Dick De Mott in his diary. "Taking off at 0845 to exercise ourselves and try out planes after the overhaul period. Have 32 planes scheduled[,] but by the end of the period there are only 23 left. Guys drop out left and right to go back for forced landings from one cause or another."[6]

Ensign Bill Redmon was one of those guys. He was strapped into the carrier air group commander's personal plane. The Vought F4U-1D carried a full load of .50 rounds in its trays, 230 gallons of fuel in the internal tank, another 150 gallons of fuel hanging from the port pylon in a belly tank, two 5-inch rockets strapped to one wing, and special camera and radar equipment installed on the other wing. With nearly three hundred stick hours in the bent-wing birds and two months of combat under his belt, Redmon was ready.

Left: Ens. William Kaneb in his own creation
Right: Ens. William Redmon. *Courtesy of Bill Redmon*

The big Essex-class carrier turned her bow into the wind. It was a good day for flying, since the ceiling was unlimited, the seas were calm, and the wind was mild. After several birds had left the nest ahead of him, Redmon brought BuNo 82626 forward to the position directed by "Fly 1," the carrier air group's takeoff signal officer. "On deck there was lots of noise and wind. Hand signals were used when they got me into the takeoff spot. 'Fly 1' checked out the plane for visible problems and to be sure the deck was clear. He gave me the wind-up signal to bring it to full throttle, but then he had me shut it down."[7]

"Fly 1," who had moved Redmon into the same takeoff spot as the previous planes, was commanded by the carrier's air officer over the address system to move the plane farther forward. "Fly 1" responded that everything was fine the way it was. This was not the response the air officer (a member of the ship's company and not part of the air group) expected. Insisting that he was in charge, the air officer ordered Redmon spotted farther up the deck to speed up takeoff times. "I was moved forward on the deck and went through the process again." As the bow came up, the takeoff officer slashed his checkered flag downward. "He gave me the signal to take off, but there was not enough deck. When I left the bow, I didn't have enough flying speed. I left the deck with wheels down and full flaps."[8]

As it cleared the deck, the Corsair began to settle immediately. "The torque from that 2,000 hp engine pulled me to the left." Redmon retracted the wheels immediately, but the left wing dipped farther even though full right rudder and aileron were applied. Over 5 tons of nose-heavy fighter plane corkscrewed toward the Philippine Sea as the *Shangri La* maneuvered to starboard. "I hit the water upside down."[9]

Inverted, the airplane became a submarine as 13 feet of Hamilton prop pulled the aluminum albatross underwater. Seawater poured through the cowling, surged through the oil cooler and intercooler intakes, got past the Browning's ports, and jetted into the wings at the folds, where it coursed through the hollow spaces and lightening holes in the wing spars. Bubbles spurted from the six ammunition casing ports while more buoyancy was lost as the fuselage belched its air through the tailwheel's doors. BuNo 82626 was well on its way to the ocean's floor, 3,300 fathoms below.

The difference between life and death depended on Redmon's actions in the next few seconds. Stunned and injured, Redmon struggled to escape the cockpit crypt.

Time spent in the Dilbert Dunker had been time well spent. Designed by Ens. Wilfred Kaneb, the Underwater Cockpit Escape Device was known among the pilots as the "Dilbert Dunker." A simple device, it featured the cockpit of an SNJ mounted atop a pair of rails. Pilots with full gear strapped themselves into the machine and then slid down at a 45-degree slope until it hit the end of the ramp at the surface of a swimming pool. Recalled Redmon seventy-three years after his first use of the training apparatus, "It was quite a little ride. When you hit the bottom, it just threw you out. It took a few seconds to get your wits."[10]

Two years later, reflex conquered panic: "I first checked my hatch. It was open when I took off but had closed partially. I couldn't move, so unbuckled my parachute, seat back, and raft pack." As the plane was swallowed by the dark depths, he disconnected his communication cable and then felt for the opening between the canopy and the windscreen. Redmon finally broke free: "I wiggled through the hatch opening but was then caught on the antenna. I didn't have time to think things through. I might have had a little breath left, but I was dragged deep underwater."[11] Redmon popped one of the two CO_2 cartridges on his Mae West. "I shot up like a cork."[12]

The newly minted frogman broke from the seas just as the fantail of the mighty carrier steamed past. Members of the carrier's crew crowded the rails to see if he had survived. Kapok-filled life jackets were hurled over the side. "They threw a raft from the fantail, but the wind took it away. I tried to swim for it when I realized my leg was broken."[13] The tibia and fibula were shattered. With lacerations both to forehead and scalp, the taste of iron from his blood mixed in his mouth with the salted seas. Entering shock, the twenty-year-old pilot bobbed alone in the ship's white wake. An unused dye packet hung on his vest, forgotten in the haze.

Redmon's attention was elsewhere until salvation arrived, "I was semiconscious at this point. I had no idea the destroyer was coming until it was almost on top of me. A sailor jumped from the destroyer to help me get aboard, but when he saw how badly I was injured, he had the whaleboat dropped to get me aboard." After the motorized launch was secured on the davits, the pilot was carried to deckhouse sick bay aboard the USS *Frank Knox* (DD-742). Its doctor performed the initial treatment in the warship's meager medical facilities: "Once aboard, they gave me morphine and cut off my shoes to save my leg."[14]

The ensign's time with the tin can sailors was brief. Less than an hour after rescuing the pilot, the *Frank Knox* was steaming alongside the *Shangri La*. Lines were shot across the warships and secured by crews on both sides. "Despite feeling a bit 'dingy' from the morphine, I reminded them to get their ice cream. From the destroyer, they high-lined me in a litter back to the carrier."[15] From the *Shangri La*'s gedunk, 10 gallons of ice cream—the standard booty for the return of an aviator—were sent as thanks for the rescue and return of Redmon.

Doctors went to work on Redmon: "They set my leg, cast it, sutured my wounds, and fixed the rest. The air officer that really was the cause of the crash was not even man enough to see me in sick bay, but the ship's new captain [Richard Francis] Whitehead did."[16]

The air accident report, perhaps to protect the senior CVG officers, found no fault with Redmon. They penciled "100% undetermined" as the cause of the plane loss.[17] Redmon did not fly again in World War II.

Redmon was transferred to the USS Rescue (AH-18) before being later transferred to a naval hospital at Guam on August 18, 1945. The Iowa native was still there when the Missouri *steamed into Tokyo Bay for the surrender ceremonies. He stayed in the USNR until released in 1956. Redmon passed away in 2019.*

The USS Frank Knox *rescued four more pilots before the war ended, the final a British Corsair pilot from the HMS* Victorious *on August 10, 1945.*

Ens. Wilfred Kaneb passed away in 2016 at the age of ninety-six. During World War II, thousands of Navy and Marine pilots took rides in his Dilbert Dunkers. Kaneb's contribution to the war effort saved untold numbers of pilots during the war and the years that followed.

Blown Away

Ens. Arthur B. Hiser. *Courtesy of the Hiser family*

Before dawn's first rays, the flickering exhausts from the two Corsairs spotted just ahead pierced the dark. Light rain on the windshield compounded the image. The slipstream buffeted the bird, pulsating off the skin, passing underneath the wings. The twenty-one-year-old pilot kept his feet on the brakes. In an instant, his Corsair lifted off the deck. Gunners on the stern 40 mm mount were startled by the sight of the dark-blue Corsair hovering over the fantail before collapsing into the phosphorescent wake of the carrier.

The day did not start well for the air boss aboard the *Essex*. Carrier Air Group 83 had been in combat just ten days. March 28, 1945, promised to be another full day of air operations. Planned for the first series of launches were two divisions of VF-83 Hellcats and a division of VBF-83 Corsairs for the target CAP; two photo F6F-5(P) and two night F6F(N) Hellcats were staged; forty-two more Hellcats, Corsairs, Avengers, and Helldivers were poised to strike Minami Daito Jima. But just ten minutes into launches, an F4U-1D preparing to launch slid across the wet deck into two other Voughts. Three Corsairs were scratched. Two were immediately jettisoned over the side. A few minutes later, a fourth Corsair began its takeoff run when it, too, skidded on the wet deck as it approached the forward elevator. It toppled off the deck onto the port catwalk. Flames lit up the scene. Lt. j.g. William "Bucky" Harris scrambled to unstrap himself before diving out of the cockpit. The fire would rage for almost thirty minutes before his plane could be cut free to fall into the Pacific.

Prepared for their CAP launch were Lt. j.g. Edward "Pap" Pappert and his wingman, Lt. j.g. Vernon Coumbe. Ens. Arthur B. Hiser's mount was spotted between the other two Corsairs.

We are holding the brakes and revving the engines to full throttle. The plane chatters. The engine is going full speed. The chains and brakes hold the plane into position. I look back. Whoa—the backwash from Coumbe's plane and mine lifted Hiser's plane into the air and blew him off the fantail and into the drink. I call the tower. "Plane overboard," I yell. "We know," answers the tower. "The plane stuck in the catwalk but the pilot is ejected and is in the water."[18]

Pappert tried again to explain the situation: "No, not the one taking off. There is one off the <u>back</u> of the ship."[19]

Trailing *Essex* Was the USS *Chauncey* (DD-667)

Serving as the plane guard, the destroyer's captain, Lt. Cmdr. Preston B. Haines Jr., saw the events unfold: "We sighted flames on *Essex's* flight deck at 0540 and closed the scene."[20]

While Harris, who was suffering from burns on both his arms and legs, was bobbing in the seas, twenty-one-year-old Hiser impacted the dash when his Corsair smashed into the seas. Staggered, Hiser attempted to escape the sinking bird as it descended into the dark depths. Gloved hands fumbled to release him from the straps. The saturated uniform and flight gear weighed him down. "Well, after I hit the drink, I can remember that I was under the water, and I got out of the cockpit and brought the chute with me. I swam toward the surface. It seemed like an awful long time to get there."[21]

After surfacing, the Kansas native was able to inflate his raft, but "When I first got up, I looked back at the carrier, and it had turned 90 degrees from where I left it. After I got in the raft, I got the veri-pistols [*sic*] and shot off a couple of shots."[22]

Lt. Cmdr. Haines backed down the engines as a cargo net was laid over the side to retrieve the wounded pilot. "I had eleven fractures in my jaws, one eye was out of the socket." Despite the pain of his injuries, Hiser was able to grasp the net and climb his way to the deck. From there he was taken to sick bay, where "They gave me something or other. Anyway, it knocked me out. I wasn't awake for a few hours after that. I don't know, my memory wasn't too good then."[23]

Minutes later, Harris was also recovered. He was transferred back to the *Essex* later that day. Hiser, however, was transferred to the battleship USS *South Dakota* (BB-57). Its large medical department would begin the process of putting him back together. For Hiser, who had just two combat missions under his belt, his war was over.

William "Bucky" Harris eventually added four more victories to his tally. His first kill came when he had flown an SB2C Helldiver with VB-17. Harris was the only ace during the war to notch his first kill in a dive-bomber. He was killed when a bomb tipped with a proximity fuze exploded midflight just a few days before the war ended. Harris was the last ace to be killed during World War II.

Hiser stayed aboard the South Dakota until May. He eventually was transferred stateside for further medical care. He was still healing at a Texas hospital when the war came to its end.

Funeral Pyre

Danger on deck was a fixture during carrier landings. Bounding seas and rookie pilots only added to the risk. Lt. j.g. James Sakellariades returned to the USS *Essex* after achieving a rookie fighter pilot's dream: two kills and one probable during his first combat mission. Sakellariades's bird absorbed debris when one of the Zekes blew up. After he came back aboard, the damaged VBF-83 plane jumped the barrier and plowed into planes spotted ahead. The engine buckled, the wing tips were smashed, and the fuselage broke off behind the cockpit. Despite the wild ride, the Washington, DC, native and the deck crew were uninjured in the deck crash.

Any ordnance or tanks affixed to the birds were liable to break free and hurtle down the deck. As hooks grabbed wires and planes deaccelerated, drop tanks could continue forward. As they passed underneath the turning props, inevitably a fire ball would erupt. On occasion, pilots failed to turn the gun safety switches to "safe," thus leading to friendly fire when they accidentally sprayed the deck with .50-caliber rounds.

The HMS *Illustrious* was hunting for Japanese warships in the Bay of Bengal during early March 1944. After landing, Norman Hanson of 1830 Squadron taxied over the lowered barriers. He parked forward, raised his wings, and shut off his bird. The barriers rose behind him in anticipation of the next landing. Hanson described the scene behind him: "Joe Vickers had drifted off to port on his approach. Probably because Joe had lost sight of the batsman [LSO], he ignored all signals from Hastings to go around again. . . . Joe hit the port after deck group of 4.5-inch guns. He then careened up the port side of the deck until he crashed heavily into the great steel stanchion of the no. 1 barrier, slewing the tail around to rest across the nets, with the nose pointing towards the island."[24]

Crashes were off-limits to untrained personnel by order of the captain. As firemen sprang into action, others mounted the plane in an attempt to help Vickers out. Casual observers, known as "goofers," watched the scene without too much concern. Spontaneously the gas tank blew up. One rescuer was killed, another was blown to the deck, and a third (who was enveloped in flame) was blown overboard. Vickers didn't stand a chance. As more firemen tried to extinguish the inferno, the Brownings erupted, spraying the deck with .50-caliber rounds. Burning oil and gas leaked into an ammunition compartment below deck, causing severe burns to three more sailors. Magnesium in the engine kept the inferno raging. Vickers's bird became his funeral pyre.

Left: Lt. j.g. Sakellariades's VBF-83 Corsair after jumping the barriers
Right: The drop tank of Lt. Cmdr. Freddy Charlton, FAA, explodes. *Imperial War Museum*

Air Pilot

> *Up, through boundless, unknown places,*
> *He climbed the air-steps of the sky—*
> *Through Corridors of endless spaces,*
> *Until he saw God standing by.*
> *Then, one day came a message saying,*
> *Your brave son's loss—regret to tell*
> *I know that he with God is staying;*
> *It was but just his plane that fell.*

—Sara R. Stansberry

Into the Gray

And he was gone.

The ancient Greeks believed that three fates controlled birth, life, and death. The fate Atropos, who determined the time and manner of an individual's death, arrived without notice. And so it was for Lt. j.g. Charles W. S. Hulland on April 23, 1945, while on a combat air patrol in the waters east of Okinawa.

Mythology would have suggested that the fate Clotho, the provider of life, was on hand in October 1918 during Hulland's birth in Illinois. The second fate, Lachesis, the determiner of destiny, would have been ever present as he earned his gold wings in 1943. She warded off Atropos when Hulland and VF-74 deployed to the Mediterranean for the invasion of southern France in August 1943. Six "Flying Wolfhounds" were sent on a reconnaissance mission inland. As they crossed the coast into enemy-held France, a German convoy became the target of repeated strafing runs: four tanks, fifteen troop carriers, and one command car. Following this attack, Hulland and his buddies attacked another column of fourteen enemy trucks. It was not a one-sided battle. Turning away from the skirmish, black smoke emanated from Hulland's Hellcat. As the oil pressure dropped to zero, Hulland jumped from just 1,600 feet. Both pilot and bird hit the ground within a hundred yards of each other. As he gathered his parachute, his buddies headed away from the scene lest their presence alert the enemy to Hulland's whereabouts.

Hulland was able to contact the French Resistance before eventually making his way back into Allied hands. He was awarded the Navy Cross for extraordinary heroism. After his return to America, Hulland was assigned to VBF-85 and transitioned into gull wings.

Eight months later, flying on a routine CAP, Hulland's division was orbiting the USS *Shangri La* until the call came in that a bogey was approaching the task group. Immediately, the division split into two sections of two, one section high and one low, as they flew through an overcast sky. Hulland's wingman identified the unknown plane as a "friendly." The division leader and his wingman turned to starboard to rendezvous, as did Hulland's partner. But it was apparent less than a minute later that Hulland had not made the turn to join up.

Fate's hand had intervened: despite a methodical search of the area, Hulland was never found. His engine may have shut down due to rust in the carburetor, or some other momentary distraction provided enough time for the fate Atropos to have her chance. He was declared missing in action. The US Navy declared Hulland dead in 1946.

Give as Good as You Get

South of Okinawa, the British Pacific Fleet Task Force 57 was charged with suppressing air attacks from the islands of the Sakishima Gunto, the chain of islands that hopscotched from Formosa northeast to Okinawa. On May 16, 1945, HMS *Victorious* launched "Ramrod" (ground-target) missions against the Mikayo Jima airfield. Squadron 1836's Corsairs worked over the airfield and other targets before turning their attention to a troop convoy. While Lt. D. T. Chute, RNVR, sprayed the trucks with his Browning .50s, the soldiers returned the Brit's salutes with their Arisaka rifles. They gave as good as they got: the whistling death bird was sent away, smoke erupting from its engine as it shuddered in its death rattle, its oil pressure dropping to zero. The group leader knew he had to ditch immediately.

The Corsair Mk. IV didn't make it far. Preparing to ditch close to the island, Chute dropped his flaps, released the drop tank, turned the injured bird into the wind, and made a dead-stick landing, gliding along the waves until the nose dropped and the ride ended. He had time enough to disconnect and dismount from his steed. After inflating the yellow dinghy, the Welshman cut off the shrouds of the parachute, saved the silk, and awaited rescue. The hour was late and the light began to recede.

Chute was covered by his mates for a time while wingman Rob White (RNZNVR) radioed requests for a lifeguard sub. Declining fuel levels forced the birds to head back to the nest. Darkness descended on Chute.

After a few hours, the outline of a boat was seen. With rescue on the horizon, the twenty-four-year-old pilot fired a flare and waved a waterproof torch back and forth as a beacon while praying the boat was friendly.

Ignoring the shallow depths and risking shelling due to their proximity to the enemy shore, USS *Bluefish* pulled within 3,000 yards of the beach. Chute was hoisted from his raft less than two hours after ditching. Climbing down the conning tower, he joined the rest of *Bluefish's* private air force: two Grumman Avenger crews, one British and one American, both rescued during the sub's eighth war patrol. The host provided "medicinal" brandy, a warm shower, and a hot meal.

The zoomies stayed aboard until June 1, when the Bluefish *returned to Subic Bay. Chute eventually found his way back to the 1836 by hitchhiking rides on British planes all the way to Australia. Both Chute and his squadron returned to the fight against the Japanese Empire soon thereafter.*

Studs and Duds

The service life of a carrier-borne fighter plane was not long. Hard landings, battle damage, salt air, and a lack of maintenance time during combat ops took a toll on the birds. Those planes that could fly, but would not be used for combat missions, were swapped out as "flyable duds." They were flown to smaller escort carriers (CVEs), which ferried replacement planes and pilots for the fleet and light carriers. "We would leave the *Bunker Hill* by destroyer and be transferred to a supply transport carrier. A 'breeches buoy' on a line would move us from ship to ship[,] and that was exciting in itself," recalled Marine ace 2Lt. Dean Caswell.[25]

The replacement Corsairs were covered in "Cosmoline gunk" for protection against saltwater on the voyage. And, when we catapulted off the small carrier, that stuff would be blown all over the plane and our windshields and canopy by the propeller. It was almost a blind landing on our carrier because of the filthy oil/tar concoction. That's the way we got replacement planes in the middle of the Pacific[,] and it was probably as dangerous as a raid on a Japanese airfield.[26]

More Unfriendly Fire

April 16, 1945, was another day of "flash red" alerts for the ships surrounding the empire's pathway, the Ryukyu Islands. In the previous ten days, Japan had launched two of the largest kamikaze attacks of the war. Known as *kikusuis*, these massed air assaults were designed to overwhelm the defenses of the fleets, destroy the landing craft, cripple the American and British carriers, and destroy the ships stationed around Okinawa Jima as radar pickets. On April 6–7, after nearly seven hundred enemy aircraft were sent aloft, six American ships were sunk by kamikazes, and an additional twenty were damaged. The USS *Hancock* (CV-19) was sent home after a kamikaze crashed her deck, cartwheeling through the Hellcats and *Corsairs* spotted aft. Six days later, eleven more ships were struck.

The third of ten *kikusui*s commenced on the sixteenth. VMF-451 was nested on the USS *Bunker Hill* (CV-17) along with their brothers, VMF-221 and VF-84. Several "flash reds" brought the ships to general quarters early in the day. Maj. Herbert "Trigger" Long led one of the two divisions launched to beef up the CAP. They were vectored out to radar-picket position #3 between the big island and Task Group 58.3.

Long was part of the group of marine pilots that fought early in the war, flying from the 'canal in their tough barrel-chested Wildcats. He scored three times while flying with VMF-121 and matched that total again when he flew Corsairs with VMF-122 in 1943.

His division arrived on station as the ships below were under heavy air attack. The skies bloomed black clouds as US Navy 5-inch shells tried to keep the enemy at bay. First Lieutenant Ray Swalley netted the first kill when he brought down a Val. Long pursued another Val through the angry clouds before he was able to shoot down his foe. The victory was his tenth of the war, thus making Trigger a double ace.

The proximity fuzes of the 5-inch shells from the USS *Beale* did not discriminate between friend and foe. Long's bird was hit and entered a spin. The veteran pilot wasted no time abandoning his steed. Taking to the silk, the ace landed in the cold waters off Okinawa.

After fending off her attackers, the destroyer escort USS *McClelland* came to Long's rescue. After he was aboard, the twenty-six-year-old major was so incensed by having been shot down that he had an order transmitted to the destroyer that had claimed his bird: all gun mounts would have a Corsair painted on the side. If he could help it, never again would a destroyer shoot down a Corsair!

The indignity of having to hit the silk due to friendly fire gave way to his return to the nest. After finally making his way back to the *Bunker Hill*, Long was summoned to the carrier's medical department. Anyone who had spent time ashore was subject to delousing. Rank provided no privilege: Long underwent delousing.

Trigger Long flew ninety-five combat missions. He was awarded the Legion of Merit with combat "V" device, eight Distinguished Flying Crosses, seventeen Air Medals, and two Purple Hearts. He passed away in 2001. Long is buried at Arlington National Cemetery.

CHAPTER 10

ESCAPE AND EVASION

PART I: ESCAPE

Ambush! Torches flushed the night from the rice paddy. "Merde! Se lever! Suis moi! Se dépécher!" In his excitement, the legionnaire chief yelled in his native French at the airmen. "Damn it! Get up! Follow me! Hurry!" He led them toward the cover of the jungle. The crack of Japanese rounds filled the air. Picking himself up from the mud of the rice paddy, Rocky Lynch grabbed the old bolt-action rifle and headed for the sounds of the battle. He had joined the Marines to fly a fighter plane. Instead, that career was suspended as he fought with the French Foreign Legion during their escape from Indochina north to China. The Japanese were hot on their trail.

The retiring sun lit up the green leaves of the palm trees just before they scraped the ventral skin of his Vought. Second Lieutenant Joseph O. Lynch reflexively pulled the nose back up and raised the flaps. The marine's actions bought him a few more seconds of airtime before his bird descended to earth and plowed through the rice paddy just a few miles west of Saigon. Lynch stood and grasped the mud-soaked canopy, stepped out of the cockpit onto the wing, and stepped back in time.

Just a month earlier, Marine Fighting Squadrons 124 and 213 embarked sixty officers, 120 enlisted Marines, and thirty-six new bent-wing birds aboard the USS *Hollandia* (CVE-97). From Oahu, they steamed westward to join the mighty aircraft carrier armada, Task Force 38, at the fleet anchorage in the Ulithi Atoll in the Carolina Islands. They dropped anchor on Christmas Day 1944. As additions to Carrier Air Group 4, the marines embarked on the fleet carrier USS *Essex*. A new assignment for US Marine aviation in World War II lay in store.

Suiciders. Kamikazes. *Tokubetsu Kōgekitai.* The Divine Wind thundered across the Philippines starting in late October of that year. In the span of a few weeks, over a dozen US carriers were impacted. As part of a change in US Navy tactics to counter the aerial threat, the request was sent to VAdm. John "Slew" McCain, Commander Task Force 38, to change the balance of the carrier air groups in order to smother the wind: "Greatly increased number of VF [fighter planes] needed to insure [*sic*] 100% kill on interceptions and still satisfy requirements of VF sweep CMA strikes and continuous target CAP."[1]

When the USS *Essex*, as part of the Fast Carrier Task Force 38, stormed out of Ulithi on December 30, 1944, for planned missions against the enemy airfields and targets on Formosa, Luzon, Hong Kong, and targets surrounding the South China Sea, gone from her hangar decks were the Helldivers of Bombing Squadron 4. Carrier Air Group 4 carried the fifty-four Hellcats of Fighting Squadron 4, fifteen Avengers of Torpedo Squadron 4, and the Corsairs. And so, for the first time in the war, marine squadrons were flying with their golden-winged navy brothers from a carrier deck. It was an appropriate choice of squadrons: VMF-124 and -213 had introduced Vought's best to combat in the skies over the Solomon Islands in the spring of 1943.

The marine fighters stumbled initially. On the first day out, 1Lt. Tom Campion's mount stalled after clearing the flight deck. The drop tank from his Corsair ignited a funeral pyre upon the Pacific. The next day, 2Lt. Barney Bennett received the wave-off from the LSO. Bennett overcorrected trying to gain air. His F4U dived into the ocean. The St. Louis native perished with his plane.

The squadron commander, Lt. Col. Bill Millington, led his squadron into its first combat as two marine divisions escorted seven navy Avengers during strikes against central Formosa on January 3, 1945. Millington also became the first marine to draw blood during the tour, when he nailed a Yokosuka P1Y Frances. But another marine pilot was lost when 1Lt. Robert "Moon" Mullins failed to return from the mission. Weather conditions were so poor that later strikes were canceled. The next day, the weather was even worse. First Lieutenant Donald Anderson was spotted climbing into the clouds by the American destroyers on picket duty. It was the last time he was ever seen. The losses would continue.

Rocky Lynch finally got into combat on the seventh. He left the *Essex* as part of two divisions of "Hell Hawks" assigned to fly target CAP over Luzon. The weather was again foul, and it wasn't long before the mission had gone awry. After emerging from the clouds that extended from the deck to 20,000 feet, flight leader Capt. Wilbur "Gus" Thomas realized that the flight was scattered. Finding himself alone, he eventually made his way back to the *Essex*. The twenty-five-year-old Lynch was also forced to fly the trip solo, as did a third pilot. But five pilots became lost in the soup and ran out of gas. The destroyer USS *Cotton* collected Lts. Cloward and Green, but the three other marines were never found.

Left to right: Capt. Gus Thomas, unidentified, 2Lt. Rbt. Dorsett, 2Lt. Lynch. *Courtesy of the Lynch family*

Nine days after their departure from Ulithi, attrition was high for the VMF squadrons. The *Corsair* had yet to earn the nickname "kamikaze killer." For the time being, the pilots were just trying to survive training at the "Formosa Instrument Flight School."

"Welcome to the South China Sea," Tokyo Rose cooed to the sailors and marines of Task Force 38. "You will not get out alive!" Overnight on the tenth, the fast carrier armada turned west and sailed into the cauldron of fire where no US Navy surface warship had ventured since the beginning of the war. Japanese held airfields ringed the sea. "It was a bold action; anything might have happened; we were ready for it."[2]

In search of the hybrid Japanese battleship-carriers *Ise* and *Hyūga,* the task force fueled at sea on the eleventh as they pointed their bows toward French Indochina. "Tomorrow we may have a golden opportunity to completely annihilate an enemy force," Third Fleet commander William "Bull" Halsey alerted TF 38. "You all know that is what I expect you to do. Give them hell and God bless you all."[3]

Before dawn on January 12, the fighters, bombers, and torpedo planes of Task Group 38.2 were fueled and armed. Launched into squally weather just 45 miles from Cam Ranh Bay, they hunted for the remnants of the Imperial Japanese Navy's battle fleet. Task Groups 1 and 2 sent nearly six hundred sorties against targets along the coastline and the airfields inland. Task Group 3, following the other two groups, tasked its planes with searches, sweeps against enemy airfields, and attacks on surface targets of opportunity. Another 330 combat sorties were flown by her pilots.

The American surface striking group of battleships never got to battle their Japanese peers (who had previously been moved from these waters to Singapore), but the fliers struck gold when they found several enemy merchant shipping convoys. Four heavy strikes were flown. But the *Essex,* with its two marine squadrons, launched the Corsairs to provide top cover for Group 3 while the navy flyboys roamed the coast laying waste to the oil fields, airfields, and shipping. It wasn't until after noon chow that the marines got in the game, flying a fighter sweep against the airfields at Biên Hòa and Long Tranh.

For Lynch, though, his time was spent flying CAP patrols over the task group. His recovery by the *Essex* was his thirtieth carrier landing. And it would be his last. "I had two combat air patrols that day. When I landed from the second one, I was told that Gus Thomas, my flight leader, was going to lead an eight-plane fighter sweep in the Saigon area to find and destroy a force of twenty-four Japanese planes that were sighted by a returning flight from another carrier."[4]

There was no better choice to lead them than Capt. Gus Thomas, USMCR: none of the squadron ready rooms found in the dozen Task Force 38 carriers had a pilot with more kills. Thomas was one of the best-skilled fighter pilots to ever fly in an American uniform. The triple ace notched his 16.5 kills over the skies of Rendova, Vella Lavella, Kahili, and the Shortland Islands with the -213 "Hell Hawks" back in 1943. When he scored, he scored in multiples, by threes and fours. Before his twenty-third birthday in October of that year, Thomas was the leading Marine ace in the war.

After VMF-213 left the South Pacific in December 1943, several more Marine pilots moved past Thomas on the kill list. But by 1945, Pappy Boyington was missing in action, Bob Hanson was dead, and the rest were stateside. Thomas remained as the eighth-greatest hunter in a US Marine uniform, the thirteenth ace to wear the wings of gold, and the sole triple ace with the fast carriers.

Maj. James M. Johnson, from -124, led three "Hell Hawks" while Thomas's division took to the air at 1430. "The weather was fairly good[,] with low overhanging clouds," noted Lynch months later.[5]

As the special fighter sweep approached the coast, towers of black smoke from the burning Standard-Vacuum and Shell Oil storage facilities pointed the way to Saigon. "We could see there were many, many fires burning."[6] Johnson took his division north to Cape St. Jacques while Thomas continued onto Saigon.

It was a fighter pilot's delight: parked at the Tân Sơn Nhứt airfield, dozens of enemy fighters were discovered refueling. The ace led his charges for pass after pass. Thomas burned four planes by himself, and several other pilots ignited others as they poured .50 cal. rounds across the runways, hangars, and nearby wooded areas adjacent to the field.

Despite a day of attacks against their shipping and airfields, the Japanese defensive forces sent meager antiaircraft fire against the "Hell Hawks." Second Lieutenant Powhatan Kehoe's bird was punctured three times in one wing, but he suffered just a small loss of hydraulic fluid. But another Corsair was mortally wounded over Thủ Dầu Một city.

"I felt a jolt in the cockpit," recalled Lynch. "The propeller immediately stopped with one blade straight up. I pulled the nose up and opened the canopy and started to bail out." Thomas spotted the danger. Himself the survivor of two ditchings in 1943, he took charge: "Gus came over the radio and yelled, 'Don't bail out here. See if you can crash[-]land straight ahead[,] and we'll cover your withdrawal.'"[7]

Already at low altitude, time was short. There was no possibility of making it out to sea to ditch. Lynch was 3 miles west of the town of Tràng Bàng when he went down:

I nosed over and re-strapped myself into the cockpit and headed towards an open rice paddy about a mile or a mile and a half from the airfield. Without the engine running, the noise of the anti-aircraft fire and the planes firing to cover my setdown became quite loud. I started to milk the flaps down about five hundred feet. From the point of intended letdown, I could see I was going much faster than I wanted to be able to get into the rice paddy.[8]

The day's late sun lit up the blue bird as Lynch descended: "As I felt contact with the trees, I pulled the nose slightly up and pulled the flaps up. This created a high rate of descent[,] and I splashed into the rice paddy which was about two or three feet deep." Blue became brown. "The mud spray was quite loud for a few seconds[,] ending with a sharp jolt and silence."[9] Lynch disconnected from his plane, turned to activate the destruct switches on the IFF ("identification, friend or foe") transponder, and climbed out onto the wing as his teammates flew over him and the airfield at low altitude to distract the enemy. As Lynch jumped off the wing into the paddy, he leapt into another era. One of the most incredible escape-and-evasion odysseys in World War II had begun.

Safety or Threat?

Standing knee deep in the flooded field, Lynch eyed the Annamites—members of the local indigenous population—encouraging him to follow them in a direction away from the airfield. He acquiesced. At the edge of the field, he ascended to a dirt road. The group took off at a run. Adrenaline prevented Lynch from feeling the wound on his right shin.

After twenty minutes he was faced with another choice, one that flew in the face of the Escape & Evasion training given to marine and navy pilots: Not sure of whether those that found him were truly rescuers, Lynch granted them his trust and followed them into a hut. As his eyes adjusted in the dark haze, he found three old women, all smoking cigarettes. The tall American opened his flight suit to show the thin, dark natives the American flag and the "blood chit" with Chinese characters he had been given in case he was shot down. The voucher garnered no recognition as both American and Indo-Chinese eyed each other with confusion. But Lynch was reassured in broken English, "We are friendly; we are friendly. Wait, wait."[10]

Into the hut entered a man wearing a Japanese uniform blouse and jacket. Lynch was leery of a trap. The stranger pointed to the jacket, repeatedly stating, "Japanese." Lynch realized that the jacket was Japanese but man was not. He motioned for Lynch to follow him. Before exiting, Lynch left his American cigarettes with the native women. In the distance, smoke arose from the rice paddy where Hellcats had strafed Lynch's mount, BuNo 57381.

As the sun began to descend on the French colony, Lynch again put his trust and life into the hands of another. After twenty minutes of walking, the pair arrived at a temple-style building. Once again, he was reassured: "You are safe," Lynch was told. "We wait."

It was not long before a group of Vichy French soldiers, distinct in their pillbox hats, emerged from the trees. One who spoke English, asked, "Are you American? We're French. Come with us. We take you to safety."[11]

The latest guardians led Lynch down the road to where a pair of 1934 and 1936 Ford touring convertibles were parked. Lynch was given a cotton robe to wear over his flight suit, along with a plantation-style helmet. Dressed as a monk, the pilot was cautioned to "say nothing. Say nothing. We'll do all the talking."[12] With sun at their backs, the converted coal-powered cars were driven southeast to Saigon.

The enemy. Though the Vichy French government administered the colony and collected the taxes, the Japanese military dominated the country. The two countries were allies by treaty only. Tensions were strong between the two governments. The roads were filled with Japanese military vehicles. As the Fords tried to pass through an intersection at the same time as the Japanese, yelling and swearing in two languages erupted, gesturing back and forth commenced, while vehicle horns added to the din. Lynch kept his head down and tried to disappear into the seat. Instead of evasion, he found himself surrounded by Japanese in a foreign land. Escape was not even a thought.

"I was taken into Saigon to the French army headquarters and fed a chicken wing before being questioned," stated Lynch. "I told the French I was from an aircraft carrier and that I thought maybe a landing was imminent."[13] He continued the deception by telling Lt. Jacques Metifeu, an intelligence officer, that the task force was so large, it could not be seen from end to end. After saying that the carriers had sent 3,000 airstrikes against targets that day (an exaggeration of 300%), the French military realized that no Japanese planes had risen to oppose the strikes. Smoke clouded the horizon; the smell of burning oil drifted into the city. For the Vichy French, the news could not have been more dangerous.

With the liberation of France after the invasion of D-day in June 1944, the Vichy French government in Europe was thrown from power as the Free French regained control of their country. In their Southeast Asia colony, the local government was aware of the Axis downfall both in Europe and the Pacific. They walked a tightrope. Bound by treaty to aid the Japanese, nevertheless it was apparent after the recent American invasion of the Philippines that time was short for the Vichy government to decide whether to honor its treaty with Japan or change sides and align themselves with the Allies. The Japanese were aware of this too.

In order to preserve control over Indochina, the governor-general, Admiral Jean Decoux, allowed downed Allied fliers to be turned over to the Japanese. He had a change of heart when an American fighter squadron attacked Vichy officials in retaliation for the death of one of their pilots by the Japanese. The arrival of the large American carrier force at its shores only served to reinforce his decree. Orders were given by Decoux that any American fliers captured by French Indo-Chinese army, Indo-Chinese guards, or administrators should not be turned over to the Japanese. And so, to Lynch, his ruse had its desired effect: "They were impressed and took me a women's prison in Saigon for safekeeping from the Japanese."[14]

Lynch was locked in a cell on the second floor, just down the hallway from the native female prisoners. After settling onto a bunk draped with mosquito netting, Lynch could not help but notice the contrast between his cell and his stateroom on the USS *Essex*. Both were a world away from his St. Cloud, Minnesota, home. Marooned in French Indochina, Rocky Lynch had survived a day that had started with American military dominance but had ended with an unknown future in a foreign land doomed to erupt.

French voices and a rattling of the keys in the lock startled Lynch as another flier entered the cell. Lt. j.g. Elmer G. Stratton from the USS *Hancock* had also been shot down. After crash-landing in a field west of the Hóc Môn district of Saigon, "Bones" Stratton cleared his plane and escaped into a nearby farmhouse. His Fighting Squadron 7 wingman strafed the downed Hellcat before returning to the carrier. The Saigon Fliers Club continued to grow.

Not long after Stratton's arrival, three more Americans were led to the cell. Ensign Peter Lambros and his flight crew—Richard Fetzer (ARM3c) and Edward Santopadre (AMM3c)—had bombed an oil terminal in Saigon's Nhà Bè district despite intense and accurate antiaircraft fire bracketing the VT-45 Avengers. After the contingent had finally gone to sleep, Lt. j.g. Horace B. Moranville was brought to the jail. Rabbit—as he was known to his buddies—had attacked Tan Son Nhut airfield in late afternoon. Like Lynch, he was able to ditch his Hellcat in a rice paddy. His VF-11 buddies stayed overhead until he was seen to make contact with natives at Tân An, in the Mekong delta. The six-kill ace was interrogated by Lt. Metifeu at the woman's prison before being transferred to the main prison in Saigon.

The Saigon Six compared their day's experiences long into the night, before exhaustion took charge. Despite facing internment and an uncertain future, they were the lucky ones. Some pilots had not survived their crashes. Those who did survive crashes were turned over to the Japanese. In the hands of the empire, they faced an even less certain future.

As the sun set on the fast carriers, the special fighter sweep returned to the *Essex*. Gus Thomas reported to the air combat intelligence officer, 2Lt. Leo Pambrun, for debriefing. Though dozens of enemy planes had been strafed, one of their own had not returned. Rock Lynch was "last observed standing by his plane."[15] The Navy declared him as "missing in action."

Captivity: Day Two

On Saturday, January 13, "The day dawned bright and clear," noted Rocky Lynch. "There was not a cloud in the sky." Allowed out of their cells, the Saigon Six ventured to the barred windows for a glimpse of their surroundings. Not far away, Japanese planes flew in and out of the Tân Sơn Nhứt airfield without challenge. Gone was the pall of black clouds from burning ships, antiaircraft fire, and storage depots. No American carrier planes brought death or destruction to the city. And the Americans realized that McCain's fast carriers of Halsey's Third Fleet had steamed forth to their next missions elsewhere, leaving Saigon, French Indochina, and them in their wake.

The Hunt Was On

With several downed carrier planes littering the landscape, and no corresponding corpses to be found, the Japanese military was acutely aware that there were several American fliers in the vicinity. Searches for them came up empty, but Vietnamese agents working for the Japanese military intelligence confirmed their capture by the French.

It Was a Marriage of Distrusting Partners

The day after the Japanese attacks against Allied forces at Pearl Harbor, Wake Island, Guam, Hong Kong, and the Philippines, Admiral Decoux declared neutrality in alignment with the Vichy government in France. A common defense pact had previously been signed by Decoux with the Japanese. Exports of rice, rubber, and other supplies to China had already been cut off. The Vichy French had allowed the Japanese to establish military bases in their colony in exchange for the sovereignty of French Indochina being maintained.

As the war progressed, the Japanese worked to undermine the local government while Decoux struggled to keep the colony in French hands by a number of acts of collaboration, the most odious of which was the surrendering of American and British POWs to the Japanese. By 1944, it was apparent that the Axis had little chance of winning the war. Decoux turned a blind eye toward the passing of military intelligence regarding the Imperial Japanese Army activities to the Allies.

Friday, January 12, had brought an apocalypse to Decoux's doorstep: the oil facilities were burned, numerous Japanese warships had been sunk, dozens of merchant vessels had been destroyed, railway bridges and facilities were damaged, and the Japanese airfields at Tân Sơn Nhứt and Biên Hòa were attacked. Even the old French cruiser *Lamotte-Picquet* lay capsized in the Donnai River south of Saigon, an epithet for the prewar French forces in Indochina. And the Japanese military had been helpless to respond.

When a Japanese delegation demanded the next day that the Governor-General Decoux's forces hand over the Saigon Six, Decoux pressed his right to imprison them for destroying French property and killing Indo-Chinese personnel.

The Saigon Six Were in Danger

French officials came and went from the women's prison throughout the thirteenth. In order to prevent a Japanese coup de force, a French army 6-by-6 truck with a canvas-covered bed backed up to the doors of the jail at 2200 hours. The aviators were spirited away to a new destination under the cover of darkness. Upon arrival, they were escorted inside the prison Maison Centrale de Saigon without delay. The guard detail had been quietly reinforced. Orders were given that the internment of the special prisoners was to be kept absolutely secret. Drinks of rum and water were offered to the prisoners by the commandant, a portly Frenchman, when he greeted the six. The salutations were brief. Guards escorted the Americans to their cells. "It was a pretty bleak and depressing evening," recalled Lynch. "We thought, well, here we are, but at least we're safe. This concluded our second day in French Indochina."

The French underground in Saigon fed intelligence regarding the Japanese armed-forces activities in the south. With the arrival of the Saigon Six, communication began with the north to save them. The plan was simple: the six would be transferred to the military base at Tong, where they would either be transferred to India or China in order to be reunited with American forces or kept under French guard. Either option depended on Japanese pressure, but the execution of either plan was not possible.

It Was the Worst-Kept Secret in the War

As the Fast Carrier Task Force steamed northward in preparation for attacks on the South China coast, Hong Kong, Formosa, and Hainan, word was received by Monday, February 5, that the missing aviators were safely in the hands of friendly French forces.

Adm. McCain's carriers would not return to French Indochina again.

The Stone Walls and Ceilings Were Painted Black

The humidity intensified the rank smell of too many men packed tightly in a building with few windows. The Maison Centrale de Saigon—the Central Prison of Saigon—had stood for sixty years. An imposing three-story building of colonial design, the cell blocks surrounded three courtyards and took residence next to the Palais de Justice, the courthouse. The inmate population had risen over time, but the facilities lagged. Sanitation was poor. Inmate riots occurred over the years, as a facility designed to hold hundreds had been incarcerating thousands of prisoners. The overcrowding had been multiplied by Admiral Decoux's efforts to round up forces that posed a threat to his colonial regime. However, the six new prisoners were moved here not so much to keep them in but more to keep the Japanese military out.

The Saigon Six Were Special

It was apparent almost immediately by the privileges extended to them. In the overcrowded prison, they were segregated from the main population. "We were taken through the central courtyard down into another area. There were three adjacent cells with two beds each," recalled Lynch. "These were rearranged so that the middle cell served as dining and living quarters. . . . We decided that the central cell would become our meeting room. It also had the shower and a little hole in the floor[,] which were to be our restroom facilities."[16] The fighter pilots—Lynch, Stratton, and Moranville—took one cell for themselves, while the third was taken by Ens. Pete Lambros and his crew, Richard Fetzer and Ed Santopadre. But, the Maison de Centrale was still a prison: "All the worst prisoners were housed there," noted Santopadre. "There was screaming all night. It was awful."[17]

"Good morning," greeted the man from outside the triumvirate of cells. "I am Joseph Francisque. I will serve as your interpreter." Before the six stood the special "guard." Of Indian birth and with French citizenship, he spoke with a British accent. Rumored to be an employee of the American consulate, his help was invaluable. "Through Francisque, we learned that the Free French were trying to secure the release of the American fliers for movement to American hands in China," reported Lynch. At the same time, Francisque kept the fliers abreast of developments on the outside.[18]

As with all prisons, life was regimented, the days interned at the prison routine. The six were allowed to wear their flight suits rather than prison garb. Three hot meals were served them daily, usually fare of pork or chicken with sweet potatoes. Lynch's leg wound was tended. "We were treated fairly well here," recalled Lynch. "The French were very solicitous of our health."[19]

Special privileges and gifts became commonplace for the six: The commandant was persuaded to give them a table for their middle cell. Cigarettes, books, cards, cologne, and alcohol were delivered. At one point, even a radio was provided. Though the amenities made life in the prison easier, at least their safety was ensured.

"This lifestyle carried on for about six weeks," detailed Lynch.[20] Access was granted into the courtyard, sometimes at night so the other political prisoners would not see them, other times after lunch. Rabbit Moranville, the senior ranking of the six, organized calisthenics for the group. "We would have an hour to an hour and a half while the prisoners and their guards all had their siestas," recalled Lynch. "We would amuse ourselves in the quadrangle by wandering around and examining what we could."[21] The warden kept two barracudas in a fishpond there. "We delighted in the throwing of things into the pond and watching the barracudas snapping up whatever we put in there. It was a very vicious fish."[22] Like the pisces, the fliers survived at the whim of those who held them.

A Japanese delegation called on Decoux daily to demand he turn the Saigon Six over to them. Decoux continued to stall.

Departure

Saturday, January 20. Very few Japanese planes had taken to the air against the American planes and carriers rampaging across the South China Sea. During the fast carriers' ten-day foray, devastating attacks had been sent against Formosa, Luzon, French Indochina, and Hong Kong. It was the high-water mark for US Navy and Marine aviation during World War II: a record tonnage of Japanese merchant ships were sent to the depths of the seas. Under the cover of night skies, VAdm. McCain withdrew his forces from the South China Sea. They would never return to the cauldron of fire.

Escape was a tantalizing hope for the six. In the books and magazines that were smuggled to their cells, secret communications were received from a civilian resistance network. "They wanted to take us out of the country through Hanoi and turn us over to the American authorities," according to Lynch:

The director and the Vicci [sic] French refused to relinquish our control to them [Japanese forces] because they felt that we were the one lifeline that they had for safety if and when the Americans came in Indochina. We all pursued the tactic and the line of reasoning that when the Americans came in—they had this massive invasion force poised off the coast of Indochina—that we'd tell them that these people were our saviors and they have saved us from the Japanese.[23]

Their efforts seemed to have an effect on warden Victor Castille: "He was scared to death for his life. He came to see us occasionally or we went up to his office[,] and he would plead with us to tell the Americans how he had saved us, that the Japanese knew we were in there[,] and they came to the door daily to demand our release to them or just to talk to us, and he would keep refusing, saying that we were his prisoners and he would protect us."[24]

However, the safety of the six came from the top. Without a guarantee of conditions and treatment for prisoners of war (as specified in the Geneva Convention) forthcoming by the Japanese, General-Governor Decoux kept the Americans interned under his protection.

Rumors

The Saigon Six worried about what awaited them outside the walls of the prison: "Francisque had told us several tales of plantation owners and other French citizens who had harbored downed American fliers from the January 12 raid." Lynch continued:

One particularly gruesome tale was about a Navy lieutenant that the Japanese had shackled behind a truck. They forced him to follow the truck through the city of Saigon in the area where the suspected hidings existed. The lieutenant finally collapsed and was dragged—or rather his remains were dragged—through the street with hopes of striking terror in the hearts of the French. The French knew that the penalty for hiding one of the American fliers was beheading.[25]

American bombers returned to Saigon on Saturday, January 27, 1945. Even within the confines of the thick stone walls, the Americans recognized the sounds . . . phump, phump, phump in rapid succession. Tremors were felt through the stone floor. Dust and bits of mortar sprang from the walls. A threat had returned to the skies above Saigon. Tasked with striking Japanese targets, twenty-two Boeing Superfortress bombers dropped their bombload wide of the target. In the aftermath, hundreds of civilians were killed or wounded, but the Saigon Six were safe in the bowels of Maison Centrale. Without seeing a plane, without having to ask Francisque, they knew there were American bombers in the air overhead. While they were proud of their brothers' efforts, the bombing did nothing to help their plight.

It Was a Message They Hoped That They Would Never Receive

It was already Tuesday in Saigon when a teenage boy, bundled against the winter cold of Minnesota, hopped off his bicycle before ringing the bell at the home on Monday, February 5, 1945. He passed a telegram addressed to Mr. and Mrs. Joseph L. Lynch.

Deeply regret to inform you that your son Second Lieutenant Joseph O. Lynch is missing in action in the performance of his duty and service of his country. I realize your great anxiety but details not now available and delay in receipt thereof must be expected. To prevent possible aid to our enemies do not divulge the name of his ship or station. Letter follows. A A Vandergrift Lieut General USMC Commandant of the Marine Corps.[26]

It was a scene repeated in five other homes around the country that day.

The Explosion Echoed off the Stone

The star arched out of the prison walls as it lit up the night sky. White-hot light flickered as it descended slowly before coming to rest near the home of Francisque. After darkness had returned, the interpreter slipped out of his home and returned to the prison. Chaos had erupted within its walls.

"What have you done? What have you done?" demanded Francisque of the Saigon Six. Feigning innocence, the Americans denied any knowledge of how a flare had been launched from the prison. But the courtesy extended to them of keeping their uniforms was the downfall of their alibi. In an act of boredom, Moranville had fired a miniature Very gun he had kept hidden. Francisque continued his interrogation: "Do you know where the fire landed? It landed in front of my house[,] and the Japanese officer who lives next door came running to see what the explosion was!"

Their American flight gear was replaced the next morning by prison shorts and T-shirts.

Air Raid!

On Wednesday, February 7, 1945, "We were awakened by the roar of aircraft passing over the prison. We all gathered in the breezeway of our cell block and cheered as we looked up to see American B-29 aircraft flying over," said Moranville. "However, the cheering soon changed to cursing."[27] The building shook as shrapnel ricocheted off the prison walls. The distant phump, phump, phump of a few weeks earlier had been replaced by an immediate WHUMMP! WHUMMP! WHUMMP! Pressure waves forced wind through the cell blocks. The raid by forty-four B-29 bombers from the 20th Bomber Command was "carried out under covered weather[,] and without precise bearings of the objectives, several French military buildings were hit," wrote French artillery captain Jacques Beauvallet. "In particular, at Saigon, the case of Ileme RIC and the headquarters of the Cochin China-Cambodia Division (in particular my personal office was destroyed)[,] and we had some victims."[28] Once again, hundreds of civilians were wounded or killed by the attack. No Japanese military personnel were harmed. However the English-speaking intelligence officer Lt. Jacques Metifeu, who had interviewed the six, was killed in the raid. Danger remained omnipresent for the Americans.

Pawns

The Saigon Six were aware of their status as internees in a prison run by a stranded colonial government. The American carrier forces were long gone. American B-29 Superfortresses were raining bombs down randomly on the city. China was 600 miles away. "We had two contacts with outside Free French in the director's office. Several occasions in trying to arrange our release ended in failure[,] and we'd go down to our cells and discuss how desperate the situation was getting," explained Lynch. "We felt it was just a matter of time before the Japanese came to the door and demanded our deliverance to them."[29]

"Since escape was always considered a possibility, we spent a lot of our time on our nightly sojourn to the courtyard casing the prison and its goings on," described Rabbit Moranville. "We knew that every time the guard changed, the off-going guards would turn in their weapons and count ammunition. We also knew that they were pretty loose about locking up the gun case." Routine provided an opportunity: "We had also found that if any of us wandered to any part of the prison other than our cells and the courtyard, the guards would chase us back to the courtyard."[30] A plan was hatched.

One night, four of the six wandered into different areas that were off-limits. As the guards herded them back to their designated areas, Rocky Lynch slipped into the guard room while another of the six stood watch. "Rocky picked up a 9 mm revolver and stuck it under his shirt and returned to the courtyard." As soon as he could, Lynch snuck the weapon into one of the cells and stashed it in the dry tank of an unused toilet. "We had a great laugh and turned in for the night."

It was just after midnight when mayhem broke out in the prison. "The commandant and most of the senior guards as well as several junior guards descended on our cells," recalled Moranville. "Since they weren't speaking English, it was easy for us to act like we had no idea what the problem was. However, as usual[,] within five or six minutes here came Francisque screaming at us, 'What have you done? Where is the gun? We know you have it!'"[31] The Americans protested their innocence. Searches of the cells failed. Over the course of the next week, the six were subject to random searches. Their courtyard privileges were revoked.

The standoff continued until the six decided the pistol was of little value without any bullets. Moranville continued the tale: "When we gave the gun back to Francisque and told him that we got it for a planned escape, he was aghast. 'How would we get over the wall?' 'We'll throw a mattress over the wire and glass and drop to the street.' And although we weren't exactly sure where he lived, we told him we were going to come to his house and make him help us! Anyway, after we returned the gun, our privileges were restored."[32]

Japanese Troops Poured into the Country

On paper, the Indo-Chinese army was a significant force of 90,000 men, but fewer than 15,000 were of European descent. The officer corps was understaffed. The military lacked for modern weapons. The armories held but a few weeks of ammunition should conflict arise. The purchase of modern Grumman Wildcat fighter planes from the United States was canceled over a year prior to the attack at Pearl Harbor. The French forces had to make do with the existing inventory of fabric-covered biplanes. Significant resupply from Europe did not emerge. Hitler's armies were being routed, and so both the Vichy French and the Japanese expected the latter would attempt to seize control of the French colony.

The Japanese sent a patrol to Maison Centrale to secure the American prisoners. All they found were three empty cells.

"Get Your Stuff Together. We Are Taking You to Hanoi."

Monday, February 26, 1945. Shortly before midnight, Francisque appeared at their cells to initiate their escape. The Saigon Six did not protest. Their prison garb was exchanged for Foreign Legion uniforms. "Needless to say, it didn't take us very long to throw our toothbrush and a couple pairs of extra socks into a bag and jumped into the back of a six-by-type vehicle,"[33] recalled Lynch. Moranville continued the tale: "We piled into the back of an Army truck and left Saigon. We were all very happy to be on the move and anticipated that we would be out of Indochina in a very few days."[34] Their expectations would be doused by reality.

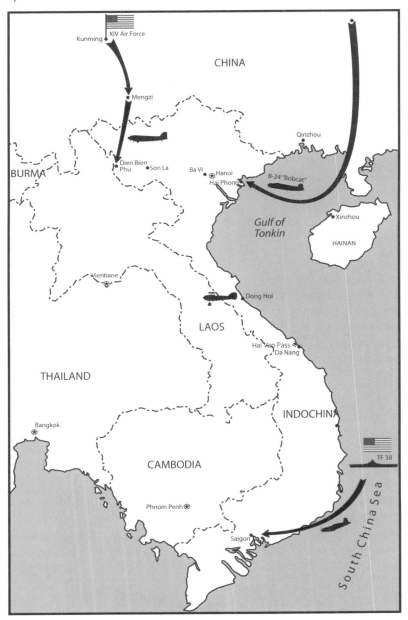

Map of escape and evasion, Indochina

Grounded

Six weeks after their last flight, the fate of the Saigon Six had been transferred to two soldiers from the French army's aviation corps, Lt. Rene Pellegrin and the chief mechanic, Sergeant Chief Jean-Antoine Frau. There lay 600 miles of dusty roads between the prison and Hanoi. Hidden under the canvas cargo cover over the bed of the small truck, they were finally on the move. "We really didn't have any idea where we going," explained Moranville. "Only that we were heading north[,] and that was the way to China."[35]

The difficulties of escape emerged. "We hadn't gone very far before we six Americans decided that they were extremely incompetent drivers," groused Moranville. In the back, the Saigon Six were continually thrown around as they sweltered under the canvas. "They were constantly getting off the pavement onto the gravel shoulder and also hitting the curbing along the approaches to the bridge. Of course the highway was very narrow[,] and there were literally hundreds of extra-narrow bridges to cross."[36]

For the pilots, rank had its privileges. Noted 2Lt. Lynch, "When we had a flat tire, they could not get the tire pumped up with the little hand pump they had. The two drivers were not physically capable of handling the hand pumps as we could. So it ended up that the two enlisted personnel [Fetzer and Santopadre] did most of the pumping."[37]

Each day's travel ended after they arrived at the safety of a French army outpost.

The fighter pilots were used to seeing their enemy from a distance. It was rare that they were face to face with their opponents. Rabbit Moranville was an ace with six kills to his credit, but Lynch had been tasked with CAP missions during his brief time aboard the *Essex*. He hadn't even encountered an enemy plane in the air.

The Japanese army was on the move throughout the colony in preparation for the coup. Main roads were few. "There were numerous encounters with the Japanese troops throughout the journey," recollected Lynch:

> Some were decidedly hair raising to say the least. We had one close brush with the Japanese at one of the ferries when the French[,] with their typical driving skill[,] and the Japanese[,] with their belligerence[,] brushed vehicles at the entrance of the road going down to the ferry. Again, there was much shouting, very reminiscent of my entrance in Saigon where they shouted loud phrases at each other and gestured as if they were going to engage in combat, which seemed to be their way of doing business.[38]

While both sides waited, the French contingent ate lunch. Over the French and Japanese conversations, one voice broke through: "Hey, Peter," demanded Santopadre in English, "tell that guy to hand me another piece of chicken!"[39]

Despite the *faux pas*, "We were finally allowed onto the ferry and were taken over to the other side."[40]

Roadblock!

Wednesday, February 28, 1945. Halfway between Saigon and Hanoi, the Japanese convoy climbed the winding roadway across the Hải Vân Pass in the Annamite mountain range north of Da Nang in the south-central coastlands. A coup was in the air, and both partners of the uneasy alliance had little trust left for the other. The main roads were especially crowded with Japanese troops entering the country or being reassigned to positions closer to French army outposts. As the convoy attempted to cross the bridge at le Col des Nuages— *the Pass of the Clouds*—their progress was halted by a lone army truck stopped on the span. A pair of French troops could be seen outside the vehicle, but the bed canopy remained closed. In the hills overlooking the Da Nang Bay, it was an ideal site for an ambush.

The brakes of the Japanese convoy squealed as the trucks came to a halt. The sounds of slammed doors, booted men running forward in response to commands in Japanese, and the bolts of rifles being retracted and then slammed forward again reached the six in the back of the truck. Through the flaps in the canvas, enemy troops were seen approaching. Tensions rose. With suspicion of sabotage, the officer in charge angrily ordered Lt. Pellegrin to move his vehicle immediately.

Savoir faire, the ability to rise to the occasion, took hold. Pellegrin explained that his truck was stalled due to vapor lock, the result of the poor alcohol-based petrol they were forced to use. Perhaps the Japanese could offer mechanical assistance, the lieutenant suggested, so that their own trucks laden with troops and materiel could pass. After surrendering his bill of lading, Pellegrin encouraged the Japanese officer to inspect the truck for himself.

With his personal guard, the Japanese officer marched to the rear of the truck while a group of his soldiers inspected the bridge. "*Korehanandesuka??!!*" "What is this?" As the canvas flap at the tailgate was pulled aside, the Japanese officer was startled to find six more troops sitting silently. He demanded to know why these soldiers were not pushing the truck clear of the bridge. Lt. Pellegrin explained that part of his mission was to deliver sick Foreign Legion troops to a hospital at Sa Pa, near the Chinese border, for treatment of communicable diseases.

The Japanese officer eyed the six with suspicion. Unlike the colonial French troops, these six legionnaires were not deeply tanned. They were younger than the French troops he had encountered previously. One even had red hair. The Saigon Six just sat mutely as they had been previously instructed. Not satisfied with the explanations proffered by the French, the Japanese officer still had his own mission to accomplish. "*Tochu de torakku o oshite kudasai!*" At his command, Japanese troops pushed the Citroën backward off the bridge and onto the side of road. No blood had been spilled before the enemy convoy sped past. Capture had been averted.

Close Brushes with the Japanese Continued

Each passing mile along the north-central coast brought the six closer to escape and safety. But several days into their evacuation, good luck—that period when opportunity and ability collide—presented itself as they bivouacked at a French army post between the cities of Hué and Hanoi. "It was a very picturesque military outpost highlighted by the fact they had a large biplane, which was an old Potez," related Lynch. "It was one of the last two-seater French fighter planes from World War I, from an era of Spads, Newports, Fokkers, etc."[41] Its pilot, Lt. Hubert Coquard, was quite enthralled both with his piloting ability and the capability of his steed.

The Potez 25 design was very much like the Stearman N2S Kaydet biplane used for Navy pilot primary training. Lynch himself had soloed in a Stearman. Conspiracy took hold in the minds of the American pilots. With a wingspan greater than Lynch's Corsair, the Potez 25 was a large biplane. "We considered maybe commandeering this plane."[42] The idea flamed out quickly: "The plane could only hold two people[,] and we really had no idea how far it was to China," added Moranville.[43] The Saigon Six had come this far together. They were determined to escape to safety together. The antique plane was left unmolested.

They were tired and sore from a week of travel in the truck during the long days north. But horns honking, the foreign chatter in the streets, and the smells of the city indicated their arrival in Hanoi. Another step on the road to escape was completed. Francisque had shared tales about the city to the north before they left Saigon. "We kept trying to peek out as much as we could through the canvas sides[,] watching the people of Hanoi," recalled Lynch. "It was considerably different than Saigon, an altogether different climate and dress. And, also, it looked to us like the natives were different looking."[44]

With the large Vietnamese army headquartered in Hanoi, the city was also a target for potential attack by the Japanese. The six did not stay long.

Sunday, March 4, 1945

The Citroën headed west. Lynch recalled, "A little way out of Hanoi, estimated ten to fifteen miles, we climbed another large hill[,] and, when we stopped, we were at Mount Ba Vi, which was the central command headquarters of the Foreign Legion based in the Hanoi area. There was a legionnaire camp there and some provincial French troops."[45] Red Fetzer recalled they had been told in Saigon that they would be placed in a hotel after they arrived in Hanoi.[46] The promise was a carrot.

"The compound was part of a chain of French outposts in the area[,] and living conditions were primitive."[47] Lynch described that they "had a large[,] fenced-in, barbed[-]wire compound which was supposed to be an internment area. The small barracks were off to the side housing the French troops, and a small cabin inside the compound was where they placed us."[48] The latrine was located outside the wire; thus, if Mother Nature called, the Americans were forced to yell and pound on the door at night to attract the attention of the guards. "We were told we would remain there until we would be freed or find out what further action was to be taken."[49]

As they entered the stockade, they discovered eight cots and two other Americans.

Alarm!

Monday, January 1, 1945. 0230 hours. On its return leg to Kunming, China, the B-24J bomber headed northwest through the night after completing a sweep of the Tonkin Gulf and the South China Sea. Over Hainan Island, shipborne antiaircraft fire found its mark: the "bail out" bell rang through the pencil fuselage. The Bobcat's eleven-man crew poured out of the escape hatches, taking to the silk in the dark night skies over French Indochina. Some found safety; others endured capture.

While three men were taken prisoner immediately by Japanese forces, the majority fell into friendly hands. Six of the Army Air Force men were able to make their way back to Kunming within three weeks. Two others with leg and ankle injuries sustained in the fall were taken to a civilian hospital in Hanoi. But as Japanese forces continued the search for the remaining airmen, the two Americans were moved to the Foreign Legion camp at Mount Ba Vi for safekeeping.

The band of brothers at Ba Vi had grown. The Six were introduced to SSgt. Hugh C. Pope and Sgt. George Uhrine from the Bobcat. Both were big men, and both were recovering from their injuries. While Pope could walk, Uhrine was still hobbled after eight weeks interned at the camp.

As a Marine, Lynch was used to the hand-me-downs that the Navy discarded to the Corps. It was not altogether different at Ba Vi, since the Foreign Legion was a more austere

B-24 Bobcat crew. *Back row:* SSgt. Hugh C. Pope, nose gunner, *second from left;* Sgt. George Uhrine, top turret gunner, *second from right. Courtesy of Michael Hernandez*

organization than the French army. While the Saigon Six had a fair amount of privilege while being held in colonial Saigon, their time at Ba Vi was radically different. The relatively good food provided in Saigon was gone. At Ba Vi, both the legion and the detainees ate chow that consisted mainly of pork fat or fish heads and rice.

Posted at Ba Vi was the 7th Company, 2nd Battalion, of the 5e *Régiment Etranger*, the 5th Foreign Regiment or 5e REI. They were a mixed lot of soldiers. Of the 250 legionnaires, the majority were German or Russian but also included Austrians, Poles, and Hungarians. Even a few Englishmen were found in their ranks. They were led by French officers.

Most legionnaires were over thirty years old and had arrived long before war had broken out between the Allies and Axis. The 5e REI had been stationed in Indochina back in 1930, but no further troops had arrived after 1941. They had been in garrison for years. Hence, they were a regiment of exceptionally old soldiers in a game where combat is measured by the spilled blood of youth. Since the fall of France, they had received exceptionally little resupply. Much of their equipment, like the Potez 25, was old World War I era. The climate exacted a toll on their weapons and equipment. The 65,000 FIC troops were in worse shape due to a lack of supplies and training. Thirty-eight thousand of these French troops were concentrated in the northern Tonkin region, of which 7,500 were Europeans. The Japanese, however, had a high percentage of combat-hardened troops within the ranks. They bore modern weapons.

He Ended Up Being Their Savior

The Saigon Six could not have known it at first. "We were introduced to a very impressive[-] type person there, an old legionnaire chief," wrote Lynch of their meeting with Adjutant Chief Augusté Andérés. "He spoke very little English and, as far as we knew, didn't understand English. He was a remarkable person. He was about six-foot-three or four, a powerfully built man with a mustache."[50] His uniform was distinguished by the highly polished *puttees*—leather leg bindings—he wore.

Andérés wasted no time getting the six Americans back in shape: "He would take us on walks every day. We didn't know this at the time[,] but he was physically preparing us for a lot of walking. We would walk for about two hours up and down the countryside and hillside of Ba Vi," recalled Lynch.[51] The young American fliers could not match the stamina of the elder legionnaire. Though clothed with the uniform of the legion, the six still wore the footwear of the US Navy and Marines. Comfort on deck did not translate to comfort on the trail.

Other than the marches with Andérés, there was little daily activity for the Americans. During the day they had freedom to roam the compound, but at night the stockade was secured. They whiled away their idle time with conversation and games of "Red Dog" poker as they awaited the next step of their journey to freedom.

The thunder of explosions crept up the Red River delta from the east on Friday, March 9. The Saigon Six and the two Army fliers had already settled in for the night, but the sounds drew them to the barred windows. "We really thought it was the Army bombing again[,] and we hoped it was both the Japanese and the French who were being bombed," wished Rabbit Moranville.[52] Lynch agreed that there was "an awful lot of gunfire and commotion down at the bottom of the hill in the direction of Hanoi."[53]

Disarm or Fight!

Friday, March 9, 1945. Several weeks earlier, the Japanese had presented Governor-General Decoux an ultimatum. With the Japanese high command viewing an Allied invasion of Indochina as inevitable, it demanded that Decoux sign a treaty that ensured the French would resist such an attack with the Japanese. Decoux had stalled for time, but March 9 became the ides for his colonial French government. France would no longer rule Indochina during World War II.

Acting on the orders of General Yuitsu Tsuchihashi, a coup d'état commenced as reinforced Japanese troops attacked French military positions across the country. French troops in Saigon surrendered after their commander was arrested. Positions in Hanoi were overrun. At Lang Sơn, a series of fortresses were attacked by Japanese foot soldiers and tanks. The French positions fought bravely but were eventually lost. Thousands of French and indigenous troops were either killed or taken prisoner. At Đồng Đăng, the soldiers held out for several days against Japanese attacks before they were defeated. Many survived the battle only to be bayoneted to death or beheaded.

The legion was not immune. The 5e REI's headquarters in Tong was invaded. The legionnaires guarding the ancient Citadel of Hanoi suffered heavy casualties. In the Hà Giang province, only five legionnaires survived of the eighty-seven who fought the battle. At Vinh and Tiên Kiến, entire platoons were wiped out. The coup was a rout for the Japanese.

At Ba Vi, providence smiled on the legionnaires of 7th Company, 2nd Battalion, for the briefest of times.

PART II: EVASION

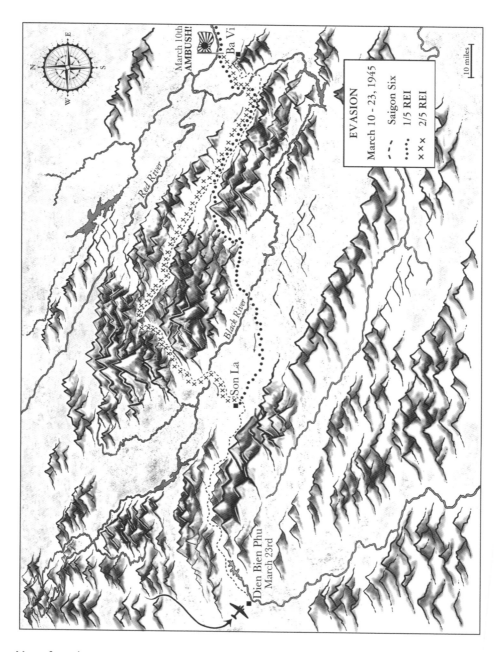

Map of evasion

Saturday, March 10, 1945

"The Japanese are attacking." 7th Company commander Capt. Maurice Courant, accompanied by Adj. Chief Andérés, told the Americans that the company was marching to Tong. "If you want to come with us, you are welcome. Or you can stay here."[54] Scattered across the Red River delta, numerous 5e REI battalions and companies had survived the previous night. Communication to the south was nonexistent, while the forces in the north were in disarray. The surviving French, colonial, and legionnaire troops were to gather and retreat to safety in China. Moranville summed it up for the American contingent: "The decision to go along was immediate and unanimous."[55]

From the armory, the Americans were issued weapons of another era, French-made *Lebel MLE* 1886 bolt-action carbines. Just thirteen rounds of ammunition were issued with each *Lebel*. A heavy blanket completed their gear. From the stockade, they gathered their few personal belongings before joining the legionnaires on the parade grounds.

The legionnaires stood in formation around the flagpole as the blue, white, and red colors were lowered. The band played "*La Marseillaise*" while the troops rendered salutes. *Aux armes, citoyens! Formez vos bataillons! Marchons! Marchons! Grab your weapons, citizens! Form your battalions! Let us march! Let us march!* The next phase of their odyssey had begun.

The Foreign Legion column of 250 legionnaires and the eight Americans exited through the camp's gates. "The pace was set by the captain [Courant,] who had a little white pony," described Lynch. "We thought at the time that he was a little devil[,] and we all took an immediate dislike to this captain."[56] A donkey bearing Sgt. George Uhrine, still unable to walk without difficulty, brought up the rear. Rocky Lynch led the beast along the way. The company marched down Ba Vi on a road heading east.

The legion did not get far: a woman and a French nun with a child from the nearby Ladies of Notre Dame orphanage warned them that there were enemy soldiers at the foot of the mountain. Per Moranville, "We changed our direction and evaded the Japanese."[57] They marched back to their camp. Said Lynch, "We all went down the west side of Mount Ba Vi heading towards the Black River."[58]

Moranville described the difficulty of the march:

When we started, we were walking along a road[,] but before we had gone very far, we turned headed back up into the mountains and into the jungle. We spent most of the afternoon in the jungle. It also became evident that Sgt. Uhrine was not going to be able to continue with us because the terrain was such that the horse could not make it. At sunset[,] when it was becoming dark, the troops started marching again through the jungle[,] and we were forced to leave Sgt. Uhrine behind with quite a few legionnaires who were also unable to hike the terrain. It was an extremely emotional situation when we departed. It was impossible for Uhrine to go along[,] but there was no logical reason for any of us to remain with him. It was a pure matter of probability that whoever stayed would certainly be captured and possibly would be killed by the Japanese.[59]

The Saigon Six finally departed the collection of stragglers, deserters, and Uhrine. They would never see him again.

Uhrine was bitter at being left behind. Pope was to continue on with the Saigon Six. None of the ten legionnaires spoke English, but Uhrine, a first-generation Hungarian American, made a connection with a Hungarian legionnaire. Uhrine had learned the language from relatives in their Michigan home. He was advised to throw away his dog tags and never speak English again.

The march out continued into the evening. Recalled Lynch:

> The Foreign Legion . . . was a tough outfit. They marched to objectives. Objectives were not eight-hour or ten-hour marches, but they went from point to point; whether it was twenty hours or twenty-eight hours to reach it, they walked until they got there. About every hour and a half, they would stop for about ten minutes and take their shoes and socks off and rub their feet. If they had something to drink in their canteen, they'd take a drink. If they had any food or any rations, they would take a couple of bites and off we'd go. Adjutant Chief Andérés was not as close to us on this march as he had been during our stay at Mount Ba Vi.[60]

The column continued the overland march into and through the night. The Americans, who were out of shape, lagged behind the legion column as they descended from the jungle toward a rice paddy.

Ambush!

Bamboo torches lit up the night as gunfire erupted across the paddy. The column had marched into the trap laid by Japanese forces. The Americans were unsure of their next move as the firefight commenced in the distance. "We had our guns out," recalled Lynch. "The Navy pilots had thrown their guns away because they were too heavy. I had mine all loaded and ready to fire at anything that might have shown."[61] The gung-ho marine Lynch decided to join the battle but was restrained by his fellow Americans.

"Adjutant Chief Andérés came up and shouted something at us[,] and we tailed in behind him,"[62] said Lynch. "We stopped and hid in the jungle again," recalled Moranville.[63] The sound of battle continued behind them as they moved off the trail after running for twenty to thirty minutes to seek safety.

Sunday, March 11, 1945. It was a night without sleep or comfort. At daybreak, Andérés referred to a map stored in his tunic: "I think I remember this area. I was here ten years ago. We'll go in this direction here."[64] He led them down a mountain pass. "We headed back in the direction of where we'd come the night before[,] and we went over the remains of the area where we had been ambushed by the Japanese," stated Lynch. "Approximately fifty men from different scattered locations fell in behind us."[65]

Andérés re-formed the surviving legionnaires, reduced from a company down to a reinforced platoon. He led them back to the temporary safety of their legionnaire outpost. The adjutant chief left the Americans there so he could continue to gather up additional survivors from the ambush site. That was the last the Americans would ever see of their savior, Andérés.

By this time, Captain Courant had reappeared with more remnants of the legion company. The Saigon Six and Pope joined Courant's contingent as they escaped Ba Vi down to its western base bordered by the Black River.

The ranks thinned as legionnaires fell out: "We were all in our early twenties[,] and they were in their forties or fifties. When they became exhausted or couldn't continue, they just waved to the rest of the force[,] and we'd go on and they'd sit alongside the road."[66] An English legionnaire, Nobby Clarke, explained to Lynch: "Don't feel bad. The Japanese prefer the legionnaires much over the French soldiers because the legionnaires were about 80 percent German. He said the Japanese and the Germans were allies[,] so they the treated the legionnaires very humanely."[67] It was an optimistic sentiment.

The Odds of Survival Were Poor

Brigadier General Marcel Alessandri's forces were faced with a mission they were ill prepared to execute. Following the Japanese attacks of the ninth, he marshaled the surviving troops at his disposal in the provinces where the Black River and Red River conjoin west of Hanoi. It was a mixed group: French and colonial troops, *tirailleurs tonkinois*—a corps of Tonkinese light infantry—and various elements of three battalions of the 5e Etranger, 850 legionnaires in all. Their goal was to reach China, nearly 500 kilometers away. But to do so, they had to evade the Japanese while navigating the difficult mountainous terrain that shoulders the Red River. They had no supply column, no air support, and little artillery. What few vehicles they had were worthless once they reached the river. The jungle and the Japanese would oppose them the entire way. The march commenced two days later. Though epic in attempt, Alessandri would not emerge as a modern Hannibal.

Under the cover of darkness, Courant's forces forded the Black River. Heavy weapons were discarded. Fetzer was a witness to the tragedy that occurred: "We were trying to get away from the Japanese all the time. When we crossed the Black River some of the Frenchmen couldn't swim and they drowned. It was horrible."[68] Fetzer made it to safety only by holding on to the tail of Captain Courant's horse.

As they pushed northwest into the mountainous Sip Song Chau Tai region that flanked both sides of the Black River, they had no radios and few supplies and were unaware of General Alessandri's plans. Ironically, the Saigon Six and Pope were initially placed with an aviation detachment for safekeeping. They joined forces with other elements of 2nd Battalion of the 5e Etranger, commanded by Captain Guy de Cockbourne, Courant's predecessor as commander of the 7th Company. The column included other colonial forces who had evaded the Japanese. They trudged through the Black River valley. Time and topography were against them. Lynch described the area as "some of the most mountainous terrain that I've ever seen. We'd walk four or five hours, then we'd stop. The legionnaires would always sack out along the road resting."[69] Ahead of them lay hundreds of miles of mountainous terrain on the trail to freedom.

The forces of General Alessandri were fortunate that their gathering had been undetected by the Japanese. But after the march had begun, rear-guard skirmishes were fought so the column could advance. The column in the Black River valley had not retreated far when Cockbourne's 2nd Battalion legionnaires and the aviation troops were detached to prevent the Japanese from advancing up Provincial Highway 41. Lynch complained that "The captain and his horse had disappeared!"[70] Left behind with the colonial troops, Pope and the Six were orphans again.

The Retreat Took Its Toll

The aviators had become foot soldiers. Their US Navy footwear was not designed for an overland march. Blisters developed. Some cut away portions of their shoes, but that caused foot ulcers and lacerations to fester. Of the few items they carried from Ba Vì, extra socks proved to be the most important. They continued their march toward Điện Biên Phủ.

During the retreat, mosquitoes and leeches added to their misery. Palm fronds served as bedding at night, but as Moranville pointed out, "There was little time for sleeping or dallying along the way because we knew that the Japanese were trying to find us and intercept us."[71]

But the group remained as the hunted. Enemy snipers picked off several Frenchmen. Contact and skirmishes with Japanese patrols, even in the cover of the jungle, became commonplace. The group dwindled in size and strength. Within days, food was in short supply.

"Legionnaires, popularly called pirates, foraged food from villages and natives[,] but often the party had none," said Lynch. Moranville recalled:

Whenever we would come into a village, the troops would just take whatever food they wanted. Chickens, ducks, pigs, goats, and whatever the troops could find was fair game, and they would just take it, cook it, and we'd eat it. Rice was the one staple that we would get every night. It was also the food we would carry with us the next day for breakfast and lunch. Everyone would gather a couple of hands full and press it into two balls about the size of a baseball and put in your pocket or wherever and eat it while we walked the next day.[72]

The farther west the group progressed, the farther it was from the graces of the villagers who supported the French. "Whenever we approached a village, you could hear the natives shooing their livestock out of the village and into jungle so that we could not steal it. It was really quite amazing how well the jungle telegraph warned them of the plundering herd. Although we always seemed to find plenty of quantity to eat, the quality left much to be desired. Nearly all of the meat, whether chicken or pork, was cooked a minimum so that it was always almost raw." Moranville continued, "Sanitary conditions were nonexistent, too, but, so what—it became a matter of expediency—eat it that way or starve."[73] The Americans were pressed into servitude cleaning pots and mess kits for the colonial troops.

Fresh water was no less an issue than food: "When we first started, none of us had a canteen for water[,] and if you asked for a drink from one of the soldiers, they would usually tell you that it was all gone[,] so we would drink from the streams that we were crossing all of the time," described Moranville. "Here again, it was better to get bugs and get out than not drink and perish in the jungle."[74]

"The fliers' teeth and gums became very uncomfortable from lack of cleaning," recalled Lynch.[75] They turned to shards of bamboo as makeshift dental floss. "Nearly everyone was ill within days from exposure, poor food, and lack of sleep. The weather turned against the group[,] but there was no choice except to slog through the heat and dust[,] which turned into rain and mud."[76]

Emotional burdens were carried by the young Americans. It was likely that the USS *Essex* had already discharged its squadrons at the end of their combat tour. Their buddies were probably on their way home to America. The Saigon Six and Pope might perish in an attack high in the hills of this foreign land, the jungle to become an anonymous graveyard. If so, there was little probability that their families would ever know what had happened to them.

Wednesday, March 21, 1944: Kunming, China

A brown Douglas C-47 taxied across the steel matting before the twin Pratt & Whitneys were shut down after the brief 100-mile flight from Mengtze. The next day, an intelligence officer trained to save downed pilots was welcomed aboard. The pilot set their course for Điện Biên Phủ.

The rescue attempt had begun.

Spy School

It was known as "P.O. Box 1142," a covert training facility for American military intelligence. Hidden near Ft. Hunt's coastal artillery batteries overlooking the Potomac River, the US Army's Captured Personnel and Material Branch trained soldiers in the art of escape and evasion when shot down or captured behind enemy lines. Its operatives assisted downed fliers by sending maps, radios, and compasses hidden in common objects. Escape networks were established with the local resistance fighters. The covert Escape and Evasion program was known as MIS-X.

The MIS-X shop in the China-Burma theater was established at the 14th Air Force's main airfield at Kunming, China. The secret intelligence program was known as the Air Ground Aid Section (AGAS). Manned with just a few dozen personnel, the section was tasked with providing escape-and-evasion training to pilots and aircrew stationed there. Its efforts to establish escape routes across China were highly successful, to the frustration of the Japanese.

Word of the capture of the Saigon Six on January 12 filtered to the AGAS in short order. The Commander Air Group 4 aboard the *Essex* was notified of their capture by the fourteenth of January. Rescue planning commenced in Kunming, 1,000 miles from Saigon. But, it was not until the Potez pilot, Lt. Hubert Coquard, evacuated an American army pilot from Sơn La to Mengtze on March 16 that the AGAS learned the Saigon Six were moving toward Điện Biên Phủ. A rescue team was sent from Kunming to Mengtze.

When requested to transport a portable radio back to Sơn La to help in the rescue efforts, Coquard agreed. A simple code-and-communication plan were devised so that Coquard could signal the rescue team to fly into Indochina. He took off in his old biplane. Coquard was never heard from again.

No Flag Flew over the Airfield

The transport plane from the 27th Troop Carrier Squadron of the 14th United States Army Air Force circled Điện Biên Phủ several times on March 22 before the pilot, Maj. James H. Rasmussen, finally landed on the dirt runway atop the hilltop plain. Several World War I–era French biplanes sat off to the side.

It was a dangerous assignment. The mission had to be flown with inadequate maps. No up-to-date intelligence about the battles on the ground had been given to Rasmussen. For the mission, he handpicked his crew: MSgt. Bill Coldren and radioman Sgt. Harry "Bud" Leam. "We were going with the best we had. We were giving it our best shot," remembered Leam. "Coldren was the top-of-the-line crew chief in Engineering."[77] An Air Ground Aid Section officer, 1Lt. Edmund "Ned" Carpenter II, accompanied them.

Taking no chances, Rasmussen ordered Coldren and Leam onto the wings of the plane with Thompson submachine guns. The whole time he kept the engines running. "If anyone even looks like they want to get close, do not hesitate to shoot them."[78] He taxied the gooney bird toward a small hangar. Explicit instructions were given to Carpenter to stay in front of the plane, within eyesight of the pilot.

Carpenter was met by a small contingent of Frenchmen. "*Ou sont les pilotes americains? Where are the American pilots?*" The conversation was inaudible to Leam over the engine noise, but it was apparent by the gesturing and the frowns that the meeting did not go well. None of the Navy aviators emerged. The groups separated. A wounded legionnaire shared that the Americans were still at Sơn La, 60 miles east of Điện Biên Phủ. It would be at least a day before they arrived.

Back aboard the plane, Carpenter informed Rasmussen, "They're not here!" The pilot responded that he was not waiting on an enemy airfield for the Saigon Six to arrive at an unknown time. Carpenter told Rasmussen he would stay behind and radio for a return flight when the Saigon Six arrived. The C-47 took off for Mengtze without him.

Ned Carpenter was uniquely qualified for his role with the AGAS. He held a private pilot's license, was fluent in French, had traveled abroad before the war, and had attended Princeton University. The athletic officer possessed a keen mind. A renaissance man, Carpenter was a fan of opera and literature. He was not loud but stood firm in both conviction and actions.

The twenty-four-year-old intelligence officer was left to his wits and special training.

The pilot pointed at the old teapot in the store, but the Sơn La shopkeeper wished to sell him a new teapot instead. They haggled before the aviator traded his broken US Navy–issue wristwatch for the used teapot and a new rattan caddy to carry it. It seemed like a prudent deal, and several other Americans left the shop with new teapots too.

The French column had entered Sơn La the day before, March 21. "As we started down

First Lieutenant Edmund N. Carpenter II *(second from right)*, AGAS Shop, Kunming, China

the other side of the last mountain range, we ran into better weather. We were getting pretty hungry and were pretty beaten up as far as our physical condition was concerned," recalled Rocky Lynch.[79] Cockbourne's 2nd Battalion arrived at Sơn La from another direction after fighting rear-guard actions against the Japanese the entire way. They were exhausted and tattered. The elements had been their other enemy. In the lowlands, leeches had attached themselves to legionnaires. Chiggers—an enemy of all foot soldiers—brought typhus with its accompanying fever, rashes, and headaches. Malarial mosquitoes had taken their bites.

But for a brief period, the Saigon Six and Pope were reunited with the legionnaires from Ba Vi. Recalled Lynch, "Lo and behold[,] coming up to us with hands out and all smiles, like we were old friends, was our captain friend who deserted us at the ambush two weeks previous to this! He got very little satisfaction from us."[80]

Nobby Clarke (one of the English legionnaires), who enjoyed the company of the Americans, especially the outgoing Lynch, kept them informed of events and translated orders from the top.

The day spent at Sơn La afforded the colonial troops and the legionnaires a brief period to eat and resupply. Throughout the village and on the roads nearby, Free French soldiers were preparing to battle the Japanese. They had been parachuted into the valley from China. Their uniforms were French army, their weapons American. For the rear-guard action, they built barricades and prepared bridges with explosives. Their plan was to make a fighting retreat back up the provincial route. In contrast, most of the Americans had already long discarded their Lebel carbines during the march up.

It was decided that the Saigon Six and Pope would be evacuated with the seriously wounded to Điện Biên Phủ to the west. "I'm sure we looked quite stupid to all the French troops who were preparing to fight a war[,] and we were walking around with tea caddies," noted Moranville. "The next morning we all mounted a military truck and were driven to Điện Biên Phủ. . . . Along the way we noted that the new French troops were wiring all the bridges with explosives in order to destroy them to slow the Japanese advance."[81] But for the Saigon Six and Pope, the end was almost within sight.

Both rows left to right. First row: Pope, Lambros, Lynch, and Santopadre; second row: Moranville, Fetzer, and Stratton. Courtesy of the Lynch family

No Response

The rescue team at Mengtze took turns cranking the radio set to try to contact Carpenter at Điện Biên Phủ on the twenty-third. Sgt. Leam recalled that the plan was "as soon as our Navy personnel were located, we could fly back down and pick them up."[82] The exhausting work was in vain. "We would crank until we could crank no more."[83] No response was ever received from the radio given to Coquard, nor did they hear from Carpenter. Rasmussen and Col. Nathan H. Ranck—assistant operations officer of the 69th Composite Wing—decided they could wait no longer. The team boarded their C-47 and returned to Kunming. The decision to leave was not popular with the AGAS. "[They] wanted us to stay. Major Rasmussen advised that we had more[-]important things to do."[84]

March 23: Sơn La

The Saigon Six and Pope boarded trucks for the last leg of their evacuation. It took just a few hours. "We came into this valley that looked very peaceful," said Lynch. "It was the end of a near-epic journey. I was told that we had walked 300 miles in thirteen days across some of the roughest geography in Southeast Asia. We were told this was Điện Biên Phủ, which at that time was of no special significance to us except that it was the end of our search and it was the objective we were hoping to reach. What was there at that time, we did not know, only that this is where we were supposed to be."[85]

Disappointment. There was no rescue plane awaiting the convoy.

Another American Emerged at Điện Biên Phủ

Carpenter introduced himself to the Six and Pope before explaining his role in the rescue mission. "He said that he persuaded the colonel to leave him down there so he could radio them when we arrived," recalled Lynch. "He was a very upbeat, young intelligence officer, very likeable, and boy, was he a Godsend to us!"[86] But the radio that was to have been brought there by Lt. Coquard perished with the pilot when his Potez crashed on its return flight from Mengtze.

The weather was also against them. "Heavy clouds came into the area[,] and it was almost zero/zero on the ground every day. Điện Biên Phủ is in a valley," reported Lynch. Twice daily for five days, reconnaissance P-38 long-range fighters from Kunming flew over Điện Biên Phủ. The sound of the twin Allison engines could be heard through the clouds. "They'd circle for about a half hour and return. They felt that they just could not risk bringing a plane into this area under the weather conditions with no radio facilities. They kept this up every day[,] waiting for the weather to break."[87] Storms drenched the valley.

The enemy continued to battle its way toward Điện Biên Phủ. "We knew the Japanese were coming."[88] Điện Biên Phủ was a target since the Free French paratroops were head-quartered there. More and more of their casualties streamed into Điện Biên Phủ. But Carpenter had been unable to find a radio. He resorted to going into Điện Biên Phủ to send telegrams written in code from a commercial telegraph office.

Recalled Lynch, "We were getting pretty discouraged to know after all this effort we'd put in and four and a half months of uncertainty, fear, et cetera, all of the physical hardships we'd gone through, it should end up we'd still be captured by the Japanese."[89]

On their sixth day there, the weather broke.

A telegram arrived in Kunming from Carpenter. In plain English it stated, "Come desperately. Everything's all taken care of. We're ready to go."[90] Maj. Rasmussen gathered his best crew again and flew his C-47 back to Điện Biên Phủ. They were accompanied by Lt. Robert Ettinger, a spy from the Office of Strategic Services. "We were down in a small village eating peanut brittle about 2:00 in the afternoon[,] and old Bones Stratton yelled, 'Hey, listen to that!' We heard this noise. There was a broken cloud cover at one of the valley[,] and through this little maze of sunshine we saw this C-47 or R4D came through the valley, wheels up," reported Lynch. "We took off and made a mad dash for the landing strip."[91]

From the air, Sgt. Bud Leam, who had flown on the first rescue flight attempt, provided witness to the scene:

Circling the strip[,] we could see that it was obvious that there had been heavy rains the past few days, in as much as the strip was dirt. Rasmussen got into a big discussion with the OSS [Lt. Ettinger] as to whether the landing should be attempted. At that time the six individuals, looking like Americans, came out of the building and started running around and waving. We decided to take the chance and land. We almost nosed over[,] and the major said we were in trouble for as we attempted to turn off the strip we were sliding and slipping.[92]

Lynch continued, "By the time we got there, the plane had circled, put down its gear, landed, and was taxiing to where we were. At that time we saw the stars on the wings and on the fuselage. You could just imagine our happiness and joy."[93]

Sgt. Leam and MSgt. Coldren emerged from the mud-splattered fuselage. Once again, they mounted the wings with the Thompson machine guns and additional ammo. As Leam clutched his weapon, the extra magazines vibrated on the wings as Rasmussen kept the Pratt & Whitneys turning. The Saigon Six, Pope, and Carpenter boarded the Douglas. Said Leam, "They were in extremely poor physical condition but elated to see us."[94]

Lynch's buddy, the English legionnaire, also tried to board. "They pushed poor old Clarke off."[95]

Ettinger remained behind. His mission was to begin coordination of air attacks against the Japanese by American forces from China.

Sgt. Harry "Bud" Leam in rear hatchway of a C-47. *Courtesy of Harry J. Leam*

Landing had been the easy part. Getting out safely was another. Leam recalled:

Ready for takeoff, we all knew we were in trouble due to the muddy field. Rasmussen told Coldren to walk alongside as we taxied to note how far we were sinking in mud[,] as he was using a lot more power than usual. Returning to the aircraft[,] Coldren advised that our wheels were sinking about six inches and that sometimes the wheels were sliding nor [*sic*] rolling. Rasmussen then took the ship back as far as possible[,] and with Ranck's and his feet pressing on the brakes as hard as they could[,] he went into full power[,] thus lifting the tail off the ground and causing the wheels to slip. He had advised that we all sit forward and with no moving. While the aircraft shook rattled and rolled (and sliding)[,] we gave all we had. The very short strip had a fence and small shack at the end of the runway. Standing between the pilots, same was growing bigger and bigger. Rasmussen then called for flaps at one half, then three quarter[,] and finally full and pushed the throttles all the way. I thought the engines would blow. He red-lined them. I think we hopped over the shack—it seemed like we were going to take it out. Both pilots had white knuckles and they were sweating. The radio operator was praying.

As it became clear we were airborne[,] there was a loud cheer from the rear. As we circled the field you could see two ruts in the dirt looking like they ended inside the hut.[96]

The Saigon Six took turns coming forward to the cockpit to thank the Army fliers: "They remarked that they never knew a ship could shake and make so much noise on takeoff." Leam responded, "Me too!"[97]

Clearing the valley, Rasmussen turned the cargo plane northwest toward Kunming. Two hours later the Saigon Six and Pope were back in Allied hands. Recalled 2Lt. Joseph Lynch, "It felt great to be the first Marine pilot out of French Indochina."[98]

Điện Biên Phủ fell to the Japanese two days later.

Another telegram was delivered to the house in St. Cloud, Minnesota, on Friday, April 6, 1945: "ALL IS WELL AND SAFE. ANXIETY UNNECESSARY. HOPE TO SEE YOU SOON. JOSEPH LYNCH."

The Saigon Six were flown to Hawaii. Lynch received a hero's welcome and a party in his honor from his flying buddies. He was pressed into service to give a lecture about his perils in Indochina. His Corsair was the only one to touch French Indochina soil in World War II. Postwar, Lynch stayed in the Marine Corps and served in Korea. He was not allowed to deploy to Vietnam. Lynch passed away in 2008.

Ned Carpenter was awarded the Bronze Star for the rescue at Điện Biên Phủ. He parachuted into China at the end of the war to help recover four of the Doolittle Raiders who had been held as POWs. Carpenter never revealed his exploits to his family. He passed away in 2008.

Tân Sơn Nhứt airfield, now Tân Sơn Nhứt International Airport, is the busiest airport in Vietnam.

Author's note: In various interviews and writings, Lynch confused Augusté Andérés with a legionnaire named Gunther. Andérés's name has been inserted where appropriate.

CHAPTER 11

SALVATION AT KURE

The veteran Avenger pilot fought to keep his plane airborne. He worked the stick to compensate for the tail that was breaking apart. Where his radioman should have been, instead, flak had punched holes through the plane's skin. Smoke escaped from the cowling. Fuel was rapidly burned. Still over Japan, it was apparent they would never make it back to the carrier. Without warning, an enemy fighter dove from the clouds at them.

By mid-March 1945, the Marine pilots of VMF-451 "Blue Devils" had already experienced a month of combat. Not all had survived. On their very first mission, Lt. Forrest Brown had been shot out of the sky over Tokyo. The stress grew with the missions, the battle damage, and the losses. A plane that went down meant that the pilot was probably gone forever. First Lieutenant Philip S. "Pots" Wilmot described the frustration endured by the pilots: "You don't save guys. They get shot down. You see them go this way [down] or you see them not pull out of a dive. That's what you see. You come home with holes in your formation and you think, 'Thank, God, it's them and not me.'"[1]

"Okay, Boys, We're Going to Strike Kure"

Maj. Hank Ellis, the CO of VMF-451, briefed his pilots on March 19, 1945. As the news was absorbed by the pilots seated in their ready room aboard the USS *Bunker Hill*, Pots Wilmot recalled, "Boy, we knew it was going to be tough."[2] It was. Three-quarters of a century later, Wilmot declared it was both the worst and best day of his life.

The Kure Naval District was one of the Imperial Japanese Navy's most important anchorages. It was home to large capital-ship construction shipyards, armories, munition production factories, and other support services. By this point in the war, the glorious IJN no longer roamed the Pacific at will. American submarines had starved the island nation of needed petroleum. Most of the IJN's surviving carriers and battleships were anchored in the sheltered harbor.

In the weeks prior to Operation Iceberg, the invasion of Okinawa, Task Force 58 was tasked with reducing the ability of Japanese planes to attack the invasion forces. Targets included airfields on the Ryukyu Islands and Kyushu, and the destruction of the Japanese fleet. The day prior, fighter sweeps were sent to Kyushu, where it was believed most of the Japanese air strength was concentrated. It was a banner day: 102 enemy aircraft were claimed as destroyed in the air, and another 275 were reported destroyed on the ground.

On the nineteenth, the carriers *Bunker Hill*, *Essex*, and *Cabot* prepared to send large strikes against Kure. From the *Bunker Hill*, eighteen Corsairs from Air Group 84 were sent forth to escort twenty-six Avengers and Helldivers. The *Essex* also sent a similar strike of its Air Group 83 fighters and bombers

Lt. Ray U. Plant Jr. and James Papazoglakis, AMM3c

The fighters carried eight HVAR rockets. The bombers and torpedo planes each carried four 500-pound bombs. Some of the *Cabot*'s TBMs carried propaganda leaflets to be released north of Kure. Aboard the *Essex*, twenty-six-year-old Lt. Ray Upson Plant Jr. piloted an Avenger. James Papazoglakis, a nineteen-year-old Brooklyn boy, served as his gunner. As a sacrifice to distance, they left their radioman behind to save weight. As dawn's first rays spread light across the Pacific, Plant and Papazoglakis were launched. The strike assembled and headed northwest across Shikoku.

After circling north above the base, the strikes rained down from the southeast. Though bogies in the area refused to mix it up with the Americans, the antiaircraft guns had no such hesitation. Nearly two hundred heavy flak batteries protected Kure. As the strike force began the attack, multicolor bursts of red, yellow, white, green, black, and purple punctuated the skies from deck level all the way to 14,000 feet. Guns on the warships opened fire as well. "It was a Roman holiday of AA fire,"[3] noted the "Blue Devil's" air combat action report. Planes crisscrossed the sky. Chatter from nervous pilots overwhelmed the radio circuits.

One AA burst nearly collected Wilmot: "We got over Kure about 9:00 in the morning. The whole sky lit up with antiaircraft fire. One went right off right by my wing. It was so close I could hear it go 'BANG!' It pushed my airplane sideways."[4] The explosion rattled Wilmot: "I opened my eyes and I was still flying, so I said, 'Okay, I'm alive.' My oil pressure was still good, so I continued the attack."[5]

The bombers made their bombing runs while the fighters unleashed their 5-inch high-velocity aircraft rockets (HVAR). Major Herbert "Trigger" Long was intent on adding to his score. Just the previous day, the "Blue Devil" ace had earned his seventh kill. At Kure, he planned to sink a carrier. His rockets punctured the carrier *Ryuho*, causing death and destruction. The "Holy Moses" rockets put the light carrier out of commission.

Pots Wilmot flew wing on the squadron's greatest ace, Maj. Archie Donahue, who already had nine kills to his credit: "The major said, 'Okay, let's go.' He pulled up and started his dive. We all followed him. I was right on his wing. I was a good dive-bomber, and I could always hit the target. I always fired my rockets in a dive-bomb because the damn rockets, I could never make them to go right. They'd go and drop off. I could never get them to the target! So, I figured, I'll just dive-bomb them."[6]

Wilmot got into position: "I get upside down and I let the nose fall and I corkscrew around. I put the curl of my cowling on the target. Well, the wind is different and drifts you out, so you have to keep corkscrewing around to get the wind exactly right to keep the cowling on the target. Then when you accomplish that, you better pay attention because you're coming down at 500 miles per hour. I got my fix and then salvoed my rockets—I had eight rockets.[7]

"'Sweet Ed' Fuller was the tail-end charlie. He saw my salvo hit the carrier. When we got home, he told 2Lt. Johnny Nayman, the squadron's intelligence officer, that 'Pots got rocket hits on the carrier!' Nayman wrote it up and I got a medal! The Navy loved sinking ships. It's the best thing you can do."[8]

While the fighters had the advantage of speed and smaller size, the Avengers had a different experience. Forced to approach in low glides, the big birds were large targets. James Papazoglakis, AMM3c, recalled that as they approached the target, "Everything went to hell in a handbasket"[9] as the wall of flack arose. At one point the enemy bursts caused him to lose sight of the target. As Lt. Ray Plant piloted the Avenger through the fire, Papazoglakis was at work in the rear turret: "I cannot forget spinning around firing the machine gun and being so close to those ships that I could see the whites of their eyes."[10]

At the precise moment, Plant released the bombs. "He pulled back hard on the stick to avoid flying straight into the water and retreat from the dive."[11] The enemy guns followed.

Grumman Avengers had earned a reputation as tough birds that were able to absorb a tremendous amount of punishment and still bring their fliers home. But Plant's plane was struck at its most vulnerable point: "Flack hit the tail section of the plane. It threw me hard against the canopy and gave me a headache. The sound was incredibly loud," recalled Papazoglakis. Where a radioman normally would have sat, flak had punctured the plane's skin. Smoke was coming from the engine. "I looked around and realized the tail section had been shot up."[12] Pieces of BuNo 68641 pulled away in the slipstream.

"Plant was an incredible pilot, calm and very skilled, even after we had been hit."[13] But Plant had his hands full. As his plane shuddered and smoked, he struggled to control the yaw and pitch. If he stalled, there was little rudder available to recover. Mountainous Shikoku lay ahead of them, and the carriers were nearly 150 miles farther. Fuel burned prodigiously with the throttle kept in "Auto Rich." Mental calculations of fuel, altitude, and distance weighed heavily on Plant. Even if he could reach the carriers, he would have to ditch because the turkey would probably stall on approach. Worse, the tail empennage could break away at any point. Plant and Papazoglakis wondered if the plane would hold together long enough for them to get to safety. Jumping or ditching at sea appeared to be the only choices. Even knowing where the lifeguard submarine was supposed to be positioned didn't guarantee survival. Often, enemy planes drove the lifeguards back underwater.

The organized strikes that had flown into Kure were in disarray. With numerous targets enveloped in flak, a condition known as "group grope" was in full effect. Flight elements had broken down; radio discipline had given away to the excited chatter of young pilots. Radio calls giving bearings and distances to American ships and bases were transmitted in plain English. "Bogies were repeatedly reported without the reporting pilots identifying himself."[14]

After his rockets were salvoed, Pots Wilmot became part of the grope: "I pulled up and I was separated—I lost my major. I saw this Corsair over there, and I scooted over there and joined up with him." The white vertical arrow on the tail showed it to be another Air Group 84 plane. "I look in and it's 'Wonderful Wee' Brown! I thought, 'God, I'm gonna live!' This guy can navigate and fly instruments. I just stuck with him."[15]

As the pair of "Blue Devils" headed east, they came upon Plant's plane. "We were under the clouds, and all of a sudden a TBF came out of the clouds, smoking and losing altitude. Wee Brown and I joined right up with him and started going down with him to protect him in case anything happened."[16] Seeing the holes near the canopy and just two men aboard the plane, Pots assumed the radioman had been killed.

In an air war, attacks were violent, often very short, and usually without warning. Flying over Kure were pilots of the 343rd Naval Air Group, a fighter group composed of exceptional veterans flying the Kawanishi N1K2-J Shiden-Kai. Code-named "George" by the Allies, it was a modern navy fighter that could go toe to toe with Hellcats and Corsairs. It was often confused by American pilots with the Imperial Japanese Army's Nakajima Frank, another exceptional fighter plane.

With any luck, Plant would find the rescue submarine. But, Pots Wilmot recalled, "Sure enough, this damn Frank came right out of the clouds right at the TBF. He was going to finish it off. Wee Brown turned into him and immediately fired a burst. The tracers go out past the nose. [Brown] just let his nose slide down, and he started getting hits on the engine and in the cockpit. The thing started to smoke and it was gone. He got it, and so we stuck with the TBF."[17]

The marine escorts continued with the Avenger but kept their distance in case the plane should blow up. About 25 miles past Shikoku, Brown radioed to Plant, "There's the lifeguard sub down there on the surface."[18] If Plant didn't ditch, the Navy fliers would have been on their own. Wilmot recalled, "We were following the TBF down, and there's this sub on the surface. The TBF went right over there and plopped in the water. The two guys jump out. They scrambled up on the sub so we knew they were safe. I said, 'Wee, let's go home.' He said, 'Okay, Pots,' and away we went!"[19] The Corsairs continued east toward the safety of the *Bunker Hill*.

Things were not so sure for Plant and Papazoglakis. There was no guarantee the *Avenger* would hold together during ditching. Even if the Japanese surface fleet was impotent, Japanese subs still patrolled the home islands. Nevertheless, there was no other choice.

After ditching in the Pacific, Papazoglakis grabbed the raft pack as he and Plant scrambled from the plane. As it inflated, they held the sides as they swam away from the plane to avoid being sucked under. With the unknown sub silhouetted on the horizon, the veteran pilot unholstered his Smith & Wesson. The fear of capture by the Japanese weighed heavily on pilots' minds. First Lieutenant John Hansen of VMF-422 stated postwar, "It was common knowledge in the military what the Japanese did to prisoners. We'd heard stories of how they treated downed pilots by torture and beheading. I know now that a lot of it was propaganda[,] but there was no doubt the Japs were merciless and cruel. We never talked about it among ourselves[,] but there was a sort of grim fatalism that we had better not be taken alive."[20]

Papazoglakis recalled:

Growing up in Brooklyn as a "city boy," I could barely swim, and suddenly I have been shot out of the air; I have watched my airplane coming apart, wondering if we could make it to safety and live. Now I am sitting in this little raft in the middle of the ocean. It was the first time I felt I could breathe, and then Plant pulls his pistol, cocks it back with the barrel placed behind his ear as he is looking over his shoulder, and says, "Unless that is the bars and stars, Jimmy, it has been good flying with you."[21]

The sub turned toward them to close the 500 yards.

When the *Essex* boys finally saw the American flag flying, Plant holstered his pistol. Breathing a sigh of relief, Papazoglakis thought, "We're going to make it."[22] They were helped aboard the USS *Bowfin* (SS-287), their salvation complete.

The Bowfin *returned to Guam with the Navy fliers a few days later. Papazoglakis and Plant boarded an escort carrier bound for the Fast Carrier Task Force. They were transferred back to the* Essex *one day ahead of the largest kamikaze attack of World War II. VT-83 finished its tour aboard the* Essex *in September 1945.*

Ray Upson Plant Jr. was awarded a Navy Cross for the mission on March 19, 1945. Both Plant and Papazoglakis earned a DFC and an Air Medal with two gold stars for their service during the war. Postwar, Plant returned to his native Connecticut to work at Connecticut General Life Insurance. He was promoted to squadron commander of VT-786 at nearby Floyd Bennett Field. Plant passed away in 1975.

Papazoglakis returned to Brooklyn and shortened his surname to "Pakis." Using the GI bill, he earned a degree in industrial engineering. Pakis worked in the aerospace industry and later with the US Defense Logistics Agency. He passed away in 2015 at age ninety-two.

In an interview done in March 2018, Pots Wilmot acknowledged that March 19, 1945, was the worst and best day of his life. He had come close to dying, but he had saved another. He wondered if the Navy fliers in the Avenger had survived the war. On the seventy-third anniversary of the attack against Kure, Rev. Thomas Papazoglakis thanked Wilmot for saving his father.

That August, Wilmot and Papazoglakis met in person. Wilmot reflected on his time in combat: "You don't save guys. They get shot down. You see them go this way [downward hand motion] or you see them not pull out of a dive. That's what you see. You come home with holes in your formation and you think, 'Thank, God, it's them and not me.' That's what you saw. [As tears were welling up] Sometimes you cried. You know it was terrible out there. I guess that's why I was put here, to save Rev. Tom's dad. That's my ultimate achievement."[23]

CHAPTER 12

A TORPEDO
FOR MY BUNK

Tossed by the strong seas running, the two Marine fliers held tightly to their personal rafts. Strapped together, the two Goodyears were buffeted by waves as the skies turned dark. The division leader was in shock and not fully coherent. But upon hearing the sound of engines, his wingman fired tracer rounds from his .38. And magically, a submarine appeared in the chop.

His time in the air spanned the entire war. As America sat on the sidelines, France fell and Britain was under siege. For an American teenager who wanted to fly against the Axis, the pathway was through Canada. Like many of the Marines' "first team" of fliers in the Solomons, Thomas Mayburn Tomlinson's entry to the fight was his selection into the Royal Canadian Air Force. From there he was supposed to head to Europe. Instead, Japan's visit to Oahu early one Sunday morning ended that plan. The lad from Montana joined thousands of aviators who had already earned their wings and come back to the States in the spring of 1942. The Marines had just 592 pilots at the start of the war. Tomlinson was one of just a handful of pilots who received a Marine commission into their expanding ranks. With gold wings on his tunic and a single gold bar on each shoulder, his introduction to combat came in the Solomons rather than over the English Channel.

In its first incarnation, VMF-214, then the "Swashbucklers," took to the air with Grumman Iron Works' stubby F4F. From Guadalcanal, they waged war in the spring of 1943. The "Threadbare Buzzard" and his mates transitioned to Vought's machines before their second tour that year, but they lost their first birdcage when Tomlinson's Double Wasp quit during a practice strafing run. Overland, he turned his mount back out to sea. As he hit the waves, the canopy slammed shut. He struggled at first to reopen the glass while water poured into the plane. As he emerged, the seat-pack life raft lanyard became entangled on the throttle quadrant. While he fought to free himself, 02683 settled beneath the seas. Tomlinson was finally able to extract himself and surface, his equipment intact but with wounds to his head. The crash boat was his savior.

Just a week and half later, three divisions of "Swashbucklers" were sent as cover for eighteen B-24s' run on Kahili. Seven of the Corsairs turned around short of the target. Vought's birds had been rushed into combat. Flying early-edition dash-ones from primitive airfields carved out of island jungles, it was not unusual to have many pilots turn back from missions due to mechanical difficulties.

At altitude, Tomlinson's mount lost manifold pressure following a loud noise erupting from under the cowling. He dove to keep the Double Wasp running before finally setting the Vought down on an uncompleted field at Seghi on New Georgia. He came in hot but managed to keep the bird in one piece as it hopped down the rough strip.

There were no aviation mechanics on hand, but that was not an impediment. Much of America's youth had grown up on farms during the Depression. Mechanical aptitude was second nature for them. With the cowling of the dash-one removed, it was apparent that part of the engine's ductwork had a hole where there shouldn't be a hole. In short time, a patch was installed. To Tomlinson, "It looked suspiciously like the bottom of a tin tomato can."[1] The field repair held, and Tomlinson was able to bring his bird home.

First Lieutenant Tomlinson nailed a Zeke on August 15, just weeks before -214 completed their second tour. He finished out his time in the Solomons as a member of -215 before heading back to the States in early 1944. The silver bars on his collar were doubled, and so he served as a

Tomlinson flying escort duty over Munda, 1943. *Courtesy of Larry Rowley, trustee*

flight instructor first at El Toro and then at Jacksonville before heading to Miramar the next January. It wasn't long before he joined -213, which was training as a carrier replacement squadron at Ewa.

The Fast Carrier Task Force was an unstoppable phalanx. An armada of carriers and warships, it roamed the Pacific at will, choosing when and where to bring the fight to the enemy. But in October 1944, the enemy sent forth an unimaginable weapon: the kamikaze.

Only two Corsair squadrons, the Marines' VMF-124 and -213, had flown from Halsey's carriers. But with the change in enemy tactics, the need for their Corsairs was great: "Give us carrier planes with improved performance. If we are to continue to dig the enemy out of his foxholes, wherever he may be, we must have better implements. The SB2C, the TBM, and F6F-5 are obsolescent, overloaded planes. If we cannot have these planes, then send us more and better replacement pilots, because, by God! we will need them," cited a Carrier Air Group 7 report.[2] The brass felt the same way. In February, the task force sortied for attacks against the Japanese home islands, Iwo Jima, and Okinawa. Many of the fleet carriers carried squadrons with a mixture of Vought and Goodyear Corsairs.

Attrition was dramatic after the March raids against Japan. To keep the fast carriers in the fight, the replenishment Task Group 50.8 brought forth smaller jeep carriers with replacement planes and pilots. Tomlinson's division (Lts. Sager, Lewis, and Garlock) was aboard the USS *Admiralty Islands* (CVE-99) when a request came for a division that could fly the Navy Corsairs aboard the USS *Essex* (CV-9). Advised that only a division of Marine pilots was available, "'We'll take anything' was the ungracious reply from Air Group 83."[3]

The interservice rivalry continued as the pilots were transferred from the jeep carrier to the fleet carrier by way of the destroyer USS *Haynsworth* (DD-700). Carried by a highline on March 28, the tin can sailors were surprised to have Marines aboard. Before the transfer to the *Essex*, the thought in the minds of the deck force was "Dip them down, spin them around, and give the Marines a bath," a baptism into the black-shoe navy. The antagonism was mutual. "A pox upon them," cursed Tomlinson.[4]

On board the *Essex*, the pace was hectic. With the invasion of Okinawa, the air squadrons of the Fast Carrier Task Force were tasked with a variety of assignments: night combat air patrols, daytime CAPs, target CAPS, radar-picket CAPs over the destroyers, dumbo escort, fighter sweeps, mission strikes, and bomber escort duty.

The pilots were put to use right away, some days flying multiple missions, as they protected the fleet and aided in the advance of the marines and soldiers on Okinawa. Four days after the invasion, word came down that the Japanese would retaliate in force against the surface fleets on either side of the big island.

Experience had shown both opponents that there was no more deadly time for a carrier than to be caught with a deck load of armed planes. "The order was passed during the night of April 5 to de-gas and de-bomb all VT-VB aircraft, strike them below on the hangar deck, and to have all fighter planes in readiness to intercept the Nipponese sky-train, believed due to arrive at dawn the following morning."[5]

"However, the morning of April 6 came and went with only a modicum of enemy activity taking place. The ready rooms buzzed with speculation and regret at the unreliability of the Jap schedules. Came the mid-afternoon and things began to happen."[6] When it became apparent that massed attacks were not going to arrive as expected, the mission planners turned their focus back to supporting the invasion forces and reducing the threat of northern enemy-held airfields. By midday, with their -1Ds racked with 1,000-pounders and drop tanks, Tomlinson's division along with another Navy Corsair division joined a dozen Hellcats, a dozen Helldivers, and fourteen Avengers of Air Group 83, all headed due north to bomb the Wan airfield on Kikai Jima. Wan was suspected of being a staging base. Enemy planes could come down from Kyushu or Korea to refuel and rearm there before aiming their pippers at the ships of the Fifth Fleet.

As half of the *Essex's* plane complement was on its way to Kikai, little did they know that the largest kamikaze raid of World War II was about to commence, a thirty-hour battle that would culminate in the deaths of hundreds of sailors and leave more ships damaged than the attack at Pearl Harbor. Seven hundred enemy planes were sent down the Ryukyu Islands chain, half of them with the mission of driving their planes into the steel of the fleet. From Japan, the largest battleship ever built was about to begin its own suicide run against the invasion fleet.

Small groups of enemy planes appeared on combat information centers' radars at midday. With the midmorning destroyer CAP returning to the steel nests for refueling, the eight Corsairs protecting the *Essex* mission to Kikai, Tomlinson's and Lt. Cmdr. Frank Patriarca's divisions, were ordered to intercept enemy planes. Their bombs were dropped, their drop tanks released, and all six Brownings were charged as they peeled away in the hunt for bogeys.

As a rampart for Carrier Group 58.3, the USS *Haynsworth* was serving on forward picket duty 12 miles ahead of the main force. "Spotting a medium[-]sized incoming raid of bogeys, we vectored our CAP onto them," reported the tin can's executive officer, Lt. Cmdr. Scott Lothrop. "Our fire control radar was locked on throughout the dogfights, but we held our fire lest we shoot down our own people."[7]

In the low cloud cover, olive-drab Zekes were spotted by the two divisions of Corsairs. Tally ho! Patriarca led the charge. The division leader, formerly a Dauntless pilot who had earned a Distinguished Flying Cross during the battle for Midway, unleashed his guns against the first bandit. Following behind, Tomlinson added lead to the attack. Scratch one Zeke. Patriarca and Tomlinson gave chase to a second bandit, with similar results. Both division leaders claimed the kills.

Second Lieutenant Harold M. Sagers.
Courtesy of Steve Sagers

The battle in the clouds was heard by the sailors at general quarters on the tin can: "The sound of dog-fight and MG [machine gun] fire was heard and could be tracked from port bow to beam. A Judy or Zeke was then seen splashed 1,500 yards on our port quarter. The sound of fire shifted onto the starboard bow, almost overhead." An enemy plane "appeared in a very steep dive, out of the clouds with two friendly Corsairs, one on each side."[8]

The Americans pushed the throttle forward to activate the water injection to close the distance to the bandit. As the kamikaze attempted to turn away from the Marine division, Tomlinson's wingman, "Mo" Sagers, had the bandit in his crosshairs. At close range he opened fire, his rounds finding purchase in the enemy plane's engine and fuselage. The Zeke hit the waves and exploded with Sagers close behind, flying through the detritus. Having burned through their fuel and ammo, the two Corsair divisions returned to the *Essex*.

But during the fight, one of the enemy planes had escaped. Aboard the destroyer *Haynsworth*, Fire Controlman Tom Scott witnessed the raider get away: "There were no impediments to our seeing to starboard. It was a low ceiling; we heard the planes above us as if they were having a dogfight . . . Zoom! Zoom! Zoom! Then 'the' plane came out of the clouds[,] heading away. . . . Then he saw us."[9]

Cmdr. Stephen Tackney maneuvered his ship so as many guns as possible could be brought to bear against the enemy plane. During the attacker's twenty-second run to the destroyer, 20 mm, 40 mm, and 5-inch guns opened fire, but it was for naught. At the last moment, the raider pulled up and drove his plane into the tin can's superstructure. The radio shack imploded as a fireball embraced the starboard side of the ship. The butcher's bill was twelve sailors dead and dozens more burned and injured. The largest kamikaze raid of World War II had taken its first victims.

Hundreds of attacks against the fleet emerged from the air over the next six hours. By day's end, twenty ships had been struck by the Divine Wind. Six of these ships were sunk. Nearly four hundred sailors were killed, while over four hundred more sailors were wounded. But Kikusui No. 1 was not over.

As aerial duels swirled in the skies of the Ryukyu Islands, a new threat emerged. Breaking from its anchorage at Tokuyama in midafternoon on the sixth, the *Yamato*, the largest battleship in the world, steamed south to destroy the American invasion forces on the west side of Okinawa. Despite her main 18-inch guns and thick armor protection, it was a suicide mission for the Imperial Japanese Navy. With the aerials attacks concentrated on wiping out the American carriers, the *Yamato* and her train did not have air cover. In a plan that was already injudicious, this was the fatal flaw.

The *Yamato* with her attending cruiser and destroyers had not traveled far before they were discovered by two American submarines positioned in the Inland Sea as night fell.

Response from Fifth Fleet commander Adm. Raymond Spruance was swift: an opposing armada of six battleships, seven cruisers, and twenty-one destroyers were sent northward to prevent the Japanese battle force from engaging the invasion forces. The Fast Carrier Task Force commander, Adm. Marc Mitscher, recalled one of his three carrier groups from its replenishment activities so they could rejoin the other two groups. The next day would be one of maximum effort, with a singular focus of sinking the *Yamato*.

At first light, *Essex* launched three divisions of F6F-5s and two divisions of F4U-1Ds. The Hellcat divisions were sent on search missions for the Japanese force. Meanwhile, the Corsairs were to station themselves at high altitude as communication relay teams 100 and 200 miles from the carrier force. Their positions allowed VHF transmissions to be relayed between the task force and their pilots. Tomlinson's division flew to the latter position, flying through thick overcast skies. Navigation, never a strongpoint for Marine fliers, proved to be their Achilles' heel as the day progressed.

At 0815, the enemy armada was discovered. Waiting for the announcement were hundreds of fighters, bombers, and torpedo bombers on the wooden carrier decks, fully gassed and armed for the long-range attack against the largest remaining jewel in the IJN's crown. The swarms commenced launching at 1000, headed northwest in groups large and small. It would be a two-and-a-half-hour journey.

In a series of attacks that started at 1232, the battleship and her attendants were under heavy air attack. In just fifteen minutes the guard ships were decimated while the *Yamato* was severely wounded as bombs, torpedoes, and strafing rounds found their mark. Back in the ships of the carrier force, the air battle was broadcast over the ships' speakers, to the glee of its listeners. A second wave of planes arrived fifty minutes later to lay waste to what remained of the armada. After another thirty minutes, the last wave of planes delivered the coup de grace as torpedoes punctured the exposed underbelly of the listing battleship. Finally, at 1423, *Yamato* capsized. Explosions from her magazines shattered the leviathan.

Meanwhile, kamikazes and bombs rained from the skies against the steel fleet around Okinawa. Just before the *Yamato* was first attacked, the carrier USS *Hancock* was bombed. Her decks and planes erupted in fire as sailors and airmen jumped into the sea to escape the conflagration. Four other warships were hit by kamikazes; 152 sailors became eligible for Purple Hearts, while an additional 104 families in America would learn of the death of their loved one and their posthumous Purple Heart medals.

While the air armadas laid waste to the enemy, Tomlinson's division battled the weather. Due to the heavy overcast, the fliers climbed higher than expected to break through the clouds. In the process of attaining their station, they entered the northern subtropical jet stream. At the time, jet streams were a little-known phenomenon, but the Japanese had been using them tactically since the previous year. In the same airspace as the Marines, the Japanese had been launching large paper balloons festooned with explosives. Traveling across the Pacific in just a few days, the balloons were designed to descend over America. At low altitudes, long fuzes ignited that detonated explosives or incendiaries. The goal was to burn American forests, depress morale, and divert resources away from the war effort. Though hundreds of the weapons of terror descended on America, their impact was low. The FBI ensured the attacks were not publicized.

Meanwhile, hours at altitude had increased fuel consumption by the Double Wasps. When finally relieved, Tomlinson's division was low on fuel and unaware they were terribly off course. Fellow VBF-83 pilot Lt. j.g. Ed Pappert followed the unfolding drama: "The marine division failed to return to the ship at the expected time. I went to the control room. There was a large circular screen on which the aircraft showed up as a lighted blip on the screen. We could see where they were. They had been blown off course about 300 miles. We could hear them talking to one another. The ship would not contact them for fear that the Japanese could locate our fleet."[10]

Unable to get a fix on the fleet, Tomlinson was offered alternate routes but finally received a final wish that was as much curse as it was blessing: "Good luck."[11] They were on their own.

Lost, Tomlinson brought the group down through the clouds. Their only choice was to ditch in enemy waters. Second Lieutenant John Garlock's plane was the first to run out of gas. It plowed into the sea, but he emerged in the pounding swells. Section leader Thomas Lewis was trying to help his wingman when he, too, succumbed to an empty fuel tank and ditched. Trying to keep his team together, Tomlinson and his wingman, Sagers, turned their mounts into the wind, dropped their flaps, and prepared to drag their tails through the wave tops.

Sagers recalled the landings:

Our division captain, Tommy Tomlinson[,] was next to ditch his plane; he got out alright [*sic*] but I could see he was having trouble getting into his raft. I crash[-]landed real close to him, thinking I would help him into his raft, in fact I was afraid for a moment I had landed right on top of him. However the sea was so rough, some waves being sixty feet high, that I was in my raft from about ten o'clock in the morning until about five that afternoon before I spotted him again.[12]

Tomlinson's Mae West hadn't fully inflated. With the temperatures of the running seas hovering around 60 degrees, he fought to stay afloat. But after a futile struggle to get into his raft, for Tomlinson, physical exhaustion and immersion in the cold saltwater seas took its toll. The malarial protozoans injected by mosquitoes in the Solomons continued to sap the pilot's strength. Hours after ditching, Sagers came to the aid of his division leader: "We both came up to the top of a big wave together[,] and I grabbed his raft. He still wasn't in his raft, but hanging onto [*sic*] the side, exhausted. He was very sick and weak[,] having swallowed a great deal of saltwater. The water was very cold and he was shaking with the chills."[13] Tomlinson's hypothermia was followed by vomiting and dehydration.

Exhausted and with just a few ounces of water left in his canteen, Sagers sought nourishment and replenishment from the survival packs: "I had been thinking of a nice steak dinner on the carrier[,] as I was very hungry[,] so decided to examine my small ration pack. Both the captain and I found our rations gone, undoubtedly some hungry sailor had helped himself to them aboard ship."[14] In actuality, the air group commander had ordered the cans of water and food stripped from the rescue packs to save weight. The Air-Sea Rescue service had become so successful (a squadron of rescue PBM Mariners were stationed south of Okinawa) that the need for these items was no longer considered essential. No one had envisioned a scenario where a division of fliers would be blown hundreds of miles off course and far from the rescue capabilities of the Fifth Fleet.

There had been no sightings of either Garlock or Lewis as the stormy day dissolved into night. Sagers recalled that "The first night on the raft was very cold. I couldn't keep dry[,] and the wind worked like a refrigeration unit on my wet clothes. When I was climbing into my raft[,] my knife had slipped out and punctured the bottom of my raft[,] and I had also lost my helmet[,] so the sun baked my head by day and the wind chilled it at night.

But, if nothing else, the twenty-two-year-old pilot was determined to survive. Periodically they fired flares from their Very guns in the vain hope they would be seen. Sagers jury-rigged his parachute into a net in an attempt to catch fish but, for his troubles, fell out of the raft. He struggled to climb back into his little boat but never let go of Tomlinson. After a seagull ventured near, the pilot turned to game hunting, but just a few feathers were the profit of his shooting. He refrained from drinking the few remaining ounces in his canteen and worked to keep Tomlinson alive: "The captain was in a semi-conscious condition by the second day[,] and it became increasingly difficult to hang onto [*sic*] his raft. I had made up my mind to hang on to him[,] however[,] even if he should die."[15]

The efforts exacted a toll both mental and physical on the pilots. Sagers initially saw a crate of cans full of stewed tomatoes bobbing on the seas. With an aversion to those victuals, he debated whether death was better than their consumption as the hallucination drifted by. His own death seemed close by:

I got very seasick and vomited so much that I lost nearly all of my digestive juices. I can remember at one time hanging my head over my raft and in my agony calling out, "Mother! Mother!" As improbable as it might seem, my mother at this very time was lying asleep at home when she suddenly sat bolt upright in bed and said, "Something is wrong with Monroe." My father tried to comfort her and told her she was just having a bad dream, but she insisted something was wrong and told him she heard me calling to her.[16]

During the second day of their ordeal, Tomlinson and Sagers agreed that a chance of rescue was impossible. "Due to the storm, our carrier wouldn't be able to estimate our position. The captain knew I was a Mormon[,] and finally he said that Mormons knew how to pray[,] and asked me if I would please pray for both of us. I had said many silent prayers and was very glad when he asked me to pray aloud. After the prayer I felt much better."[17] As on the ancient Sea of Galilee, the storm was calmed.

Sagers's relief was short lived. "The captain went unconscious and I thought he was dead. Accepting of his fate, Sagers drifted off, but when he awoke, the horizon was filled with a fleet of American ships. The mirage steamed past without pause as Sagers tried to figure out why the warships would not stop to rescue them.

Lost at sea, the second day finally ended. The vibrations of the Pratt & Whitney, the rush of the wind over the gull wings, and the radio static in the headphones had been replaced by just the lap of the raw seas against the rubber boats. The horizon was open on all sides as Sagers crouched shivering in his raft, desperately trying to hold on to Tomlinson's boat. The division leader was unconsciousness or dead, they were hundreds of miles from their last known position, adrift on stormy seas, and there had been no sighting of Lewis and Garlock. All of their flares had been launched without notice or return. They thought they were near Okinawa but in fact were 250 miles southeast of Kyushu. There lay 6,000 miles of empty Pacific Ocean between the fliers and North America. Their chance of survival was as dark as the night sky.

The hunting had been good for Cmdr. Ralph Style's boat during its third war patrol. Assigned to patrol in the Yellow Sea between China and Korea, the USS *Sea Devil* (SS-400) had expended her torpedo load against an enemy convoy on April 2. By the end of the battle, the submarine had torpedoed six ships, sunk five floating mines, and taken three Japanese sailors as prisoners on the high seas.

After fifty-six days at sea, on April 5, she was ordered to return to Midway. On patrol south of Kyushu, word was received just hours after the attack on the *Yamato* to be on the lookout for downed aviators. Three evenings later, Lt. j.g. Vernon Crosby had the watch as officer of the deck:

We were cruising along in the blackest, blackest night I can remember. All of a sudden there was this red rocket that went up right alongside of me. I was the only one up on the bridge that saw it. No one else saw it except me. I asked the captain to come up to the bridge. He asked me what I saw[,] and he asked who else saw it[,] and I said I don't think anyone else saw it. He said let's turn around and go back. So we did. Then he ordered the searchlight out on the bridge. That knocked my socks off because we were not that far from Tokyo.[18]

Styles ordered the boat to begin a search for the source of the pyrotechnics.

Day turned to night. During the second night lost at sea, Sagers noticed, "The clouds began to drift apart and I saw a star I thought was an airplane. I then heard what I thought was the motors of a plane. Excitedly I grabbed my pistol and shot a tracer bullet into the air. . . . I then fired some more straight up."[19]

With the hope that downed aviators were close, Styles ordered green stars from Very guns fired every two minutes in response to the tracer rounds from Sagers's .38 Smith & Wesson. "At this time[,] a flare shot up from the water on my right and then in a moment one on my left," reported Sagers. But initially the Marine wasn't sure who was responding, Americans or Japanese. "I was very frightened; with flares on both sides I thought I must be right in the middle of the entire Japanese fleet. I lay very quiet. I had no desire to become a Japanese prisoner."[20]

Following the exchange of tracers, the searchlight on the sub came upon the two Goodyears lashed together. "We're coming to help you, Yanks," a voice called out. "I could then see the outline of a ship and the people on deck. They looked too tall and husky for Japanese[,] so I decided to take a chance and called out to them," responded Sagers.[21]

The approaching sub threw a line out to the bent-wing drivers. Concerned that Tomlinson might not have survived, Sagers had him taken aboard first. After being told the pilot was still alive, Sagers came aboard. He told the sailors of the silent service that he could walk under his own power, but "When they let me go of me[,] I fell flat on my own face."[22]

While one section had been saved, another two pilots, Garlock and Lewis, were lost on the seas. Plans were made to search for the next thirty-six hours. Despite the risk of detection and their proximity to the shores of Japan, Cmdr. Styles had the searchlight sweep the dark while green flares were launched every fifteen minutes into the dark night.

An hour after the search had commenced, a light was spotted off the port beam. While flashing "SOS" with the flashlight, Lewis also blew the whistle attached to his life vest. Fifteen minutes later he was headed down the conning tower to rejoin his buddies. Three pilots rescued.

However, Tomlinson was suffering from shock and exposure. The sub's medical department, PhM2c Anthony Valenzuela, determined that intravenous plasma was the necessary treatment. Having never used the remedy before, Valenzuela had the XO, Lt. Ralph Pleatman, read the directions of how to insert the IV line. He administered the plasma until the Missoulan finally came around.

Eight hours into the search, the radarman detected a bogey heading toward the sub from a distance of 11 miles. No signal was detected from an IFF (identification, friend or foe) transponder. Deep in enemy waters and just 70 miles from the coast of Japan, Styles ordered the sub to crash-dive. The boat flooded its tanks and descended into the cold depths while compartments were made watertight. Sagers pondered his fate: "That first dive in a submarine was a real thrill, but I felt I might be safe[r] in the raft again than down under the water with depth charges exploding around us."[23]

Following the all-clear signal, the boat, along with other Allied subs and aircraft, started a combined search for Lt. Garlock, but their efforts were in vain. Cmdr. Styles lamented in the *Sea Devil*'s report of War Patrol Number 3:

> Searched over four hundred square miles unsuccessfully for remaining pilot. Also, with many friendly planes in vicinity and no word over VHF of sighting a Goodyear. Reluctantly decided to abandon search and resume course to Saipan. The rescued pilots seemed very doubtful that the lost pilot has been able to inflate his rubber boat. If his boat were afloat, I'm sure I would have seen it during the day. The seas were calm and there was unlimited visibility.

Self-preservation was also a factor in the sub commander's decision: "Once you're driven down the first time, why they know that you're out there.[24]

No trace of Garlock was ever found.

During the journey, the pilots shared quarters with the prisoners: a cramped torpedo room served as the makeshift bunkhouse, with the POWs handcuffed at night. Exhausted after their ordeal in the seas, "It seemed a little odd to think of sleeping with a torpedo on one side of you and a Japanese prisoner on the other, I slept wonderfully well. How wonderful it was to stretch my legs out full length after having them doubled up under my chin for so long. To me that bed was more comfortable than the finest suite in the Waldorf-Astoria," explained Sagers.[25]

Four days later, the *Sea Devil* arrived at Saipan on its journey to Midway. Cmdr. Styles reported that initially the POWs "were so scared, for two days they couldn't even eat. They thought for sure we were going to kill them."[26] The oldest prisoner was forty-five years old, the youngest just seventeen. Eventually they became accepting of their fate. The POWs pitched in and worked cleaning the sub and helping the cooks. They watched movies with the crew. They were drafted into the interservice enmity between the sailors and the pilots. S1C Hugh Radner recalled, "We taught them to say, 'Marines no good.'"[27]

Fear of leaving the sub was palpable. After receiving fair treatment during the short voyage, the Japanese sailors were unsure of their fate. "These tough[-]looking Marines came aboard, put sacks over their heads," recalled Ens. Axel Petersen.[28] "I know when the Marines in Saipan came down to take them, this one Japanese just fell flat on the deck and grabbed me by the legs. He didn't want to go with the Marines at all," recalled Cmdr. Styles.[29] After watching the POW crawling on his knees to the sub's skipper, crying all the while, Capt. Tomlinson couldn't help but wonder how things would have turned out if he had been captured by a Japanese submarine instead.

The three Marine pilots, the last survivors of the World War II's largest kamikaze attack, departed their savior. Adm. Marc Mitscher, commander of Fast Carrier Task Force 58, praised Cmdr. Styles: "Maybe it is routine for you fellows, but your rescue of our Marines is considered quite extraordinary in this Force. Many thanks." The accolades continued from VAdm. Charles Lockwood: "Well Done from Commander Submarine Pacific Fleet to Styles and his eagle-eyed crew for rescuing three Marine pilots during the night." Only one other Marine Corsair pilot would be saved by an American sub during World War II.

For the triumvirate, ahead of them lay a long series of flights to America. But for Tommy Tomlinson, who had been flying the bent-wing bird against the Japanese since 1943, the shooting war was over. Safe and onshore, he had survived the battles against the enemy and the loss of four Corsairs. For Lewis and Sagers, their brief but intense period in combat had come to a conclusion. The first night in California, the Marine pilots were still wearing their only uniform, the salt-stained khakis that had carried them across the Pacific. Word eventually got back to Commander Styles about their evening: "When we got into Midway[,] they told us, there was an officer there that had just come from San Francisco[,] and he said he'd been at the Top of the Mark the night before he left[,] and he said there were three Marine aviators in there buying drinks for anybody that had a submarine pin on!"[30]

Capt. Tommy Tomlinson was assigned to Quantico when the war ended. He earned the Distinguished Flying Cross and the Air Medal with five Gold Stars and was credited with two kills. He never was given credit for the two kills he claimed during the great kamikaze raid,

Kikusui No. 1. He commanded VMF-216 postwar. He retired as lieutenant colonel in 1959. Tomlinson passed away in 2018 at the age of ninety-six.

After landing on April 6, 1945, deckhands pulled debris from the dogfight out of 2Lt. Moe Sagers's Corsair. Sagers had the souvenir from the Zero kills fashioned into a bracelet for his wife, Carol. After Sagers's rescue and return home to Idaho, mother and son determined that the dream occurred on the same night that the Marines were lost at sea.

Cmdr. Ralph E. Styles was awarded his second Navy Cross for heroism during the Sea Devil's *third patrol. The citation highlighted the rescue of Tomlinson, Lewis, and Sagers. The* Sea Devil *received a unit commendation from the Navy. Years after the rescue, the submarine captain, Cmdr. Ralph Styles, continued to stay in touch with Sagers. Tom Lewis attended several USS* Sea Devil *reunions.*

CHAPTER 13

THE ESCAPE ARTIST

As he scanned the heavens, the warship convulsed as the guns were turned loose on the raiders above. With both the cannons and the machine guns firing, it felt as though the whole vessel would come apart. Awarded more than his fair share, luck had allowed Lohan to escape harm in the air. This time it was different: the kamikazes were targeting the ship that had saved him.

As he worked through his preflight check on Christmas Eve 1943, 2Lt. Junie B. Lohan, USMCR, could not have predicted his time behind the stick of a Corsair would routinely be interrupted by the loss of his plane. But the tale of the reverse ace began that afternoon.

VMF-112 was stationed in Santa Barbara. Back in the US from a tour flying Wildcats and Corsairs in the air wars in the Solomon Islands, the squadron was integrating new pilots into the flock. Lohan had two flights in the big bird under his belt when he took off on a training-familiarization flight.

With confidence to spare, Lohan engaged in a series of high-speed acrobatic maneuvers. After his steed failed to complete an Immelmann at 9,000 feet, "Airspeed was lost to an extent that the aircraft fell off into a normal left spin."[1] Despite his efforts to recover, the Vought dash-one went into a flat spin after falling 7,000 feet. Lohan attempted again to recover but abandoned the effort when the bird fell another 1,200 feet. He took to the silk. The twenty-three-year-old aviator survived, but his Corsair was demolished. One hundred percent pilot error was the conclusion of the investigation.

Seven months later, Lohan was part of a group of four birds returning from a cross-country navigational flight, when suddenly the section commander, Maj. Robert Cyrus Kennedy, lost altitude. Kennedy attempted to bail out of the descending plane, but his chute became entangled on the plane's tail while he was trapped in the cockpit. His Goodyear -1A crashed and exploded near Flagstaff.

Lohan and 1Lt. Randolph Smith headed for the Army airfield at Winslow to secure aid, while the fourth pilot orbited the crash site. Lohan's and Smith's Goodyears crashed on landing. The pilots were taken to the Indian Sanitarium in Winslow. Lohan was diagnosed with a concussion but was cleared to fly again.

Training continued in Southern California. After a bombing-and-strafing mission on August 27, the birds returned to the nest. Second in line to land, Lohan, flying a Brewster F3A-1, followed 2Lt. Lawrence Sowles. But as Sowles was landing, the control tower cleared a Lockheed R50 Lodestar to land on an intersecting runway. With the twin-engine plane crossing in front of him, Sowles could not clear the runway. Lohan brought his bird back onto the tarmac. Danger lay ahead.

Without a warning from the control tower, Lohan taxied his bird into Sowles's Goodyear FG-1A. The Hamilton prop dug into Sowles's plane and kept slashing until it finally stopped just behind the cockpit. Sowles barely avoided dismemberment. Lohan's prop, engine, brakes, and engine cowling were lost. Lohan's culpability was assessed at 25 percent for failing to stop his aircraft in time.[2]

As Lohan returned to Marine Air Corps Station Goleta after a mission in September, the pastor's son brought his Brewster dash-one down at a high rate of speed. His bird floated down the length of the airstrip until the wheels finally touched down with just 900 feet of surfaced runway left. Lohan locked up his brakes for the last 100 yards before hitting soft dirt. The Brewster nosed up and over. The birdcage was smashed, the engine and propeller destroyed, the fuselage buckled, and the hood, radio mast, right wingtip, stabilizer, and tires ruined. The finding was attributable to 100 percent pilot error.[3]

Alternately cursed and blessed, Lohan had completed the trifecta of destroying Vought, Goodyear, and Brewster Corsairs while still being able to walk away and tell the tales. He may have been the only marine to do so in World War II.

Lohan's adventures continued following VMF-112's entrance to the fight in the Pacific aboard the USS *Bennington* (CV-20). They were part of the first air attack against Tokyo since the Doolittle Raiders had risen from the *Hornet* three years earlier.

The fast carriers sailed into harm's way in March during raids against the Japanese home islands. Before dawn's first light on the eighteenth, the USS *Bennington* launched sixteen of VMF-112's birds for an attack on the Kanoya airfield on the southern island of Kyushu. Pilots had already manned their planes when the klaxon clanged out the alarm for general quarters. As the antiaircraft guns of the carriers and their attendants opened fire, pilots were recalled to the ready room, but two stayed topside. From the cockpits of their Corsairs, Lieutenants George Murray and Lohan watched as a Betty bomber targeted the carrier island. At the last moment, the guns found their mark and the shattered kamikaze plummeted into the sea. For Lohan, it was his first close call with a kamikaze, but it would not be the last. Far from it.

After the interruption, the flight was launched. As it approached Kanoya, the Wolfpack descended for its attack, but out of the sun came an equal amount of Zekes, Oscars, and Tojos. For thirty minutes a maelstrom of maneuvering and lead followed. The Japanese airmen were shut out. The Marines claimed nine kills and seven damaged in the air and on the ground, against no losses of their own. Lohan, recently promoted to first lieutenant, took his first blood when he flamed a Zeke after raking its left wing and tail with his Brownings.

Several days later, the Fast Carrier Task Force moved to what would become its home for almost three months: Okinawa. On the twenty-eighth, seventeen of -112's birds returned to Kanoya for a late-afternoon run on the airfield with a pack of Grumman F6Fs from the *Hornet*. Emerging out of the heavy clouds, a sole Kate torpedo bomber suddenly found itself in the same airspace as the Hellcats. Two took a run at it. Their .50s could not find purchase. Watching the contest, Lohan "pulled back on his throttle, sucked his Corsair in behind the Kate[,] and opened fire."[4] The rounds found their mark. The Nakajima B5N became a flaming comet as it hurtled toward the earth. Lohan had earned his second kill.

Another day, another -jima or -shima, another attack against an airfield along the "Kyu" chain. Four days past the invasion of Okinawa, the *Bennington* boys were back up in the air. The mission for April 5 was an afternoon strike package of thirty-eight planes targeting the airfield on Tokuno Shima, a staging base for enemy air attacks against Okinawa. Corsairs, Avengers, Helldivers, and a solitary Hellcat were launched. Each Corsair carried 5-inch rockets and a single 500-pound bomb. Word had come down that the Japanese were planning a major air attack.

After dropping his bomb and then returning to fire his rockets, Lohan returned a third time to strafe the airfield. A gunner had his Vought in the crosshairs. An oil line was severed. Smoke emanated from the cowl, and oil covered his windscreen, as Lohan turned his mount back toward the seas. He made it 30 miles before he had to put his plane down on the waves.

As soon as Lohan ditched, the Marines with the aid of VB and VT planes from Air Group 82 started their rescue procedure. One plane climbed, turned on the emergency IFF, and transmitted the message. Other planes circled Lohan, who by this time was out of the plane and in his life jacket. Almost immediately the torpedo bombers began to drop lifeboats, dye markers, and smoke lights. However, in the rough seas, the pilot lost his knife, boat pack, and parachute. Lohan had considerable difficulty sighting any of the rafts, and it was not until one fell within 20 feet that he swam to it and climbed aboard. With water temperatures in the 60s, the risk of hypothermia increased as the day wore on.

Another pilot, 2Lt. Robert B. Hamilton, left to find a destroyer. "He found the USS *Colhoun* (DD-801) with the very appropriate radio call name 'Helpmate' about forty miles from Lohan's position. He quickly transmitted the message and led the DD to Lohan."[5]

The pilot spent less than two hours on the water. "It wasn't long afterward that the mast of a destroyer appeared over the horizon. I cried with joy. They tossed me a line, pulled me toward the ship. Two men lifted me over the side. I was frozen."[6]

Lohan was the sixth pilot pulled from the seas by the destroyer. He had just minor injuries, and the ship's doctor, Lt. Byron J. Casey, gave him a clean bill of health and a shot of whiskey. After hot chow, a steaming shower, a set of clothes borrowed from an ensign, and a pair of slippers donated by the doc, getting some sleep was the next order of the day. Lohan finally hit the sack at 0130. While Lohan had escaped death once again, he was not safe.

In the dark night, the klaxon called the sailors to their battle stations. The *Colhoun* was posted to radar-picket station no. 2, just north of Okinawa. The call to arms was the beginning of a twenty-four-hour nightmare for the pilot. The largest kamikaze raids of World War II had commenced on April 6, 1945. The destroyers would suffer from the brunt of the attacks.

At 0230, three large bogey raids appeared on the radar in the destroyer's combat information center (CIC). Sailors scrambled from their racks. Ammunition was broken out from the storage lockers while sailors hustled to the magazines below deck to keep the guns fed. In the firerooms, firemen changed out the burner nozzles and brought up the steam in the four boilers. Fast and nimble, a Fletcher-class destroyer such as the *Colhoun* bristled with guns along its entire 376-foot length. It carried five 5-inch/.38-caliber guns in single mounts. These were the weapons to keep the enemy at bay. Five pairs of 40 mm Bofor antiaircraft guns were the second line of defense. They were deadly at the intermediate ranges. The last line of defense, the "Say your Hail Marys and hope they hit home" guns, were the seven 20 mm machine guns. They were quick to react but provided only minimal short-range protection. Hearing the 20s, sailors tightened the straps on their life jackets.

Every fifteen minutes for nearly four hours, small groups of planes attacked the tin can. The destroyer slowed to 10 knots to reduce its wake while crossing the "T," to allow as many guns to bear as possible against the invaders. Raid after raid was repelled.

Lohan was helpless. The machines guns he normally controlled had gone down with his plane. "You felt like you're sitting in the middle of a huge gun turret with guns firing from all angles. The whole ship shuddered as each barrage goes forth. In the rooms, light bulbs break. Glass shatters everywhere. Drawers come open, crash on the floor. The destroyer is a seaborne gun platform. The roar nearly deafens you."[7]

In the bowels of the tin can, the magazines were emptying rapidly as nearly 500 rounds of 5-inch shells had been fired against the enemy. Darkness and radar had been the destroyer's allies. Despite the onslaught against them, no enemy bombs found purchase in the steel decks and sides of the can. But dawn's early light would bring a different story.

Throughout the morning, word was received of intruders probing the invasion fleet and the fast carrier task groups. Just after the noon hour, the first kamikaze found its mark. The USS *Haynsworth* (DD-700) was on picket duty for Task Group 58.3, sailing northwest of Okinawa. It was a cloudy, dreary day at the time, and their radar picked up bogies closing fast. Two divisions of Corsairs from the *Essex* were sent to intercept the birds.

The roar of planes zooming past and machine gun fire in the low clouds were heard by the sailors on deck. Off the stern, a burning Zeke tumbled from the skies. A split second later, a Judy dive-bomber ripped from the clouds and headed over the destroyer's bow. Two bent-wing birds were hot on its tail. The gunners continued to hold fire as the destroyer maneuvered to bring the maximum number of guns to bear against the raider.

The American fliers pulled up into the clouds after the Judy. It wasn't safe on the deck for them as the tin can's guns trained on the enemy bird. With the advantage of cloud cover, the Yokosuka D4Y pilot winged his bird over and headed back to the ship. The Judy was the fastest dive-bomber in the Pacific, capable of nearly 350 mph. As the plane closed the mile to the ship, time slowed down in the eyes of the wide-eyed sailors.

First 20 mm, then 40 mm, and finally the 5-inch guns erupted. One 5-incher exploded close enough that the oversized bomb strapped to the *Suisei's* underside was knocked off. The small machine guns were finding the mark, but there was not enough time to stop the bandit. At the last second, the flaming plane pulled up and drove through a 40 mm mount before puncturing the radio shack. A churning fireball rose from the ship as the destroyer went dead in the water. The butcher's bill would be a dozen sailors killed. The largest kamikaze raid of World War II had taken its first victims.

Raids of various sizes appeared on the radars of the steel fleets. By midafternoon, the USS *Bush*, stationed on radar-picket duty west of the *Colhoun*, was the in the bull's-eye. Notified of her partner's potential demise, the *Colhoun* turned up the steam and headed at maximum speed to the assistance of the *Bush*. The combat air patrol managed by the wounded destroyer finally ran out of fuel as it fought off attackers. Reinforcements were sent in its place.

"This division of four planes did outstanding work splashing bandits right and left[,] but they[,] too, ran out of fuel and ammunition. At about 1545[,] established voice contact with 'Beaver 5[,]' who had a total of 12 planes with them. The whole area was filled with bogies[,] and this CAP encountered so many en route that a general melee developed about 12 to 18 miles to the southward of us."[8]

By 1630, the *Colhoun* and LCS(L) 64 were on station to lend assistance. The sight they found was startling: "Closed *Bush* who was dead in the water, smoking badly, and down by the stern. She still had remains of what appeared to be a Betty [bomber] on her starboard side amidships. She was being circled by a group of enemy planes, consisting of three Zekes at about angels 10, seven Vals at angels 7, and two Zekes at angels 5."[9]

The small landing-craft support ship closed the sinking destroyer to remove personnel. The *Colhoun* maneuvered to keep the swarm of raiders at bay. Eventually the LCS cast off her lines to move several thousand yards away so the triumvirate could unmask as many guns as possible against the raiders but the numbers of hornets was too great to contain.

The Navy drafted a marine when Cmdr. George Wilson had Lohan brought up to the bridge to utilize the flier's plane identification capabilities. The *Colhoun* was at flank speed. The engines made 35 knots. Wilson's gunners were giving it their all. Their fusillade brought one down, but more followed: "Jap planes were everywhere, and one started to dive on us. He came in at about 300 mph and it didn't take more than a glance to realize this guy was a suicide pilot. He was going to bring his bomb right to us—deliver it personally, giving up his life for a hit. Our gunners swung on him. Everyone else ducked for cover."[10]

Wilson ordered full left rudder to counter the Zeke. Lohan bore witness:

I was too fascinated to move an inch, I just stood by the rail and watched him come racing toward us. I wasn't afraid. Guess I wanted to see what another pilot was going to do. I reckon he couldn't hit us, but he did. He hit with a terrific whack forward of amidships. Parts of the airplane went everywhere. It tore up the deck, kindled fires . . . I don't believe I'll ever forget the noise that plane made as it came racing in. It was a horrible sound.[11]

The raider smashed across the port deck. Its engine and bomb penetrated the main deck before exploding in the after fireroom. Fire broke out topside. Lohan was pressed into service to bring the wounded down to the officer's wardroom, which doubled as an emergency treatment area and surgery. "Doc Casey and I had just begun to carry the worst cases into the wardroom for treatment when another suicide plane hit us. The ship shuddered, then plunged forward, all guns still firing."[12]

Another raider was shot down close aboard, but its belly tank broke free and smashed into the destroyer. Flames broke forth across the tin can. Ammunition stored in the 40 mm ready racks began to cook off while burning steam from the fireroom scalded victims. Damage control parties attempted to bring hoses aft from the bow, but much of the fire-fighting equipment was destroyed by the attacks.

Swirling above the wounded destroyers, the kamikazes probed for weak spots. After one hurtled downward, others waited to follow. The *Bush* absorbed another attacker on its shattered decks. Aboard the *Colhoun*, Cmdr. Wilson ordered all personnel belowdecks but the gunners. Meanwhile, Lohan's focus was momentarily lost when he thought of his new footgear issued by Doc Casey, now soaked through by the seas: "Damn it, if I don't get out of these wet slippers I'll get pneumonia."[13]

It should have been the least of his worries. In its dive, another kamikaze had the destroyer in its sights. It escaped the efforts of the surviving 40 mm crews. The plane passed through the starboard motor whaleboat before puncturing the forward fireroom. The destroyer was paralyzed when the bomb exploded above the keel. With its spine broken, a large hole punched below the starboard waterline, the boilers out of commission, and fire consuming flammable material topside, the destroyer was dying.

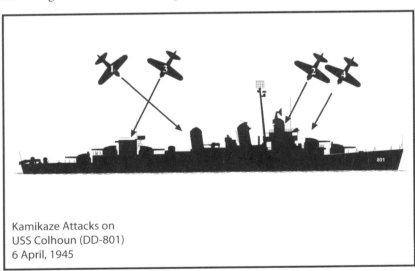

Kamikaze Attacks on
USS Colhoun (DD-801)
6 April, 1945

"We crouched with the wounded—and prayed. The plane hit directly amidships. The bomb he was carrying burst on impact[,] and there was death and destruction everywhere. Our ship was stopped dead in the water."[14] The marine could see that the tin can was punctured. "The fire rooms were the hardest hit. Only one man emerged alive from each one. You could see the horribly burned bodies floating in the blackened water. It was terrible. Awful. I gave blood plasma. The doc was everywhere."[15]

Herculean efforts were expended by the living to save the ship. Torpedoes and depth charges were jettisoned. Personnel doused fires with small, handheld CO_2 canisters. The wounded overflowed the wardroom, so the chief petty officers' quarters in the bow became a treatment area.

As a pilot, Lohan was used to the remote battles of destroying enemy airplanes rather than the up-close confines of a destroyer. "The noise, the diving planes, the barrages, the moans of the dying, the cries of the wounded and burned jarred your senses, upset your mind."[16]

As the smoke cleared, though, the tin can became a target again. Her guns were now in manual control after the electrical system had been knocked out. Communication from the gunnery officer was handled by sound power phones or sailors relaying instructions by voice. The kamikazes restarted their fatal dance. A Zeke was flamed, but a wounded Val lost her belly tank against the aft stack. Burning gasoline rained down on the decks again. As the dive-bomber sank, its bomb exploded underwater. Another hole was punctured below the *Colhoun*'s waterline. The seawater that mushroomed over the deck extinguished some of the fire. The third attacker changed targets and kamikazed the *Bush*. Another Val followed. *Bush* was struck again. "After that it was just plain hell. I thought about my wet feet, though. Thought surely I was going to catch cold. Funny how little things like that keeping buzzing through your head."[17]

The brawling continued in the heavens above as Hellcats and Corsairs chased enemy planes. On the *Colhoun*, attempts were made to stop the leaks, while topside, all nonessential weight was tossed overboard. Despite the efforts, the ship was slowly sinking, down 3 feet by the stern. *Colhoun* listed 23 degrees to starboard. "We figured we were about done for now. We got the rafts together and lashed them with rope. We wanted to be together—we wanted to be sure the stretcher cases, they were multiplying now, were going to go along with us."[18]

The maelstrom wasn't finished. This time a Japanese pilot had the American pilot in his crosshairs: "I went back to the bridge. Another suicide-mad Jap came boring in. He was aiming for the bridge. Coming like hell. I figured this one had my number. I crouched behind the bulkhead, all unnerved."[19]

A smoking Hamp fighter dived at the pilothouse. Its wing struck near Lohan before the plane flipped into the seas alongside the port beam. After his brush with death, Lohan saw his attacker again: "I stood up and looked over the side. I could see the dead Jap pilot floating by us. He was dressed in some kind of a silken robe. It had a big anchor embroidered on it. He didn't look a day over fourteen years of age."[20]

Soon after, the call went out to abandon ship. Except for a skeleton crew to stay and try and save the vessel, all remaining souls, over two hundred sailors, were evacuated to a pair of amphibious landing craft, LCS(L)s.

That ride was a nightmare. There were still plenty of Jap planes around. And we knew that if just one singled us out and dove for us—well, everyone will be killed. . . . It took hours. We couldn't turn. The LCS skipper was afraid a turn might capsize the ship. We prayed silently. We prayed aloud . . . I tried to sleep sitting down—but sleep wouldn't come. I kept seeing the Japs diving at us. I kept remembering the courage of the kids whose burned bodies we'd left behind.[21]

The *Bush* sank; eighty-seven of her crew to remain forever on duty. The *Colhoun* lost thirty-five of her ship's company. Most were teenagers who had joined the Navy just the year before. Eventually another destroyer, *Cassin Young*, delivered the coup de grace. Her

5-inchers finished what the kamikazes had started against the *Colhoun*. All told, twenty-six ships, the majority of them destroyers, were struck by kamikazes during Kikusui No. 1. Six vessels were sunk; nearly five hundred Americans were killed. Over three hundred Japanese planes were shot down by the Hellcats, Corsairs, and gunners of the 5th Fleet.

For the twenty-four-year-old Marine pilot who had escaped numerous brushes with death while flying Corsairs, the impact of his escape from kamikazes was poignant. After telling his tale to a Navy journalist and the task group's admiral, Lohan told his squadron mates this: "There's one thing I won't forget. I don't want any of you guys to forget it either—that's the courage of the men who man those destroyers out there. We owe a hell of a lot to them—more than any of us can ever repay."[22]

First Lieutenant Junie Brooks Lohan eventually made his way back to his squadron. He earned his third and final kill on May 14, when he shot down a Tony. The "Wolfpack" returned to America in June. For reverse ace, escape artist, and temporary tin can sailor, Lohan was awarded a Distinguished Flying Cross and the Air Medal with six gold stars. He passed away in 1973.

CHAPTER 14

THE HUNTERS BECOME THE HUNTED

The pilots grasped the lifelines of the seaplane tender as they surveyed the scene before them. The anchorage had become a cemetery for American warships damaged by kamikazes. Little did they realize that soon they would become the targets.

Friday, May 4, 1945: USS *Shangri La*

VBF-85 flew into battle just days after the largest kamikaze attack of World War II, Kikusui No. 1. In the two-day air battle on April 6–7, over three hundred kamikazes attacked the US Navy's Fifth Fleet. In the month that followed, nine more large kamikaze raids were launched against the steel fleets protecting the American servicemen on the Ryukyu Islands. The carriers sent regular raids against the airfields of the surrounding islands, in the hope of catching Japanese aircraft on the ground and to lay waste against the runways. North of Okinawa, Kikai Jima was a regular target for the birds of Fast Carrier Task Force 58. Lt. j.g. William H. Marr was one of four Corsair fighter-bombers sent on a mission to bomb the airfield on Kikai. Though they encountered very little AA, some found its mark. Marr was able to put 10 miles between himself and Kikai before he was forced to ditch. The impact knocked him briefly unconscious. The Goodyear FG-1D slipped quickly into the sea, taking Marr's raft pack with it. The Tennessee native inflated his Mae West and pulled the tab on a dye marker while his band of brothers circled overhead.

The call went out for the dumbo. From the Kerama Retto seaplane base southwest of Okinawa Jima, two Martin PBM Mariners from Rescue Squadron 3 (VH-3) were flying on standby, ready if the need called for an open-sea rescue.

Crowded skies resulted as the Allies tightened the noose around the Japanese home islands: large formations of B-29s flew from Guam and Tinian; B-24 Liberators flew from Guam, and their fraternal twins, Navy PB4Y Privateers, were flying out of Iwo Jima, Tinian, and Okinawa; massive PB2Y Coronado seaplanes flew patrols, strikes, and tracking missions from Kerama Retto. From the same anchorage, Martin PBM Mariner patrol-bomber squadrons were sent on day and night patrols to attack enemy warships, freighters, and bomb targets. PV-1 Venturas from Tinian also flew patrol and bombing missions. Finally, Fast Carrier Task Force 58 had been on station east of Okinawa since late March. With upward of a thousand single-engine fighters, torpedo planes, and dive-bombers, they, too, filled the skies over the Ryukyus.

The rescue squadrons (VH) filled a gap with their PBMs in the Navy's recovery efforts of its downed pilots. Destroyers saved the lion's share of pilots who crashed near the carriers, but their effective range was limited. Lifeguard submarines were on station during large strikes but were forced underwater whenever suspected enemy aircraft were in the area. Like the destroyers, their range was limited.

The little Vought OS2U Kingfishers carried on the sterns of cruisers and battleships were not designed for open-sea rescues. Their brave pilots did rescue a dozen Corsair pilots from Fast Carrier Task Force 38/58, but each landing and takeoff was dangerous. The PBY Catalinas that saved many airmen in the Solomons and other theaters had primary missions of search, transport, and bombing enemy targets. They operated from fixed bases. Open-sea rescue missions were never their primary role, especially since the Cats were prone to damage during ocean landings.

Before the invasion of Okinawa Jima, the lightly defended Kerama Retto was captured from the Japanese. Just 30 miles southeast of Okinawa, the protective anchorage served as a seadrome. Several VPB (patrol-bomber) PBM squadrons arrived in its lagoon two days later, along with their seaplane tenders. And for the first time, Rescue Squadron (VH) Mariners brought dedicated open-sea rescue capabilities to the fight. It marked a new era in air-sea rescue.

The Martin Mariners were large birds. Gull winged with twin tails, the double-decked seaplane was distinctive. Compared to the PBY, the PBMs were substantially larger and faster. The Mariner's deeper hull made it more suitable for open-sea rescues than the Cats.

Their engines also sat higher and farther back from the bow than those of the PBYs, which commonly lost props and engines during open-sea rescues. The squadron's PBMs were well suited for open-sea rescues. And unlike the Cats, their hulls did not leak or sustain structural failure during these landings. The VH-3 pilots were all former PBY pilots.

By May, VH-3 had upgraded to PBM-5 models, which replaced the two Wright Cyclone engines found in the older Model 3 with a pair of the more powerful Pratt & Whitney R-2800 Double Wasps like those found in the Corsairs.

Since their only mission was air-sea rescues, VH-3 regularly rehearsed rescue drills. Stripped of combat gear, they were stockpiled with rescue equipment: life rafts, shipwreck kits, food kits, signal kits, Gibson Girls radios, float lights, smoke lights, medical litters, medical kits, and parachute flares. Special ladders were designed to be hoisted over the side to help waterlogged pilots to get on board. The PBMs were long-legged birds and could easily stay on station over a downed pilot until rescue occurred.

Their goal was to facilitate rescue but not necessarily to be the rescuer. If at all possible, surface craft would be directed to pull the downed pilots from the sea. But, failing that, the larger bent-wing birds would set down on the seas if possible.

The VH-3 PBMs did not fly alone. Rescue combat air patrols escorted them.

The Navy had experimented with jet-assisted takeoff (JATO) units on Corsairs during January 1945 over several days on the USS *Bunker Hill*. "They worked," recalled 1Lt. Philip Wilmot of VMF-451. "But it took so long for the smoke to clear from the deck that they weren't practical. We never used them in combat."[1]

But for the PBMs, JATO proved its ability to get the large birds off the ocean and into the air every time. Takeoff times were reduced to under ten seconds when the minirockets were used, thus limiting the chances of damage when compared to long, open-sea takeoffs that Catalinas faced.

Rescue 10 Miles from Kikai Jima

The rescue of Lt. j.g. William Marr started with a hitch. After becoming airborne, an escape hatch on the VH-3 PBM blew off and injured a crew member. The pilot, Lt. Robert S. Dorton, had to return to the seadrome to exchange PBMs. Delayed by the accident, Dorton flew onto Kikai Jima. Orbiting Corsairs guided him to Marr, who was held above the waves by just his life vest.

After landing on the Pacific, Dorton shut down one engine as the PBM slowly taxied toward the pilot floating in a patch of dye. A sea anchor was dropped on the opposite wing to keep the plane from traveling in circles. Floats extended down from the wings to keep the seaplane on an even keel. A rescue ladder was attached to the side from an open hatch. When Marr missed the life ring hurled to him, a crew member jumped into the sea and swam out to the pilot. Marr was quickly brought aboard. Hatches near the tail opened as crewmen swung the JATO racks out on both sides of the rear fuselage. Two JATO rockets were loaded on each side.

Dorton restarted the engine that had been shut down, and brought the bird into the wind. He pushed the throttles forward. Pratt & Whitney R-2800 engines pulled the PBM-5 across the waves. As the Mariner crested a swell, Dorton pushed a button atop the yoke. The mighty bird jumped into the air as the JATO roared. Ninety minutes after he entered the water, Marr was airborne again. His elation after the rescue would be short lived.

Kerama Retto

The anchorage had become a graveyard. Over four weeks, five large kamikaze suicide raids had targeted the US Navy in Okinawan waters. As Dorton flew between the hilly islands to land, the destruction rained upon the Fifth Fleet was apparent. Broken ships, especially destroyers, were moored around the anchorage. What was left of the USS *Aaron Ward* (DD-486) had slipped in the day before. It appeared that kamikazes had beaten her with mighty hammers: most of her deckhouse was gone, as were the gun director towers, the torpedo racks, and many other gun emplacements. One funnel was completely missing, the other eviscerated. She was barely afloat.

Other warships were victims of Kikusui No. 5: The destroyer-minelayer USS *Shea* (DM-30) limped into the anchorage. Earlier that morning, an Ohka suicide rocket had slammed into her superstructure. Later that evening, the wounded USS *Ingraham* (DD-694) steamed into Kerama Retto following a kamikaze attack. Two other destroyers, the USS *Luce* (DD-522) and the USS *Morrison* (DD-560), did not make it that far. They sank in the Pacific as a result of the explosions from the kamikazes. Two Landing Ship Medium (Rockets) also slipped beneath the waves. The ships wounded in the day's attack that could still fight stayed at sea. By 2400 hours, 472 officers and sailors of the Fifth Fleet had died from the day's kamikaze attacks.

PBM rescue, 1945. Note that starboard engine has been turned off before the pilot is brought aboard.

Marr was transferred to the tender USS *St. George*. There, he was given the once-over by the seaplane-tender's doctor. Medicinal whiskey was issued as a standard remedy for overcoming the loss of one's plane. Marr had the opportunity to rest, shower, and get some chow.

The night was marred by the call to general quarters. The anchorage itself had been a regular target during the five weeks the PBM squadrons had been assigned there. Flying kamikazes came by day; suicide swimmers and boats came by night. Jumpy sailors on deck fired Thompson submachine guns at anything that might be a potential threat. A quarter moon shined on the anchorage, so smoke was laid across the harbor to hide the ships from heckler flights.

Midmorning, May 5, 1945

A day after Kikusui No. 5 brought 160 kamikazes to the Ryukyus, a division of bent-wing birds were sent from the *Shangri La* to suppress further kamikaze flights from Kikai Jima. Each plane carried a 500-pounder. Each wing carried two 5-inch HVARs on the rails.

Arriving an hour later, the birdmen found the runways were substantially cratered by previous attacks. In glide runs, they toggled their iron from 1,500 feet and then turned to launch their rockets against revetments and an AA emplacement. While the airfield lacked planes, its gunners did not lack experience. The duel between .50-caliber and 20 mm guns was won again by the Japanese. Two of the four Corsairs fled the attack, metal skin and engines punctured by shrapnel. They did not get far.

Already at low altitude when they were hit, the fighter-bombers made it only a few miles offshore before they hit the water. Lt. j.g. Owen Payne and Lt. j.g. Leonard Welch scrambled out of their sinking birds, took to the rafts, and watched as Cmdr. W. Sherrill, the Carrier Air Group 85 commander, circled above. The forth Corsair climbed to a higher altitude to turn on its IFF. Another call for the dumbo was sent.

From Kerama Retto, a VH-3 Mariner broke with the water and headed northeast. Its pilot, Lt. Edgar Palm, landed the PBM 3 miles offshore to recover Lt. Payne and then taxied another mile to pull Lt. Welch from the seas without incident. The Corsairs provided escort for the bigger bent-wing bird before finally returning to the steel nest with just a couple dozen gallons of fuel left in their tanks.

After returning to Kerama Retto, Payne and Welch were transferred to the seaplane tender USS *St. George* (AV-16). Another pilot from the *Shangri La* arrived too. Lt. j.g. Frank Siddal was shot down in a dogfight over Okinawa when the 20 mm cannons on his F4U-1C froze. The contingent from Air Group 85 had grown to four.

Plans were made for their eventual return to the *Shangri La*. Until that time, they endured numerous calls of the klaxon horn to general quarters as more threats emerged. The "flash red" alerts continued through the night.

Sunday, May 6, 0832 Hours: USS *St. George*

Another "flash red" alert was received. On board the tender, gunner's mates, loaders, and pointers hurried to the ten 40 mm and sixteen 20 mm mounts, and the two 5-inch/.38-caliber guns. As ammunition was broken out of lockers, the sailors stood ready. They had proven their talent just a week earlier when a Suisei D4Y dive-bomber targeted the moored ship. At the last second, a 5-inch round with a proximity fuse exploded just ahead of the Judy. Ship saved.

Fourteen minutes after the klaxon screamed out its alarm, fire was commenced against a kamikaze closing from 10,000 yards out. First the 5-inch guns roared, then the 40s. Vibrations shook the hull. The firing from the 20s at short range was desperate. Despite the wall of lead and explosives sent forth against it, the Japanese raider managed to penetrate the screen before crashing through the starboard-side seaplane deck near the crane. Three sailors were killed immediately. Dozens more were injured.

Without a battle station, the kamikaze hunters had stayed belowdecks in their stateroom. Welch and Marr were sitting on their bunks, exchanging their rescue tales, when fire punctured the compartment. From the hell of conflagration, Welch was engulfed in flames. He beat them down with his hands while suffering second-degree burns in the process. Marr's uniform was on fire too. Despite the burns on his hands, Welch beat out the blaze on Marr's clothing.

With severe burns to his hands and face, the Idaho native Welch was transferred with other wounded sailors to the USS *Gosper* for medical care. The attack transport had recently been converted into a casualty evacuation transport. Complete with surgical suites and a full medical staff, its medical department took charge of the wounded men. Many of the men were charred black; skin dangled from limbs between shredded pieces of clothing. They suffered from shrapnel wounds, fractured bones, and concussions.

The seriously wounded were administered the new antibiotic, penicillin, along with as much plasma and saline as could be tolerated. Burns were covered with petroleum jelly. Morphine was injected without hesitation, while brandy was provided liberally for consumption. Open wounds were coated with sulfa powder. Despite the ghastly wounds and burns, Welch and all the other evacuees survived as much from medicine as from "the diligence and faithfulness of the corpsmen."[2]

Their stay on the *Gosper* was short. The next day the destroyer USS *Charles S. Sperry* retrieved the pilots. They were returned to the *Shangri La* on May 8. The hunters returned to the hunt.

Left to right: Siddal, Payne, Welch, and Marr. Note bandages on Welch's head and hand. *Courtesy of Lt. j.g. Dave Lawhon, VF-85*

VH-3 rescued 183 airmen during the war during seventy-six open-sea landings. Rescue by the VH squadrons' PBMs proved to be the most-effective means of recovering airmen in the Pacific during World War II.

Lt. Robert S. Dorton, the VH-3 pilot who had rescued Lt. j.g. Marr, was awarded the Navy Cross for a rescue performed on June 2, 1945. A PB2Y Coronado capsized while attempting to rescue a VBF-9 pilot who had ditched in Kagoshima Bay, Kyushu. Dorton landed in rough water just a half mile from land. Though under fire the entire time on station, Dorton was able to bring them all home. Lt. j.g. William Marr was killed the same day. His F4U-1C spun in during takeoff from the Shangri La. *Marr drowned while attempting to swim to the rescue-destroyer USS* Mertz *(DD-691). He was one of nine pilots who died during VBF-85's deployment.*

CHAPTER 15

SEABORNE SAVIOR

Ducking low in his little raft, the pilot tried to paddle away from the island as fast as he could. A cacophony of gunfire filled his ears. Shore batteries were walking bullets up the waves toward him. In return, Corsairs were strafing the beach. Over his head, automatic-weapons fire from the sea targeted the island. Closing the distance to him was Landing Craft Support 11, the seaborne savior of downed Corsair pilots in the waters off northern Okinawa.

USS LCS(L)(3)-11. *National Association of USS LCS(L)*
1-130 photo

Guns per ton, there were no more heavily armed US Navy ships in World War II than the Landing Craft Support (Large) (Mark 3) warships. They were puny vessels, even compared to destroyers or destroyer escorts, but they packed a wallop. Designed to provide fire support during amphibious invasions, the "mighty midgets," as they came to be known, were slow but deadly. They carried two pairs of twin 40 mm guns, one positioned forward and another aft. Four Oerlikon 20 mm and four Browning M-2 .50-caliber heavy machine guns were positioned amidships. Ten rocket launchers added to their punch. A 3-inch/.50-caliber dual-purpose gun on the bow filled out the offensive capabilities. Their flat hulls and shallow draft allowed them to be close to the shore. They could be beached if necessary.

At just 158 feet long, with a beam less than 24 feet, their small size allowed the mighty midgets to be quickly and inexpensively built. They were expendable. The Navy didn't bother to name them. The little gunships were pressed into service in a role unimagined at the start of the Okinawa campaign: first defenders against kamikaze raids.

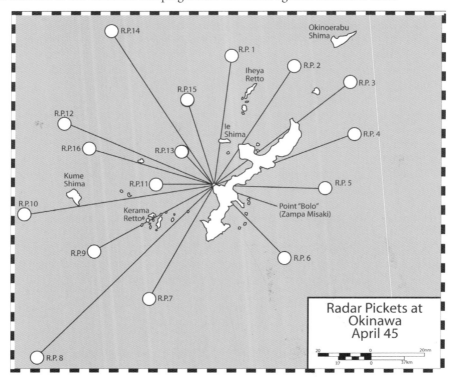

Radar-picket positions

The kamikazes had unleashed their terror in late October 1944 against the US Navy steaming east of the Philippines. The attacks continued through early January 1945 with the invasion of Luzon. In response to American carriers being forced to withdraw due to damage, Marine Corsair squadrons were attached to Air Group 4 on the USS *Essex* (CV-9) beginning in early 1945. Their top speed and rate of climb bested the vaunted Hellcats.

Kamikaze raids during the invasion of Iwo Jima were relatively light, but the Navy's brass had no illusions this would remain the situation with Operation Iceberg, the invasion of Okinawa. Both Marine and Navy Corsair squadrons filled the hangars of seven fleet carriers.

To provide defense against enemy air raids, traditional and kamikaze, a network of radar-picket positions were set up surrounding Okinawa Jima. Destroyers manned these ramparts. Each had a fighter-director team to control its own combat air patrol. The missions were known as "target CAPs." By the end of April, six additional Marine Corsair squadrons were stationed on the captured Okinawan airfields at Kadena and Yontan. Their inverted gull wings made them easier to identify by the trigger-happy gunner's mates.

First Lieutenant Philip Wilmot of VMF-451 (USS *Bunker Hill*) recalled, "The northern radar-picket positions were the most dangerous. They were the first ships seen by the kamikazes as they came down from Kyushu."[1] No truer words were spoken. Kamikaze attacks against the Fifth Fleet began before the first marine had stepped foot on Okinawa. These initial small attacks were dwarfed by the start of the *kikusui* series of massed attacks beginning on April 6, 1945. Twenty-six American warships were struck. Seventeen of these were either destroyers or destroyer-minelayers, including the destroyers at radar-picket positions 1 and 2. Despite the CAP, the northern pickets were under constant pressure. Many tin cans were sunk. The anchorage at Kerama Retto filled with damaged destroyers. "We were being briefed for a target CAP mission one morning," said Wilmot. "I asked if we would be covering a destroyer again that was code-named 'dormouse.' 'No,' I was told. 'Dormouse is dead.'"[2]

Traditional and kamikaze raids during March and early April forced three carriers with four Corsair squadrons to withdraw for major repair. It was apparent that the ramparts needed reinforcement. Multiple destroyers were positioned at some of the picket positions. Their guns were supplemented by the firepower of LCS(L)(3) ships.

They were odd couples. Destroyers were eight times the tonnage of the support ships. The greyhounds of the sea could steam at twice the speed of an LCS. But the tin cans were bigger targets too.

What the mighty midgets brought to the dance was their weaponry and first-responder damage-control capabilities. They could generate smoke to screen damaged ships, lay water on fires, rescue sailors from the sea, and evacuate casualties. Further, they provided pumps, air pressure and electric power, and medical supplies to wounded cans when necessary.

The ramparts needed reinforcement. On the second day of the largest kamikaze attack of World War II, Kikusui No. 1, LCS-11 was sent to reinforce the ramparts at radar-picket position 12. Five days later, nearly five hundred enemy planes flew against Allied forces during Kikusui No. 2. The guns of LCS-11 brought down a Val dive-bomber. A Japanese battle flag was painted on the conn. But an LCS at another RP was one of the two ships sunk by kamikazes. Nine more warships were damaged.

Kikusui No. 3 commenced on April 16. Once again, massive enemy air forces appeared throughout the day and evening. Fast Carrier Task Force 58 was prepared. Its TBFs and SB2Cs remained in the hangar decks with wings folded as the fighters responded to numerous attacks that occurred throughout the day.

It was a turkey shoot: 155 planes were shot down by the American fighters. The enemy birds were easy prey; the kamikaze pilots had minimal flight training, and their planes were outclassed by the American planes. Radar often provided early warning of their flights. Eleven Hellcat pilots became aces. American flying losses were light. Nine planes did not return; six pilots were lost.

From the Kadena airfield, VMF-322 sent Corsairs forth on fourteen CAP missions. One of its early missions was over RP12, when the fighter director aboard the destroyer USS *Cowell* vectored them to intercept bogies approaching from the northeast. In the ensuing air battle, two Vals were destroyed, but a CAP pilot was forced to bail out of his Corsair.

The *Cowell* was underway to rescue 2Lt. John H. Peterson but was diverted to RP14 to assist in the fighting there. The rescue mission was reassigned to LCS-11. The little gunboat saved the pilot on a day where six warships, including two other LCS ships, were damaged and the destroyer USS *Pringle* was sunk at RP14.

LCS-11's routine became one of many days of service on the picket line before returning to Hagushi Bay for a few days. Then, after fuel, provisions, and ammo were taken aboard, the mighty midget returned to radar-picket duty.

April 28, 1945

Though it was Saturday, there was little to distinguish the day from any other day of the week except the XO's "Plan of the Day," typed and posted by the yeoman. The red alerts kept coming; the sailors on the tiny warship kept manning their battle stations. The skies continued to fill with enemy vultures. From their vantage point on the RP line, sailors aboard the "Lucky Eleven" could often see attacks against other radar-picket positions. Enemy planes out of the range of its batteries were tracked.

Midafternoon, the *Bunker Hill* sent VMF-221 Corsairs aloft for the target CAP. After taking station over the picket ships, they were vectored toward incoming bogies closing from the north at angels 25. Jettisoned external tanks marked the "Fighting Falcons" path. They encountered Zekes flying in smaller groups. The battle was on, fifteen Corsairs versus thirty Zekes. The final score was lopsided: fourteen kills and one probable for the Marine pilots against just one loss.

First Lieutenant Earl W. Langston was leading a division of three Corsairs toward a group of five enemy fighters when he was jumped from above. Enemy tracer rounds were his first indication that he was in trouble: "I instinctively pushed over into a dive to escape my unknown assailant, only to discover two Japanese 'Val' dive[-]bomber[s] and one "Zeke" fighter escort about 2,000 feet below me[,] diving toward our fleet of ships. Their mission, in all probability, was a kamikaze attack. These pilots were so intent on their suicidal missions that they were completely unaware of my presence, thereby making my task relatively simple."[3] After shooting down the Vals, Langston targeted the Zeke. His rounds passed beneath the Mitsubishi. Alerted to Langston's presence, the lithe fighter pulled up into a steep climb. Langston followed, thus committing a major mistake: "By doing so I violated one of the cardinal rules given us by our squadron command: Never dogfight with a Japanese fighter."[4]

In a few seconds the enemy pilot was able to turn and bracket Langston's bird. The rounds hit home. Langston pulled the stick, only to find that his plane was stuck in an inverted position as it rapidly descended toward the sea. "I jettisoned the canopy, released my safety belt[,] and fell free of the plane, falling headfirst for the ocean below."[5] Without waiting to become upright, he pulled the D handle. The rapid bloom of the chute jerked the inverted pilot upright.

Langston initially blacked out. But as he regained consciousness, he discovered that the enemy pilot was intent on finishing the job. His life was hanging by threads. Langston endured two strafing runs, the second so close he had to pull his knees to his chest to avoid amputation. He prayed for his survival. The Zeke banked and came back for a third run: "By this time all my strength was gone—I hung limp in my chute and accepted my fate. At the completion of this run[,] he evidently discharged me as dead because he flew away happily rocking his wings."[6] Langston landed in the sea and took to his raft.

The prayers for survival by the preacher's son had been answered, but he would be tested again.

LCS-11 continued steaming at the tip of the spear, RP1. She was relieved midday to recover Langston. Sailors in the whaleboat hauled in their catch, a sore but grateful Marine pilot. Raids continued against the northern approaches. Steaming by herself in no-man's waters, LCS-11 was caught off guard by a low-flying *Nate* fighter. Without surrounding fire support from other ships, she just had seconds to engage the kamikaze. The .50-caliber Brownings took the first shots, quickly followed by the 20 mms and then the Bofors 40 mm as the little gunship took a hard turn to port to unmask its guns. "When the command was given, I thought the radios would shake off the bulkheads in the radio shack," recalled Lawrence B. Smith. "I could feel the vibrations of the ship and hear the roaring of the guns."[7]

In the last seconds before impact, one of the plane's wings broke off. The fighter careened into the sea just 30 yards from LCS-11. Shrapnel and aviation fuel scattered across the decks. The only casualty was the enemy pilot, but the Marine pilot Langston was topside during the attack. According to Smith, Langston "had been crouching behind our rear deck housing. After it was over, he emerged a shaken man and said to us, 'My God, get me another airplane so I can get back up where it's safe.'"[8] The captain invited Langston to the wardroom for some "medicinal" rum. Another Japanese flag was painted on the conn.

Getting Langston back to the *Bunker Hill* was an exercise in logistics. He was transferred from ship to ship to ship before finally arriving aboard the seaplane tender USS *St. George* at Kerama Retto. A TBF was sent to fetch Langston on May 4, 1945. He and fellow VMF-221 pilot 1Lt. Walter Goeggel (who had been rescued by an OS2U Kingfisher from the USS *Astoria* earlier that morning) were returned to the *Bunker Hill*. With a back injury from the poor bailout, Langston was transferred to sick bay. The preacher's son was trapped there when two kamikazes hit the carrier on May 11, 1945. He eventually escaped unharmed from that attack.

First Lieutenant Earl Langston. *Courtesy of Col. Dean Caswell, USMC (Ret.)*

Another turkey shoot started early, when the Japanese unleashed Kikusui No. 5 on May 4. Sixty-one enemy planes were downed by Corsairs. Four of these pilots became aces.

LCS-11 was on patrol with LCS-19 just north of the northernmost tip of Okinawa. About 3 miles northwest of them were the destroyers *Massey* and *Lowry*, steaming between stations 2 and 3. From a group of six enemy planes, four attacked the destroyers while a pair dove toward the two LCSs. One plane came in high, the other low. The "Lucky Eleven" sprayed fire and knocked down the low-flying Nate. It crashed 50 yards astern of the ship. The second kamikaze then made a run toward the destroyers, but the target CAP from the *Shangri La* had arrived. A Corsair ended the kamikaze's mission. That evening a third Japanese flag was painted on the conn, but not until the "Lucky Eleven" rescued another pilot.

Lt. j.g. Saul Chernoff was one of twelve VF-85 pilots flying F4U-1Cs vectored to intercept large groups of bogies. Two divisions battled Zekes at 17,000 feet. Chernoff reported:

We went on a vector for about ten minutes when Ensign E. L. Myers, USNR, my wingman [Eugene L. Myers], spotted the bogeys behind us and above. I immediately gave the lead and followed. About a mile from the bogey[,] which appeared to be a large group of Zekes in two formations, Ens. Myers pressed home his attack. I don't believe he saw the second formation as he made his attack on the first group. I saw he would be in a very bad way from the second group, so I made an attack on them.[9]

Chernoff was fortunate that he was the only pilot who had all four cannons working. Three other Corsairs had frozen guns. The Hispano-Suiza AN/M2 20 mm autocannons were never as reliable as the Browning .50-caliber machine guns found in the -1D models. Chernoff fought on, unaware that the other pilots had disengaged: "It was a low[-]side attack, coming from underneath. I don't believe they saw me[,] as no evasive action was taken. I gave a short burst to the lead plane[,] and his port wing came off and he spun in. Still coming up, I gave a short burst to the second plane[,] and he blew up. I skikked to one side and came down in another run on two more planes. They started evasive action, making a hard turn to port. I fired about three bursts on the second man[,] and he, also, blew up. I closed on the first but couldn't turn inside of him."[10]

After initiating his attack, Chernoff failed to jettison his belly tank. It worked against him when dogfighting the more maneuverable Mitsubishis: "At that time[,] I looked behind and saw three Zekes on my tail so immediately did a split 'S.' Going down[,] I was hit and my engine was smoking very badly and oil completely covered the windshield. My oil pressure started dropping and then my prop governor went out."[11]

Chernoff was forced to shut down the engine. As he glided south, he called out his mayday and turned the IFF setting to "emergency." Two of his "Sky Pirates" comrades escorted him down before he ditched. "There was quite a jar[,] but I didn't receive any injury. My life raft, which I had loosened in the air, fell to the bottom[,] and I couldn't get it out so jumped into the water with just my Mae West."[12] The other two Corsairs stayed on station to guide LCS-11 until they were relieved by a VBF-85 division. After two and a half hours, the seaborne savior arrived to save Chernoff. Another VF-85 pilot, Lt. j.g. Frank Siddal, was rescued by a Martin PBM.

The "Sky Pirates" claimed fourteen kills, thus preventing carnage at the radar-picket position 2. The *Lowry* suffered two killed in the action, but at other positions, two destroyers and two Landing Ship Medium (rockets), LSM(R)s, were sunk. Three other destroyers were struck by kamikazes. An LCS on picket duty was damaged. It proved to be one of the deadliest days for the sailors manning the radar-picket sites. By days end, nearly eight hundred sailors qualified for Purple Heart medals. Half of them would be awarded posthumously.

May 6, 1945

The soldiers and marines on the ground were into their fifth week of fighting. Their campaign would slog on for six more weeks. But for the Navy and Marine pilots, it was a relatively quiet day. No massed kamikaze raids appeared on the radar screens. No warships were struck by enemy planes. Corsair squadrons flew ground support flights, attacked airfields on the Sakishima Islands, and flew various CAPs. The radar-picket CAPs had been beefed up following Kikusui No. 5. LCS-11 was on its sixth straight day of picket duty as it guarded RP 2 with LCS-19 and two destroyers.

Maj. Edward F. Cameron of VMF-322 was flying a CAP mission between radar-picket positions 2 and 3 when rounds impacted his Corsair. As he struggled to maintain control of the damaged bird, another Corsair dove past completely out of control. The second Corsair crashed into the sea. Second Lieutenant George S. Karl of VMF-312, who had mistakenly identified Cameron's plane as the enemy, never emerged.

The "friendly fire" had fatally damaged Cameron's plane. Kadena airfield was too far. Instead Cameron turned toward Yoron Jima and took to the silk, under the impression that he had been downed by a Zero.

Sailors topside on LCS-11 saw Cameron's plane crash and the blossoming parachute. They were directed to rescue the pilot. But the Japanese on Yoron had seen Cameron too. Just a half mile from the beach, small-arms fire erupted from the island as Cameron climbed into his raft. LCS-19 stood ready nearby to provide support fire. The destroyers *Massey* and *Lowry* steamed 2.5 miles offshore, their guns trained toward the island.

To rescue the pilot, the gunship had to close the beach. LCS-11 radioman Lawrence Smith recalled, "When we approached the shore, we saw Japs running to a boat in an apparent attempt to get the pilot, who, in his little bright-orange raft, was paddling toward us as hard as he could. We fired on the beach to give him cover, setting several dwellings on fire with tracers from our guns."[13]

Cameron was caught in the crossfire. The 20 mm and 40 mm rounds screamed overhead as enemy rounds splashed near him. Four Corsairs dove toward the beach, spraying their 0.50 cal. rounds before pulling up and circling around for another strafing run.

The overwhelming fire support eliminated the threat against Cameron. With its shallow draft, LCS-11 was able to get in close to rescue the pilot. Cameron seemed surprised by the response he had initiated, having believed that "Yoron Jima looked like a friendly little island, so he tried to pancake there."[14] By evening, Cameron was back on Okinawa.

Her crew called the USS LCS(L)(3)-11 "The Lucky Eleven." She brought them through the war unscathed. Just 189 Navy and Marine Corsair pilots were shot down in air-to-air combat during World War II. Incredibly, four of these Corsair pilots were lucky enough to be rescued by the same unlikely seaborne savior.

CHAPTER 16

DEATH OF THE ACES: KAMIKAZES AGAINST THE BUNKER HILL

Open Letter to a Carrier Pilot (from a Battleship Sailor)

Blessings on you, little man
Fly, fly boy, with coat of tan,
Though still damp behind the ears,
Actions count far more than years.
We were just an also-ran.
You, who rogered TOJO SAN,
May you in your hour of need
Never lose your flying speed!

Sea-bound sailors, we have gone
To our stations in the dawn,
Watched you rise at break of light,
Watched your plane limp home at night.
Angels orbit 'round your sack!
We appreciate you, Mac!

You, when we were in our sacks,
Kept the bogies off our backs,
And, (Uah, Sharlie, ve vos dere)
Combed the Bettys from our hair.
So when we return from sea
Fly, fly boy, have one on me!

Uncle Sugar's in your sights.
Happy days! (and happy nights).
May your whiskey all be Bond,
Only ground you with a blonde.
Fortune, watch this little guy
As he watched us from the sky,
And whatever he's about,
Keep him flying! Roger. Out!

—*The Monument,* USS *Bunker Hill* newsletter, 1945

By early May 1945, the USS *Bunker Hill* (CV-17) with Fast Carrier Task Force 58 had been patrolling the waters east of Okinawa for seven weeks. Her squadron complement was an unusual mix: sixty-three Corsairs for the three fighter groups—one Navy (VF-84) and two Marine (VMF-221 and -451). The bombing and torpedo squadrons brought fewer birds to Air Group 84 so that there would be more room for Vought's best. In addition, VF-84 had ten Hellcats for night and photo missions. The Corsairs were carried as kamikaze killers, a response to the attacks that commenced in 1944 over the Philippines. Their rate of climb and speed bested the Hellcats. They provided coverage in an assortment of combat air patrol (CAP) roles as well as serving as fighter-bombers during sweep and strike missions up and down the Ryukyu Islands.

Though the Navy wanted the Corsairs on the carriers, there was a gap of combat-ready Navy squadrons in early 1945. As a plug, Marine squadrons began to fly from the carriers for the first time. They were rushed through carrier qualifications. From attacks on the Japanese home islands, the invasion of Okinawa, and suppression of Japanese air attacks from the Ryukyu Islands, the hunting had been good.

Each flight was logged in the pilot's personal Aviators Flight Log Book, a small book issued by the Navy. Records of date, aircraft, hours flown, and comments were logged. At the end of the month, the squadron flight officer would sign off on the accumulated tallies. The little brown books became an extension of the pilots' identities. "Your logbook was everything," recalled 1Lt. Philip "Pots" Wilmot. "Nobody knows anything. Nobody remembers anything, and you never saw your gun film."[1]

During World War II, 371 Navy pilots became aces—a pilot who had five air-to-air combat kills. The Marines added another 118 members into that fraternity. On his initial combat mission, Wilmot and his section leader were credited with half a kill each when they shot down a Jake floatplane over Tokyo. Half of a Japanese rising-sun flag was drawn in red ink in each pilot's logbook for February 16, 1945. The path to glory as an ace seemed promising. Wilmot believed that "Hey, this is going to be easy!"[2] As luck would have it, this was his only score of the war, but the ranks of aces within Air Group 84 grew with the steady weeks of combat.

Air Group 84 had sixteen aces. VMF-451 "Blue Devils" senior pilots included two aces. Maj. Archie Donahue with fourteen kills to his credit. He was an "ace in a day" on April 12, when he downed five Japanese planes. Maj. Trigger Long had ten kills. In the next ready room was VMF-221 "Fighting Falcons." Medal of Honor recipient Capt. James Swett had added one kill to his South Pacific tally for a score of 15.5. Capt. Bill Snider, who was already an ace from his time in the Solomons, became the Marine's first carrier-based ace. His 6.5 kills during his time on the *Bunker Hill* brought his tally to 11.5. Two more of the "Fighting Falcons" captains earned "acedom," but a pair of rookies were proficient too. First Lieutenant John McManus notched six kills and the self-described dangerous 2Lt. Dean Caswell had blasted seven enemy planes from the skies.

The Navy boasted eight aces within the ranks of VF-84, the "Wolf Gang." The squadron had been built around a core group of ten fliers from VF-17, the first Navy fighting squadron to fly shore-based Corsairs in combat. Lt. Cmdr. Roger Hedrick was promoted to command the air group after the loss of Cmdr. Bunky Ottinger. Hedrick added three more kills to bring his total to twelve. Lt. Doris "Chico" Freeman had achieved acedom, as did Lt. j.g. John Malcolm Smith. Lt. j.g. Cyrus Chambers, who had 3.33 kills in Hellcats with VF-6, had joined the ace fraternity. Lt. j.g. John J. Sargent, who had 4.25 kills flying Hellcats with VF-18, added another score in one of the VF-84 photo-recon F6F-5P Hellcats. Three more rookies (Lts. j.g. Lewin Maberry and John T. Gildea plus Lt. Willis G. Laney) had brought down five, seven, and five enemy planes, respectively. The pilot logbooks for Air Group 84 contained 192 red-inked Japanese flags.

A full day of missions lay ahead. Air Group 84 was busy on Friday, May 11, 1945: combat air patrols over the carriers, strike missions against targets on Okinawa, target CAP missions above the picket destroyers. At dawn, ten VMF-451 Corsairs escorted Avengers and Helldivers. The strike package crossed the big island to drop bombs and fire rockets against caves holding Japanese troops. The flight was recovered by 0855. Normally the "Blue Devil" pilots would have returned to the ready room. These small compartments were sandwiched between the flight deck and the top of the hangar deck adjacent to the island. The squadron offices were nearby. "I was just coming in with my flight from the morning cover flight," Donahue recalled. "We were all tired, and since we'd seen and done nothing that morning, I just wanted to release my men from duty, telling the intelligence officer, 'We're not going to debrief.' Hank Ellis [-451 CO] was going to turn me in at the bridge, but nothing happened—Ellis canceled the briefing."[3] Ellis prepared for his own mission. Most of the marines returned to their racks in their staterooms near the bow. A pair lingered behind in the "Blue Devil" ready room. First Lieutenant George Petersen was intent on finishing a letter to his wife, Catherine.

Hell Had Broken Loose

The sixth massed kamikaze attack, Kikusui No. 6, against the Allied ships at Okinawa had commenced. Sailing northwest of Okinawa, the destroyers USS *Hugh W. Hadley* (DD-774) and the USS *Evans* (DD-552) were caught in a maelstrom of kamikazes. *Hadley* downed twenty-three of the attackers, the *Evans* another nineteen. Bombs, an Okha rocket, and multiple kamikazes struck the destroyers. Though the tin cans survived, their casualty lists were long. Corsairs from the carriers and Yontan airfield on Okinawa did what they could to ward off the attackers, but they ran out of ammunition and fuel before the enemy ran out of planes.

It was a banner day for Navy and Marine pilots in the skies over the Ryukyu Islands: nearly a hundred enemy planes were shot down by the Hellcats and Corsairs of the Fast Carrier Task Force and the land-based Marine squadrons on Okinawa. The kills commenced at 0730. VF-9 from the *Yorktown* nabbed twenty-two invaders. Lt. Bert Eckard scored five to enter the ace-in-a-day club. Lt. Eugene Valencia scored three kills, bringing his total to twenty-three and securing second place on the all-time Navy ace list. Several other Hellcat fliers joined the ace ranks or added to their totals. From the *Shangri La*, Lt. Joe Robbins picked off three Zekes to enter the ace fraternity.

The Corsair pilots of the *Bunker Hill* earned their share too. On target CAP near Kikai, two divisions of the "Wolf Gang" commenced an early-morning turkey shoot: Thirty enemy fighters passed 3,000 feet beneath the Navy pilots. Chico Freeman, an old VF-17 hand, attacked and shot down two planes. Lt. j.g. John M. Smith became a double ace with a triple kill. This action earned Smith the Silver Star. Lt. j.g. Gene Powell also scored twin kills, while singles were notched by Lieutenants Caleb Kendall and Charles T. Larsen. Lts. j.g. Wayne Horner and Gil Roberts each earned their first and only kills of the tour.

Low on fuel, the VF-84 divisions returned to the *Bunker Hill*. They trapped back aboard with the VMF-451 Corsairs and the other planes from the cave strikes. Sixteen more Corsairs were launched for the Kikai patrol. Most of the "Wolf Gang" pilots returned to their ready room. For Kendall, his victory followed news that his son had been born the day before.

It Didn't Stand a Chance

On a separate target CAP, seven "Fighting Falcons" orbited at angels 12 when a lone Yokosuka Frances passed nearby. First Lieutenant Walter Goeggel, flying an F4U-1C with 20 mm cannon, finished off the twin-engine bomber. Thirty minutes later, Capt. Jim Swett spied a Japanese bomber. Despite the antiaircraft fire from a nearby destroyer, he pressed home the attack and earned another kill to cement his record as a triple ace. Swett's division ended the patrol by attacking a Betty bomber laden with a Baka bomb. First Lieutenant Ralph Glendinning scored the most hits, and so he was awarded the kill when the Mitsubishi spiraled into the sea and exploded. After two hours on patrol, the marines headed back to base.

They were being followed.

Two divisions of "Blue Devils" strafed villages and launched rockets against boats in the harbor while on patrol over Amami. First Lieutenant John Norris nabbed a sole Zeke. Around the same time, the destroyers USS *John W. Weeks* and *Wallace L. Lind* brought down an enemy plane on the ramparts of the *Bunker Hill*'s task group, 58.3.

After trapping aboard after their early target CAP over Kikai, aces John Smith's and Chico Freeman's divisions returned through a hatch in the island to the "Wolf Gang" ready room for debriefing. The ready rooms were designed to keep the pilots comfortable. Air-conditioning and reclining chairs eased their time awaiting the next mission. Underneath the island, they were just steps away from the flight deck.

The ready room was the carrier equivalent of a sport locker room after missions. "You might lose one pilot, but the guy who got the victory; well, his feet weren't on the ground!" recalled Pots Wilmot. "There is just one thing a fighter pilot wants to do: shoot down airplanes!"[4]

On the flight and hangar decks, it was a dance of spotting planes for the next strike and recovering planes from earlier missions. White-shirted ordnancemen swapped out the ammo boxes on the fighters. Gray jeeps and Ford Mototugs—a militarized version of a farm tractor—towed planes into position as they came off the elevators. Blue-shirted plane handlers assisted. The faster fighter planes were spotted at the head of the pack as the slower Avengers and Helldivers were spotted farther back. Blue-gray smoke drifted toward the stern as the plane captains started up the engines for a brief check before shutting them back down again. Just before Strike C was to launch, the call went out for pilots to man their planes. The brown-shirted plane captains fired the birds back up again and helped the pilots and crews into their mounts.

Danger Approached

Capt. Jim Swett's division was orbiting the *Bunker Hill* at 1,500 feet, awaiting their turn to come back aboard, when Swett spotted enemy planes above them. He immediately turned his division toward the two planes, but there was not enough time to intercept them. Keying his mike, Swett screamed, "Viceroy Base. There are two kamikazes right over you!"[5] The first plane was already in a dive against the carrier. Despite being out of range, the marines fired on the second plane in hopes of driving it away. In succession at 1005, the enemy planes crashed the crowded amidships and aft flight deck of the *Bunker Hill*. Conflagration arose.

The *Bunker Hill* Was Ill Prepared

No enemy planes had been identified on the radar. At "Condition One Easy," the guns were manned and the fans were blowing to provide ventilation through the carrier. The gun crews had little warning. They failed to stop the kamikazes. The first crashed the deck just aft of the number 3 elevator. It skidded through the Strike C planes, wreaking carnage before tumbling over the port side, taking Lt. j.g. John C. Milholland's Corsair with it. The 551-pound bomb penetrated the flight deck before exploding near the gallery deck. Seconds behind the first, a second kamikaze released its 551-pound bomb before crashing at the intersection of the island and the flight deck. The second bomb also exploded on the gallery deck.

Moments later, a third kamikaze made a run at the wounded carrier. By now the task group was alerted. The *Bunker Hill*'s guns opened up, as did those on other warships. After taking hits, the Japanese pilot altered his course and aimed for a destroyer in the vanguard. He missed and was absorbed by the Pacific.

On the *Bunker Hill* the concussion from the second bomb vented in three directions: upward to the flight deck, downward into the hangar, and into the gallery deck spaces. Fires ensued on each deck. So close to the pilot ready rooms, the concussion caused considerable damage and loss of life. Survivors of the blast had to fight through the thick smoke from the fires that was being pulled into the spaces by the ship's blowers.

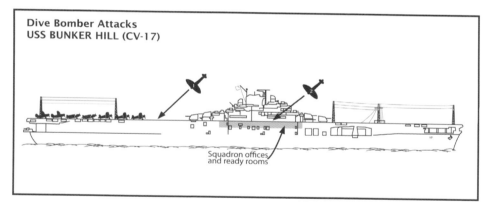

Dive Bomber Attacks
USS BUNKER HILL (CV-17)

Squadron offices
and ready rooms

"Wolf Gang" pilot Lt. j.g. John Pini was almost ready to take off with Strike C: "As we were being strapped in, I noticed a plane making a run on us. I told the plane captain that the guy was crazy to buzz the carrier. It never occurred to me that it was a kamikaze because we were not at general quarters."[6] Lt. j.g. Stan Abele, a fellow "Wolf Gang" pilot, was preparing to mount his Corsair: "At first I thought it was one of ours[,] and I was worried he would get shot down," said Abele. "Then I realized it wasn't[,] and yelled, 'It's a Jap![,]' but it was too late. The plane clipped the upraised wings of my plane and crashed into four other planes next to me on the fantail, destroying every one of them and killing the pilots inside."[7] The "Wolf Gang" CO, Lt. Cmdr. Raymond "Ted" Hill, whose Corsair was nearly struck by one of the kamikazes, escaped from his cockpit. Pini was also able to clear his bird. Lt. j.g. M. T. "Mac" Daniel emerged from his Corsair: "He was black. The flash fire that swept back had ignited his g-suit[,] and the burning nylon made him look a lot worse than he was."[8]

The Corsairs of Lts. j.g. William "Flip" Gerner (VF-84) and John C. "Bud" Milholland were warming up their engines before the next strike. "The Zero clipped the upraised left wing of Gerner's Corsair before crashing hard into the next plane and ramming Bud Milholland's Corsair. Gerner watched Milholland's plane rip violently over the side, locked with the kamikaze." Milholland escaped from the sinking Corsair only to emerge in the burning waves. "It burned so hot that the fingers of his left hand fused together into a swollen, oozing mitten."[9]

The Birds That Had Carried Them To War Had Turned Against Them

Gas tanks exploded. Burning fuel flowed across the deck. Oxygen bottles fed the fire while rounds cooked off. The highly pressurized hydraulic lines that snaked through the planes to drive the main gear, actuating rams, and other connections going through the wheel wells to the wings for the guns, the wing-lifting and flap mechanisms, were punctured. They sprayed combustible fluid into the inferno. Tires exploded and burned. The canvas that covered wing surfaces and the rudder was set on fire. The Grumman, Curtiss, and Vought birds had become bombs that fueled the devastation. Air Group 84 personnel and the ship's company suffered the consequences.

Abele bore witness: "Everywhere planes were exploding. Rockets and munitions on the surprised American planes were detonating[,] and the entire flight deck and island of the carrier were on fire. It was a raging inferno, a flaming holocaust, and everywhere was the stench of burning fuel and flesh."[10] Burning fiercely, the wounded carrier fell out of formation. Explosions rocked the ship. Roiling black smoke engulfed the carrier's after end. It flowed over the deck and towered high into the sky.

Left: View of the Bunker Hill from the USS *Bataan. Courtesy of the National Archives, photo 80-G-274266*
Right: Air Group 84 casualties asphyxiated in a passageway

As the kamikazes impacted the *Bunker Hill*, Pots Wilmot was in his stateroom, forward and near the bow: "Just as I was getting ready to get into my bunk, I heard the 20 mm guns. When the 20 mm guns start, you know the enemy is close. Right after that the ship shook and we got hit by the first plane. He went into a whole bunch of navy guys getting ready to launch. Right after that, the second one hit at the base of the island, and the bomb came off and went through the flight deck. It exploded down in the navy ready room, about 50 feet from where we had been for our debriefing."[11] Wilmot and another pilot evacuated the compartment and headed topside to the flight deck: "Everything was on fire. I tripped and looked down. It was a cooked sailor. There were sailors all over the deck, and they smelled like they'd been cooked. I was shocked; there was fire everywhere. We looked over the side and there was a kid hanging from a knotted rope. He looked up at us and his eyes were as big as silver dollars. So, we pulled him up."[12]

Two "Blue Devils" had lingered behind after the other pilots returned to their staterooms: "George Petersen was in the ready room with Alvin McConville. When the kamikazes hit, Alvin went out through a back hatch towards the flight deck. He was surrounded by fire. He grabbed the railing, which burnt his hands, and jumped overboard. A destroyer rescued him," recalled Wilmot. "Petersen stayed in the ready room to write a letter to his wife. He left the ready room when the first kamikaze hit, but got as far as the Navy ready room when the bomb exploded. He was a good pilot. The other four replacement pilots were shot down, but Petersen had two kills."[13]

Another "Blue Devil," 1Lt. Al Simkunas, had already proven himself to be an adept survivor. His Corsair had been shot out from under him over Okinawa in March. He survived ditching on another date after his Corsair stalled just before landing. "We kept our whiskey down in two cells that belonged to the squadron. I was the alcohol officer," explained Pots Wilmot. "Simkunas was down with the whiskey when the ship got hit!"[14] "[Simkunas] was quite a character," recalled 1Lt. Richard Wood. "He was in the middle of the ship[,] and there was so much smoke you couldn't see where you were. He and some sailor following him found a porthole open. They climbed out. There was a fixed ladder on the outside of the porthole[,] and they climbed up on that."[15] Added Wilmot, "Simkunas coughed for a week."[16]

"Fighting Falcon" 1Lt. Earl Langston was in sick bay after a back injury from the deployment of his parachute on April 28. "The sick bay was located one deck below the hangar deck[,] and before I could make my way through the darkened passageways to a ladder that would take me to the hangar deck, the damage control people had secured the water tight hatches, thereby cutting off all means of escape. I was trapped there along with hundreds of other men for what seemed like an eternity, not knowing at what moment we would be committed to a watery grave."[17]

Several "Fighting Falcons" were in the armored officers' mess compartment. It was just one deck beneath the hangar deck. Two of its rookie aces, 2Lt. Dean Caswell and 1Lt. John McManus, had been drinking coffee when disaster struck. According to Caswell:

No warning was given and all the lights went out . . . no one turned off the big blowers that brought fresh air to the lower decks. This caused the lower decks to be flooded with thick oil smoke coming from the Flight and Hangar decks where everything was burning or exploding. . . . John and I, in a dazed shock, were in the Officer's Mess and were suddenly immersed in deadly black smoke that was being pumped into the carrier's lower decks by the air blowers.[18]

They donned their gas masks with two others as they attempted to make their way topside. Emergency battle lanterns could not cut through the thick smoke, forcing them to crawl through the blind and tortuous passageways. Their progress was interrupted as bodies of collapsed sailors and pilots blocked their path. Eventually they found a ladder, but the hatch at the top was dogged close. They pounded it with the battle lantern before it was finally opened. Dense smoke followed them out as the group broke free. "Only four of us crawled out, almost totally asphyxiated, but the crowd behind us had already succumbed."[19]

Pilots, unlike every sailor on the ship, were not trained in damage control procedures. With life and ship at stake, many, such as Pots Wilmot, did not hesitate to assist:

Our executive officer was Cmdr. "BeNo" Dyson. We called him BeNo because every morning he would come on the horn and announce, "There will BE NO this or BE NO that on this ship . . . so we called him BeNo. He saw us and told us to grab a hose. We grabbed a hose and he said to follow him. He went right into that damn fire. We followed him until the heat got unbearable, then we turned back and got out of there. Cmdr. Dyson was in there fighting the fire. I thought, "My God, that guy is fearless."[20]

Though outwardly intrepid, "Blue Devil" ace Archie Donahue recognized any mission could be the last. Recalled Wilmot, "Archie always dropped a coin into the lap of the Buddha he kept in his stateroom before a mission as a sacrifice."[21] Donahue was in his stateroom when the attacks occurred. "I ran topside and went along the ship with the chaplain, Father [Lt. Cmdr. Robert Edward] Delaney, who was giving last rites."[22]

Fellow "Blue Devil" 1Lt. Ray Swalley manned another hose. Magnesium parts of the Double Wasps were difficult to counter: "What was so amazing about the fire was engines that were burning metal and you'd put the hose on and the fire would go out. You'd put your hose on another one and you went back and it would start it up again."[23]

Other pilots joined in the efforts. Aces 1Lt. John McManus and 2Lt. Dean Caswell, having survived the hell of climbing over the corpse-littered passageway, braved *Dante's Inferno*: "We found out that such a hose, with some 150 pounds of water pressure, is a 'living thing' and difficult to hold."[24] Another "Falcon," 1Lt. Charlie Nettles, also fought both the hose and the fire:

I ended up on the flight deck trying to help put out the fire. The first fire hose we uncoiled was rotten and of no use. We finally found one that was usable[,] and I was on the nozzle end. When they turned on the water it flopped me all over the deck. Finally, a big black fellow grabbed the hose behind me and saved the day. What an experience. We were not organized and we didn't know what to do.[25]

Confusion reigned. "The flames and smoke were horrendous. The carrier was listing badly. Two DDs [destroyers] were spraying water on the flames[,] and it seemed like an eternity until the fire came under control. One thing I will always remember is the smell of burning flesh."[26]

The *Bunker Hill* was still capable of steaming under full power but began to reduce speed so that pressure could be maintained in the fire main lines. Though the fires were burning upward, water was pouring down. It pooled and collected in compartments and spaces. Initially, Capt. George A. Seitz ordered the carrier turned into the wind to clear the smoke from the deck. Radical turns were executed to clear water and fuel from the hangar deck. Forty minutes later, three destroyers and a cruiser came alongside to help fight the fires. Sections of hose and rescue-breathing apparatuses were transferred to the *Bunker Hill*. Down in the raging hangar deck, planes were pushed onto the number 1 elevator. Brought up to the bow, many were pushed overboard to prevent becoming further accelerants for the fires. Fires erupted in the flight deck magazines and ready service lockers. The inferno raged from amidships to its stern.

"Wolf Gang" pilots Pini and Daniel had escaped their planes and run to the catwalk. With smoke billowing around them, they were lost as to where to go. A sailor came across the pair and led them to the fantail. Like many others, they crossed over to the cruiser *Wilkes-Barre* as it fought fires from the carrier's starboard side.

At 1056, the task group commander, RAdm. Frederick Sherman, ordered the *Bunker Hill* to operate independently with her attendant screen. Air operations took precedence as large groups of enemy aircraft continued to emerge over the Okinawan skies.

In the "Fighting Falcons" ready room, ace Capt. Don Balch, 1Lt. Blaine Imel, and the air combat intelligence officer, 1Lt. Leo Pambrun, were with a mess steward who had brought them sandwiches and coffee. They fought the smoke and darkness: "Lt. Pambrun yelled to hit the deck and crouch low holding hands. Thinking the catwalk was aflame, someone yelled to head for the gun turrets for escape. When this narrow passage started glowing orange[,] we knew our only chance was the catwalk, recalled Imel. "The smoke was choking us and we were moving fast. At this point I do remember making my amends to the maker."[27] The kamikaze that had crashed aside the island caused fire to rage through access passageways and ladders within the island leading from the gallery to the flight deck.

Left: Starboard, aft. The mast of a destroyer can be seen through the smoke portside.
Right: USS *Charles S. Sperry* (DD-697) sprays water on USS Bunker Hill.

A group of thirty men led by Balch found themselves on the small catwalk aft of the island and below the flight deck. A nearby fire hose turned out to be rotted. "When we were hit[,] we went out on the catwalk[,] where all hell was breaking loose—lots of smoke, heat[,] and noise of exploding ordnance. I lined the three of us [pilots] up and started unloading aircraft rockets from the ordnance locker room and throwing them overboard."[28]

Trapped. With fire behind them, no alternatives for escape. The Pacific lay 75 feet below. The group jumped overboard. The pilots had been trained on how to enter the water, but the mess steward had not. "He was cut in half by the trauma of hitting the waves incorrectly."[29] Trailing in the carrier's curving wake, Blaine Imel recounted, "I remember watching as the big listing and smoking ship become smaller and smaller."[30]

Lt. j.g. Stan Abele joined a group of fifteen to twenty survivors on the catwalk near the fantail. "Every hatchway they attempted to open accosted them with toxic fire and billowing smoke."[31] They finally jumped overboard to escape the conflagration. The jump was made not only from perilous height but from a ship turning 20 knots, a frothy wake trailing behind.

Within minutes of the attack, four destroyers stopped to rescue survivors on the seas. Rafts were jettisoned and life jackets were thrown overboard in hopes that sailors who had jumped from the carrier might be saved. Other carriers pushed empty belly tanks and float lights into the water when men were spotted. Some were rescued immediately. For others, it would take hours. For some, there would be no salvation.

With so many sailors in the sea, Capt. Jim Swett ordered his division to drop their raft packs and Mae West vests. Don Balch witnessed pilots saving pilots: "Some of our returning planes dove on us to show the destroyers where we were located in the water."[32] After three months of combat plus having been previously rescued at sea himself, 1Lt. Ralph Glendinning was in the habit of carrying extra dye markers with his flight gear. "We then spent an hour circling men in the water, leading destroyers to them as best we could, as the rest of the fleet steamed away. Flying low with my canopy open, I dropped four dye markers at different locations where there were groups of men in the water to aid the destroyers in locating them."[33]

After four hours, damage control parties and volunteers had contained the fires with the assistance of the cruiser USS *Wilkes-Barre* and the destroyers *English* and *Charles S. Sperry*. The carrier's days of battle in the Pacific were over.

After the carnage was extinguished, the reckoning began. The pilots sought their brothers and flight logbooks. A haunting sight was encountered in the "Wolf Gang's" ready room. Rescuers discovered numerous pilots still in their seats. The bomb from the second kamikaze had penetrated the flight deck and exploded in the neighboring squadron office. Lt. j.g. Wilbert "Beads" Popp had been napping on a wardroom couch ahead of a patrol mission. He found the rest of his division dead in the ready room. A fiend had stolen the watches from several of the deceased.

Pots Wilmot recalled that in general, fighter pilots subscribed to several different philosophies of combat, though each believed they were the best pilot. Squadron leaders considered themselves invincible. With previous combat experience, they feared no enemy. "There isn't a Jap pilot that can shoot me down." Others held the belief of fait accompli—"If your name is on a Japanese bullet, there's nothing you can do about that."[34] Ace Lt. j.g. John J. Sargent fell into the latter category. The initial attack had not roused him from the compartment. In his Texas drawl, he had said previously to Popp, "Relax, Petah. If it's going to hit you, it will hit you."[35]

The reality of what happened to their fellow pilots hit home as Wilmot and others returned to the squadron ready rooms: "In another compartment we saw Navy guys. They were dead in their seats."[36] The "Wolf Gang" was decimated. Numerous other pilots died in the compartment. Lts. Caleb Kendall and Wayne Horner had each scored their first kills earlier that morning. Lt. Chico Freeman had scored his eighth and ninth kills too. In an air group built around aces, Freeman had climbed into seventh position.

Of Chico Freeman, Pots Wilmot recalled: "He spent lots of time in our ready room talking to the majors. He was the most humble pilot I ever met. When I saw him, he was blue gray. He was dead."[37]

"The Marines, we were lucky; we had the hop that day that we were hit," remembered 1Lt. Wesley Todd from VMF-221, "because the Navy was in the ready room being briefed for the next hop, and when those bombs hit, and I heard from somebody who was aboard and got out of it alright [sic], that these guys were still sitting in their chairs, dead—but it's the vacuum that collapses your lungs—there's a vacuum immediately after that, and it exploded your lungs actually." Emphasized Todd, "But we were lucky."[38]

Earl Langston, who had already survived being shot down and being strafed twice by a Zeke and then survived a kamikaze attack on the picket ship that rescued him, survived again: "It was almost three hours before the raging inferno above deck was brought under control enough to allow the hatches opened leading below to where we were trapped. It was a scene of death and destruction that greeted us as we came out onto the hangar deck."[39]

"Blue Devil" Ray Swalley recalled the carnage:

> Later on in the day we were down getting people out, the people that were dead. They would go down. You had to take a blanket. One would get on the upper part of the torso[,] and the other get the legs to put him on the blanket and drag him out. Some of them were just like they were in a pressure cooker because of the heat below and the water in there, the steam and all. You'd go to pick them up by the legs to put them on[,] and the legs would just come off, just come apart.[40]

For the pilots, two missions were paramount: saving their buddies and finding their logbooks. "John [McManus] found a firefighters suit, one of those silver suits with headgear and glass face, a good protection against fire. He insisted on donning the suit and climbing a ladder from the hangar deck into the fire[-]engulfed pilot's ready room," recalled Dean Caswell of VMF-221. "Despite others telling him not to go, and this included me, he climbed the ladder and fought his way into the inferno with our hoses on him, to return saying he couldn't see anyone alive. This was a fiercely brave thing to do[,] and [he] totally disregarded his life in hopes of saving others."[41] McManus was later awarded the Marine Corps Medal for heroism involving voluntary risk of life for his actions.

The same thought was on the mind of the "Blue Devils": "Checker [Hodson] and Ray [Swalley] looked down into our squadron office through a hole in the deck and saw our logbooks in the office, which they retrieved," recalled Pots Wilmot.[42] "Your logbook was everything. Nobody knows anything, nobody remembers anything, and you never saw your gun camera film. They gave them to the guys of our squadron. Our logbooks were scorched and had to be glued together when we returned to El Centro."[43]

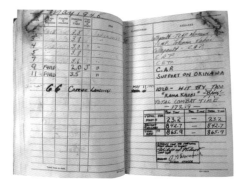

Homeless

Several Air Group 84 flights were still airborne as the fires raged: "Flying Falcon" ace Capt. Bill Snider had been leading his division:

The scorched and water-soaked Aviator Log Book of VMF-451 pilot 1Lt. Philip Wilmot.
Courtesy of Phil Wilmot

Our mission was a strafing and rocket attack on military installations on Tokuna Airfield. About 1030, our mission was completed with good results, and when all my planes were accounted for, I attempted to make radio contact with the *Bunker Hill* to give them a flash report of the attack. It was impossible to "raise" the ship, and I immediately told my division fliers that I feared something had happened to our carrier. About 11 a.m.[,] huge columns of smoke from the carrier area come into view. We knew it was the *Bunker Hill*.[44]

Snider led his division back to the carrier. "A few minutes later, we flew into the carrier landing circle. It was the first suicide attack results I have ever seen. The big carrier which had been our home and our airbase for ninety days was a flaming surface from the flight deck 'island' to the stern. Billows of smoke poured from the hangar deck[,] and we could see the crew working frantically with fire hoses."[45]

First Lieutenant Wesley Todd was flying in Snider's division. "We looked at each other in disbelief and then at our fuel gauges, wondering where we were going to land."[46]

Jim Swett's division was in the same predicament: "We were stuck in the air with no place to land. When we got low on fuel and began declaring an emergency, they told us to land on the USS *Enterprise*. This was the old *Enterprise* with a narrow flight deck. They had never received *Corsairs* aboard, but now we had twenty of them coming in, plus two F6F Hellcat photo planes."[47]

The *Enterprise* took the fifteen "Fighting Falcons" Corsairs aboard. It wasn't a moment too soon. Several of the Pratt & Whitneys coughed and died from lack of fuel as they taxied past the barriers. The carrier *Randolph* landed a division of Navy Corsairs plus the two photo-recon F6F-5P Hellcats. Majors Hank Ellis and Trigger Long led their divisions of "Blue Devils" to the *Enterprise* as well. The Marines had invaded another Navy carrier.

They did not stay long. The next afternoon the twenty-one Air Group 84 fighters were launched to a new home. "And so then we flew to Yontan Airfield," recalled "Fighting Falcon" 1Lt. Wesley Todd.

We flew over there and gave 'em our airplanes. And as a matter of fact, one of the guys on the way back said, "Let's hit Amami O Shima". . . because we knew this was our last day of combat. And finally, we decided not to do it. Why take a chance and lose somebody, you know, on your last day? So, we just landed on the coral runway at Okinawa, gave 'em our airplanes, and then we had to wait for transportation back to where the *Bunker Hill* would eventually pull in.[48]

Lt. Glen Wallace, a Corsair pilot from Air Group 83 on the *Essex,* joined them on May 12. He wrote in his diary: "Flew air support over Okinawa. Had engine failure over front lines. Made dead-stick landing at Yontan Field. Saw all the boys from the *Bunker Hill.* They were going back to the states."[49] Their existence with the frontline marines was meager. The hell of the carrier was no better than the hell on land. They slept on the ground. K rations replaced meals served on green linen tablecloths by stewards. Dust from the coral runway choked the air. "Saw lots of dead Marines and Japs," recalled Wallace. "The stink was awful."[50]

The Marine pilots feared they would be incorporated into the Marine *Corsair* squadrons stationed at Yontan. First Lieutenant Ralph Glendinning of VMF-221 recalled, "Gen. Wallace wanted to keep us on Okinawa to meld in with another squadron since we hadn't been overseas the required eighteen months."[51] Adm. Mitscher, the Fast Carrier Task Force commander, sent word that his pilots should be reunited with their squadrons. An R5C Commando flew them to Guam.

The tin cans were lifeguards. Hundreds of sailors and pilots had entered the seas. Some perished due to wounds suffered from the explosions. Others were injured by the fall. Some drowned initially; others, after a period of time. A band of four destroyers swept the *Bunker Hill's* path, but with the carrier turning 20 knots, it was a large patch of ocean. Stan Abele's group of fifteen to twenty that had leapt from the catwalk were left behind as the wounded carrier steamed away. Initial thoughts of rescue passed with each subsequent minute. They were in the water for five hours before being rescued by a destroyer. Abele and the others climbed a cargo net to safety.

By late afternoon, the USS *The Sullivans'* decks were crowded with 166 rescuees. The USS *Stephen Potter* accounted for an additional 107 saved. Many of the men had sustained serious burns. The immersion in salt water added to their agony. In the crowded wardroom of the USS *Waldron* (DD-699), Lt. Joe Perry, a gynecologist in civilian life, treated the wounded among the twenty-one souls brought aboard. The USS *Ault* (DD-698) pulled twenty-nine men from the unforgiving Pacific. All told, the tin cans saved 321 souls.

Like the wayward *Corsair* pilots, VAdm. Marc Mitscher (commander, Task Force 58) and his staff were transferred by a bosun's chair to the *Enterprise* by way of the destroyer *English*.

Return to the *Bunker Hill*

The sun shone brightly the next morning. The sea was calm. The air above the convoy was free of enemy planes. The USS *Bunker Hill* was 200 miles east of the Fast Carrier Task Force. But the nightmare continued. "When I got out on deck the next morning, I saw all these white blankets, nearly four hundred blankets, and under each blanket was a dead sailor with a 5-inch shell wrapped inside," reported Pots Wilmot.[52]

Through the morning, destroyer attendants returned the rescued carrier men and pilots. The hospital ship USS *Bountiful* (AH-9) came alongside to receive the wounded both from the *Bunker Hill* and the destroyers. Her white paint and large red crosses contrasted against the scarred and blackened carrier. After the transfers were completed, the destroyers departed on a high-speed return to Okinawa.

Three days later the *Bountiful* transferred *Bunker Hill* casualties to the fleet hospital at Guam. Among the nearly one hundred patients were four VF-84 pilots, including Bud Milholland and "Fighting Falcon" 1Lt. Leo Pambrun, the squadron's air combat intelligence officer. For Pambrun, the wounds brought an end to his three and a half years serving in the Pacific.

Their return to their ship did not ease the pain and suffering. Questions of who had survived and who had not were paramount in the minds of the returning pilots. After transfer in a bosun's chair, 1Lt. Blaine Imel's senses were overwhelmed: the ship reeked of the dead. The stench of burned fuel and smoke permeated the air. "We could see the damage and disheartening cleanup of our once[-]proud ship. When we came aboard, we saw our lost comrades laying [sic] in long rows on the deck. . . . Don [Balch] and I surveyed the area where we had been, probably without saying, to justify our actions. One view of the twisted catwalk and charred ready room was all we needed."[53]

VF-84's Beads Popp was detailed with the task of taking a crew of forty-five enlisted below deck to recover corpses from compartments that had been secured during the attack.

It was a macabre mission. They discovered that many of the victims had fought in vain to escape the smoke-filled compartments. When the assignment was completed, only five members of the work detail were still present.[54]

Navy pilot Lt. j.g. Stan Abele's reaction was similar: "When I came back on board, I wasn't prepared for what I saw. The hangar deck had hundreds of dead bodies on it[,] covered with canvas tarps. They were being readied for burial at sea. A tractor was pushing wrecked airplanes over the side."[55] Amid the wreckage and carnage, Abele searched the victims. "I tried to find my best friend, Gene Powell, and went from body to body before I couldn't take it any more. I lifted up one tarp[,] and the poor fellow was so badly burned that his arm fell off."[56]

Eventually Abele gave up the search. Abele's last memory of Powell was the morning before, down in the ready room celebrating his two victories.

At 1230, funeral services began. They would continue until sunset. The colors flew at half-mast as the corpses slid from the palls. Pots Wilmot bore witness: "They had a board on the edge of the flight deck with a couple of Marine guards with rifles. They'd put a body on the board, the Marine guards would present arms, they'd tip the plank, and the sailor would slide off. They did this all day, about four hundred times."[57] 2Lt. Caswell was in charge of the identification. It was a grueling process for the Marines' greatest carrier ace. He was just twenty-two years old: "Then we buried the dead. There was a number but lost in the doing. At that point, very few cared, including me."[58]

Casualties line the deck. The Corsairs brought up from the hangar deck have smoke-blackened canopies.

The brunt of the losses was borne by Air Group 84. The deaths of 137 of its pilots, officers, flight crews, and mechanics was the single greatest loss of an air group during World War II. Over one hundred men had died in the gallery passageways and compartments. The Purple Hearts sent to the parents and widows at home were distributed unevenly. VMF-221 "Fighting Falcons" suffered no pilot deaths but lost eleven of their mechanics in the blaze. Another mechanic was never found. Brother Marine squadron VMF-451 lost just one pilot. VB-84 lost two pilots and nineteen enlisted. VT-84 suffered ten officers and fifteen enlisted crew killed. With a large proportion of its pilots on the flight deck or in its ready room, VF-84 lost nineteen of its pilots. On no day during World War II were more aces killed. The same was true for Corsair pilots.

Three who slipped from the canvas palls were brothers from the fraternity of aces: Lt. Doris Freeman, Lt. j.g. John T. Gildea, and Lt. j.g. John J. Sargent. Freeman had earned his final two kills just the day before. He and Sargent had started on the path to acedom in the Solomon Islands back in 1943.

Three aces: Lt. Doris Freeman, Lt. j.g. John T. Gildea, and Lt. j.g. John J. Sargent. *The Slipstream Mark II & III*

The cleanup of the detritus continued for several days. Dean Caswell recalled: "There was no sleep for three days[,] and exhaustion put us out of business with the nightmares that follow such horror. Fire and smoke have bothered me ever since."[59]

A safe harbor was reached on May 15, when the *Bunker Hill* finally anchored at the Ulithi Atoll. At this weigh station on its journey home, Air Group 84's lost lambs were reunited with their squadrons. "We finally got our ride in a DC-3 from Okinawa back to Guam," explained 1Lt. Wesley Todd. An overnight flight brought them to Ulithi before they hitched a ride in a Higgins boat back to their ship. They were not prepared for the sights and stench that met them. "We went back aboard the *Bunker Hill*. That's when you find out who's there and who wasn't anymore. And we had to be deloused. Anybody who had been on Okinawa had to be deloused, where they squirt you all over your body to make sure you don't have lice."[60] For ace Maj. Trigger Long, it was his third return from Okinawa to the carrier: he had been shot down by friendly fire in April and had once landed on the island with fouled plugs. Long had the ignoble distinction of having been deloused twice.

It was almost the last hurrah for Marine Corsairs on the fast carriers. After the departure of the *Bunker Hill*, only the USS *Bennington* (CV-20) with VMF-112 and -113 stayed in the fight. No more Marine carrier aces were crowned during their final two months of deployment. By the end of June, Marine Corsairs could be found only in land-based squadrons or aboard a few escort carriers. Over six months, from January through June 1945, the Marine Corsair pilots had proven themselves to be capable carrier-based fliers for Task Force 38/58. They destroyed 214.5 enemy planes in the air. VMF-221 and -451 aboard the *Bunker Hill* accounted for one hundred of these kills, thus making them the greatest Marine tandem team aboard the fast carriers. Because the Corsairs were better interceptors than the Hellcats, the Marines flew far more CAP missions than their Navy brothers. At least seventeen Marine pilots served as replacement pilots in Navy Corsair squadrons. From attacks in the South China Sea to sweeps over the Japanese home islands, Marine Corsair pilots kept the juggernaut Fast Carrier Task Force 38/58 fighting.

The USS *Bunker Hill* was awarded the Presidential Unit Citation. All pilots attached to Air Group 84 were later authorized to wear the Presidential Unit Citation ribbon.

Cmdr. Howell "BeNo" Dyson, the executive officer of the USS *Bunker Hill* who had disappeared into the conflagration with a hose, survived. He was awarded a Navy Cross and a Purple Heart for his actions on May 11, 1945.

Of the fifteen Helldivers aboard the *Bunker Hill*, just the seven SB2Cs on the stern were saved. None of the fifteen Avengers were saved. Of the ten Hellcats, just the two that landed on the USS *Randolph* survived. Thirty-nine Corsairs aboard the *Bunker Hill* were destroyed, were pushed overboard during the fire, or were later surveyed. Only three of the Corsairs on the bow were retained. Another nineteen Corsairs landed on the *Enterprise* and the *Randolph*. Most were later surrendered to Marine VMF squadrons on Okinawa. On the night of May 24, 1945, Japanese sappers crash-landed at Yontan. Using hand grenades, mines, mortars, and explosive charges, they destroyed many fighters, including several of the CVG-84 Corsairs that had been diverted there.

VMF-221 and VMF-451 returned to California to re-form. The war ended before they ever flew another combat mission. Second Lieutenant Dean Caswell was the highest-scoring Marine carrier-based ace of the war, with seven kills. Both Capt. Bill "Luke" Snider and Maj. Archie Donahue earned the unique distinction of earning acedom both on land and sea. Donahue was also the US Marines' only carrier-based ace-in-a-day pilot.

The Marine pilots were cleared as the cause of the destruction of their flight gear lost in the fire. No financial penalty was assessed by the Marine Corps.

"Blue Devil" 1Lt. Philip Wilmot's landing on May 11, 1945, was his last carrier landing during World War II. He stayed in the USMCR postwar. As a private pilot, he flew from 1942 to 2017. Pots still has his scorched and water-damaged Aviators Flight Log Book from 1945. With reference to the war, he said in 2018, "It was terrible out there."[61] Kamikaze attacks against the warships surrounding the Ryukyu Islands continued for six more weeks. The ten massed *kikusui* raids saw more than 1,800 kamikazes emerge from the skies. Despite the best efforts of the Corsair and Hellcat pilots, plus the gunners on the warships, 218 Allied warships were struck. Thirty-six ships were sunk. Nearly five thousand sailors and marines were killed.

CHAPTER 17

SNAFU

He listened to the radio for any reports of his brother's plane. On ground support missions, the flights usually returned together or by division, but for over an hour, Corsairs were landing in ones or twos. Requests had been coming over the radio from the pilots seeking vectors so they could find their way home, but only seven of the eleven birds had returned. The mission was SNAFU.

First Lieutenant John Denvir Stith. *Courtesy of Susan Stith*

Situation Normal: All F**ked Up

It was another acronym in a military vocabulary full of abbreviations. This particular acronym was not officially issued. Rather, it belonged to the dogfaces that faced the challenges of war in a military spread widely across the planet. SNAFU came into the lexicon early in the war. Its simplicity for describing the situation at hand led to its universal appeal and usage. It had a less forgiving brother, FUBAR.

VMF-115 had been flying ground support missions for Gen. Douglas MacArthur's 10th Corps in the Philippines since December 1944. By the time 1Lt. John D. Stith joined "Joe's Jokers" in June 1945, they were stationed on the southwestern island of Mindanao. For "Denny" Stith, the assignment was a radical departure from the combat missions he flew over the Slot with VMF-321 during 1944.

The Marine Air Group 12 fighter missions had become a routine of opportunity missed. Their CAP always returned with the same declaration: "Enemy sightings negative." Often sent to attack Japanese-held positions, failure to contact Army fighter directors became commonplace. Mother Nature was no friend either. It was not unusual for missions to be scrubbed because of her. When "Joe's Jokers" did put lead, napalm, and ordnance on target, the thick flora blocked the view to see whether the mission had accomplished its goals. On the morning of June 14, the CO, Maj. John S. Payne, briefed a dozen of his pilots about their ground support missions against Japanese targets at Guadalupe on Mindanao. Poor weather was expected. Fuel conservation would be key to a successful conclusion of the mission.

SNAFU appeared. No belly tanks were available for the flight, but then Operations scrubbed the hop. Payne's boys were advised to stand by. After a period of time, word came down that the mission was on again. But twenty minutes was lost when the ordnance section needed to attach extra rockets. After their flight was directed by the tower to taxi to the far end of the runway, the pilots mounted their steeds. A crew chief accidentally dumped 1Lt. Paul Becker's parachute. There was no time to get another, so the flight was reduced to eleven planes. SNAFU.

As they waited to taxi from the rocket attachment area, the tower held them in place as another flight of twenty-seven Dauntlesses and a single Corsair departed on their own mission. Next the tower cleared an R4D for takeoff. A twin-engine Douglas pulled out of its revetment but then parked in front of Payne's gang. Stith gave a quick glance toward the R4D's cockpit. His older brother, Dick, was not at the controls of the cargo plane.

The R4D finally took off, but then the "Jokers" were held in place as a Corsair was cleared to land. All this time, eleven big Hamilton props were turning while the hungry eighteen-cylinder Pratt & Whitney Wasps fed from the main fuel tanks. Stith was already keeping an eye on his fuel gauge.

A dozen Corsairs from VMF-211 had already dropped their napalm against enemy targets close to American troops in the Davao region. After strafing several buildings, they re-formed to return to Moret Field at Zamboanga. With the weather closing quickly, they were redirected to land at Malabang. SNAFU.

Stith's flight finally got airborne. Ceiling and visibility were not unlimited over Mindanao as the flock flew east for over 200 miles, crossing from the west side of Mindanao to the east. The weather continued to deteriorate. The ceiling dropped to 2,000 feet. Visibility was restricted to 3 miles. Course headings were changed frequently, as was altitude. The "Jokers" flew under and around massive cloud formations. Stith muttered to himself, "This weather is lousy."[1]

As they located Davao, they pulled their sticks to the left. The new course heading had them following the Agusan River north to their target area.

The flight leader radioed numerous course corrections as the birds hurried to rendezvous with the airborne army attack controller. It was for naught. The little L-5 Sentinel had been on station so long, waiting for the Marine gulls to arrive, it could wait no longer. Radioing that it was leaving the area, the army pilot directed the "Jokers" to look for two large, white "T"s on the jungle floor to indicate where the ordnance should be targeted. When the "Jokers" finally arrived over the supposed target area, no Ts could be found. SNAFU.

Major Payne turned his flight south for the airfield at Malabang rather than attempt to return to Zamboanga. They leveled off at angels 8, but 1Lt. Victor Butts soon radioed that his Corsair was running rough and its fuel levels were dropping quickly. He shed his ordnance, switched to the reserve tank, and lowered his rpm.

Stith, a man of impeccable manners, uttered again what was almost a profanity for him: "This weather is lousy."[2] Hidden in the broken clouds was Mt. Piapayungan, its peak towering over 9,000 feet. It was one of many volcanic peaks over 8,000 feet tall that rose from the floors of central Mindanao.

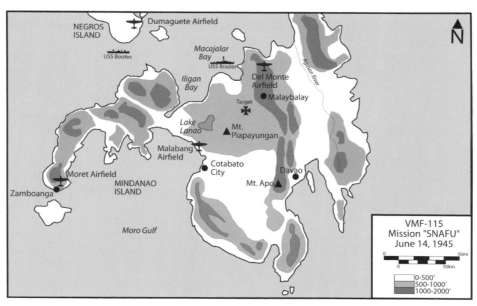

Map of SNAFU

With broken clouds behind them and a solid front ahead, Butts broke away. He dove through the overcast in an attempt to find a place to set his bird down. Major Payne pressed ahead with the flight, leading the hop into the overcast. It would be the last moment all the pilots were accounted for, as the pilots began to fragment into smaller echelons.

Second Lieutenant Chaytor Mason, the tail-end charlie, slid up close to his section leader, 2Lt. Bernard Kramer. Kramer began to pull away from his wingman. Mason, whose plane could not keep up, reached for the microphone. It wouldn't work. Kramer disappeared into the clouds. Mason was on his own. SNAFU.

Kramer caught sight of other members of the flight a couple of times, but as he weaved in and around great cumulonimbus masses, his fuel levels became precariously low. Kramer was faced with either trying to climb over the clouds or trying to find his way home on his own to Zamboanga. He turned northwest, though Payne had led the others in the opposite direction. Peacock Crystal–Zamboanga continued to feed him vectors. Kramer eventually broke out of the overcast north of Mindanao. As he sought the American-held Dumaguete airfield along the coast of Negros Island, he used up his remaining fuel. Still in radio contact with Kramer, 2Lt. Lawrence Lawson advised him to ditch near a ship. As an American warship came into view, Kramer radioed Lawson that he was forced to make a water landing, "just in case somebody went to look for me sometime."[3]

Kramer tried to turn on his emergency IFF (identification, friend or foe) transponder but discovered that the ground crew had secured the switch with wires that were too thick to break. SNAFU.

The gunners were trigger-happy aboard the ammunition-filled cargo ship after two previous brushes with kamikazes. As a lone plane descended upon the USS *Bootes* (AK-99), the barrels of the single 3- and 5-inch guns tracked its course. Gun crews on the 20 mm and 40 mm machine guns did likewise. No IFF signal was received from the plane. Fortune finally smiled on Kramer: The sailors of the watch recognized the profile of the Vought and held their fire as Kramer circled the ship at just 100 feet above the sea. He rocked his wings violently to show he was in trouble. With flaps down, he dragged his tail across the calm sea for a textbook ditching.

The whaleboat crew pulled Kramer out of the water. The ship's doctor infused the sopping-wet pilot with medicinal whiskey, Schenley's Black Label, or "Black Death" as it was known. The captain and crew unceremoniously stripped him of his flight gear, first-aid kit, compass, and life raft pack.

He found himself alone. After entering the overcast, 1Lt. Paul Chambers had stayed near Butts until he broke formation to find a place to land. Repeated calls to have someone form up on him went unheeded. After changing altitudes several times, Chambers found himself over Lake Lanao. He had been flying northwest instead of southwest. It was then that he discovered his gyrocompass wasn't working. SNAFU. Chambers called Zamboanga and requested a vector to guide him to Malabang.

Butts was running out of fuel. After he left the formation, his bird had burned through 80 gallons of fuel in just forty-five minutes. With the Double Wasp losing power, he jettisoned both the rockets and the bombs to shed weight. Finally, his engine turned under power for the last time while he was at angels 8. When he emerged from the clouds, there was solid jungle below him. Expert piloting allowed the twenty-one-year-old pilot to put his Corsair down in a small field, the underside of the Vought clipping the trees as it descended. Wheels up, the plane skidded for 50 yards before it halted abruptly. Discovering that he was still in one piece, Butts radioed the flight that he was alive and unhurt. He destroyed the IFF transponder. Whether he had landed in enemy-controlled territory or not, he was unsure.

Second Lieutenant Lawrence Lawson, who had followed Butts down, waggled his wings when Butts radioed that he was unhurt. Lawson climbed through the soup. Circling as top cover, Stith saw Lawson emerge from the clouds. Lawson advised Capt. Stith that he was going the wrong way. "I don't know," said Stith. "Okay, if you know the way, I'll follow you."[4] Though he was an experienced combat vet, Stith was flying his first mission with VMF-115. He joined up on the rookie lieutenant Lawson.

But after a period, Stith got his bearings. After flying wing on Lawson, he said, "Follow me and I'll get you there."[5] They made a course correction in the opposite direction. They tried to keep each other within sight. Stith keyed his mic as he glanced over at Lawson. "This is lousy weather."[6] Stith jettisoned his napalm. Lawson kept his ordnance attached. They were on their own.

His flock was lost. The squadron commander already had three aerial kills to his credit, along with another seven destroyed on the ground from the Solomons campaign. By the time Maj. John S. Payne assumed command of VMF-115 in late May 1945, his dress uniform was adorned by a Purple Heart, the DFC, and several air medals. Two weeks later, his flight was scattered despite his assurances to them that if they stuck with him, "I'll get you there."[7] But Payne's flock had thinned. He and his wingman, 1Lt. John Benson, were still together when they landed at Malabang. Second Lieutenant Mason, who had been unable to keep up with Kramer, spotted the flight leader ahead and followed him from a distance to Malabang.

Flying on instruments, Stith and Lawson turned on their IFF in hopes that Peacock Crystal could guide them home. Initially, they were directed on a course due west but, after fifteen minutes, were vectored to fly southeast. As more pilots came over the airwaves requesting vectors, the two "Jokers'" own queries went unanswered. Eventually, they lost radio contact with Peacock Crystal. After contact was finally reestablished, they were vectored on a path northwest. Their fuel gauges did not provide reassurance. The heavens opened as they flew through showers.

Chambers was in a sweat. The bent-wing birds cruised at a rate of 80 gallons per hour, and he was already low on fuel when 1Lt. Bigelow Watts and 1Lt. Horace D. Dawson pulled away. Chambers went into conservation mode. He flew at 1,475 rpm and drew 28 inches of manifold pressure. His airspeed was a miserly 120 knots. Peacock Crystal continued to feed him vectors while he descended slowly through the overcast. Cotabato City on the eastern coast came into sight. Chambers jettisoned his bomb over the Moro Gulf of the Celebes Sea before finally pranging at Malabang. The fuel tank held just a few remaining gallons of gas. He had managed to fly for nearly an hour on just 39 gallons of gas!

Flight Gamma-1 was in trouble. Since vector headings were repeatedly requested, it was apparent that the flight was scattered and lost. A crowd began to build within operations at Zamboanga. Reports were received from Malabang of individual "Jokers" touching down, but only four of eleven of the original flight had landed. Several other pilots had radioed in that they were going to ditch or crash-land. The ground support mission had gone awry. The crew chiefs and mechanics understood what had happened: SNAFU.

They relied on their maps to try to find Malabang. But at some point, Lieutenants Watts and Dawson lost 2Lt. Everett Eastman when they poured on the coals. Dawson broke through the clouds and found his bearings near Cotabato City, southeast of their goal. He and Watts followed the coastline northwest. They eventually landed at Malabang; Eastman was nowhere to be seen.

Eastman regained his bearings after recognizing Lake Lanao. He jettisoned his napalm, took a heading of 230 degrees, throttled back to conserve fuel, and let the Vought do the rest. He broke out of the soup overwater. As he dove through an opening in the clouds, Malabang appeared. He landed of his own accord.

The veteran pilot moved toward the radio in the operations shack as the crowd of younger pilots deferred to rank. Capt. Dick Stith got the word that seven "Jokers" had landed at Malabang. His younger brother, Denny, was not one of them. Instead, Denny's repeated requests for a proper heading faded in and out. Dick Stith had flown long enough to know that unlike his R4D transport plane, the Corsairs did not have long legs.

The Marine Corps Reserve's sole representative in the Lanao del Sur province found himself quickly outnumbered. After forty-five minutes on the ground, 1Lt. Victor Butts saw a squad of armed men emerge from the treeline. He kept his sidearm holstered while the native men kept their rifles at sling arms. To the relief of the twenty-one-year-old lieutenant, the men were friendly guerrillas. Butts wanted to go to Malabang. Instead, he began an overland march north to Sugud on the path to eventual repatriation.

Stith and Lawson found themselves over Iligan Bay on the north coast of Mindanao rather than over the southern Moro Gulf. The chance to return to Zamboanga or Malabang was no longer feasible. They banked right to try to find the airfield at the Del Monte plantation.

Lawson finally shed his ordnance to pare weight, but the fuel gauge was against him. Short of his goal, he finally put her down on a local road as the engine sputtered from fuel deprivation. A tree caught the plane's right wing to bring his journey to an end. He radioed that he was okay. Lawson suggested that Stith put his plane down in Macajalar Bay. Stith radioed back, "I'm not itching to land in the water. I've done that once before."[8]

Stith continued his search for a place to land.

April 8, 1944: Green Island

Eight VMF-321 Corsairs were sent to cover a large flock of Marine dive-bombers that were to attack Japanese positions at Kavieng, New Ireland. The attack was uneventful for 2Lt. John Stith, but the return home was not. Between enemy-held New Ireland and Tabar Islands, the oil pressure of his Goodyear plummeted. Stith ditched it in the seas. He had enough time to get the raft pack out of his bird before it sank 900 fathoms to the ocean floor. Drifting on the waves, Stith waved to his three teammates, who stayed on station above him. They waggled their wings in response. Eventually, with fuel levels running low, the three "Hell's Angels" were forced to return to the nest. At 30 miles from land, Stith was left with the knowledge that many Marine Corsair pilots who had ditched successfully in these waters never were recovered. No one knew whatever became of Pappy Boyington, who had disappeared three months earlier.

Word of Stith's crash arrived before the "Hells Angels" returned to Green Island. Navy Patrol Squadron 91, the "Black Cats," kept three Consolidated PBYs moored there. The rescue dumbo took off from the lagoon. After several hours of searching, a yellow dot was seen bouncing on the waves west of Tabar Island. After the big cat landed on the seas, crewmen pulled Stith in through a fuselage window blister. For the twenty-two-year-old Stith, the previous three hours had been the loneliest time in his life.[9]

In the midst of the crisis, a C-54 was cleared to land at Zamboanga. Escort fighters covered the approach of Bataan II. Brass from the headquarters were lined up alongside the runway where the Skymaster was finally parked. A door near the tail opened, a stairway was lowered, and "Attention" was called. Salutes were extended. Gen. Douglas A. MacArthur emerged from the hatchway, strode down the steps, and returned the salutes of those who had prepared for his inspection.

Time and fuel were running out. Stith had hoped he'd catch sight of Del Monte or another airfield. With the decision that it was better to land under power than in a glide, he banked his Corsair to the right so he could get a better view of the coastline. The altimeter wound down as he descended. "I circled over Macajalar Bay and decided to make a water landing near an American ship."[10]

Anchored in the bay, the USS *Brazier* (DE-345) had completed weeks of escort duty guiding supply ships following the invasion of Mindanao. At 1518, a lone Corsair circled the destroyer-escort at low level before turning toward the beach. Stated Stith, "Then my engine conked out. At the same time I spotted a clearing near the beach, so I glided toward it."[11]

Stith kept his wheels up. "I shoved the nose in and came in on my belly."[12] He plowed across a supply dump. "My plane came in so quietly that two soldiers working among the boxes didn't see me until I almost on top of them. Then I saw them," reported Stith, "They were running like hell."[13] The landing came to a halt after just 75 feet. A propeller blade snagged a drainage ditch. The 34-foot fuselage went up and over on its nose and left wing. Stith's head slammed into the gunsight. "I was hanging upside down and thanked my lucky stars that I was alive. Then, I saw smoke coming from the engine." He released his belts and fell to the ground. Stith was shook up but not badly injured. Some ground-pounders came to his aid. "Even though my plane was wrecked, I considered myself pretty lucky."[14]

"Some soldiers came up and told me that they had completed an airstrip that very day!" Stith continued, "It was on one side of the dump."[15] SNAFU.

The mission was SNAFU. It ended at the cost of four Corsairs. No ordnance had been dropped on the enemy. But all eleven pilots survived, scattered across Mindanao like seeds in the wind.

The Jokers returned to Zamboanga over the next several days. Seven flew in from Malabang. Butts, who had been escorted by friendly guerrillas to an airfield, arrived at Malabang in an L-4 Cub before returning to Zamboanga. He arrived with his parachute and life jacket in hand. Kramer, who had ditched near the USS *Bootes*, was transferred from ship to ship until he hopped a ride on an R4D. From Leyte he traveled to Peleliu in the Palau Islands. It was several days before he was wheels down at Zamboanga.

It was up to another PBY to return Denny Stith to his squadron. Awaiting him was his older brother, Dick, at Moret Field. After the brothers embraced, the conversation turned to the wound on Denny's face. Henceforth, Denny would be addressed by the nickname "Gunsight."[16]

VMF-115 remained at Zamboanga until war's end. They never did shoot down an enemy plane during their tour there.

Postwar: Three pilots from the SNAFU mission would later die during three different wars. Second Lieutenant Lawrence W. Lawson Jr. was killed in July 1945. He and Kramer were on a training flight to Del Monte when Lawson struck a hill. The ensuing wreckage was scattered over a large area. Lawson's corpse, still strapped into the cockpit, came to rest in a cemetery.

First Lieutenant Bigelow Watts Jr. was killed during the Korean War during an attempted carrier landing. Capt. Watts left behind a widow and one child. Cynthia Watts gave birth to their second child five months after her husband's death.

Second Lieutenant Everett A. Eastman changed branches postwar when he joined the US Army's aviation branch. Chief Warrant Officer 2 Eastman died in Vietnam in 1967.

Second Lieutenant Chaytor D. Mason became a professor of human factors psychology at USC. He passed away in 1996.

Maj. John S. Payne, USMCR, converted to the USMC. For gallantry in action, he was awarded the Silver Star during the Korean War. He retired as a full colonel.

First Lieutenant John D. Stith finished World War II with over one hundred combat missions flown. He continued flying in the Marine Corps, first stationed in China postwar, and then later flew two combat tours during the Korean War. Stith retired as a lieutenant colonel in 1968. He passed away in 2007.

CHAPTER 18

SHEPHERDING THE FLOCK

The gangly Navy ensign stood at full attention. His eyes stared straight ahead, looking over the head of the emaciated admiral. The three silver stars on each collar could be seen peripherally. Their weight hung in the air. The twenty-one-year-old pilot had journeyed far in two years, but now he was before the carrier task force commander but for the failure of a shepherd's staff.

It had been a long journey. A year after the immediate dark days of the Pearl Harbor attack, the young man enlisted in the Navy's V-5 Aviation Cadet program. The training that started in early 1943 finally finished eighteen months later, after he earned his wings of gold at Corpus Christi in July 1944. Ens. Leon Devereaux, like most of his peers, had set his sights on becoming a fighter pilot. Instead, the Navy trained him to fly lumbering Grumman Avengers at NAS Green Cove Springs. When volunteers were sought to fly Vought F4U Corsairs, "My arm almost shot right out of my shoulder!"[1]

From the warmth of Florida, Devereaux was transferred to frigid Chicago in early December 1944. He earned his carrier qualification aboard the converted side-wheel carrier, the USS *Wolverine* (IX-64), flying SNJs fitted with tailhooks. From there he returned to the West Coast for transportation to the newly formed Bombing Fighting Squadron 100 at Barber's Point, Hawaii.

Ens. Leon Devereaux *(front row, far right)* at NAS Barbers Point, Hawaii, 1945. *Courtesy of Leon Devereaux*

VBF-100's mission was different from the traditional VF squadrons. The need for more fighters aboard carriers and fewer dive-bombers became paramount after the Japanese introduction of kamikazes in late October 1944. The -100 was a special functional unit that provided precombat training and carrier qualifications for replacement pilots destined to serve with the fleets. Their bird of choice was the Corsair.

Gunnery, tactics, dive-bombing, navigation, fighter-director (radar) tactics, and rocket training were part of the flight syllabus. In the ground school, the pilots learned more navigation, radio and radar procedures, and plane recognition, and the use of gunnery skills on synthetic devices both from movies and lectures. Escape and evasion, resistance to prisoner-of-war interrogation, flak analysis, intelligence strategy, tactics of Pacific warfare, combat hints and suggestions, fleet communications doctrine and procedures, and the tactics of the Japanese. Flight training always took precedence over the classroom efforts.

Devereaux became carrier qualified again in the bent-wing bird during the second week of March. The jeep carrier USS *Tripoli* provided the deck space. Soon after, a large contingent of the squadron's pilots were sent west to join VBF-99, another recently commissioned squadron, at Guam. There the squadron worked to maintain combat readiness for the replacement pilots through refresher training. There were significantly more pilots than there were airworthy Corsairs. After a few weeks, the unit was reassigned to Saipan, where the pilots chased incoming bogeys and escorted wounded Boeing B-29 bombers back to Tinian or Guam.

In late May 1945, thirty months after joining the Navy, Devereaux and a group of other replacement pilots along with fifty-four replacement aircraft boarded the USS *Bougainville* (CVE-100). Destination: the Fast Carrier Task Force, which had been hunting in the waters east of Okinawa for several months.

The journey was not without peril. Past midnight, the barometer started to fall on June 5. Before dawn, it had plummeted to 28.17 inches. The wind shifted to the southwest, its force reaching hurricane strength. The ocean responded with mountainous seas, and the barometer began to climb rapidly. In the pilothouse, the sailor at the helm called out to Capt. Thurston B. Clark the inclinometer readings, which qualified the degree of the carrier's rolling. The bluejackets aboard knew this device by a more practical reference: the "puke meter."

Aviators are a tough lot as far as nausea goes. But as the rolls grew deeper and the time to recovery to an even keel also lengthened, everyone aboard from bluejacket to captain took notice. At one point the warship rolled 53 degrees, past the supposed degree of no return. Ens. Leon Devereaux said silent prayers for the crew's safety: "I thought we were going down."[2]

Despite the severe pounding, the jeep carrier recovered. "It was a pretty darn bad deal," recalled Devereaux in a bit of understatement.[3] Four support beams under the flight deck were bent, several 40 mm mounts were destroyed, a catwalk was twisted by the wind like a rag, and the forward elevator was left in poor working condition. Though no men were lost, the same could not be said of the mechanical cargo: three Hellcats were swept overboard to disappear into the scud. Below, "Planes were just rattling around in the hangar deck. It was just terrible."[4] By the time the *Bougainville* had broken through the storm, fifteen other aircraft were damaged beyond repair. Stricken from the records, three more Hellcats, four Helldivers, and eight Avengers were jettisoned over the side when the seas finally calmed.

Even the heavies took a pounding: The USS *Pittsburgh* (CA-72) lost her bow. The forward flight decks of the USS *Hornet* (CV-12) and the USS *Bennington* (CV-20) collapsed across their bows.

It was a relief for the two divisions of replacement pilots (one Marine, one Navy) when they were transferred by way of a highline pulled taut between the *Bougainville* and the destroyer USS *McNair*. The journey continued with another rope and bosun's-chair ride from the tin can to the USS *Shangri La* (CV-38).

The replacement divisions were just in time for the last few days of attacks against Kanoya, Kyushu, and Minami Daito Shima, and missions in support of the soldiers and marines trying to conquer Okinawa. The carrier force retired to Luzon on June 9 for a period of upkeep and unwinding.

In early July, the USS *Shangri La* stormed east as part of Task Group 38.4, a steel armada of warships. CV-38 was partnered with her fleet carrier sisters *Yorktown* and *Bon Homme Richard* as well as the light carriers *Independence* and *Cowpens*. Three of the four biggest battleships in the US Navy (*Iowa*, *Wisconsin*, and *Missouri*) and six cruisers provided a ring of fire. Twenty-one destroyers formed an additional outer ring and provided the picket guards. Over 25,000 bluejackets and officers steamed within the phalanx. VAdm.

John "Slew" McCain, commander of Fast Carrier Task Force 38, had three more carrier task groups under his command. He flew his flag from CV-38.

McCain, now sixty years old, had earned his golden wings back in 1936, thus achieving the distinction of becoming one of the oldest naval aviators. After commanding the air campaign in the Solomon Islands during the dark days of 1942, he was assigned to lead the Bureau of Aeronautics. Slew returned to sea in August 1944 as commander of one of the Fast Carrier Task Force's groups, TG 58.1. Just a few days after the emergence of the kamikazes in late October of that year, he was appointed Task Force 38 commander. He led the fast carriers through the invasion of the Philippines and the bold foray into the South China Sea in early 1945 before passing the reins to VAdm. Marc Mitscher. Third Fleet boss Adm. Bill Halsey and McCain spent the next four months planning the missions for the second half of 1945. The invasion of Japan was on the horizon.

But the only interaction the pilots of Carrier Air Group 85 had with the older pilot was spotting him overseeing flight operations from his perch up on the carrier island. He was known to be a cantankerous leader who preferred confrontation to consolation.

The four groups of the task force emerged in the waters off the home islands on July 10. Tokyo was at the receiving end of that day's mission. Refueling exercises and weather prevented another attack until the fourteenth.

It was to be a show of massed aviation power as Task Force 38 launched over a thousand sorties to northern Honshu and Hokkaido, against targets that the B-29s from Saipan could not reach. Moving to within 80 miles of the coastline, the first missions were catapulted before dawn's first light at 0330. Another sweep and strike were launched in the hours that followed.

Midmorning, eight Corsairs were brought up from the hangar deck. As they were spotted aft, a ribbon of hydraulic fluid trailed one Goodyear dash-one D, Bureau Number 87834. Amid a continuous dance of takeoff and landings, the deck force's focus was elsewhere.

The two divisions were sent aloft. One division, led by Lt. j.g. Elvin "Unk" Hatfield, was sent out as part of the combat air patrol (CAP), an aerial guard, to protect against enemy interceptors and snoopers that might follow the American planes back to the task force. Two hours into their patrol, while flying the low CAP at angels 5, they were vectored on a course of 270 degrees to intercept bogies at angels 10, range 8 to 10 miles.

Arriving on station, the bent-wing birds ambushed a pair of Mitsubishi G4M bombers. The division broke down into its two elements for the attack. Hatfield led Ens. Devereaux down in a run from above and behind. When Hatfield's guns jammed, he gave Devereaux a hands-down sign to alert his wingman. Devereaux's weapons functioned as they found their mark: rounds stitched the bomber's fuselage. The port engine began to smoke. As he dove, enemy gunners in the flying cigar returned fire, but their weapons could not find purchase. Doom was their fate.

Devereaux came back around for a second pass. By then the enemy's guns had been silenced. Once again, he laid rounds through the bomber's fuselage. As the plane began a left-hand spin toward the sea, Devereaux followed it down until it exploded against the water. No survivors emerged from the wreckage.

During the initiation of the attack, the second bomber had broken away. It escaped as gun failure also plagued the trailing second section of Corsairs. Hatfield and Devereaux were too late to catch the latter snooper. They remained on station for another three hours until the end of their patrol.

The three other Corsairs landed first on the *Shangri La*, but the cleanup spot was reserved for Devereaux after achieving his first aerial victory. As he circled the carrier, he went through the sequence needed for final approach: his shoulder harness was locked, his tailwheel was free, the landing-gear lever was set for full flaps 50 degrees, and the levers for the landing gear and the arresting hook were shifted to the "down" position. From the center span, the doors opened as the landing gear extended and rotated. Small doors in the tail opened, and the rear wheel assembly descended while the tailhook hung free. The gun switches were turned off and the gun-charging knobs were pushed into the "safe" setting before Dev rolled the canopy back. Airspeed had dropped to 95 knots. All was ready, but just a few gallons of fuel remained in the main tank. If he didn't get aboard on the first or second approach, he'd be parking in the Pacific.

As he lined up on the stern, Devereaux took the cut from the landing signal officer. Ahead of him lay twelve parallel arresting cables. Each end of the wire-covered hemp rope was attached to a hydraulic cylinder below deck that released tensioned wire to bring the planes to a halt once the tailhook snagged a cable. Compression springs on the tail assembly cushioned the jolt for the pilot.

It felt like a good landing as the bird touched down between the first and second arresting wires. But as his 4-foot-long, 70-pound steel tailhook struck the deck, it bounced back up toward its internal housing instead of staying deployed in the down position. Though all three wheels were on the deck, he continued to pass over the subsequent arresting cables. Devereaux instinctively knew something was wrong.

Spotted forward were Corsairs and Avengers that had returned from earlier strikes and patrols. Devereaux slammed on the brakes while the island aft 5-inch mounts flashed by over his right shoulder. As the plane skidded, the twenty-one-year-old pilot was out of deck.

Ahead were the barrier cables. Two stanchions stood guard on opposite sides of the flight deck. Several more pairs also stood at attention in columns behind. Each set held multiple lengths of metal cables that crossed the deck like a tennis net and blocked the path to the forward deck area. As the Hamilton Standard prop slashed into the wires, sparks flew. Divots were slashed into the wooden deck. Lethal splinters pierced the air. The Goodyear flipped forward as the tail rose from the deck to a near-vertical position, wavering between dropping back and turning turtle before the fighter settled in the vertical as it rested on its nose and starboard wing. Deckhands jumped into action to clear the wreckage. Asbestos-covered firemen were at the ready should the plane ignite.

Devereaux unbuckled his straps with one hand, the other ready to grasp the edge of the windscreen. He had braced his legs against the side panels before gravity pulled him forward. "I was not injured and was able to get out of the plane on my own."[5] Stunned, he climbed down from the bent bird while hands reached up to assist his descent to the deck. He took a final look at his injured fighter plane. There was no need to paint a Japanese flag on the side of this Corsair; 87834 was done.

As Devereaux was assisted across the deck toward the island, he was met inside the hatchway by a messenger with an order to report to flag country, three decks up. It wasn't a journey he had anticipated or sought. Recently the Carrier Air Group 85 boss, Cmdr. Wallace Sherrill, had torn into the young pilot for visiting with one of the plane bosses, an enlisted man from Devereaux's hometown of Bend, Oregon. Fraternization among the pilots with nonofficers would not be tolerated. "I thought I was going to be reprimanded again."[6]

Still wearing his flight gear, Dev was led into the compartment used by the task force commander, the senior sailor and the cog of the Fast Carrier Task Force. As the 6-foot-tall ensign came to rigid attention and proffered a salute, there stood VAdm. John McCain.

The crags in his face made him appear much older than his years.

The short, skeletal, and rumpled officer returned the salute but did not issue the expected reprimand. Instead he offered his hand. "Great job," praised McCain. "You are one for one, eh!" With the loss of his own plane after shooting down the enemy bomber, Devereaux recounted later, "That's all the praise you get from an admiral!"[7]

A postmortem of FG-1D BuNo 87834 revealed that the dashpot reservoir, a chamber of hydraulic fluid that kept the tailhook in the down position, was cracked and empty. Devereaux was absolved of any responsibility for the loss of his plane but was never given this information. He would not learn this news for seventy-one years, until the aircraft accident report was finally located.

Of 1,391 sorties flown on July 14, 1945, by the pilots of Task Force 38, only Devereaux shot down an enemy plane over the carrier armada. On July 24, he participated in the attacks against the remaining Japanese capital warships moored in Kure Harbor. His fighter sweep cleared the decks of the battleship Haruna *with their .50s and 5-inch rockets before the fighter bombers arrived. Devereaux's final flight in the Pacific was as part of the massive Tokyo Bay flyover at the end of the surrender ceremony on September 2, 1945. His return to the* Shangri La *marked his ninety-third carrier landing. After collecting three Air Medals for his service, Devereaux returned to Oregon after the war, married, and raised a family. He worked for a lumber company as well as served as the town's mayor for a time. Devereaux passed away in 2020.*

VAdm. John McCain was in poor health by the time he had Devereaux brought to see him. His weight was down to 100 pounds at war's end. McCain begged off attending the Tokyo surrender ceremony, but Third Fleet commander Adm. Halsey insisted he attend. McCain died of a heart attack a few days later. He was sixty-one years old. He was posthumously promoted to full admiral in 1949.

VBF-85 Corsair in the barrier, December 6, 1944, USS *Shangri La*

CHAPTER 19

LAST BIRDMAN SAVED

While Vought was hurriedly working to develop and produce its Navy fighter, the fastest-level flight bird in production, the company was also building one of the slowest birds, the Kingfisher. The two machines would often share a symbiotic relationship in the expanse of the Pacific.

After five months of combat, VBF-83 was worn out. After boarding the USS *Essex* during the spring of 1945, they had flown through the ringer: the March Tokyo Raids, the kamikaze season at Okinawa, the *Yamato* mission, and months of attacks against various -jimas, -shimas, and -daitos. Their scoreboard listed hundreds of kills in the execution of their profession. But they had bled too. Twelve of the squadron's original fifty-four pilots had been killed.

Five other carriers with Corsairs crowding their decks had steamed from Ulithi with them in March. But, one by one, VBF-83 witnessed the departure of the wounded *Franklin*, *Wasp*, *Hancock*, *Intrepid*, and *Bunker Hill*. All were victims of Japanese bombs and suiciders. The Marine Corsair fliers aboard the *Bennington* had completed their tour in June. VBF-83 remained as the senior Corsair squadron on station with the Fast Carrier Task Force. The invasion of Japan loomed.

Carrier Air Group 83 was formed in May 1944. Its fighter-bomber squadron (VBF-83) was carved out of the fighter squadron. Instead of Grumman Hellcats, the VBF boys flew the -1D model Vought Corsairs.

When they came aboard the *Essex*, three pilots from one division (Glen Wallace, Ed Pappert, and Vern Coumbe) were assigned a stateroom along with Clinton "Clem" Wear. They were a tight clan, spending most of their days together, including flying time. Despite the size of the carrier, the pilots were confined to just a few spaces: the ready room, the wardroom, the "island" to watch landings, and their stateroom. The stateroom served as their home away from home. After the day's flying was over, they retired to the compartment to play cards, read, nap, write letters, and relax. Photos of their gals hung inside their lockers.

Left: Ens. Clinton Everett Wear. *Courtesy of the Wear family*
Right: Lt. j.g. Vernon Coumbe

The missions were wearing them down though. By early August, Vern, Pap, and Wallace had over 120 flights recorded in their flight logbooks. They had been lucky: the fraternity of VBF-83 pilots continued to shrink due to injuries, accidents, or combat deaths. Some pilots were missing in action. At least one was suspected to have become a prisoner of war. The number of familiar faces in the ready room lessened as anonymous replacement pilots filled the empty chairs. Regardless, they answered the calls to man their planes without hesitation. But each pilot was aware as he strapped himself into the cockpit that any mission could be his last. The old hands had seen too much combat to assume otherwise.

Wednesday, August 8, 1945

Steaming 160 miles from Honshu, Task Group 38.3 was stymied by the weather. All flights were scrubbed. It was rumored throughout July that they were headed home to Uncle Sugar. The expected dates of departure came and went with regularity. By August 3 the *Essex* was being cannibalized for parts needed by other carriers that were to stay in theater. Instead of packing their bags, CVG-83's pilots prepared for further missions against Japan. Just two days earlier, the flight surgeon tried to ground the entire air group due to combat fatigue. He was overruled by Captain Roscoe L. Bowman. Air Group 83 would remain in combat. "Damn that scuttlebutt," cursed Glen Wallace. "We didn't go home as planned again."[1]

The famed explorer Adm. Richard E. Byrd was highlined aboard the *Essex* from a destroyer to observe Air Group 83 flight operations. In exchange, a mailbag was sent back to the tin can. In it was a letter written by Clem Wear the day before to his bride and new baby. He was in the habit of writing Pat several times weekly. This was the last letter she ever received from him.

VBF-83 Returned to Combat on Thursday, August 9, 1945

After nine days of routine CAP missions, strikes were launched against airfields on northern Honshu and shipping in the Tsugaru Straits. Morale took another blow when word came back to the ready room that Lt. Bucky Harris, one of the squadron's three aces, was lost that morning when his proximity-fuze-tip 1,000-pound bomb blew up en route to the target. Another casualty for the yeoman to record, another letter for the CO to be written home to a pilot's family.

Late morning, minutes after a B-29 dropped an atomic bomb on Nagasaki, the *Essex* and the *Randolph* launched a large strike of Corsairs, Hellcats, and Helldivers against Ominato Naval Base. The 300-mile distance to the target and back taxed their fuel tanks and stamina. Vern Coumbe recalled, "So the pilots manned planes, praying they would come back and set foot in the ready room once more after that last hop."[2] As he had for nearly a year, Coumbe flew wing on Pappert.

The *Randolph's* birds went first, dropping bombs on the IJN cruiser-minelayer *Tokiwa*, a freighter, and a pair of destroyer escorts. By the time the *Essex* birds were able to begin their attacks, the antiaircraft batteries were alerted and ready. As 500- and 1,000-pounders began to rain down, intense AA crisscrossed Mutsu Bay. One VB-83 Helldiver was hit: trailing white smoke, Ensign Paul Bacci turned his plane out to sea. As he retired from the attack, his plane abruptly rolled over and hit the water. No survivors emerged.

Pappert and Coumbe had the misfortune of being the final planes to dive. Pappert scored a hit on the *Tokiwa*, and his wingman followed. After Coumbe released his bomb, 25 mm fire ripped across the nose and right wing of his bird. The oil cooler was sheared from the wing root, breaking through the thin skin of the cockpit before it struck Coumbe in the head and arm.

At low altitude, the twenty-four-year-old pilot was in trouble: the Pratt & Whitney had seized. "Bobcat 305," Coumbe radioed, "This is Bobcat 208. I'm going to land in the bay near where the bombs went in."[3]

Fighting the controls, Coumbe managed to ditch. He scrambled to unplug and unstrap himself from the plane as it quickly settled. Before exiting, the pilot had to lift the severed oiler cooler off his lap and throw it over the side. Coumbe popped the raft and climbed aboard as his Vought sank.

Despite tight fuel supplies and a long journey back to the task group facing them, Ed Pappert was undeterred: "Godson, this is Pap. Let's go back and look for Coumbe."[4] Another squadron mate radioed that he had seen Coumbe in the raft. Finally the fuel gauges forced them to depart. Word was sent back to the task group by way of the submarine CAP that Coumbe was alive but just 5 miles south of the Ominato Naval Base.

Coumbe didn't give up hope of rescue. He paddled against a strong west wind to keep his position in the center of the bay. As the hour grew late, none arrived. The *Essex* was scheduled to depart the task force the next day.

It was nearly 1430 when Pappert and VBF-83 ace Lt. Lindley Godson had departed Mutsu Wan. If a rescue plane was launched immediately, it would not arrive until at least 1830. The odds of rescue at that hour were poor.

Aboard the battleship *North Carolina*, two Vought OS2U Kingfisher pilots, Lieutenants Raphael Jacobs and Almon Oliver, were ready. With so many American planes attacking Japan, it was inevitable that many would not return. But no rescue mission was launched: "Weather was again bad: rain, fog, low ceilings[,] and poor visibility. Some eleven pilots had been shot down in the area of Ominato. We had the rescue duty and were prepared for a long flight into the area in the late afternoon[,] but it was cancelled due to darkness."[5]

Discouraged

After the long flight back, the VBF boys caught the wire, climbed down the right wings, and headed for the ready room. Exhaustion infested the compartment. As they hung up their flight suits, they were under the impression that their war was over, that their months of combat were completed. No rescue mission would be sent to Mutsu Bay. "Over the ticker comes word—a change in plan. Tomorrow is another strike day." Pappert was not alone in wondering, "Why can't we be relieved? Why can't the *Essex* be sent back as she was ordered? We have already flown our share—and a little more."[6]

Pappert, Wear, and Wallace eventually returned to their stateroom. One bunk was empty. That night the mood was somber: "No acey-deucy is played, no card games. Everyone is too tired or too disillusioned to stand another's company."[7] For Clem Wear, the postponement meant one more day before he can return home to his wife, Pat and their six-month-old daughter he has never held.

But for all the losses, both of men and machines, there was still hope, a silent prayer that something good could come from something bad. The missions of the next day brought a silver lining: The *Essex* would remain on station. It fell to Clem Wear, the resident jokester in the stateroom, to give hope definition: "You know, Pap, we might be able to save Coumbe," suggested Wear. "If he can get to shore and hide in the bushes tonight, then swim back out into the bay, it can be done."[8] Wear had reason for optimism. Four months earlier he had been shot down in an attack against targets in southern Japan. He was left adrift 9 miles east of Japan. The following day a dumbo rescued him 22 miles from where he went down.

By this point in the war, air-sea rescue had become a science. At least 60 percent of downed pilots were recovered.[9] Destroyers on plane guard or picket duty had been retrieving pilots since carrier air warfare had commenced. Before missions, pilots were given the coordinates for the lifeguard submarines. Air-sea rescue squadrons were flying mighty Martin Mariners from Okinawa. But only the little Kingfisher had a chance to land in the confines of Mutsu Bay. Aboard the *Essex*, the CVG-83 commanders argued their case to launch a rescue mission. Their request was granted.

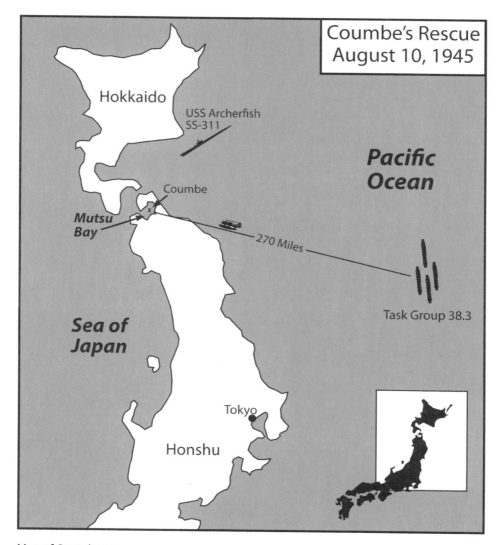

**Coumbe's Rescue
August 10, 1945**

Hokkaido

USS Archerfish
SS-311

Coumbe

**Pacific
Ocean**

**Mutsu
Bay**

270 Miles

Task Group 38.3

**Sea of
Japan**

Tokyo

Honshu

Map of Coumbe rescue

Coumbe stayed at sea for most of the night, fighting against the surf that threatened to drive him ashore. As the dark receded, he discovered the beach was just a mile away. Coumbe paddled to shore before hiding himself and the raft in a patch of dense trees. His one-man invasion of Japan had commenced.

The Vought Corsair Had an Older Brother

The sea version of the OS2U Kingfisher was small and ungainly, a catapult-launched scout-observation plane. It sat on a large center pontoon with two wingtip floats. For defense there were just two .30-caliber machine guns, one in the nose, the other mounted on a rotating ring in the rear of the fuselage fired by the observer/radioman. The OS2U's little Pratt & Whitney R-985 could make only 450 horsepower, less than a quarter of what the R-2800 could produce for the Corsairs. It was slow, but unlike its muscular brother, it could remain on station for long periods of time. The two planes were very different but shared one trait: they were both ruggedly built. The Kingfishers could withstand the punishment of a catapult launch and land in seas with swells up to 9 feet.

Both had been built at the Vought factory in Stratford, but the Corsair forced its brother out of the house. Production for the Kingfishers was shifted to the Naval Aircraft Factory at the Philadelphia Navy Yard due to the greater need for fighter airplanes.

The amphibious Kingfishers were carried on sterns of the cruisers and battleships with the Fast Carrier Task Force for artillery-spotting and antisubmarine patrols. The little bird was used to deliver message bags to other ships, thus allowing the phalanx to maintain radio silence. Often they were the only option to save downed pilots and crew. By late in the war, over fifty airmen of the Fast Carrier Task Force 38/58 had been saved by the little Voughts. Aboard the USS *North Carolina,* a veteran pilot stood by to answer the call.

Lt. j.g. Almon Oliver was one of the youngest aviators in the US Navy, having enlisted just days after his eighteenth birthday. He had earned his golden wings at the tender age of nineteen. By the time he was twenty he had been awarded the Air Medal for outstanding courage while spotting shellfire from enemy antiaircraft guns during the invasion of Iwo Jima. He routinely flew ASW patrols twice a day. Come August, the twenty-one-year-old pilot was an old pro.

Friday, August 10, 1945

As Coumbe paddled toward shore, the *Essex* began to send her birds forth. Roused from his sleep, Pappert hurried to the ready room. To his dismay, the rescue mission had been scrubbed. Instead he was part of a strike force of a dozen Corsairs against Hachinohe airfield. But the flight was on its own, unencumbered by slower bombers. The *Essex* was also 40 miles closer to the target than it had been the day before. It was decided that after VBF-83 attacked the airfield they would fly the extra miles north to Mutsu Bay and search for Coumbe.

The distinctive notes of the Double Wasps brought Coumbe out from his hiding spot. Ens. Joe Jones spotted him: "There he is on that rock[,] waving a white handkerchief."[10] Morale rose instantly with the discovery. The *Essex* was notified of the sighting. With great reluctance the VBF-83 pilots kept their distance for fear of giving away Coumbe's location to the enemy. They eventually turned back to the nest.

0840 hour: In preparation for the rescue, the *North Carolina's* Kingfishers had the rear seat armament removed. No back-seaters would fly. Aboard the stripped and lightened OS2U, Oliver's salute indicated he was ready. A black-powder charge propelled the bird down the 68-foot catapult that had been swung out into the wind. As it cleared the rail, the Vought was already doing 70 mph as it became airborne. Jacobs joined up on Oliver as they pointed their birds northwest.

Immediately after Pappert's strike was recovered aboard the *Essex*, a rescue CAP led by the squadron commanding officer, Lt. Tom "Ham" Reidy, was launched. Lt. j.g. Clem Wear's request from the previous night was approved: he was behind the stick of one of the other Corsairs sent to rescue his friend. VBF-83 was going back into the lion's den to recover one of their own.

Coumbe had taken a position on the northern edge of the woods so he could easily spot any rescue attempt. Failing rescue from Mutsu Bay, he was faced with crossing the peninsula and trying to find the rescue sub 15 miles offshore, a nautical needle in a haystack.

Midday, the sounds of Double Wasps brought Coumbe out of his hiding place and back to the beach. Circling overhead were two Kingfishers guarded by three Corsairs and a Hellcat. The white diamonds on their tails indicated they were from Air Group 83. Coumbe waved madly before dashing to the beach. He took to the water, fighting high winds and surf in an attempt to be rescued.

Breaking from the CAP, two of the Corsairs came in low over the bay. The canopy of one plane was rolled back as the pilot banked to keep Coumbe in sight. As he tried to toss a raft to Coumbe, it was believed that the pack became ensnared on the throttle control unit. To Coumbe's horror, the Corsair plunged several hundred feet before crashing into the water.

The antiaircraft batteries across Mutsu Bay had been alerted by the early-morning visit of the VBF-83 birds. Across the bay, chaos was erupting: "By this time the destroyers at the naval base, and anti-aircraft fire from the airfield and Army bases[,] opened up with a fury," recalled Lt. j.g. Oliver. "There was a strong wind blowing into the beach[,] and the surf was quite high. Lt. Jacobs landed to pick up the pilot while I tried to dodge anti-aircraft fire."[11]

As Lt. Jacobs taxied within 50 yards from shore, 5-inch shells began to bracket his Vought. "I saw that Coumbe couldn't breast the heavy surf[,] so I stood up and tried to toss him a line." Tragedy struck: "An unusually heavy comber shook my aircraft violently, tossing me from the cockpit into the water."[12] Jacobs's foot accidentally pushed the throttle forward. The Kingfisher began to taxi across the bay without him. Now two pilots needed rescue. Large-caliber rounds began to geyser in the water nearby as they swam toward shore.

Oliver watched the events unfold: "After some time the plane started a take-off run, but soon it was porpoising badly and unable to get airborne. I then flew alongside and discovered no pilot."[13]

The runaway bird became the center of attention for the enemy. Shore fire turned away from the pilots and toward Jacobs's plane. Lt. Reidy's Corsair made a low pass and flamed the bird as Oliver brought his Kingfisher down to attempt a rescue: "Both pilots were wildly waving from the beach. I landed, taxied to the beach, blipped the engine with full flaps[,] and backed through the surf onto the beach. I told Jacobs to help the other pilot into the plane and I would send help for him."[14]

Another Kingfisher from the USS *Pasadena* (CL-65) was in the area, but Jacobs was not persuaded. Jacobs climbed into the back-seat position. Coumbe was forced to sit on his lap. Shellfire shifted toward Oliver's plane. The twenty-one-year-old pilot taxied off the beach before getting his tail-heavy bird airborne from the rough seas. For the first time in the war, an American plane had taken off from Japan.

Due to flight distance, Oliver's initial plan was to make for the lifeguard sub. Instead he rolled the dice and turned toward the fleet. As the hours passed, the fuel gauge continued to drop. It registered "empty" as Oliver made his landing approach. The *North Carolina* had already turned 90 degrees in an attempt to make a suitable slick for landing. No go. Oliver was forced to burn more precious fuel as he went around for a second attempt. This time he managed to bring it down, catch the tow sled, and be hoisted aboard. After seven and a half hours in the air, the tanks held but a cup of fuel.[15]

Oliver was greeted by the ship's doctor and presented a bottle of medicinal brandy. He retired to his stateroom and slept for two days after the arduous mission.

Vern Coumbe stayed aboard the *North Carolina* for a day before being transferred back to the *Essex*. "There was no great response when Vern came back," stated Pappert. "He was welcomed, but we had just lost two pilots."[16] For Coumbe, relief to be alive was replaced by horror when he was told that it was his buddy Clem Wear who was killed while attempting to save him. Wear left behind a widow and a new baby girl. Once again, the time to grieve was brief.

A Hero Crowned

Tuesday, August 14, 1945. Radio stations and newspapers across America spread the news of the US Navy pilot who single-handedly invaded Japan and was later rescued. Lt. j.g. Vernon Coumbe was hailed as a hero. A headline later in the *Chicago Tribune* declared of Coumbe, "Credited as the First Yank to 'Invade' Japan."[17]

Tuesday in America was Wednesday, August 15, in Japan. The *Essex* had not turned east to depart Japanese waters. Because he was uninjured, Coumbe was back in combat. He and Pap were sent as part of a strike against Honshu, since there was no reprieve for CVG-83. With the primary target socked in by bad weather, Ham Reidy was leading the flight toward the secondary target when word was received from the fleet: Drop your bombs at sea and return to the carrier. The Japanese had just accepted the terms of surrender.

World War II was over. Lt. j.g. Vernon Coumbe was the only Navy carrier pilot saved from the shores of Japan during the war.

Lt. j.g. Jacobs *(second from left)* and Lt. j.g. Oliver *(third from left)* receive their Distinguished Flying Crosses. *Courtesy of Battleship North Carolina*

Lt. j.g. Vernon Coumbe was awarded the DFC and an Air Medal with seven stars for his service with VBF-83. He was credited with one kill. During the weeks following the surrender, the Coumbe-Oliver tale of rescue was published in numerous papers across America and memorialized in a True Comics strip. Frequently asked to retell the story of his rescue, Coumbe was never able to complete the account without breaking down due to the loss of his best friend, Clem Wear. Postwar, Coumbe and his bride, Helen, headed to the Alaska territory to seek an adventurous new life for their young family. Lt. Cmdr. Vernon T. Coumbe, USNR, passed away in 1960 and was laid to rest at Arlington National Cemetery.

Almon P. Oliver's rescue mission was the final time he ever flew a Vought Kingfisher. He and Jacobs were both awarded the Distinguished Flying Cross for their heroism in the rescue. Oliver made the Navy his career and retired as a commander with twenty-five years of service. Oliver passed away in 2016.

While Oliver was rescuing Coumbe, Lt. j.g. Woodrow J. Borne rescued Ens. M. W. Voss of VB-16 off the east coast of northern Honshu with his USS Pasadena OS2U. Borne was awarded the DFC for the rescue.

Lt. j.g. Clinton Wear was posthumously awarded a Gold Star in lieu of a second Distinguished Flying Cross along with his nine Air Medals. He was credited with three kills. Wear's daughter participated in an unsuccessful scuba search for her father's plane in 1997.

Lt. j.g. Ed "Pap" Pappert was awarded the Silver Star for a direct hit against the Japanese cruiser Tokiwa on August 9, 1945. In addition, Pappert was credited with one kill. He was awarded the DFC and seven Air Medals. He served as Coumbe's best man postwar.

Lt. William H. Harris Jr. earned many distinctions: Harris was the only ace in World War II whose first kill came behind the stick of a Curtiss SB2C Helldiver. He was the final Navy ace, final Corsair ace, and last American ace killed during World War II.

Carrier Air Group 83 amassed a legendary record: 228 Japanese planes destroyed in the air and another 107 on the ground. The Essex carried thirty-six Corsairs in March 1945. By the end of the war, nearly triple that amount had been brought aboard as replacements for Corsairs damaged or destroyed. There was a greater cost: thirty-five pilots and thirteen aircrewmen of Air Group 83 were killed. The Essex finally departed Japanese waters on September 3, 1945.

CHAPTER 20

FROM ŌFUNA TO INFERNO

Few escaped the hornet's nest: airmen captured in eastern New Britain were subject to interrogation and torture. When their usefulness waned, the Japanese left them to slowly starve. High-value prisoners Marine majors Gregory Boyington and Donald Boyle, with four other airmen, were evacuated to Truk before transfer to Japan for further interrogation. They arrived at the naval fortress in the midst of an American Navy attack during mid-February 1944. Safety was never guaranteed.

The Conditions Were Inhumane

Majors Boyington and Boyle and the four other prisoners were moved into cramped jail cells at the devastated Dublon Seaplane Base at Truk on February 21, 1944. There was no room to lie down. The small hole in the floor used as a lavatory was in constant use by Boyle, who was suffering from dysentery. What was to have been a way station during their transfer to Japan had become a fixed hell. So complete was the US Navy attack on February 16–17 that there was no transportation available to evacuate the prisoners.

The same day, 1Lt. Edward Croker, the Avenger pilot with whom Boyington had shared a cell, was executed at Rabaul. More executions followed on March 4 and 5. As retribution for large bombing raids, thirty-one Allied prisoners held at the Tunnel Hill POW camp south of Rabaul were executed. Two Corsair pilots (1Lt. Walter Mayberry [VMF-217] and 1Lt. Roger Hugh Brindos [VMF-321]) were among the victims. Three other Corsair pilots remained captive.

A New Hell

The tires screeched as the Tabby touched down in Honshu, Japan, on March 7. From inside, several Allied prisoners emerged along with the interpreter who had arranged their transfer from New Britain. They had flown almost 3,000 miles from Rabaul during several stages and three weeks of journey. The late-winter air stung the captured airmen. They still wore the dank clothing from their captivity at tropical Rabaul. Majors Boyington and Boyle set foot on Japanese soil. They would spend the next seventeen months enduring prison camps on Honshu.

More Corsair pilots would join them as the Japanese Empire collapsed toward the home islands.

Ōfuna Interrogation Camp

Boyington hobbled down the road with Boyle and the other prisoners. The shrapnel wounds he endured two months earlier when he had been shot down had not been treated. Before them appeared the Ōfuna prison camp. Through its wooden stockade gates, they entered hell.

The Ōfuna camp was unique among the prisoner-of-war camps on Honshu. Most were administered by the Imperial Japanese Army. Instead, Ōfuna was run by the Imperial Japanese Navy. The prisoners were known as "captives," and so no notification of their imprisonment was released to the Red Cross. The prisoners brought to Ōfuna were considered to be high-value intelligence targets. The majority were airmen, submariners, or technicians.

All efforts were spent to break the POWs: New prisoners were put either in solitary or cells that held just two or three men. They slept on straw mats with thin blankets. New prisoners were not allowed to talk with each other or congregate. Prisoners were forced to maintain a lotus sitting position during daylight hours if they were in their cell.

POWs received just three-fourths of the standard meager POW rations. Any personal request, such as using the latrine, required permission from a guard. There was little else to occupy their time, since no other assignments were given. Reading materials were not available, nor were letters written. Unlike in the IJA-run POW camps, no pay was issued to the prisoners for work, nor was there a canteen available to buy toiletries.

The plumbing was fifteenth century. In the latrine, a wooden trough urinal sat atop a gravel-lined floor. Feces dropped into pails that had to be collected. The waste would then be used to fertilize gardens. Prisoners were assigned the task of cleaning both the prisoner "benjos" and the camp personnel's benjo. For every 100 shit flies caught, prisoners earned a cigarette.

Despite the efforts to break them, the prisoners remained defiant. Part of the camp routine was to face northeast toward the Imperial Palace during the morning salute to the emperor. Prisoners and guards alike bowed, but the POWs would also spit in the snow. When the guards yelled their ritual phrase, the prisoners, too, would yell, "Cigarettes for Roosevelt,"[1] which sounded similar to the guards' exclamation. Defiance, even in small ways, helped steel the prisoners.

Savage. Cruel. Stupid. The guards were considered to have been scraped from the bottom of the IJN barrel. Most spoke no English. Many enforced the camp rules with brutal authority. Nicknames were issued by the prisoners to match their personalities or physiques: Weasel, Indian Joe, Flange Face, the Slugger, Gargoyle, Bench Legs, Shithead, Swivel Neck, Metal Mouth. The Olympic runner 1Lt. Louis Zamperini wrote, "Those who worked in the camps were mostly moronic farm kids and misfits not fit for combat."[2] Boyington even caught one guard using a pocket mirror to practice scowling.

Rank was not recognized, but celebrity became notoriety. The guards took delight in harassing or giving extra beatings to famous prisoners such as Zamperini, Boyington, or other high-ranking officers.

Compared to their prisoners, the guards were small. The equalizer was the *bimbo,* a club wielded by the guard for infractions, either real or imagined. Made of solid wood, it was 3 feet long and 3 inches in diameter. Lt. j.g. Eugene Tougas described one of the two beatings he received with the *bimbo*: "I was hit on the back of the legs with this club[,] and it was swung as one swings a baseball bat. I was so sore I was unable to sit down for three days without a great deal of pain."[3]

Boyington was slow to adopt the prisoner rules. "He was braggadocious and liked to throw the bull a lot," recalled Zamperini. "Pappy was stubborn and wanted things his own way; he caused some trouble in camp and suffered the same mistreatment and starvation as the rest of us. After being caught smoking during a nonsmoking period, he was beaten pretty badly. It took a few bumps on his head, but he finally began in his own bulldog way to conform to the submissive POW lifestyle."[4]

"The worst beating I ever had just about one week after I was able to stand up on my feet without the aid of a crutch," recalled Boyington. "I was taken out in a circle and beaten with a baseball bat. After one guard tired with a heavy club, a second guard started with a smaller club."[5] Standing defiantly, Boyington internally prayed he would not lose face and collapse. He was held at the position of attention until nightfall.

"One form of cruel and unusual punishment was described as the 'co-prosperity brace.' Men subjected to this torture were forced to stand with knees bent and hands back of heads," reported Maj. Boyle. "Compelled to hold this position for seemingly unending periods of time, they were lashed when they weakened."[6] Jean Balch, ARM3c, captured after his Helldiver was shot down over Hong Kong, recalled, "These things would last nearly all day. They would have you sitting on an imaginary stool . . . They would have you in a push-up position. If you ever sagged they would . . . well, these guys carried tree limb-sized clubs, and they beat the hell out of you."[7]

Punishments for one POW often meant punishment for all. Other times, beatings were random. Victims often collapsed into unconsciousness. Boyle recalled postwar that even though there were only about a dozen guards, he was beaten by all of them at one time or another.

One guard stood out for his evilness: Sueharu Kitamura. Tagged by various nicknames (the Quack, the Painter, Kongocho, or Congo Joe), Kitamura was an enlisted pharmacist mate who "ran" the camp. He was not an officer but was born of high social status and knew some English. His medical treatment of the POWs was sadistic.

Kitamura thrilled in "treating" the wounded. With shrapnel embedded in his leg, Boyington underwent surgery by Kitamura, who thought he could find the metal with a magnet. Fellow Marine major Boyle recalled that Boyington "submitted to an 'operation' by a Japanese medical corpsman. The corpsman 'operated' with a scalpel and squeezed the fragment out. The whole thing was done without an anesthetic. It took four of us to hold him down and he bled a lot, but he never let out a sound."[8]

Lt. Cmdr. George E. Brown, a survivor of the sinking of the USS *Sculpin* (SS-191), testified postwar:

No proper medical supplies were available at this camp. For a period of nine months I acted as the medical orderly and interpreter for the Japanese pharmacist's mate who was stationed at this camp. Very often I was severely beaten and disciplined for endeavoring to wash or clean the bandages that had been used many times before by other guards because they personally disliked the Japanese pharmacist's mate. I volunteered to perform these duties. . . . I observed that the bandages used by the Japanese pharmacist's mate were never washed or properly sterilized and that extreme disregard of all sanitary conditions prevailed, therefore I volunteered to assist the Japanese pharmacist's mate in his medical duties[,] and I washed the bandages and endeavored to sterilize his instruments as best I could[,] and even this was futile in obtaining any sanitary conditions and worse than would obtain in even the worst possible dispensary in the United States. The same bandages that had been applied to a gangrenous wound or scabies or infected wound, would be applied time and time again to other flesh wounds after only the slightest rinsing.[9]

Brown further testified: "I also noted the Japanese pharmacist's mate treated one man for piles and use[d] the same tweezers to treat another man for an infected throat."[10]

A Navy PBY pilot was brought into the camp. He had been badly burned. During his short time in solitary, the wounds festered as the rank stench filled the barracks. He died. No treatment was ever offered. Another pilot who had arrived with a crushed rib cage died soon after. The guards used his corpse for bayonet practice.

Though the death rate for the camps on Honshu was much lower than for POWs held by the Japanese across the ragged remains of the empire (10% vs. 25%), it paled in comparison to the safety of Allied aviators held by the Germans. Of the five British Fleet Air Arm Corsair pilots captured by the Germans, all five survived the war in Luftwaffe-run stalags. Other than the fifty escapees who were executed after the "Great Escape," very few Allied airmen died in German camps. But three FAA Corsair pilots captured after raids on the oil refineries at Palembang, Sumatra, in January 1945 were beheaded. Another FAA Corsair pilot died in captivity after being shot down over Formosa.

Though prisoners were forced to keep their cells and the barracks and grounds of the camp clean, they were not allowed the same personal accord. No new clothing was issued. The clothes on their backs became ragged with time.

It was intelligence that the Japanese sought from their captives. English-speaking interrogators regularly quizzed the POWs. Lt. Cmdr. Lawrence Savadkin, the engineering officer aboard the USS *Tang* (SS-306), testified that initially, new prisoners were interrogated daily. Most of the interrogators were graduates of American universities:

> They were wearing excellent American clothing. They sympathized with us very much, but all they did was offer us their sympathies, they did nothing to improve our living conditions there[,] which were none too good. As time passed on[,] the interrogations became less frequent and their nature incidentally was technical, all about the machinery, the ship, the radar gear, the engineering department, communications. I believe that we all successfully kept information to ourselves and gave them a lot of nonsense. They seemed to realize it but were perfectly content to fill reams and reams of paper up with information, much of which they must have known was entirely erroneous.[11]

Boyington's Fame Preceded Him

The "Black Sheep" leader was the most famous flier in the Pacific. His face and name had graced newspapers, magazines, and newsreels through the second half of 1943, until his disappearance over Rabaul. In case he was tempted to lie about his identity, Boyington was reminded of this fact. As he was prompted by the interpreter Chicky Honda at Rabaul, Boyington clung to consistent lies throughout the quizzing.

The world did not know that the greatest Marine fighter pilot was still alive. Prisoners held in the initial isolation section of Ōfuna would communicate with others in the non-isolated part of the camp by using a system of closed fist / open palm as a rudimentary Morse code. When Army flier 2Lt. William Dixon came to the camp, the first message transmitted to him by another POW was "Tatsumi Boyington is here."[12]

The rations were not enough to sustain any man at a healthful weight. Most of the prisoners lost 40 percent of their body weight. Three meals of soup and barley were doled out each day. The soups might contain vegetables, greens, potato slices, or bean paste. Occasionally a minuscule piece of fish or meat might appear in the soup. So could maggots. Conditions were bad enough that after a prisoner discovered a tangerine floating in urine while on benjo duty, he pocketed the citrus for later consumption. Wrote William Dixon, "This was not funny or disgusting[,] as no one really knows what a person will do when he or she is starving like we were."[13]

For men on the sick list, the ration became half. For those with dysentery, food was cut off altogether as a poor means to bring the condition to a quicker end.

Food, or the lack of it, was the most popular topic of conversation. Some men made mental lists of the foods they wanted following their release. Louis Zamperini shared recipes from his mother's Italian kitchen. Though Boyington thought that they were just made-up hooey, others enjoyed the distraction. Boyington himself went to bed with dreams of his favorite foods. He and Boyle promised each other that they would install soda fountains in each room of their homes after they returned to America.

The Red Cross did bring food packages at Christmas 1944, but each prisoner received just a part of a box. The guards kept most of the bounty. Some prisoners managed to locate the storage room for the bundles. At great risk, they pilfered food from the packages during nighttime raids.

As Boyington's internment transitioned from new prisoner to regular prisoner, he was given a job in the kitchen, preparing the prisoners' food. Service there offered a chance to pinch food for himself. The fires provided warmth that the thin blankets in his cell could not. Boyington had dropped to 110 pounds, but after he began working in the kitchen, he began to add pounds to his frame.

The chief cook was Tatsumi Hata, but the prisoners called him "Curly." When fresh supplies of rice and meat were delivered to the camp, Curly and the Quack would sell portions on the black market. Vegetables that were intended for the prisoners' meals were allowed to rot. Boyington claimed though that he and other kitchen helpers were stealing food from the guards' meals to put into the food for the POWs.

Despite these brazen thefts of military supplies by its own personnel, the camp administrators turned a blind eye. Not so the prisoners: two sailors from the USS *Tang* were caught stealing food from wounded Navy pilots. Other prisoners turned to Pappy Boyington to address the problem after the *Tang* captain, Cmdr. Richard O'Kane, did not. Boyington, though not the ranking officer in the camp, gained the loyalty and respect of those close to him. The Marine major sternly reprimanded the sailors. Boasted William Dixon, "Pappy Boyington was our lead honcho[,] and no one else counted regardless of rank."[14]

Like the prisoners, guards, too, were transferred in and out. Few of the guards learned any English, but the prisoners began to pick up some Japanese. A few prisoners learned Japanese written characters. Japanese papers accurately described events in Europe but put a strong propaganda spin on their own losses in the Pacific. Between filched newspapers and new prisoners coming into the camp, the POWs had a good sense of what was happening in the war.

Fortress Rabaul

First Lieutenant Moszek Zanger, VMF-222, was captured on May 5, 1944, after bailing out during a midair collision. He was executed by the Japanese. Ten days after Zanger was captured, 1st Lt. Charles C. Lanphier, a member of Boyington's "Black Sheep" Squadron, died of disease and neglect. He had been held captive since August 28, 1943, after crashing while flying through a heavy squall. Three months later, on August 8, 1944, 2Lt. John J. Fitzgerald, VMF-215, who had been shot down in January 1944, died of pneumonia while held as a prisoner on New Britain. Of all the Corsair pilots who had been taken prisoner at Rabaul, only VF-17's Lt. j.g. James L. Miller remained alive.

It Was the Beginning to the End

A single F-13, the photoreconnaissance version of the new Boeing B-29 Superfortress bomber, surveilled Tokyo on November 1. Its presence went unnoticed by the POWs in the camps. Three weeks later, 111 20th Air Force B-29s took off to bomb Tokyo. Few of the bombers hit the target area, but it marked the first time that bombs had been dropped on Tokyo since April 1942, when Col. Jimmy Doolittle led sixteen small Army bombers from the decks of the USS *Hornet* to bomb the capital of the empire. This second appearance of Superfortresses was noticed by the citizens of Tokyo, the Japanese military, and the prisoners of war. The silver birds' presence was significant: ten months of storms followed as bombs rained down on the industrial and military targets in Japanese cities. The drone of the Wright Duplex Cyclone R-3350 engines that powered the Superfortresses overhead became "music" to the prisoners.

Ōfuna: Winter 1944–45

Despite the cold temperatures of winter near Tokyo, the prisoners were not given any extra blankets to keep warm in the unheated barracks. No coats or cold-weather gear was issued to the POWs whose clothes were ragged. Even with snow on the ground, they were forced out of the barracks during the daylight hours. Sometimes prisoners had to perform calisthenics, *taisō*, in the snow. In efforts to keep warm, the starved men would shuffle in tight coils, allowing each man some warmth and protection at the center of coil before moving back to its perimeter and the cold. They kept the huddle as much in the sun and away from the wind as was possible.

These efforts to keep warm provided only meager protection from the elements. "I do remember a Maj. Boyle who was never without a dripping nose," recalled William Dixon, an Army Air Corp bombardier. "Some of us would take bets on when the nose drop would fall."[15]

As the cold of winter blanketed the Tokyo region, permission was granted so the prisoners could sing Christmas carols. The calendar turned from 1944 to 1945. The outlook for the prisoners would soon change.

Corsairs to Japan!

Friday, February 16, 1945. Positioned 120 miles southeast of Tokyo, the mighty Fast Carrier Task Force 58 launched attacks against the Japanese home islands as part of Operation Jamboree. It was a feint for the invasion of Iwo Jima scheduled in three days' time.

The Navy, which had rejected the carrier use of the Corsairs in 1943, had adopted *Corsairs* in a big way by 1945: nine Corsair squadrons flew from the decks of four fleet carriers (*Essex, Bunker Hill, Bennington,* and *Wasp II*). Each of the flattops carried two Marine fighting squadrons. The *Bunker Hill* also carried Navy Fighting Squadron 84, which flew mostly Corsairs. One hundred sixty of the bent-wing birds were available for sweeps, strikes, and combat air patrols.

Some of these squadrons were new to combat. Others had returned from the Solomons to America to refit and re-form. Experienced leaders led rookie pilots who were mostly just twenty-one or twenty-two years old. The eager young pilots were more anxious about staying with their leaders than worrying about capture. "It was a real adventure," recalled 1Lt. Phil "Pots" Wilmot, who flew as a wingman. "I didn't know anything about anything."[16]

In the officers' mess aboard the *Bunker Hill*, 2Lt. "Nick" Nickolaides, VMF-221, noted that "something special was about to happen, when the morning was introduced at breakfast with steak and eggs, a very unusual event for the pilots readying for combat."[17] Stewards served the hearty breakfast to the pilots. Each place setting included china, silverware, and a silver napkin ring. It was no secret aboard the carrier that it was headed to attack Tokyo. "We thought a strike on Tokyo was wonderful, because we didn't know what war was about," reminisced Wilmot seventy-four years later.[18]

When called to man their planes for their first combat mission, the pilots found the conditions less than ideal. First Lieutenant Ray Swalley, VMF-451, recalled, "The USS *Bunker Hill* was taking water over the bow when I got up, so I knew it was going to be a tough take-off with the freezing weather icing the flight deck. Didn't feel good about that[,] but I knew we would go, one way or another."[19]

With the cold, Wilmot traded out his regular Marine boondockers for fleece-lined boots. Cold rain pounded the windshield. The low ceiling and numerous squalls made launching the inaugural carrier attacks difficult: groups could not find each other in the soup. Scattered divisions from different carriers joined up to form new strike groups. When the pilots climbed to higher altitudes, the weather improved. American fighter planes dominated the skies.

Over Sagami Bay on the approach to Tokyo, 1Lt. James Anderson of VMF-451 spotted an Aichi 13E floatplane below him in the fog. Anderson dove on it, scoring some hits as he flew by. His wingman, Wilmot, finished the job by sliding in behind him. His Brownings hit the seaplane's right wing root. The Aichi flamed and crashed into the sea. On the prospect of becoming an ace, twenty-one-year-old Wilmot thought to himself, "Hey, this is going to be easy!"[20]

Ōmori Prison Camp, Tokyo

There were no stewards, no linen, no silver napkin rings. *Tobins*—POWs serving as food handlers—distributed watery soup, barley, and tea for breakfast. Lucky prisoners found a daikon in their soup. Air raid sirens sounded at Ōmori, a large POW camp on a man-made island in Tokyo Bay, 11 miles northeast of Ōfuna. Robert Martindale, a captured Army flier, witnessed the attack: "The steady drone of B-29 engines was replaced by the high whine of fighter engines. When we heard the sounds, everyone came out to watch the show of carrier planes attacking selected targets in the Tokyo-Yokohama area. The low-flying aircraft appeared to be concentrating their attentions on the airfields. Bob Tusken remarked that they were coming over our back fence as they made their runs on the Haneda airfield and seaplane base a few miles south of us."[21]

Unaware they were flying over a prisoner-of-war camp, many of Adm. Mitscher's flyboys chased targets: "Three F4U fighters streaked over the camp and dived in on the Japanese navy airstrips about two miles south," remembered Louis Zamperini. "A Hellcat chasing a Zero came in low over the camp before it broke off and headed back to TF58."[22] Prisoners watched the duels from the depths of their air raid trenches.

As the sirens wailed at Ōfuna, guards kept the prisoners in their barracks. Carrier dive-bombers were seen beginning their runs on the Yokosuka Naval Base. The thunder of the explosions echoed across the hills. Cmdr. Richard O'Kane of the USS *Tang* commented, "As before, a glance to the skies meant a beating from the guards, but the sight of torpedo bombers just yards away was worth it."[23]

Drawn by the familiar sounds of Double Wasp engines, Boyington slipped outside from the kitchen. It was a year to the day that Boyington and Boyle had landed at Truk during the carrier attacks. During that time, the two Marine majors had endured hell together at Rabaul, Truk, and Ōfuna.

Boyington found himself once again close to the action:

What a sight, I thought, as I saw a Zero scooting low along the hilltops directly over our camp, being chased by a Navy F6F, An old familiar feeling came through over me, causing a tingling to run through my body, as I watched the F6F pour his 0.50[-] caliber machine guns into the hapless Zero, which belched flame and crashed into a hillside as the F6F pulled skyward. . . . I was thrilled by the sights of two more shoot-downs before one of the guards finally shooed me inside the back door of the kitchen.[24]

Task Force 58 continued its attacks again on the seventeenth. The flying conditions remained poor: a heavy cloud cover, low ceiling, and squalls made large attacks difficult. When nine VMF-451 Corsairs engaged enemy fighters, two-thirds of their Brownings were frozen. Further attacks were canceled by midmorning. The fast carriers withdrew to prepare for the invasion of Iwo Jima. Adm. Nimitz announced that 509 enemy aircraft had been destroyed in the air or on the ground. Several enemy warships had been sunk, while vital airplane factories has been heavily damaged.

The Doolittle Raid on Tokyo in April 1942 had raised the morale of Americans at home. The Task Force 58 raids three years later raised the morale of the Allied POWs on Honshu. The extended attacks indicated that the US Navy had conquered the Philippines, since they were able to steam at Japan's doorstep. Prisoners knew more raids would follow. They became bolder in their attempts to steal food. Predictions were quietly made as to how many days before Japan would be defeated. The will to live grew stronger.

Chichi Jima

Four days past the February 19 invasion of Iwo Jima, the USS *Bennington* launched a dozen VMF-123 Corsairs on a fighter sweep against the Susaki airfield on Chichi Jima, an island 150 miles to the north. Second Lieutenant Warren Vaughn's bird was struck by heavy AA fire. He bailed out. He was last seen by the other pilots swimming toward shore. The Navy declared Vaughn to be "missing in action."

The Childress, Texas, native was taken prisoner by the Japanese, interrogated, and then moved to a wireless station. The Japanese planned to use Vaughn to decode messages. After several days, it was announced that he would be executed. Vaughn told the Japanese that he was prepared to die. Blindfolded, Vaughn was decapitated by sword in front of a large group of officers and sailors. Lieutenant Kanahisa Matsushita, the surgeon for a torpedo boat squadron, was ordered to remove Vaughn's liver. Two Japanese officers split the organ, each taking part for their own personal consumption.

Vaughn's death at the hands of the Japanese navy was one of many such atrocities. Intent on boosting the morale of IJN sailors on desolate islands, captured American airmen were tortured, bayoneted, beaten to death, or decapitated. The cannibalization of livers or flesh skinned from the corpses by IJN officers was commonplace. The Bonin Islands were the scenes of numerous heinous tragedies.

The Corsairs and other warplanes of TF 58 paid another visit to the emperor on February 25. The raid was a great success as seventy-five victories were claimed by the American fliers. Only a handful of fighters were lost to the enemy.

Four days from finishing his combat tour, 2Lt. Don Carlson of VMF-124 crash-landed his Corsair in a field after AA hit his fuel tank. He was imprisoned by the military police of the IJA, the Kempeitai. During his forty days in solitary confinement, Carlson was starved, suffered numerous beatings, and lost several teeth.

The deadliest bombing attack of World War II started on Friday night, March 9, over Tokyo. The carrier raids during the previous weeks laid the path for the Army bombers. Nearly three hundred B-29s roared over the city in a daring low-level attack. Napalm bomblets rained down on the city. Most of the structures were constructed of wood. As antiaircraft rounds streaked glowing paths in the dark, searchlights lit the night skies seeking targets. The fires raged, and soon walls of flame rose into the chilly night skies. At Ōmori both prisoners and guards alike watched transfixed from the island camp. The inferno drove rats across the causeway onto the island.

At Ōfuna, the prisoners huddled in their barracks. Wrote Boyington, "The B-29s came over low, at around four to six thousand feet. We could hear them swoop down and dive, the engines roaring. We didn't know where they were, didn't know when to duck. We could just put our faces down into our cotton blankets—and hope."[25]

The inferno raged through the night. About 16 square miles of Tokyo were consumed by the flames. Estimates were that up to 100,000 residents died. The stench of death hung in the air as the city smoldered for days. Charred corpses lined the streets. More floated in the rivers and channels. Tokyo had become a funeral pyre.

INFERNO

The Fast Carrier Task Force returned to the seas southeast of Japan on March 18, 1945, after two weeks of refitting and replenishment at Ulithi. The Japanese home islands were in the crosshairs again. The largest invasion of World War II, Okinawa, was two weeks away. Adm. Mitscher sought to destroy enemy airpower and sink the vestiges of the once-proud IJN.

Before dawn, the command came for pilots to man their planes. From the decks of the armada's fifteen carriers, hundreds of missions were flown against a multitude of enemy military targets on the Japanese home islands.

The USS *Franklin* (CV-13) carried seventy-two of Vought's kamikaze killers. Thirty-six belonged to VF-5. Marine Fighting Squadrons 452 and 214 brought aboard eighteen birds each.

VMF-214, famous for its South Pacific air duels in the *Slot* under ace Pappy Boyington, was back for its third combat tour after a fourteen-month absence from fighting. Only a handful of Pappy's "Black Sheep" remained in the squadron. Many, such as 1Lt. John P. Stodd, were rookies flying their first sweeps and strikes.

The "Black Sheep's" CO, Maj. Stan Bailey, led a flight of sixteen Corsairs from the *Franklin* to target the planes at the Izumi airfield. Each bent-wing bird carried 2,400 rounds of .50-caliber and four 5-inch HVARs. Crossing the coast at 15,000 feet, snow-covered mountains and fields lay below. Each division sought its own preassigned target.

HVAR 5-inch rockets from the Corsairs were exchanged with antiaircraft fire from the field. Stodd's -1D absorbed rounds before the engine seized and he was forced to put his plane down in the bay. Stodd escaped the cockpit but was soon captured by an enemy patrol boat. His brothers in the air wisely left him alone, believing that being the aggressor at this point would bring certain harm to their squadron mate. Stodd became the first VMF-214 pilot lost in combat since Pappy Boyington disappeared at the end of the squadron's second tour.

Lt. William "Country" Landreth, an experienced hand formerly with the original Navy Corsair combat squadron VF-17, was in combat again with Fighter Bombing Squadron 10 aboard the USS *Intrepid*. He was part of an early-morning strike against targets on Shikoku. They turned their Brownings on freighters in Yawatahama Harbor. Landreth came out of his dive and pointed the hog's nose toward an island with some small storage tanks and buildings. He let loose with his remaining rounds. One of the buildings erupted

Left to right:
Former VF-17
pilots Lt.
William
Landreth and
Ens. James C.
Dixon. *Courtesy
of the National
Archives,
photos 80-G-
220740 and
80-G-220720*

in a ball of fire reaching over 300 feet into the sky. The leatherneck raced through the churning conflagration at 400 knots. The shock from the apocalypse fractured a lower vertebra in his back. At the same time, the lube oil system of the -1D was terminally wounded. Landreth turned the dying bird toward the open sea, with the hope that he could reach a lifeguard submarine. He wouldn't get that far.

As he was trained, Landreth jettisoned his canopy, turned into the wind, and dropped his Corsair onto the water. Despite his injuries, he escaped the plane, inflated his Goodyear, and camouflaged himself with the blue-colored tarp.

For several days Landreth floated undetected, but the numbing March weather took its toll on the twenty-three-year-old pilot. With freezing rain pelting him, pneumonia raging in his lungs, a damaged esophagus, hypothermia numbing his body, and a broken back, circumstances took their toll. Landreth finally surrendered to a Japanese patrol boat. Like "Black Sheep" Stodd, Landreth became his squadron's first combat casualty. With three and a half kills to his credit, his air war was over.

INFERNO! USS *Franklin*, March 19, 1945, 0708 Hours

From the heavens a Japanese dive-bomber broke through the clouds to drop a bomb on the crowded aft flight deck of "Big Ben." Thirty-three fully armed and fueled planes exploded. Twenty more planes were in the midst of being prepped in the hangar deck below. Above and below, many of the Corsairs had a new type of bomb attached to their center pylon: "Tiny Tim" 11.75-inch, air-to-ground rockets. Each carried nearly 150 pounds of TNT. The combination of high-octane fuel, bombs, and explosions were the ingredients for the greatest conflagration that a carrier was to ever survive.

Fire and explosions racked the *Franklin* for hours. For fighters returning from their missions, the nest was dead in the water, listing heavily, and holed throughout her flight deck. Three-quarters of her crew either had abandoned ship in the face of encroaching fires, had transferred to other ships, or were among the dead and wounded. Several of the other fleet carriers in the task force offered refuge for VMF-452's and -214's bent-wing birds. Destroyers crisscrossed the area desperately trying to save those who had jumped overboard. *Franklin*'s air war during World War II had come to an abrupt end.

His Buddies Almost Got Him

Rescued from the seas the day before, "Black Sheep" Stodd was being transferred by truck to Izumi when another flight of American birds roared down to attack the airfield. With .50-caliber lead hail pummeling the road, the blindfolded pilot was dragged into a ditch until the attack passed. It was not an auspicious start to his new life as a prisoner of war. The twenty-two-year-old pilot would eventually be transferred to Ōfuna.

Landreth was sent there too. His broken back saved him from the torture that others endured, but his bed was still the cold, dirt cell floor. As he slowly healed, Landreth endured problems swallowing. Other prisoners kept him alive by soaking hard tack in the thin rice water before feeding it to him.

As part of their training prior to the attacks on Japanese-held islands, the pilots were briefed about a new policy. Reciting only name, rank, and serial number would quickly lead to a POW's death. Instead, pilots were told to talk about anything that did not pertain to the military. Japanese captors were subject to rapt tales of college football by Landreth, a Cornhusker by birth.

He Complained of a Headache before He Died

The news of President Franklin Delano Roosevelt's death on April 12 spread across the globe. Boyington was working with his crew clearing Tokyo when he was pulled aside by a Japanese soldier who was fluent in English. He told the flier of FDR's death and offered his sympathy. The news traveled more slowly to Ōfuna. "Maj. Boyle was the only prisoner that could speak and understand Japanese, unbeknownst by the way to the Nips," remembered 2Lt. William Dixon. "He was the one who told us about the death of President Roosevelt from a Jap newspaper that was a week or so old."[26] Despite the news, there was no respite in the drive to conquer Japan.

At 5,000 feet over Tokyo, 327 B-29s roared in low for another incendiary attack on April 13. The capital city burned again. Over 11 square miles were consumed. Ōmori, surrounded by water, escaped devastation. Two nights later the Superfortresses returned. Parts of Tokyo, Kawasaki, and Yokohama became infernos.

The Kamikaze Attacks Had to Be Stopped

For four weeks, Fast Carrier Task Force 58 had pressed attacks against Okinawa, the stepping-stone islands of the Ryukyu chain, and Kyushu. A series of massed kamikaze attacks had commenced ten days earlier. The Navy was intent on killing the enemy birds in their nests. On April 16, fighter sweeps were launched against the numerous airfields on the southernmost home island. The tally for Mitscher's fliers were seventeen enemy planes shot down, fifty-four destroyed on the ground, and another seventy-three enemy planes damaged on the ground. Two more Corsair pilots joined their brothers at the "Torture Farm."

Antiaircraft fire damaged Ens. James M. Bouldin's VBF-83 Goodyear FG-1D. He lowered the flaps, kept the wheels up, and crash-landed in an open field. The Sooner staggered from the burning wreckage before collapsing. School children captured him.

In the air, Lt. James Cass Dixon of VF-84 leapt from his Vought after it was hit by ground fire. The *Bunker Hill* flier and former VF-17 pilot was quickly captured, blindfolded, and held at Kishura airfield. The torture began immediately: "If I failed to answer any question or gave a negative answer[,] I was hit over the head with a club. I was then taken

to another place in the vicinity[,] where the same treatment was received. Then I was returned to the cave[,] where the same thing happened again. I did not receive any medical
treatment for my burns for four days. During this time I had handcuffs on my wrists over
the blisters."[27] His valuables, including his Navy watch, were stolen from him.

Within days, Dixon had been flown to Ōfuna. The beatings continued at the hands
of the Quack, Metal Mouth, the Dog, and the Weasel. Dixon sought first aid from the
Quack: "I asked him to treat my burns on my right arm. The burns were 1st degree, and
were very painful. He refused. Four days later I was called into his office for treatment.
The blisters were all broken by this time[,] and my arm was a slimy, dirty, stinking mess
of wounds from my wrist (where two sets of handcuffs and a rope had cut deep into my
arm to my shoulder)."[28] The pharmacist mate "painted the burns with a white salve and
then wrapped my arms with a dirty piece of gauze. Later[,] after the wounds became scabs[,]
he delighted himself by taking a pair of tweezers and ripping the scabs off. Then he would
ask me if I felt much pain."[29] Dysentery stole Dixon's weight.

He Died of Neglect

Lt. j.g. James Miller of VF-17 had been held at the Tunnel Hill POW camp since he had
jumped from his Corsair during an attack against shipping near Rabaul on February 17,
1944, the day after Boyington and Boyle were flown from Rabaul to Truk. During his fifteen
months of confinement in the dank prison camp, Miller's weight dwindled. As he grew
weak from dysentery and beri-beri, other prisoners tried to assist Miller: "He started to
swell up from his toes upward, his face became swollen. We tried to feed him banana leaves
and grass but to no avail," recalled John Kepchia, ARM2c, a fellow prisoner. "Finally the
swelling reached his chest. It looked like an inner-tube around his chest. We knew, and he
also, that the end was near. One night he whispered, 'Goodnight, Kep,' and I whispered
back 'Goodnight, Jim,' and we went to sleep. In the morning he could not be awakened.
Three days later he was gone also."[30]

May 1945: Ōfuna

After weeks of suffering beatings, interrogation, and starvation at various Kempeitai jails,
the Corsair pilots captured during the previous two months (Carlson, Stodd, Landreth,
Bouldin, and J. Dixon) were transferred with other airmen to Ōfuna. They were joined by
a British Corsair pilot. Lt. Donald Cameron had been shot down over Italy earlier in the
war but had escaped. In the Pacific, the same fate awaited Cameron. After an attempted
escape on Formosa, Cameron was transferred to Ōfuna.[31]

There was no meeting of "Black Sheep." By the time Stodd arrived at Ōfuna, Boyington
and Boyle, the senior Corsair pilots, had been transferred to other camps. Maj. Donald
Boyle led a contingent of POWs to the industrial port city of Niigata. During the transfer,
they bore witness to the destruction caused by B-29s. Nearly every city encountered during
the journey across Honshu revealed devastation. To date, though, Niigata had been spared.
B-29s were often seen overhead, as was the accompanying antiaircraft fire. Night raids
were accompanied by the searchlights sweeping the skies. The big birds only mined the
harbor. Their eggs never rained down on the city.

Niigata Camp 5-B was much larger than Ōfuna but just as primitive. Its barracks were
overcrowded. Since there was nowhere for the *gaijins* to escape, the stockade fence was
just 6 feet high. The camp medic was cruel and often sold the camp's medicine on the black

market. There were few guards, but being so far from oversight by Tokyo, many of them were brutal. Beatings were common.

Many of the POWs had been captives since the early days of the war. They included survivors of the Bataan Death March. Nearly half the POWs were civilians. With the loss of able-bodied men to work in factories, docks, and warehouses, POWs were contracted as laborers by Japanese companies. Most worked as stevedores moving coal to and fro under dangerous conditions. Their long workdays continued year round regardless of the weather in the northern city.

Maj. Boyle stood out for his rank, his military branch, and his nationality, since there were few officers or NCOs. Two weeks after his arrival, he witnessed Lt. Tetsutaro Kato, the camp commander, beat a corporal from the Royal Scots who had threatened to strike a guard while working on the docks. Boyle later told US investigators, "I saw Kato beat Shaw with his fists about the face and kick Shaw in the face while he was laying [*sic*] on the ground. One of Shaw's eyes was just a mass of blood. Kato then called me and asked me if I knew what Shaw had done. I replied I did not. He then told me I should know as it should have been my job to know."[32]

TSgt. Stewart Stonestreet testified postwar what happened next: "Lt. Kato started beating Maj. Boyle with his fists. Maj. Boyle was knocked to the ground[,] whereupon Lt. Kato kicked him about the body and face." Stonestreet continued, "Maj. Boyle was kicked and beaten for approximately half an hour. At the end of that time Lt. Kato allowed Boyle to return to his barracks."[33] Other prisoners assisted Boyle inside. His face remained swollen and discolored for many days.

As the war continued into the summer of 1945, there was less work to be done, since Japanese industry was suffocating from the attacks by submarines and bombers. Less work also led to less opportunity to pilfer from Japanese warehouses. The arrival of more POWs strained the physical resources of the camp.

What little medical care that was available came from a captured doctor, but he rarely had medicine available. Prisoners on sick call received half rations. Those who were admitted to the dispensary rarely emerged alive. The death of a prisoner from disease was without ceremony. No services were held; no eulogies or prayers were offered. The corpses were cremated at a nearby cemetery. Camp doctor Kenneth Cambon stated, "Nobody cried."[34]

Yet, hope and defiance could not be extinguished. News of Allied success in the war filtered into the camp. During performances for camp officers, the POW band's selections would venture from Japanese favorites to choices popular with Westerners after the sake had taken hold. Eventually the band would break into rousing renditions of "*Stars and Stripes Forever.*"

Ōmori

Maj. Boyington was transferred to the main Japanese army prison camp at Ōmori. The camp was built on a man-made island that jutted into Tokyo Bay, an unintended protection against the firestorms.

Like at Ōfuna, the eight wooden barracks were unheated. Plastic covered the windows. Only a few bare lightbulbs hung from the ceilings of the 100-foot-long open-bay barracks. The usual allotment of bedbugs, sand fleas, and lice plagued the men. The latrines were of the benjo type. As spring warmed into summer, the stench from the "broth" and the accompanying flies became unbearable.

Though it was a registered POW camp, Boyington and others from Ōfuna were housed in Barrack #1, which was physically separated from the other seven barracks. B-29 crew members were also assigned to #1. These airmen were especially hated and maltreated throughout Japan. At Ōmori, they were given just half rations. They were allowed to bathe once monthly. When air raids took place, the prisoners were not allowed to take cover in the camp shelters. The sickest prisoners had to be smuggled out of their stockade for treatment before being clandestinely returned. "We were not registered as prisoners of war; we did not enjoy the few privileges that the recognized prisoners of war were given, such as reading and having sick call and also being able to fraternize with the rest of their fellow prisoners throughout the entire camp," wrote Lt. Cmdr. Lawrence Savadkin, a survivor from the USS *Tang*.[35]

For the prisoners in the other seven barracks, there was a routine. Each barrack had its own CO and XO. There was an "Officer of the Day." There were also two physicians, two dentists, and two priests. Despite having the clinicians there, POWs suffered from diseases secondary to starvation and location: malaria, boils, pellagra, beri-beri, and tropical ulcers. Respiratory diseases were common. One of the worst afflictions was "Hirohito's curse," the diarrhea and dysentery that resulted from the poor camp sanitation.

The Music Grew Louder over Tokyo

In total, 520 B-29s targeted the urban-industrial area south of the Imperial Palace and areas west of the harbor on May 23, 1945. The city became an inferno again.

22,000 Feet over Kagoshima

Four months of carrier attacks had mostly smothered the kamikaze flame. These suicide missions had been flown by pilots with very little time behind the stick. After being challenged by Allied fighters, the results were lopsided. Rumor had it that there were no good pilots left in Japan. Not so when twenty Corsairs from USS *Shangri La* were sent on an early-morning sweep to Kyushu on June 3, 1945. As they flew to Kagoshima, they were jumped by twenty to thirty Japanese fighters. Diving down from 22,000 feet, the enemy fighters flew tight formations, executed well-timed attacks, employed split-"S" tactics, and retained the initial altitude advantage.

But all fighter pilots are eager to shoot down their opponents. Divisions and sections broke down when the opportunity occurred to engage the enemy. Corsairs gave chase, following enemy fighters through their dives. Indicated airspeeds rose over 400 knots. When Lt. Siguard Lovdal tried to match their turns, the tail tore off his Corsair.

The Corsairs of Lt. j.g. Edward Dixon Jr. and Lt. John Schoff were shot out from under them. They bailed out and were captured. The VF-85 pilots' next stop was solitary confinement at Ōfuna. Like fellow prisoners Lt. j.g. James Cass Dixon and Army flier 2Lt. William Dixon, Lt. j.g. Edward Dixon faced additional punishment for his surname: "When we met a guard in the hallway or anywhere else, we had to bow to him and end his name with 'soan[,]' such as 'Sukata-soan[,]' which I believe meant mister or some word of respect,"[36] explained the Army pilot. The guards resented addressing the three pilots as *Dix-soan*. It provided another excuse to mete out punishment.

It Was a Damned Flight

Ten VMF-312 Corsairs took off to fly a CAP over southern Kyushu on July 1. Two turned back immediately with engine trouble. Three others developed oil leaks. In succession, two pilots bailed out and a third ditched. A PBM on rescue duty arrived rapidly but could not set down on the rough seas. A lifeguard submarine was alerted to the position of the three pilots but could not be on station until dark. By morning's early light, the Mariner returned and rescued two of the pilots. First Lieutenant Samuel S. Smith was not found. Captured by the Japanese, Smith endured torture at Ōmori.

Special Barrack #1, Ōmori

By the summer of 1945, it had become a defiant struggle to survive, since it was just a matter of time before the empire collapsed. Not all made it. Cpl. Arthur H. Gill Jr., USAAF, had transferred from Ōfuna with Boyington. He lost his will to survive, but Boyington made it his mission to goad Gill to hang on. He tried to force-feed Gill but lost the battle on July 2. Gill's corpse was placed on a funeral pyre at the north end of the island.

The music continued through August as B-29s rained ordnance.

Another Corsair Pilot Was Taken Prisoner

About 70 miles northeast of Niigata, Ens. John Maynard Petersen released his 500-pound bomb over the Obanazawa airbase. His VBF-6 F4U-4 absorbed its blast. Petersen managed to fly for another 12 miles before making a wheels-up landing on a plateau. A partner VT-6 Avenger circled in an attempt to find a place to land and rescue Petersen. It was for naught. Petersen was captured and sent to Ōfuna.

The sight of two B-29s high over Nagasaki on August 9 was not reason enough to sound an alarm. Several minutes later the second atomic bomb exploded over Japan. Death enveloped the city. Around 600 miles to the northeast, the prisoners of Camp 5-B were unaware of the terror unleashed over Nagasaki. Fate had intervened: Niigata had been selected as a target for an atomic bombing, but weeks earlier, Kyoto and Niigata were scrubbed from the target list.

Monday, August 13, 1945: 40 Miles North of Tokyo

Ten bent-wing birds strafed the Kashima seaplane base. Pressing their luck, the VBF-85 birds returned for pass after pass. Ens. John Chapman recalled:

> We allowed about a hundred yards between each of us in order to allow ample room to pick up targets and to insure [sic] the safety of each of the guys in front. I turned the gun switches on, armed the .50s, and put my finger on the trigger on the front of the control stick. I watched the three guys in front of blasting away at targets, then lined the "pipper" on my electric gunsight onto a row of aircraft on the ground, squeezed the trigger[,] letting loose a tremendous blast of fire power[,] and watched as a row of aircraft blew apart.[37]

Chapman's oil cooler hemorrhaged after it was pierced by antiaircraft fire. Rather than risk being shot at in a parachute, he ditched in Kasumigaura Bay. After tossing his Smith & Wesson in the water, he was captured by sailors in a small launch. Blindfolded, Chapman was brought to shore. Soon he faced interrogation by Jimmie "Handsome Harry" Sasaki, a dapper USC graduate who was fluent in English. During this session, Chapman received the first of many beatings. After the cross-examination, his next stop was Ōfuna. Chapman was reunited with fellow USS *Shangri La* Corsair pilot Ed Dixon. A VB-85 Avenger pilot and airman were there too.

This late in the war, not only were the prisoners starving, but the civilian populace was too. Sent out into the city daily as part of a work crew, Boyington spoke enough Japanese that he could barter for food with his pay. The extra rations were slipped into the daily lunch that was prepared on-site.

Rumors of peace were rampant around the scuttlebutts and in the squadron ready rooms of the fast carriers by August 15. But until Japan capitulated, combat missions were being sent forth. Task Force 38 launched their fighters, bombers, and torpedo planes for sweeps and strikes.

It was to be a repeat performance of two days earlier. By the end of the bombing, rocketing, and strafing runs, Lt. j.g. John Clifford Dunn of VBF-85 was floating in his raft in Kasumigaura Bay. When a Kingfisher arrived to rescue Dunn, he was already in the hands of the Japanese. Dunn was ignobly the last Corsair pilot to be captured during World War II. His new home was the Ōfuna camp.

The pilot assigned to fly a Myrt reconnaissance plane did not have the gods smiling favorably upon him. His Nakajima C6N1 was light and fast but was no match against Corsairs. A flight of sixteen Air Group 83 Corsairs and Hellcats were inbound to sweep the Sagami airfield. Before they crossed the coast, the Nakajima came into sight. Lt. Cmdr. Ham Reidy led the attack. Out of the sun, he turned astern while firing repeated bursts. His Brownings nabbed the game. Reidy, who had become a double ace with the kill, continued the mission. Tokyo was closed in by clouds. As Reidy pondered their next action, word was received that all strike groups should jettison their bombs and return to their carriers. Upon landing back aboard the *Essex*, the cessation of hostilities was announced to the fliers.

Midday, while flying a CAP mission over a picket destroyer, Lt. Bayard Webster and his wingman, Ens. Falvey M. Sandidge of VBF-85, were vectored toward two incoming enemy planes. Webster's attack left a Frank fighter smoking before it escaped into the clouds. Sandidge shot down a Judy dive-bomber. Sandidge had notched the 2,140th and final air combat victory by American Corsair pilots during World War II.

The Guards and Honchos Had Disappeared

Work moving coal came to a halt after the bone-thin POWs from the Niigata camp realized no one was watching them. When discovered, the guards were standing in line, bowed before a radio, and listening to a speech. Their demeanor reflected bad news. Following the broadcast's conclusion, the POWs were marched back to their camp. With the news of Japan accepting the Potsdam Declaration, several of the guards left and never returned. In quiet celebration, dinner rations were doubled for Boyle and the other prisoners.

Ōmori Prisoner-of-War Camp

As he lay sick in his barrack, Boyington was surprised when an elderly guard secretly told him that Japan had surrendered unconditionally. Soon after, the work crews returned early. One of the English details reentered the camp in jubilant song. The camp commander assembled the prisoners to officially announce the news. He requested that the former prisoners maintain discipline.

Second Lieutenant Robert Martindale recalled:

Most of the men camp spent the rest of the day and evening in happy but subdued elation. Surprisingly, there was very little of the uncontrollable exuberant behavior which normally would be expected at that time. It was a relief to have part of the trials and tribulations lifted from weary shoulders. What had been subjects of dreams and idle talk now began to have more meaning. Rescue, home, families, food, and women now assumed realities in conversations. Survival was no longer paramount nor of importance. We had survived. The sick and the faint of heart had received new vitality. The major thought in all our minds was "How long would it be until we were taken from this place?"[38]

The Japanese at Ōmori were concerned about their own survival for a different reason. Camp records were burned. Many guards got drunk in sorrow. Some wanted to kill the prisoners but found the doors to Special Barrack #10, which housed Boyington and other special prisoners, had been nailed shut from the inside. Other guards intervened to prevent a massacre.

Ōfuna Prisoner-of-War Camp

Two events convinced the prisoners that the end of the war was close. Shot down earlier in the day, Lt. j.g. John Dunn shared what had been rumored aboard ship and news of the atomic bombs. The constant carrier airstrikes had also ceased abruptly. The IJN quickly replaced their barbaric guards with new guards.

Rabaul, August 15, 1945

Warrant Officer Ronald C. Warren RNZAF had been held as a prisoner since June, when his Corsair was shot down. Despite his broken leg, he was held in a cave. "Rabbit" Warren was the only Corsair pilot among the few POWs at Rabaul to make it out alive.

The roar of low-flying American planes brought the prisoners from their barracks on August 25. The guards did not try to force them back inside. As Task Force 38 patrolled the eastern coast of Honshu, hundreds of carrier planes homed in on the "PW" painted on the roofs of the prison camps across Japan. The pilots of the first planes dropped what they had with them: cigarettes, sandwiches, and rescue packs. Later flights dropped goods donated by the carrier sailors and rescue supplies hurriedly assembled aboard ship. It was manna from heaven.

Lt. John E. Freemann Jr. piloted his VB-6 Helldiver from the USS *Hancock*: "We flew in low over Ōmori, only about 100 feet off the ground. On a roof, I saw a message: 'Boyington

Here.' The POWs were in the compound yelling and waving to us. We were so close I could see them well. My back-seater dropped bags of supplies. We came over them twice and dropped bags. The POWs ran right to the bags. We were happy to help. I waggled my wings goodbye as I pulled up to head back to the *Hancock*."[39]

For the first time, fighter planes could flat-hat across Japan without the risk of being shot at. "This is great!" recalled Lt. Ed Pappert of VBF-83. "We are like a bunch of school kids out at recess!" Though the Helldivers and the Avengers could carry large sacks of supplies, the fighters were not left out: "Wonder 21 [Pappert's Corsair division] is again part of a group of twelve Corsairs flying over the Tokyo area. A flight before us told us of paintings on roof-tops asking for food, cigarettes[,] and news," recalled Lt. Ed Pappert. "The cooks make up bags of groceries that we carry in the cockpit to drop to the prisoners of war. Flying low over the buildings we see one rooftop with the words 'VF-83.' We fly as slowly as we dare and drop the bags of food and news releases prepared by the ship[']s personnel."[40]

Many pilots dive-bombed the camps, thus forcing the makeshift Allied prisoner ad-ministrations to designate drop zones. The carrier planes reached high accuracy, but B-29s coming in at 1,000 feet or lower found that the parachutes on the barrels of supplies didn't always have enough altitude to deploy. Once again, the Allied prisoners were forced to retreat when the music of the B-29s began.

For men who had little, the drops were overwhelming: "We established our military police organization in the camp, Maj. Gregory Boyington, USMC[,] being at the head of it at that time[,] and the military police were given the job of rounding up all the supplies dropped, taking them to the proper places[,] and seeing they were properly distributed. Hungry men will probably steal any bit of food that they can lay their hands on[,] and it was necessary to regulate things," testified Lt. Cmdr. Savadkin.[41]

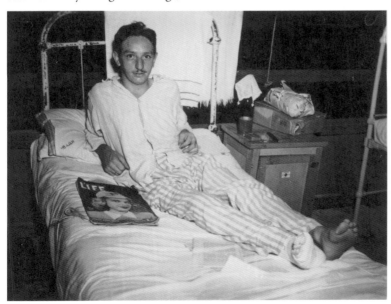

Warrant Officer Ronald C. Warren, RNZAF, recuperating at hospital, Jacquinot Bay, New Britain, RNZAF, September 8, 1945

Tuesday, August 28: Ōmori

Ens. Leonard Komisarek buzzed Ōmori in his VF-88 Hellcat. Pushing his canopy back, the Ohio native, with one kill to his credit, dropped a streamer with the message that the prisoners had long waited to learn:

> *Hi Fellows,*
> *You'll be free by tomorrow . . .*
> *Our planes have landed*
> *On field nearby. Give*
> *The girls back home*
> *A kiss for me. Loads*
> *of luck—God Bless You.*

Liberation

Word Spread Quickly

Three landing barges were approaching Ōmori. Prisoners ran from the camp, waving homemade flags. They crowded the shoreline in jubilation. Many men broke down in tears. Others jumped into the water and swam toward the approaching boats. Liberation had begun.

From its anchorage 4 miles east of Ōmori, Task Group 30.6 began its mission of liberating, evacuating, and extending medical care to Allied POWs. The cruiser USS *San Juan*, the destroyer *Lansdowne*, the high-speed transport *Gosselin*, and the hospital ship *Benevolence* formed the group. Their orders were to evacuate only the most seriously ill prisoners. The rest would have to wait until the surrender was official in a few days.

Lt. Cmdr. Lawrence Savadkin recalled:

> On August 29, ships anchored off the island—we were able to see them. Some Higgins boats came ashore and Commander [Harold] Stassen visited the camp. He told us that we would leave after the peace treaty or the surrender treaty had been signed. However, he was accompanied by a very senior Naval medical officer[,] and after they conducted an inspection of the camp, they arrived at the conclusion that the place was not [a] fit place for us to live in[,] and told us that we would leave immediately.[42]

The task group commander, Commodore Rodger W. Simpson, ordered all available landing craft to begin the evacuation. "The Japanese camp commander protested that he was not authorized to turn the prisoners over to the task unit[,] and he must await word from headquarters that the formal surrender had taken place."[43] Commodore Simpson reminded Col. K. Sakaba that he had not issued a request but an order. Landing parties began evacuating Ōmori, Ōfuna, and Shinagawa Hospital camps.

"We could see this white vessel from the shore, a beautiful sight," stated 2Lt. William Dixon about the hospital ship *Benevolence*. "Many of the more recent prisoners were able to climb up the rope net thrown over the side of the ship[,] but us old timers were too weak to manage that and had to be hoisted aboard by loading derrick."[44]

Though Boyington had managed to keep up his weight between bartering for food while on work details and the later supply drops, most of the prisoners were in much-worse shape. The majority weighed less than 100 pounds.

"Before very late that night, the night of August 29, they had all of the 516 prisoners from Ōmori Camp safely aboard the hospital ship *Benevolence*,"[45] reported submariner Savadkin.

Boyington asked the first Navy nurse he encountered for a kiss. Medical protocol interrupted. Savadkin continued:

There we were given a quick delousing, we were all full of vermin. We were given clean clothing, a quick medical screening[,] and sent down to the chow hall. They had ham and eggs, ice cream, pie and milk. I personally accounted for fifteen fried eggs, about a quarter pound of ham[,] and I don't know how much ice cream. I got sick a few hours afterward. I think all of us did the same thing, and it is my opinion that the doctors felt they could handle an upset stomach, and the effect on our morale would far offset the effect of our upset stomachs after we were all finished with it.[46]

Besides the open mess, the hot showers proved to be the second-most-popular compartments. The hospital ship's evaporators were taxed. Noted Army lieutenant William Dixon, "The PA system requested everyone to refrain from using showers until the following morning."[47]

The most-debilitated patients, such as Lt. James C. Dixon, were assigned racks on the hospital ship, while the healthier patients, such as Boyington, were transferred to other ships. The high-speed transport *Reeves* accepted 149 patients, including Boyington and Cmdr. Richard O'Kane. The USS *Wantuck* (APD-125) took two hundred more former POWs. Thirty correspondents came onboard the *Reeves* to interview Boyington and the other repatriates.

The first Corsairs landed at the Atsugi airfield, 8 miles southwest of Ōmori prison camp. Three VBF-6 Corsairs were launched for an early-morning patrol over Tokyo on August 29. Lt. Robert Thelen's bird developed a gas leak. He and two other pilots landed, thus earning them the distinction of being the first Corsair pilots to safely land wheels down on the home islands. Army Air Force C-54s were being flown into the airfield from Okinawa to liberate POWs. They had no time for the ace Thelen. His buddies returned to the USS *Hancock* when repairs could not be effected. Thelen slept under his plane's wing and ate in a Japanese relief canteen. Since he had landed without authority, the now-peacetime Navy opened an investigation. Gen. MacArthur arrived the next day to add to the commotion.

He Had Returned from the Dead

Less than forty-eight hours after a liberation team arrived to inspect the prisoners at Ōmori, papers across America reported on August 31 that Boyington was alive! In his absence, his mother had accepted the Medal of Honor and a Navy Cross. The Marines promoted Boyington to lieutenant colonel. With the news of his release, the Corps pushed its publication relations campaign up to full throttle.

Surrender: Sunday, September 2, 1945

The war began on a Sunday at Pearl Harbor, when 260 Japanese fighters, torpedo planes, and dive-bombers destroyed the battle fleet over the course of two hours on December 7, 1941. It ended on the deck of the USS *Missouri* in Tokyo Bay, when representatives of the Allies and Axis signed the surrender document. Anchored nearby was the Pearl Harbor veteran USS *West Virginia*. The Fast Carrier Task Force remained at sea. On what was already a bleak and cloudy day for the Japanese, hundreds of American fighters, torpedo planes, and dive-bombers from fifteen carrier air groups flew low over the anchorage in just two minutes. It was an impressive sight. "There were so many planes aloft, it was 'group grope.' It made the pilots nervous as hell."[48] A flyover of B-29 bombers completed the aerial show of might. Liberated prisoners on the USS *Benevolence* had a ringside seat.

Left: Former POWs aboard the USS *Benevolence*. Lt. James C. Dixon at far right. *Courtesy of the J. C. Dixon family*
Right: (left to right) Ens. John Chapman, Lt. j.g. John C. Dunn, Lt. j.g. Edward Dixon, V.Adm. John H. Towers (commander, Task Force 38), Lt. j.g. Richard W. Mann, and Robert F. Hanna, ARM2c. *Courtesy of the National Archives, photo 80-G-278829*

Eight Hours after World War II Had Ended

On the carriers, they called her the "pregnant turkey," perhaps because when she landed, you could see the full span and breadth of the 54-foot wingspan of the Avenger. Large and ungainly in its approach, a VT-85 bird was very pregnant.

September 2, Flight Deck of the USS *Shangri La* (CV-38)

A junior flier got the assignment: fly to Atsugi airfield, where former prisoners were gathering, and bring back the airmen from Air Group 85. Ens. John Chapman recalled, "We were sitting together on the ground[,] and a pilot, [Ens.] Frank Boyer, showed up." Chapman and the two other Corsair pilots, Edward Dixon and John Dunn, plus two other airmen from their air group followed Boyer. "We all walked over to his TBM[,] and somehow, to this day I don't know how, we all five managed to get in that aircraft."[49]

Air Group 85 had lost twenty Corsair pilots during its deployment. The return of the turkey changed that figure. The Task Force commander, VAdm. John H. Towers, welcomed back Chapman, Dixon, and Dunn, plus Lt. Richard W. Mann and his crewman Robert F. Hanna, ARM2c, of VB-85.

VBF-85 pilot Lt. Dick De Mott recorded in his diary:

We have a big crowd on deck to meet them. Oh, what a happy day. They pile out of the planes and we all mob them. All have lost weight, particularly Easy [Mann VB-85] and Dick [Ed Dixon]. Boy, are we happy to see them[,] and in each case it's practically the same. They were continually beaten and starved, existing in the crudest possible way. Easy has lost at least 30 pounds and looks pretty thin. Dick broke his hand when he crashed at Kure in the Inland Sea at about 150 knots[,] and how he ever got out of that is a miracle. His hand was never set properly and is sort of paralyzed as a result. It will have to be rebroken and reset but[,] after that, and some good care, should be alright [sic]. All the guys have tales to tell that are actually dumbfounding[,] and it's hard to sit looking at them and realize what they have been through. We have a party in Dunn's room and listen to him for hours.[50]

The strain of combat was telling: "It makes you so goddamn mad at the Japs to hear about their methods first hand that we regret sorely every round of ammo we didn't fire at them while over there."[51]

Niigata Camp 5-B

B-29s, the planes that might have turned the port city into a nuclear Armageddon, dropped their first loads over the city in the days before the peace treaty was signed. Like at Ōmori, C and K rations rained down. Daikons were replaced by Spam. With fresh uniforms, toiletries, food and cigarettes for barter, and time on their hands, the POWs roamed the city seeking relief from the horrors of war.

The day after the surrender in Tokyo Bay, the US Army arrived at the gates. The liberators discovered hundreds of former prisoners whose morale had soared. Barbecues and bonfires were held. With plans to evacuate the camp on the fourth and the fifth, officers had to visit the city's geisha houses to round up all the wayward prisoners. A Bataan Death March survivor was so drunk that, had he not been discovered under a blanket, he would have been left behind as the others boarded trains to Yokohama.

A Marine musician, who had been a prisoner for most of the war, blew "Taps." Maj. Donald W. Boyle marched with the last evacuees out of Niigata Camp 5-B. They had left the horror of Niigata, but the horror of being a prisoner would never leave them.

EPILOGUE

Operation Magic Carpet, the repatriation of millions of overseas servicemen to America, began its Pacific chapter in the days after the surrender. Battleships and destroyers were initially tasked, but cruiser, hospital ships, troopships, and carriers were eventually added to the task force. The kamikazed USS *Bunker Hill* had been repaired to the extent that she joined the operation. VBF-83, the fighter-bomber Corsair portion of the *Essex*'s Air Group 83, was finally released after six months in combat.

The Marine Corps, like the other branches, expedited the return of their brass and celebrities. After a long flight from Guam to Pearl Harbor on a C-54, Maj. Donald Boyle telephoned both his mother and his wife. Neither knew he was alive. From Pearl, he flew into Oakland Airport along with twenty ex-prisoners on September 10. He arrived in the company of Lt. George Estabrook Brown (the only surviving officer of the USS *Sculpin*), Cmdr. David H. Hurt (the CO of the USS *Perch*), Lt. Cmdr. Ford H. Callahan (who sent the last message from Corregidor), and Cmdr. Arthur Maher (the senior survivor of the USS *Houston*). From California, Boyle returned to his native Brooklyn. His twenty-seventh and twenty-eighth birthdays had passed while he was a prisoner of the Japanese. Waiting for him were his wife, Louise, and his daughter, Patricia, who was born while he was overseas.

Two days after Boyle touched down in Oakland, another Skymaster arrived with Boyington. After his repatriotization, he claimed two further kills during his last fateful flight at Rabaul. Without witnesses or other corroboration, the Marine Corps awarded the victories to Boyington. He moved past Rickenbacker and Foss.

Like during his days of combat in the South Pacific, Boyington became a household name again in papers, magazines, and newsreels. The national press attended a reunion of his fiercely loyal "Black Sheep" pilots. The gathering at NAS Alameda could not have been complete without a Corsair for Pappy to use as a backdrop. Recovered from his wounds two years earlier, Capt. Rollie Rinabarger flew up from El Toro with a specially marked F4U-1D. Twenty-six Japanese flags adorned the nose. For the benefit of the press and the "Black Sheep," their leader pasted two more kill flags. Boyington's legend was further cemented.

Boyington applies the last two victory flags. The Corsair was flown by Capt. Roland Rinabarger of the Black Sheep. *Farbman/LIFE Images collection via Getty Images*

The Marine Corps kept Boyington playing the star. He appeared in a war bond tour. Newly promoted, silver oak leaves adorned his uniform. In October, President Truman hung the Medal of Honor around his neck.

Boyington traveled to New York City several days later to ride in the FAdm. Chester Nimitz ticker-tape parade. He rode in a position of honor in a jeep behind the cars bearing Nimitz and his party. Boyington and his cellmate, Maj. Donald Boyle, were reunited for a few hours during the event and subsequent festivities. They had survived Rabaul and Ōfuna together. The pilots remained friends for life. Decades later, the character 1Lt. Bobby Boyle on the TV series *Baa Baa Black Sheep* was named for Maj. Donald Boyle.

The health of many of the liberated prisoners was slow to return. After returning to America from USS *Benevolence*, a hospital ship, VF-84's Lt. j.g. James Cass Dixon spent four months recuperating. It took "Black Sheep" John Stodd twelve months to gain enough strength and weight to his 90-pound frame before he could be discharged from a naval hospital.

Postwar

While many pilots left the service never to fly in combat again, many of the Marine Corsair pilots stayed in for the Corps or the Reserve. They formed the nucleus for the next twenty years of Marine aviation. Survival during the war was no guarantee for survival postwar. Two of the great Marine Corsair aces, captains Don Aldrich and Wilbur "Gus" Thomas, died in aviation accidents in 1947. Aldrich was flying a Corsair, Thomas an F7F Tigercat.

Many former Corsair pilots were called up to fly when North Korea invaded the South. Some pilots were in new roles, but many returned to combat in the Corsair. Vought continued Corsair production postwar, right into the jet age, thus making it the longest-produced piston-engine fighter in service. The French brought the final model, the F4U-7, to their war in Indochina in 1954. It was a gap of nine years since 2Lt. Joseph O. Lynch flew the only Corsair to crash-land in Indochina during World War II. The final production count was 12,571 planes.

Korea, August 10, 1950

Six weeks after thousands of North Korean People's Army soldiers crossed the thirty-eighth parallel into South Korea, 2Lt. Doyle H. Cole, USMCR, was strafing enemy targets when antiaircraft fire tore into his VMF-323 Corsair. He turned his bird out to sea, hoping to get back to his carrier. He was forced to ditch instead. A mayday call brought a Marine helicopter. Cole was winched aboard. That same day, Capt. Vivian M. Moses crash-landed his VMF-323 bird behind enemy lines. The same VMO-6 whirlybird slipped into enemy territory to retrieve Moses. A new era had begun with the first combat rescues of Corsair pilots by helicopters.

Arlington, Virginia

In a grove of trees on a sloping hillside, a slab of marble quarried in Vermont stands downhill from the Tomb of the Unknown Soldier. It is positioned almost exactly 1 mile south of the Marine Corps War Memorial. As the sun rises over the Capitol in Washington, DC, its rays brighten the gold five-pointed star inscribed on the marble face. Typically, rocks are found on the gravestone, signs of respect and remembrance from people who stopped to pay homage to Col. Gregory Boyington. Pappy never flew another combat mission again after that fateful day over Rabaul in 1944. His personal flaws ended his career. But he and the bent-wing bird remain locked together in history.

Colorado, November 2017

The elderly pilot flew his homebuilt sport plane through a series of maneuvers before landing it on the airfield below. As he picked up the tail and dragged it into the hangar, his mind drifted back to just his second solo flight. It was on December 7, 1941, over sunny Southern California. When he landed the Piper J3, his fiancée emerged from the car to ask where Pearl Harbor was. The eighteen-year-old pilot admitted he didn't have a clue. Three years later he went to war from Pearl on the USS *Bunker Hill*. After over a thousand hours behind the stick of a Marine Corsair, seventy-six years of piloting, and having cheated death on numerous occasions in the air, Pots Wilmot decided it was time to end his flying days. America's oldest active Corsair pilot had survived. He penciled the final entry into his aviator flight logbook. An era had ended.

Lt. Col. Boyington and Maj. Boyle reunited at the Waldorf Astoria in New York City. *Petersen / New York Daily News via Getty Images*

Pots Wilmot at MCAS Mojave, 1944. *Photo from the Loren Leach collection, courtesy of Colby Burl*

APPENDIXES

Kikusui Massed Kamikaze Attacks, 1945[*]

No. 1	April 6–7	355
No. 2	April 12–13	185
No. 3	April 15–16	165
No. 4	April 27–28	115
No. 5	May 3–4	125
No. 6	May 10–11	150
No. 7	May 23–25	165
No. 8	May 27–29	110
No. 9	June 3–7	50
No. 10	June 21–22	45

[*] *The Campaigns of the Pacific War: United States Strategic Bombing Survey Pacific* also cites an additional 435 kamikazes during this same time frame. All totaled, 1,900 kamikazes flew against the US Navy's 5th Fleet and the British Pacific Fleet during the spring of 1945.

USN Nav Aer M-592 Back Pad Kit Contents

1. Whistle
2. Rations: 3 cans
3. Compass & waterproof matches
4. Machete
5. Reflector (signaling mirror)
6. Mosquito head net
7. Cotton line—25 feet of 75-pound test cotton line
8. Water (2 cans)
9. Fishing kit M627
10. Waterproof adhesive tape and 6 safety pins; salt tablets

11. Pyrotechnic projector & six red Very shells
12. Salt tablets
13. First-aid kit: bandages, sulfanilamide powder & sulfadiazine pills;
       morphine syrettes; burn ointment; seasickness pills
14. Sharpening stone
15. Reversible poncho sea blue / orange yellow. Securable over bow & stern of raft.
       Can be used as a water collector or shelter on land
16. Cotton gloves
17. Jack-knife
18. Sunburn ointment
19. Burning glass
20. Kant Rust (graphite lubricant)
       Instruction Manual

American, British FAA, and RNZAF Corsair Pilot POWs

Rabaul

8/28/43	VMF-214	1Lt. Charles C. Lanphier	Died of starvation 5/15/44
8/30/43	VMF-217	1Lt. Walter Mayberry	Executed 3/5/44 (Tunnel Hill massacre)
1/3/44	VMF-214	Maj. Greg Boyington	Transferred to Japan. Survived.
1/20/44	VMF-321	1Lt. Roger H. Brindos	Executed, 3/5/44 (Tunnel Hill massacre)
1/20/44	VMF-321	1Lt. Robert W. Marshall	Died of wounds, 1/20/44
1/23/44	VMF-212	Maj. Donald W. Boyle	Transferred to Japan. Survived.
1/30/44	VMF-215	2Lt. John J. Fitzgerald	Died of pneumonia, 8/8/44
2/17/44	VF-17	Lt. j.g. James L. Miller	Died of neglect, 5/7/45
5/5/44	VMF-222	1Lt. Moszek Zanger	Executed, 6/1945
1/15/45	No. 14 Sqdn.	Flt Lt. Francis G. Keefe, RNZAF	Died of blood poisoning, 1/30/45
6/21/45	No. 20 Sqdn.	Flt. Sgt. Ronald C. Warren, RNZAF	Survived

POW Camps Honshu, Japan

VMF-214	Maj. Greg Boyington	Survived
VMF-212	Maj. Donald W. Boyle	Survived
VMF-124	Lt. Donald A. Carlson	Survived
VMF-214	Lt. John P. Stodd	Survived
VMF-452	Lt. William Landreth	Survived
VMF-312	1Lt. Samuel S. Smith	Survived
VBF-83	Ens. James M. Bouldin	Survived
VBF-83	Lt. James C. Dixon	Survived
VBF-6	Ens. John M. Petersen	Survived
VF-85	Lt. j.g. Edward Dixon Jr.	Survived
VF-85	Lt. j.g. John H. Shroff	Survived
VBF-85	Ens. John H. Chapman	Survived
VBF-85	Lt. j.g. John C. Dunn	Survived
1833 NAS	Lt. Donald Cameron	Survived

Outside Japan

VMF-123	2Lt. Warren E. Vaughn	Executed and eaten, Chi Chi Jima, 2/26/45
Squadron 1834	SubLt. J. H. J. Roberts	Unknown
Squadron 1833	SubLt. Reginald James Shaw	Beheaded, Indonesia
Squadron 1833	Ens. Evan John Baxter	Beheaded, Indonesia
Squadron 1834	SubLt. L. D. Durno, RCAF	Beheaded, Changi Prison, Singapore, 8/1945
VF-85	Lt. David Kincannon	Beheaded and shot, Kikai Jima

Held by German Luftwaffe

Squadron 1841	Lt. R. E. Dubber	Survived
Squadron 1836	SubLt. J. W. Mayhead, RNZN	Survived
Squadron 1838	SubLt. D. Robertson	Survived
Squadron 1834	SubLt. J. F. R. Ball	Survived
Squadron 1841	SubLt. H. S. Mattholie	Survived

Held by the Vichy French in Indochina

VMF-213	2Lt. Joseph O. Lynch	Rescued

GLOSSARY

US Navy Officer Ranks

Ens.	Ensign
Lt. j.g.	Lieutenant junior grade
Lt.	Lieutenant
Lt. Cmdr.	Lieutenant Commander
Cmdr.	Commander
Capt.	Captain
Como.	Commodore
RAdm.	Rear Admiral
VAdm.	Vice Admiral
Adm.	Admiral
FAdm.	Fleet Admiral

US Navy Enlisted Ranks (Aviation)

AMM	Machinist's Mate
AOM	Ordnanceman
ARM	Radioman

US Marine Officer Ranks

2Lt.	Second Lieutenant
1Lt.	First Lieutenant
Capt.	Captain
Maj.	Major
Lt. Col.	Lieutenant Colonel
Col.	Colonel

US Warships

BB	Battleship
CA	Heavy Cruiser
CL	Light Cruiser

CV	Fleet Carrier
CVE	Escort Carrier
CVL	Light Carrier
DD	Destroyer
LCS	Landing Craft, Support
LCM	Landing Craft, Mechanized
LCVP	Landing Craft, Vehicle Personnel
PT	Patrol Torpedo
SS	Submarine

American Aircraft

B-24	Consolidated Liberator bomber
B-25	North American Mitchell bomber
B-29	Boeing Superfortress bomber
C-47	Douglas Skytrain transport
C-54	Douglas Skymaster transport
FG	Goodyear Corsair fighter
F-13	Boeing Superfortress recon-bomber
F4F	Grumman Wildcat fighter
F6F	Grumman Hellcat fighter
F4U	Vought Corsair fighter
F3	Brewster Corsair fighter
J2F	Grumman Duck floatplane
L-4	Piper Cub liaison-spotting plane
L-5	Stinson Sentinel liaison-spotting plane
N3N	Naval Air Factory primary trainer
OS2U	Vought Kingfisher observation floatplane
PBM	Martin Mariner flying-boat bomber
PBY	Consolidated Catalina seaplane-bomber
PV-1	Lockheed Ventura patrol-bomber
P-38	Lockheed Lightning fighter
P-39	Bell Airacobra fighter
P-40	Curtiss Warhawk fighter
R4D	Douglas Skytrain transport
SB2C	Curtiss Helldiver dive-bomber
SBD	Douglas Dauntless dive-bomber
SNJ	North American Texan trainer
TBF	Grumman Avenger torpedo bomber
TBM	General Motors Avenger torpedo bomber

Japanese Aircraft Name Model/Type

Betty	Mitsubishi G4M bomber
Emily	Kawanishi H8K patrol flying boat
Frances	Yokosuka P1Y bomber
Frank	Nakajima Ki-84 fighter-bomber
George	Kawanishi N1K2 fighter-bomber
Hamp	A6M Zero variant
Jake	Aichi E13A recon-seaplane

Judy	Yokosuka D4Y dive-bomber
Kate	Nakajima B5N2 torpedo bomber
Myrt	Nakajima C6N1 reconnaissance
Nate	Nakajima Ki-27 fighter
Oscar	Nakajima Ki-43 fighter
Tabby	Showa/Nakajima L2D transport
Tojo	Nakajima Ki-44 fighter
Tony	Kawasaki Ki-61 fighter
Val	Aichi D3A dive-bomber
Zeke/Zero	Mitsubishi A6M fighter

NOTES

Introduction
1. *Naval Aviation Combat Statistics: World War II* (Washington, DC: Air Branch, Office of Naval Intelligence, Office of the Chief of Naval Operations, US Navy, 1946), p. 15.
2. Philip S. Wilmot, 1Lt. Interviews with the author, 2014–2020.
3. Naval Aviation Combat Statistics, p. 15.
4. "Action Report, USS *Hancock* CV-19, 1 July 1945 to 15 August 1945," p. 122.
5. Capt. Armistead Dennett, USN (Ret.) Interview with the author, October 2013.

Chapter 1: Training for the Fight!
1. Boone Guyton, *Whistling Death*, p. 45.
2. Terry Dodge, *Blue Devils: Marine Squadron VMF-451.*
3. "Whisky Bill" Reynolds, *Diary of a Lucky Leatherneck Throttle Jock*, p. 65.
4. VMF-312, *War History*, p. 8.
5. Training Division, Bureau of Aeronautics, US Navy, *Flat-Hatting Sense*, p. 12.
6. Bill Cantrell, *Friends, Dear Friends, and Heroes*, p. 203.
7. VMF-114, *War Diary 1–29 February 1944*, p. 7.

Chapter 2: Combat
1. Bill Smunk, interview with the author, October 9, 2015.
2. Henry "Hank" Bourgeois, "Becoming a Marine Aviator and Deployment to Guadalcanal," oral history, National World War II Museum.
3. Edward Humes, "Ken Walsh: Ex-Flier Credits Decoration to Experience, Luck," *Orange Country Register*, November 8, 1987.
4. Gregory Pons, *USMC Aviators*, p. 65.
5. Capt John Foster, *Hell in the Heavens*, p. 57.
6. VMF-213, *War Diary 1–30 Sept. 1943*, p. 9.
7. "Chronological Narrative and History of Marine Fighting Squadron VMF-123 (1942–1945)," Air Groups, USS *Bennington*, www.uss-bennington.org (accessed February 29, 2016).
8. VMF-215, *War Diary 1–30 Sept. 1943*, p. 9.

9. Aviation Training Division of the Chief of Naval Operations, United States Navy, *How to Survive on Land and Sea: Individual Survival*, p. 101.

10. Foster, p. 23.

11. VMF-215, *War Diary, 1–30 Sept. 1943*, p. 11.

12. Col. Rolland Rinabarger, "Capt. Rolland Rinabarger," interview by Col. Frank E. Walton, The Collection of Frank Walton VMF-214, National Naval Aviation Museum.

13. Rinabarger.

14. Dominick Pisano, *To Fill the Skies with Pilots: The Civilian Pilot Training Program, 1939–1946*, p. 88.

15. VMF-221, *War Diary 1–31 Oct. 1943*, p. 17.

16. VMF-214, *War Diary 1–30 Sept. 1943*, p. 21.

17. VMF-214, p. 24.

18. VMF-214, p. 23.

19. Frank Walton, *Once They Were Eagles*, p. 43.

20. Sgt. Bill O'Neil, "He Quadruples in 'Brass': Marine Reserve Fliers Holds Many Positions," *Oregon Journal*, October 6, 1957.

21. O'Neil.

22. Walton, p. 44.

23. Walton, p. 44.

24. Rinabarger.

25. Rinabarger.

26. Rinabarger.

27. Philip S. Wilmot, 1Lt., interviews with the author, 2014–2020.

28. Capt. John D. Stith, untitled audiotape of his flight experience in World War II.

29. VMF-215, p. 11.

30. Gregory Boyington, *Baa Baa Black Sheep*, p. 174.

31. VMF-215, *War Diary 1–30 Nov. 1943*, p. 8.

32. VMF-215, p. 8.

33. VMF-215, *War Diary 1–31 Jan. 1944: Aircraft Action Report No. 16, Sec. XII*, Jan. 27, 1944.

34. VMF-215.

35. VMF-215.

36. VMF-215.

37. Henry "Hank" Bourgeois, "Becoming a Marine Aviator and Deployment to Guadalcanal," oral history, National World War II Museum.

38. Bourgeois.

39. Bob Wilson and Sunny Wilson, "Memoirs of Sunny and Bob Wilson."

40. Wilson.

41. Bill Cantrell, *Friends, Dear Friends and Heroes*, p. 230.

42. Cantrell, p. 232.

43. Graciela Strandtman, letter to the author, February 2016.

44. Bryan Cox, F/Sgt., RNZAF, interviews with the author, 2016.

45. Nicholas Mainiero, Capt., USMCR, interview with the author, July 2016.

46. VMF-441, *Aircraft Action Report No. 159, Sec. XII*, Dec. 14, 1944.

47. S/Sgt. Theron J. Rice, "Wounded Corsair Pilot, Son of Employe [*sic*], Made 'Miracle Landing,'" *Marine Corps Chevron*, 1945.

48. Rice.

49. VMF-322, *Aircraft Action Report No. 58, Sec. XII*, June 26, 1945.

Chapter 3: The Caterpillar Club

1. Boone Guyton,. *Whistling Death*, pp. 174–175.

2. Marine Air Group 31, *War Diary 1–31 July 1945: "Friday, the 13th Ditching Experience; By 1st Lt. F. W. Edison, VMF-311, MAG-31,"* p. 35.

3. Marine Air Group 31, p. 35.

4. VMF-115, *War Diary 1–28 February 1945*, p. 15.

5. Bruce Gamble, *The Black Sheep*, p. 351.

6. Philip S. Wilmot, 1Lt., interviews with the author, 2014–2020.

7. Martin Irons, *Phalanx against the Divine Wind: Protecting the Fast Carrier Task Force during World War II*, p. 273.

8. James T. Sykes, "Overseas with a Marine Corsair, 1944."

9. Sykes.

10. Sykes.

Chapter 4: Weather You Survive

1. Marine Fighting Squadron 422, *Squadron History, 1 January 1943 to 31 December 1944*, p. 65.

2. Marine Fighting Squadron 422, p. 60.

3. Marine Fighting Squadron 422, p. 62.

4. Marine Fighting Squadron 422, p. 60.

5. Marine Fighting Squadron 422, p. 60.

6. Marine Fighting Squadron 422, p. 39.

7. Marine Fighting Squadron 422, p. 64.

8. Col. Bill Millington Collection, Flying Leatherneck Aviation Museum, July 2016.

9. Bryan Cox, F/Sgt., RNZAF, interviews with the author, 2016.

10. Cox.

11. Bryan Cox, *Too Young to Die: The Story of a New Zealand Fighter Pilot in the Pacific War*, p. 128.

12. Cox, interviews.

13. Cox, *Too Young to Die*, p. 130.

Chapter 5: Luck, Dumb Luck, Gremlins, and Otherwise

1. "Grampaw Pettibone: He Robbed Himself," *Naval Aviation News*, Sept. 1, 1945, p. 12.

2. Blimp Squadron 31, *War Diary 1–30 June 1944*, p. 4.

3. Associated Press, "Former Mandan Man Rescues Flier at Sea," *Bismarck Tribune*, May 16, 1944.

4. Tom Blackburn and Eric Hammel, *The Jolly Rogers*, p. 215.

5. VMF-114, *War Diary 1–31 December 1944*, p. 8.

6. John Sponauer, "Corsairs over Connecticut, Part 2: The Pilots Symposium," www.simhq.com/_air4/air138a.html (accessed January 17, 2018).

7. Steven K. Dixon, *Photo Recon Became Fighter Duty: Marine Observation Squadron 251 in World War II*, p. 193.

8. VMF-251, *Aircraft Action Report No. 109, Sec. XIII*, April 8, 1945.

9. USS *Helena*, "Anti-aircraft Action by USS *HELENA* against Surprise Diver Bomber Attack at 2245 Zebra, 4 January 1943," January 8, 1943.

10. Ralph B. Baldwin, *The Deadly Fuze*, p. 237.

11. Marine Air Group 22, *War Diary 1–30 June 1945*, p. 19.

12. Jefferson DeBlanc, *The Guadalcanal Air War*, p. 160.

13. DeBlanc, p. 161.

14. Bureau of Ordnance, United States Navy Bomb Disposal School, *VT Bomb & Rocket Fuzes (Recognition and Disposal)*, July 1945.

Chapter 6: Prop Chop

1. Robert McClurg, Lt. Col., and Leon Marketos. *On Boyington's Wing: The Wartime Journals of Black Sheep Squadron Fighter Ace Lt. Col. Robert W. McClurg*, p. 25.

2. Robert A. Enders, 2nd Lt., "Personal Statement of 2nd Lt. Robert A. Enders."

3. Bob Wilson and Sunny Wilson, "Memoirs of Sunny and Bob Wilson."

4. R. Bruce Porter, Col., and Eric Hammel, *ACE: A Marine Night-Fighter Pilot in World War II*, p. 199.

Chapter 7: Escape from Rabaul: The Rookie and the Ace

1. Jenny Scott, *Dumbo Diary: Royal New Zealand Air Force No. 6 (Flying Boat) Squadron, 1943–1945*.

2. United Press, "US Flier Blasts His 25th Jap Plane, Nears Record," *Salt Lake Tribune*, December 29, 1943.

3. Frank Lorey, "Corsair Pilots Tell Their Stories," www.flyingleatherneck.org/blog/corsair-and-marinepilots/corsair-pilots-tell-their-stories/ (accessed Jan. 4, 2019).

4. Fred Hampson, "Boyington Last Seen Diving to Attack," *New York Daily News*, January 9, 1944.

5. Jack Morris, *One Angel Left*, p. 58.

6. VMF-215, *War Diary 1–28 February 1944*, p. 5.

7. Morris, pp. 44–46.

8. Morris, p. 5.

9. Samuel Eliot Morison, *Breaking the Bismarck Barrier, 22 July 1942–1 May 1944*, p. 397.

10. Dub Allen and Frank Johnson, "Colonel Gregory 'Pappy' Boyington," *Air Classics Quarterly Review*, Winter 1976.

11. Morris, p. 6.

12. Morris, p. 8.

13. Morris, p. 14.

14. Morris, p. 2.

15. Morris, p. 3.

16. Morris, p. 21.

17. Gregory Boyington, *Baa Baa Black Sheep*, p. 249.

18. Boyington, p. 251.

19. Morris, pp. 26–27.

20. Morris, p. 29.

21. Lee Cook, *The Skull & Crossbones Squadron: VF-17 in World War II*, p. 125.

22. Morris, p. 29.

23. Morris, p. 29.

24. Morris, p. 29.

25. Morris, pp. 30–31.

26. Morris, p. 31.

27. Morris, p. 33.

28. Morris, p. 33.

29. Morris, p. 33.
30. Scott.
31. Scott.
32. Scott.
33. Scott.
34. Scott.
35. Scott.

Chapter 8: Qualifications
1. Philip S. Wilmot, 1Lt., conversations with the author, 2014–2020.
2. "F4U-1 #02465: Aircraft Trouble Analysis," US Navy Bureau of Aeronautics, 1943.
3. Eric "Winkle" Brown, Capt., *Wings of the Navy*, p. 87.

Chapter 9: Deck Tales
1. Martin Irons, *Phalanx against the Divine Wind*, p. 162.
2. Richard Bullis and Jack Melnick, *The History of United States Ship Waldron: Destroyer 699*, p. 16.
3. Bullis and Melnick, p. 16.
4. Irons, p. 205.
5. VMF-112, *War Diary 1–30 Sept. 1944*, p. 3.
6. Richard W. De Mott, Lt., "Diary of Lt. j.g. Richard W. De Mott," July 2, 1945.
7. William Redmon, Ens., interview with the author, December 14, 2016.
8. Redmon.
9. Redmon.
10. Redmon.
11. Redmon.
12. Redmon.
13. Redmon.
14. Redmon.
15. Redmon.
16. Redmon.
17. "F4U-1D #82626: Aircraft Accident Card," US Navy Bureau of Aeronautics, 1945.
18. Edward Pappert, *Landing Was the Easy Part*, pp. 29–30. With permission.
19. Pappert, p. 30.
20. USS *Chauncey* (DD-667), *War Diary 1–31 March 1945*, p. 16.
21. Pappert, p. 31.
22. Pappert, p. 31.
23. Pappert, p. 31.
24. Dean Caswell, Col., *My Taking Flight*, pp. 86–87. With permission.
25. Caswell, p. 87.

Chapter 10: Escape and Evasion
1. National Naval Aviation Museum, "Kamikaze," www.navalaviationmuseum.org/education/online-exhibits/kamikaze/ (accessed April 21, 2017).
2. USS *Ault* (DD698), *War History*, p. 3.
3. Robert Sherrod, *History of Marine Corps Aviation in World War II*, p. 335.
4. "French Indochina Escape and Evacuation," Collection of Maj. Joseph O. Lynch, p. 2.

5. "French Indochina Escape and Evacuation," p. 3.

6. "French Indochina Escape and Evacuation," p. 3.

7. "French Indochina Escape and Evacuation," p. 4.

8. "French Indochina Escape and Evacuation," p. 5.

9. "French Indochina Escape and Evacuation," p. 5.

10. "French Indochina Escape and Evacuation," p. 8.

11. "French Indochina Escape and Evacuation," p. 8.

12. "French Indochina Escape and Evacuation," p. 9.

13. "Lynch Debriefing at Kunming," 14th Air Force, p. 1.

14. "French Indochina Escape and Evacuation," p. 12.

15. USS *Essex, Action Report: Operations in Support of Landings at Lingayen and San Fabian, Luzon, P. I., 3–22 January 1945*, p. 3.

16. "French Indochina Escape and Evacuation," pp. 13–14.

17. Joreen Santopadre, interview with the author, March 12, 2017.

18. "Lynch Debriefing at Kunming," p. 2.

19. "French Indochina Escape and Evacuation," p. 14.

20. "French Indochina Escape and Evacuation," p. 16.

21. "French Indochina Escape and Evacuation," p. 16.

22. "French Indochina Escape and Evacuation," p. 16.

23. "French Indochina Escape and Evacuation," p. 15.

24. "French Indochina Escape and Evacuation," p. 14.

25. "French Indochina Escape and Evacuation," p. 16.

26. Lynch Collection, telegram, February 5, 1945.

27. H. Blake Moranville, Lt. Cmdr., "My Indochina Odyssey," p. 11.

28. Jacques Beauvallet, Capt., letter to M. Mickelsen, February 1, 1990. With permission.

29. "French Indochina Escape and Evacuation," p. 17.

30. Moranville, p. 10.

31. Moranville, p. 10.

32. Moranville, p. 10.

33. "French Indochina Escape and Evacuation," p. 17.

34. Moranville, p. 11.

35. Moranville, pp. 11–12.

36. Moranville, p. 12.

37. "French Indochina Escape and Evacuation," p. 18.

38. "Lynch Debriefing at Kunming," 14th Air Force, p. 2.

39. Moranville, p. 12.

40. "French Indochina Escape and Evacuation," p. 19.

41. "French Indochina Escape and Evacuation," p. 19.

42. "French Indochina Escape and Evacuation," p. 19.

43. Moranville, p. 12.

44. "French Indochina Escape and Evacuation," p. 21.

45. "French Indochina Escape and Evacuation," p. 21.

46. Vic Johnston, TSgt, "Captive," *The Flyer* (Langley AFB), March 5, 1993.

47. "Lynch Debriefing at Kunming," 14th Air Force, p. 2.

48. "French Indochina Escape and Evacuation," p. 21.

49. "French Indochina Escape and Evacuation," p. 21.

50. "French Indochina Escape and Evacuation," p. 22.

51. "French Indochina Escape and Evacuation," p. 22.
52. Moranville, p. 14.
53. "French Indochina Escape and Evacuation," p. 22.
54. "French Indochina Escape and Evacuation," p. 23.
55. Moranville, p. 14.
56. "French Indochina Escape and Evacuation," pp. 23–24.
57. Moranville, p. 15.
58. "French Indochina Escape and Evacuation," p. 23.
59. Moranville, p. 14.
60. "French Indochina Escape and Evacuation," p. 23.
61. "French Indochina Escape and Evacuation," p. 24.
62. "French Indochina Escape and Evacuation," p. 24.
63. Moranville, p. 14.
64. "French Indochina Escape and Evacuation," pp. 24–25.
65. "French Indochina Escape and Evacuation," p. 25.
66. "French Indochina Escape and Evacuation," p. 26.
67. "French Indochina Escape and Evacuation," p. 26.
68. Johnston.
69. "French Indochina Escape and Evacuation," p. 25.
70. "French Indochina Escape and Evacuation," p. 25.
71. Moranville, p. 15.
72. Moranville, p. 15.
73. Moranville, p. 15.
74. Moranville, p. 15.
75. "Interview of Second Lieutenant Joseph Lynch, USMCR," April 23, 1945.
76. "Lynch Debriefing at Kunming," 14th Air Force, p. 2.
77. Harry Leam, Sgt., USAAF, interview with the author, May 24, 2017.
78. 14 USAAF 27 Troop Carrier Squadron, "Rescued in Enemy Territory to Fly Again," www.14usaaf27tcs.4mg.com/Rescuedtofly.htm (accessed May 2, 2017), p. 1.
79. "French Indochina Escape and Evacuation," p. 26.
80. "French Indochina Escape and Evacuation," p. 27.
81. Moranville, p. 16.
82. "Rescued in Enemy Territory to Fly Again," p. 2.
83. Leam.
84. "Rescued in Enemy Territory to Fly Again," p. 2.
85. "French Indochina Escape and Evacuation," p. 27.
86. "French Indochina Escape and Evacuation," p. 28.
87. "French Indochina Escape and Evacuation," pp. 28–29.
88. "French Indochina Escape and Evacuation," p. 29.
89. "French Indochina Escape and Evacuation," p. 29.
90. Annette Woolard, "A Soldier's Story: Edmund Carpenter II, Air-Ground Aid Section, 14th Air Force," *Delaware History*, Spring–Summer 1994, p. 294.
91. "French Indochina Escape and Evacuation," p. 29.
92. "Rescued in Enemy Territory to Fly Again," p. 2.
93. "French Indochina Escape and Evacuation," p. 30.
94. "Rescued in Enemy Territory to Fly Again," p. 2.
95. "French Indochina Escape and Evacuation," p. 30.
96. "Rescued in Enemy Territory to Fly Again," pp. 2–3.

97. Leam.
98. "Lynch Debriefing at Kunming," 14th Air Force, p. 3.

Chapter 11: Salvation at Kure
1. Philip S. Wilmot, 1Lt., conversations with the author, 2014–2020.
2. Wilmot.
3. VMF-451, *Aircraft Action Report No. 11, Tactical and Operational Data*, March 19, 1945.
4. Wilmot.
5. Wilmot.
6. Wilmot.
7. Wilmot.
8. Wilmot.
9. Rev. Thomas Papazoglakis, interview with the author, March 19, 2019.
10. Papazoglakis.
11. Papazoglakis.
12. Papazoglakis.
13. Papazoglakis.
14. VT-29, *Aircraft Action Report No. 32, Sec. XII*, March 19, 1945.
15. Wilmot.
16. Wilmot.
17. Wilmot.
18. Wilmot.
19. Wilmot.
20. Col. John Hansen, USMC, interview with author Mark Carlson, 2012. With permission.
21. Papazoglakis.
22. Papazoglakis.
23. Wilmot.

Chapter 12: A Torpedo for My Bunk
1. Thomas M. Tomlinson, *The Threadbare Buzzard: A Marine Fighter Pilot in World War II*, p. 94.
2. Commander Carrier Air Group 7, *Action Reports, Aircraft: Submission of, period 30 December 1944 to 25 January 1945, Sec. XII Tactical and Operational Data*, p. 126.
3. Tomlinson, p. 213.
4. Tomlinson, p. 215.
5. Carrier Air Group 82, *War Diary 1–30 April 1944*, p. 10.
6. Carrier Air Group 82, p. 10.
7. Martin Irons, *Phalanx against the Divine Wind: Protecting the Fast Carrier Task Force during World War II*, p. 325.
8. Irons, p. 327.
9. Irons, p. 328.
10. Edward Pappert, *Landing Was the Easy Part*, p. 38.
11. Tomlinson, p. 231.
12. Harold M. Sagers, 2Lt., Unpublished account of being lost at sea.
13. Sagers.
14. Sagers.

15. Sagers.

16. Sagers.

17. Sagers.

18. Ann Styles Overbeck. "Recollections of War: Aboard the USS *Sea Devil* SS 400."

19. Sagers.

20. Sagers.

21. Sagers.

22. Sagers.

23. Capt. Ralph E. Styles, "Oral History," *Naval Historical Foundation*.

24. Styles.

25. Sagers.

26. Styles.

27. Overbeck.

28. Overbeck.

29. Styles.

30. Styles.

Chapter 13: The Escape Artist

1. "F4U-1 #17498: Aircraft Trouble Analysis," US Navy Bureau of Aeronautics, 1943.

2. "FG-1A #13669: Aircraft Trouble Analysis," US Navy Bureau of Aeronautics, 1944.

3. "F3-1A #11170: Aircraft Trouble Analysis," US Navy Bureau of Aeronautics, 1944.

4. VMF(CV)-112, *Aircraft Action Report, Report No. 48-45, Sec. XII*, March 28, 1945, p. 123.

5. VMF(CV)-112, p. 123.

6. J. Davis Scott, Cmdr., "No Hiding Place—off Okinawa," *Proceedings* 83, no. 11 (November 1957): 1209.

7. Scott, "No Hiding Place," p. 1210.

8. USS *Colhoun* (DD801), *Action Report, Invasion and Occupation of Okinawa, Nansie Shoto, April 1 to April 6, 1945, and the Loss of the USS COLHOUN (DD801)*, April 27, 1945, p. 8.

9. USS *Colhoun*, p. 8.

10. J. Davis Scott, "Jap Bait," *Flying*, July 1948, p. 46.

11. Scott, "No Hiding Place," p. 1211.

12. Scott, "No Hiding Place," p. 1211.

13. Scott, "No Hiding Place," p. 1211.

14. Scott, "Jap Bait," p. 46.

15. Scott, "Jap Bait," p. 46.

16. Scott, "Jap Bait," p. 46.

17. Scott, "No Hiding Place," pp. 1211–12.

18. Scott, "No Hiding Place," p. 1212.

19. Scott, "No Hiding Place," p. 1212.

20. Scott, "No Hiding Place," p. 1212.

21. Scott, "Jap Bait," p. 46.

22. Scott, "No Hiding Place," p. 1213.

Chapter 14: The Hunters Become the Hunted

1. Philip S. Wilmot, 1Lt., conversations with the author, 2014–2020.
2. USS *Hamlin* (AV15), *General Action Report, Capture of OKINAWA GUNTO, Phases I and II, 23 March to 17 May 1945 (June 15, 1945)*, p. 102.

Chapter 15: Seaborne Savior

1. Philip S. Wilmot, 1Lt., conversations with the author, 2014–2020.
2. Wilmot.
3. Earl W. Langston, Maj., "A Time for Miracles," p. 2.
4. Langston, p. 2.
5. Langston, p. 3.
6. Langston, p. 4.
7. Kearney Smith, *Aboard LCS 11 in World War II: A Memoir by Lawrence B. Smith*, p. 81.
8. Smith, p. 82.
9. VF-85, *Aircraft Action Report No. 13, Sec. XII*, May 4, 1945.
10. VF-85.
11. VF-85.
12. VF-85.
13. Smith, p. 80.
14. USS LCS(L)(3)11, *War Diary 1–31 May 1945*, p. 2.

Chapter 16: Death of the Aces: Kamikazes against the Bunker Hill

1. Philip S. Wilmot, 1Lt., conversations with the author, 2014–2020.
2. Wilmot.
3. Jon Guttman, "Ace in Day," *Aviation History*, July 2007.
4. Wilmot.
5. Dean Caswell, Col., *Fighting Falcons: The Saga of Marine Fighter Squadron VMF 221*, p. 161. With permission.
6. Jan Jacob and Barrett Tillman, "The Wolf Gang: A History of CVG 84," *The Hook*, August 1990, p. 84.
7. Joe Ditler, "Coronado's 'Avenue of the Heroes'. . . Commander Stan Abele, USN," *Coronado Eagle & Journal*, March 8, 2017.
8. Jacob, p. 84.
9. Maxwell Taylor Kennedy, *Danger's Hour: The Story of the USS Bunker Hill and the Kamikaze Pilot Who Crippled Her*, pp. 286–287.
10. Ditler, "Coronado."
11. Jeffrey R. Veesenmeyer, *Kamikaze Terror: Sailors Who Battled the Divine Wind*, p. 124.
12. Veesenmeyer, p. 126.
13. Terry Dodge, *Blue Devils: Marine Squadron VMF-451*, DVD.
14. Wilmot.
15. Dodge.
16. Wilmot.
17. Earl W. Langston, Maj., "A Time for Miracles," p. 5.
18. Caswell, *Fighting Falcons*, pp. 156–157.
19. Caswell, p. 157.
20. Veesenmeyer, p. 128.

21. Wilmot.

22. Guttman.

23. Dodge.

24. Caswell, p. 157.

25. Caswell, p. 154.

26. Caswell, p. 154.

27. Caswell, p. 151.

28. Caswell, p. 155.

29. Ralph Glendinning, 1Lt., interview with the author, October 30, 2015.

30. Caswell, p. 152.

31. Ditler.

32. Caswell, p. 155.

33. Caswell, p. 162.

34. Wilmot.

35. Wilbert P. Popp, LDCR, *The Survival of a WWII Navy Fighter Pilot*, 124.

36. Wilmot.

37. Wilmot.

38. Wesley S. Todd, USMC, "Oral History," Wisconsin Veterans Museum Research Center.

39. Langston, p. 6.

40. Dodge.

41. Caswell, p. 157.

42. Dodge.

43. Wilmot.

44. "Vicksburg Flier Sensed Fate of Flame-Swept Bunker Hill," *Commercial Appeal*, June 28, 1945.

45. "Vicksburg Flier Sensed Fate of Flame-Swept Bunker Hill."

46. Caswell, p. 160.

47. Caswell, p. 147.

48. Todd.

49. Glen Wallace, "Wally's War: Glen Wallace's War Diary 2—Kilroy Was Here; Remembering the War Years."

50. Wallace.

51. Caswell, p. 162.

52. Veesenmeyer, p. 133.

53. Caswell, p. 152.

54. Popp, p. 191.

55. Ditler, "Coronado."

56. Joe Ditler, "WWII Veteran Shares Stories with Visitors aboard The USS Midway," *Eagle & Times*, October 11, 2012.

57. Veesenmeyer, p. 133.

58. Dean Caswell, letter to the author, May 17, 2015.

59. Dean Caswell, Col., *Fighting Falcons: The Saga of Marine Fighter Squadron VMF 221*, p. 158.

60. Todd.

61. Wilmot.

Chapter 17: SNAFU

1. Susan Stith, interview with the author, July 13, 2017.
2. S. Stith.
3. VMF-115, *War Diary, 1–30 June 1945*, p. 12.
4. John D. Stith, Capt., untitled audiotape of his flight experience in World War II.
5. John D. Stith, Capt.
6. S. Stith.
7. VMF-115, p. 8.
8. S. Stith.
9. S Stith.
10. "Unaware of Airstrip, Crash-Lands Plane," *St. Louis Globe-Democrat*, July 30, 1945.
11. "Unaware of Airstrip, Crash-Lands Plane."
12. John D. Stith, Capt.
13. "Unaware of Airstrip, Crash-Lands Plane."
14. "Unaware of Airstrip, Crash-Lands Plane."
15. "Unaware of Airstrip, Crash-Lands Plane."
16. S. Stith.

Chapter 18: Shepherding the Flock

1. Leon Devereaux, Ens., interview with the author, December 23, 2016.
2. Devereaux.
3. Devereaux.
4. Devereaux.
5. Devereaux.
6. Devereaux.
7. Devereaux.

Chapter 19: Last Birdman Saved

1. Glen Wallace, "Wally's War: Glen Wallace's War Diary 2—Kilroy Was Here; Remembering the War Years."
2. Edward Pappert, *Landing Was the Easy Part*, p. 107. With permission.
3. Pappert, p. 108.
4. Pappert, p. 108.
5. Almon P. Oliver, Cmdr., The Almon Oliver Collection, courtesy of Battleship North Carolina.
6. Pappert, p. 109.
7. Pappert, p. 109.
8. Pappert, p. 109.
9. Commander Task Force 58, *Action Report from 14 March through 28 May 1945, Part III (11) Rescue Operations*, p. 49.
10. Pappert, p. 109.
11. Oliver.
12. "Chance Vought/LTV History," Special Collections, Library of the University of Texas at Dallas, p. 26.
13. Oliver.
14. Oliver.
15. Oliver.
16. Edward Pappert, email to the author, April 13, 2018.

17. "Credited as the First Yank to 'Invade' Japan," *Chicago Tribune*, September 23, 1945.

Chapter 20: From Ōfuna to Inferno
1. William Dixon, 2Lt., personal memoirs, chapter 5, p. 20.
2. Louis Zamperini, *Devil at My Heels: A Heroic Olympian's Astonishing Survival as a Japanese POW in World War II*, p. 140.
3. Eugene J. Tougas, Lt. j.g., "Testimony of Prisoner of War Lt. (jg) Eugene J. Tougas," Naval Air Station Jacksonville, September 5, 1946.
4. Zamperini, p. 139.
5. Gregory Boyington, *Baa Baa Black Sheep*, p. 267.
6. "Beaten with Bats," *Brooklyn Eagle*, September 24, 1945.
7. Jean Balch, "Yorktown Aviator: My Experience as a Prisoner of War by the Imperial Japanese," www.yorktownsailor.com/yorktown/pow.htm.
8. "How Japs Carved Up Boyington without Giving an Anesthetic," *New York Daily News*, September 24, 1945.
9. George E. Brown Jr., Lt. Cmdr., "Perpetuation of Testimony of George Estabrook Brown, Jr., Lieut. Commander, USNR, Third Naval District, US Navy, New York, July 10, 1946," p. 5.
10. Brown, p. 6.
11. Lawrence Savadkin, Lt. Cmdr., "USS *TANG* and USS *MAYRANT*," US Navy, February 7, 1946, p. 12.
12. William Dixon, p. 12.
13. William Dixon, p. 16.
14. William Dixon, p. 13.
15. William Dixon, p. 17.
16. Philip S. Wilmot, 1Lt., conversations with the author, 2014–2020.
17. Dean Caswell, Col., *Kamikaze Madness and Marine Fighter Pilots: A True Story of a Fighting Ship and Its Marine Fighter Pilots*, p. 40.
18. Wilmot.
19. Terry Dodge, *Blue Devils: Marine Squadron VMF-451*.
20. Wilmot.
21. Robert R. Martindale, *The 13th Mission: The Saga of a POW at Camp Omori, Tokyo*, p. 198.
22. Zamperini, p. 72.
23. Richard H. O'Kane, Adm., *Clear the Bridge! The War Patrols of the USS Tang*, p. 465.
24. Boyington, pp. 308–309.
25. Boyington, p. 320.
26. William Dixon, p. 14.
27. James Cass Dixon, Lt. j.g., "The Personal Papers of Lt. jg. James Cass Dixon."
28. James Cass Dixon.
29. James Cass Dixon.
30. John B. Kepchia, ACRM, *M.I.A. over Rabaul South Pacific*, p. 120.
31. Will Iredale, *The Kamikaze Hunters: Fighting for the Pacific, 1945*, pp. 284–285.
32. "Statement of Donald Wisner Boyle, 23Sep46," National Archives (College Park, MD), Record Group 153, Entry (A1) 143, Records of the Judge Advocate General (Army), War Crimes Division, Case Files, 1944–1949, Box 646.

33. Testimony of T/Sgt Stewart Lincoln Stonestreet, National Archives (College Park, MD), Records of the Judge Advocate General (Army), War Crimes Division, Case Files, 1944–1949, Box 646.

34. Kenneth Cambon, MD, *Guest of Hirohito*, p. 74.

35. Savadkin, p. 12.

36. William Dixon, p. 19.

37. John Chapman, Ens, "Personal History," p. 3.

38. Martindale, p. 227.

39. John E. Freemann Jr., Lt., interview with the author, April 24, 2019.

40. Edward Pappert, *Landing Was the Easy Part*, p. 118.

41. Savadkin, p. 13.

42. Savadkin, pp. 13–14.

43. Commander in Chief, Pacific, US Navy. *Report of Surrender and Occupation of Japan*, February 11, 1946.

44. William Dixon, p. 29.

45. Savadkin, p. 14.

46. Savadkin, p. 14.

47. William Dixon, pp. 29–30.

48. Leon Devereaux, Ens., interview with the author, December 23, 2016.

49. Chapman, p. 10.

50. Richard W. De Mott, Lt., "Diary of Lt. jg. Richard W. De Mott," September 2, 1945.

51. De Mott.

BIBLIOGRAPHY

Published Works

Air Branch, Office of Naval Intelligence, Office of the Chief of Naval Operations. *Naval Aviation Combat Statistics: World War II*. Washington, DC: US Navy, 1946.

Aviation Cadet Regiment. *Slip Stream Mark, Volumes II–V*. Corpus Christi, TX: US Naval Training Center, 1942.

Aviation Training Division of the Chief of Naval Operations, United States Navy. *How to Survive on Land and Sea: Individual Survival*. Annapolis, MD: United States Naval Institute, 1943.

Baldwin, Ralph B. *The Deadly Fuze*. San Rafael, CA: Presidio, 1980.

Bell, Dana. *F4U-1 Corsair. Vol. 1*. Aircraft Pictorial 7. Tucson, AZ: Classic Warships, 2014.

———. *F4U-1 Corsair*. Vol. 2. Aircraft Pictorial 7. Tucson, AZ: Classic Warships, 2015.

Bender, Bryan. *You Are Not Forgotten: The Story of a Lost World War II Pilot and a Twenty-First-Century Soldier's Mission to Bring Him Home*. New York: Anchor, 2014.

Bergerud, Eric. *Fire in the Sky*. Boulder, CO: Westview, 2000.

Blackburn, Tom, and Eric Hammel. *The Jolly Rogers*. Pacifica, CA: Pacifica, 1997.

Blechman, Fred. *Bent Wings: F4U Corsair Action & Accidents; True Trials of Trial and Terror*. Bloomington, IN: Xlibris, 1999.

Boyington, Gregory. *Baa Baa Black Sheep*. New York: Bantam Books, 1958.

Bradley, James. *Flyboys: A True Story of Courage*. Boston: Little, Brown, 2003.

Breuer, William B. *The Spy Who Spent the War in Bed & Other Bizarre Tales from WWII*. Hoboken, NJ: John Wiley & Sons, 2003.

Brown, Eric "Winkle," Capt. *Wings of the Navy*. Crowborough, UK: Hikoki, 2013.

Brown, Ronald J., LYC, USMCR (Ret.). *Whirlybirds: US Marine Helicopters in Korea*. Marines in the Korean War Commemorative Series. CreateSpace, 2014.

Bullis, Richard, and Jack Melnick. *The History of United States Ship Waldron: Destroyer 699*. Self-published, 1991.

Cambon, Kenneth, MD. *Guest of Hirohito*. Vancouver, BC: PW Press, 1990.

Campbell, Douglas E. *BuNos!* Southern Pines, NC: Syneca, 2012.

———. *Save Our Souls: Rescues Made by U.S. Subs during WWII*. Southern Pines, NC: Syneca, 2016

———. *USN, USMC, & USCG Aircraft Lost during World War II*. 3 vols. Southern Pines, NC: Syneca, 2011.

———. *VP Navy! USN, USMC, USCG, and NATS Patrol Aircraft Lost or Damaged during World War II*. Southern Pines, NC: Syneca, 2018.

Cantrell, Bill. *Friends, Dear Friends, and Heroes*. Springfield, MO: Freebooter, 1997.

Carlson, Mark. *The Marines' Lost Squadron: The Odyssey of VMF-422*. Mechanicsburg, PA: Sunbury, 2017.

Caswell, Dean, Col., USMC (Ret). *Fighting Falcons: The Saga of Marine Fighter Squadron VMF 221*. Austin, TX: VMF 221 Foundation, 2004.

———. *Kamikaze Madness and Marine Fighter Pilots: A True Story of a Fighting Ship and Its Marine Fighter Pilots*. Austin, TX: Dean Caswell, 2017.

Caswell, Dean, Col., USMC (Ret.), and Lt. j.g. Jim Stanley, USN (Ret.). *My Taking Flight*. Austin, TX: Dean Caswell, 2010.

Chittenden, William H. *From China Marine to Jap POW: My 1,364 Day Journey through Hell*. Paducah, KY: Turner, 1995.

Condon, John. *Corsairs and Flattops: Marine Carrier Air Warfare, 1944–1945*. Annapolis, MD: Naval Institute Press, 1998.

Cook, Lee. *The Skull & Crossbones Squadron: VF-17 in World War II*. Atglen, PA: Schiffer, 1998.

Cox, Bryan. *Too Young to Die: The Story of a New Zealand Fighter Pilot in the Pacific War*. Ames: Iowa State University Press, 1987.

Craig, Berry. *Marine Corps Aviation Chronolog, 1912–1954*. Paducah, KY: Turner, 1989.

Daws, Gavan. *Prisoners of the Japanese: POWs of World War II in the Pacific*. New York: William Morrow, 1994.

DeBlanc, Jefferson. *The Guadalcanal Air War: Col. Jefferson DeBlanc's Story*. Gretna, LA: Pelican, 2008.

Dixon, Steven K. *Photo Recon Became Fighter Duty: Marine Observation Squadron 251 in WWII*. Jefferson, NC: McFarland, 2016.

Doll, Thomas. *Marine Fighting Squadron One-Twenty-One (VMF-121)*. Carrollton, TX: Squadron Signal, 1996.

Dommen, Arthur J. *The Indochinese Experience of the French and the Americans*. Bloomington: Indiana University Press, 2002.

Doyle, David. *F4U Corsair Walk Around*. Carrollton, TX: Squadron Signal, 2011.

Ellis, John. *World War II: The Encyclopedia of Facts & Figures*. New York: Military Book Club, 1995.

Faltum, Andrew. *The Essex Aircraft Carriers*. Charleston, SC: Nautical & Aviation Publishing, 1996.

Foster, John, Capt. *Hell in the Heavens*. New York: G. P. Putnam's Sons, 1961.

Galdorisi, George, and Tom Phillips. *Leave No Man Behind: The Saga of Combat Search and Rescue*. Minneapolis: Zenith, 2008.

Gamble, Bruce. *The Black Sheep: The Definitive Account of Marine Fighting Squadron 214 in World War II*. Novato, CA: Pacifica, 1998.

———. *Black Sheep One: The Life of Gregory "Pappy" Boyington*. Novato, CA: Presidio, 2000.

———. *Swashbucklers and Black Sheep*. Minneapolis: Zenith, 2012.

———. *Target Rabaul: The Allied Siege of Japan's Most Infamous Stronghold March, 1943–August 1945*. Minneapolis: Zenith, 2013.

Graff, Cory. *Clear the Deck*. North Branch, MN: Specialty Press, 2008.

Guyton, Boone. *Whistling Death*. Atglen, PA: Schiffer, 1994.

Hammel, Eric. *Air War Pacific Chronology: America's Air War against Japan in East Asia and the Pacific, 1941–1945*. Pacifica, CA: Pacifica, 1998.

Hanson, Norman, Lt. Cmdr., RN. *Carrier Pilot: An Unforgettable True Story of Wartime Flying*. Cambridge, UK: Patrick Stephens, 1979.

Harvey, Ralph. *Developing the Gull-Winged F4U—and Taking It to Sea*. Ralph Harvey, 2012.

Hobbs, David. *The British Pacific Fleet: The Royal Navy's Most Powerful Strike Force*. Annapolis, MD: Naval Institute Press, 2011.

Hoffman, Richard A. *The Fighting Flying Boat: A History of the Martin PBM Mariner*. Annapolis, MD: Naval Institute Press, 2004.

Iredale, Will. *The Kamikaze Hunters: Fighting for the Pacific, 1945*. London: Macmillan, 2015.

Irons, Martin. *Phalanx against the Divine Wind: Protecting the Fast Carrier Task Force during World War II*. Hoosick Falls, NY: Merriam, 2017.

Kammen, Michael G. *Operational History of the Flying Boat: Open Sea and Seadrome Aspects*. Vol. 2, *Atlantic Theatre, World War II*. Washington, DC: US Navy, Office of the Historian, Bureau of Naval Weapons, January 1959.

Kennedy, Maxwell Taylor. *Danger's Hour: The Story of the USS Bunker Hill and the Kamikaze Pilot Who Crippled Her*. New York: Simon & Schuster, 2008.

Kepchia, John B., ACRM, USN (Ret.). *MIA over Rabaul South Pacific*. Greensburg, PA: Palace Printer, 1958.

King, Ernest J., Fleet Adm., USN. *US Navy at War, 1941–1945: Official Reports to the Secretary of the Navy*. Washington, DC: US Navy, 1946.

Knott, Richard C. *Black Cat Raiders of World War II*. Charleston, SC: Nautical & Aviation Publishing, 1981.

Lardas, Mark. *Rabaul, 1943–44: Reducing Japan's Great Island Fortress (Air Campaign)*. New York: Osprey, 2018.

Lindbergh, Charles A. *The Wartime Journals of Charles A. Lindbergh*. New York: Harcourt Brace Jovanovich, 1970.

Lockwood, Charles A., Adm., USN (Ret.), and Col. Hans Christian Adamson, USAF (Ret.). *Zoomies, Subs, and Zeroes*. Philadelphia: Chilton, 1958.

Lord, Walter. *Lonely Vigil: Coastwatchers of the Solomons during World War II*. New York: Viking, 1977.

Lundquist, John B. *The First Team: Pacific Naval Air Combat from Pearl Harbor to Midway*. Annapolis, MD: Naval Institute Press, 1984.

Magnino, L. A. *Jim's Journey: A Civilian POW's Story*. Ashland, OR: Hellgate, 2001.

Marr, David G. *Vietnam 1945: The Quest for Power*. Berkeley: University of California Press, 1995.

Martindale, Robert R. *The 13th Mission: The Saga of a POW at Camp Omori, Tokyo*. Fort Worth, TX: Eakin, 1998.

McClurg, Robert, Lt. Col., and Leon Marketos. *On Boyington's Wing: The Wartime Journals of Black Sheep Squadron Fighter Ace Lt. Col. Robert W. McClurg*. Westminster, MD: Heritage Books, 2003.

Mersky, Peter B. *A History of Marine Fighter Attack Squadron 321*. Washington, DC: History and Museums Division, Headquarters, US Marine Corps, 1991.

Miller, Milt. *Tiger Tales*. Manhattan, KS: Sunflower University Press, 1984.

Monsarrat, John. *Angel on the Yardarm: The Beginnings of Fleet Radar Defense and the Kamikaze Threat*. Newport, RI: Naval War College Press, 1985.

Morison, Samuel Eliot. *Aleutians, Gilberts, and Marshalls: June 1942–April 1944*. History of United States Naval Operations in World War II 7. Boston: Little, Brown, 1951.

———. *Breaking the Bismarck Barrier, 22 July 1942–1 May 1944*. History of United States Naval Operations in World War II 6. Boston: Little, Brown, 1950.

———. *The Liberation of the Philippines: Luzon, Mindanao, the Visayas, 1944–1945*. History of United States Naval Operations in World War II 13. Boston: Little, Brown, 1959.

———. *The Struggle of Guadalcanal, August 1942–February 1943*. History of United States Naval Operations in World War II 5. Boston: Little, Brown, 1949.

———. *Supplement and General Index*. History of United States Naval Operations in World War II 15. Boston: Little, Brown, 1962.

———. *Victory in the Pacific, 1945*. History of United States Naval Operations in World War II 14. Boston: Little, Brown, 1960.

Morris, Jack G. *One Angel Left*. Santa Rosa, CA: Canyon Creek Books, 2001.

Naval Aeronautics, US Navy. *Grampaw Pettibone Looks at the Corsair: NAVAER 00-80R-21*. 2nd ed. Washington, DC: US Navy, 1948.

Navy Bomber-Fighting Squadron 85. *VBF-85 Cruise Book*. 1946.

O'Kane, Richard H., Adm., USN. *Clear the Bridge! The War Patrols of the U.S.S. Tang*. Novato, CA: Presidio, 1977.

Olynyk, Frank. *Stars and Bars: A Tribute to the American Fighter Ace, 1920–1973*. London: Grub Street, 2008.

Pappert, Edward. *Landing Was the Easy Part*. Bloomington, IN: 1stBooks, 2002.

Pisano, Dominick. *To Fill the Skies with Pilots: The Civilian Pilot Training Program, 1939–1946*. Champaign: University of Illinois Press, 1993.

Pons, Gregory. *USMC Aviators: Marine Corps Aviators in the Pacific, 1941–1945*. Morières, France: Eden Mili-Arts, 2012.

Popp, Wilbert P., LCDR, USNR (Ret.). *The Survival of a WWII Navy Fighter Pilot*. W. P. Popp, 2003.

Porch, Douglas. *The French Foreign Legion: A Complete History of the Legendary Fighting Force*. New York: Skyhorse, 2010.

Porter, R. Bruce, Col., and Eric Hammel. *Ace! A Marine Night Fighter Pilot in World War II*. Pacifica, CA: Pacifica, 1987.

Reynolds, Clark G. *The Fast Carriers: The Forging of an Air Navy*. Annapolis, MD: Naval Institute Press, 1992.

Reynolds, "Whiskey Bill." *Diary of a Lucky Leatherneck Throttle Jock*. New York: iUniverse, 2004.

Rielly, Robin. *Kamikazes, Corsairs, and Picket Ships: Okinawa, 1945*. Havertown, PA: Casemate, 2008.

Ross, John M. S. *Royal New Zealand Air Force*. Nashville: Battery, 1955.

Rottman, Gordon L. *US Marine Corps World War II Order of Battle: Ground and Air Units in the Pacific War, 1939–1945*. Westport, CT: Greenwood, 2002.

———. *World War II Pacific Island Guide: A Geo-military Study*. Westport, CT: Greenwood, 2002.

Sakaida, Henry. *The Siege of Rabaul*. St. Paul, MN: Phalanx, 1996.

Sakaida, Henry, and Koji Takaki. *Genda's Blade: Japan's Squadron of Aces; 343 Kokutai*. Hersham, UK: Classic Publications, 2003.

Scott, Jenny. *Dumbo Diary: Royal New Zealand Air Force No. 6 (Flying Boat) Squadron, 1943–1945*. Mitchell Park, Australia, J. Scott, 2012.

Sergent, Pierre. *Les maréchaux de la Légion: L'odyssée du 5e Étranger*. Paris: Fayard, 1980.

Sherman, Frederick C., Adm., USN (Ret.). *Combat Command: The American Aircraft Carriers in the Pacific War*. New York: E. P. Dutton, 1950.

Sherrod, Robert. *History of Marine Corps Aviation in World War II*. San Rafael, CA: Presidio, 1952.

Smith, Kearney. *Aboard LCS 11 in World War II: A Memoir by Lawrence B. Smith*. Bloomington, IN: Xlibris, 2011.

Smith, Peter C. *Task Force 57: The British Pacific Fleet, 1944–45*. London: William Kimber, 1969.

Somers, Paul M. *Lake Michigan's Aircraft Carriers*. Mt. Pleasant, SC: Arcadia, 2003.

Springer, Joseph A. *Inferno: The Epic Life and Death Struggle of the USS Franklin in World War II*. Minneapolis: Zenith, 2007.

Sweet, Donald H., Lee Roy Way, and William Bonvillian. *The Forgotten Heroes: The Story of Rescue Squadron VH-3 in World War II*. Ridgewood, NJ: DoGo, 2000.

Thomas, Gerald W. *Torpedo Squadron Four: A Cockpit View of World War II*. Las Cruces, NM: Doc 45, 2011.

Tillman, Barrett. *Corsair: The F4U in World War II and Korea*. Annapolis, MD: Naval Institute Press, 1979.

———. *US Marine Corps Fighter Squadrons of World War II*. New York: Osprey, 2014.

———. *US Navy Squadrons in World War II*. North Branch, MN: Specialty Press, 1997.

———. *Vought F4U Corsair*. Warbird Tech 4. North Branch, MN: Specialty Press, 1996.

Tomlinson, Thomas M. *The Threadbare Buzzard*. St. Paul, MN: Zenith, 2004.

Training Division, Bureau of Aeronautics, US Navy. *Dunking Sense*. Washington, DC: US Government Printing Office, 1943.

———. *Flat-Hatting Sense*. Washington, DC: US Government Printing Office, 1943.

———. *Flight thru Instruments*. Washington, DC: US Government Printing Office, 1943.

———. *Parachute Sense*. Washington, DC: US Government Printing Office, 1943.

Udoff, Irv. *The Bunker Hill Story*. Paducah, KY: Turner, 1997.

Veesenmeyer, Jeffrey R. *Kamikaze Terror*. Cambridge, WI: Jeffrey, 2017.

Vukovits, John F. *The Life of Pappy Boyington*. Annapolis, MD: Naval Institute Press, 2011.

Walton, Frank E. *Once They Were Eagles*. Lexington: University Press of Kentucky, 1986.

Warner, Jeff. *US Naval Aviation Flying Clothing and Gear*. Atglen, PA: Schiffer, 2007.

Webber, Bert. *Retaliation: Japanese Attacks and Allied Countermeasures on the Pacific Coast in World War II*. Corvallis: Oregon State University Press, 1975.

Weiland, Charles Patrick. *Above & Beyond*. Pacifica, CA: Pacifica, 1997.

Wichtrich, A. R., Lt. Col. *MIS-X Top Secret*. Raleigh, NC: Pentland, 1997.

Wolf, William. *Death Rattlers: Marine Squadron VMF-323 over Okinawa*. Atglen, PA: Schiffer, 1999.

Zamperini, Louis. *Devil at My Heels: A Heroic Olympian's Astonishing Survival as a Japanese POW in World War II*. New York: Harper, 2003.

Newspapers

Associated Press. "Former Mandan Man Rescues Flier at Sea." *Bismarck Tribune*, May 16, 1944.

"Beaten with Bats," *Brooklyn Eagle*, September 24, 1945.

Christy, David. "Black Sheep? Squad Vet Bahs." *Sacramento Bee*, June 20, 1977.

"Credited as the First Yank to 'Invade' Japan." *Chicago Tribune,* September 23, 1945.

Ditler, Joe. "Coronado's 'Avenue of the Heroes'. . . Commander Stan Abele, USN." *Coronado Eagle & Journal*, March 8, 2017.

———. "WWII Veteran Shares Stories with Visitors aboard The USS Midway." *Eagle & Times*, October 11, 2012.

Hampson, Fred. "Boyington Last Seen Diving to Attack." *New York Daily News*, January 9, 1944.

"How Japs Carved Up Boyington without Giving an Anesthetic." *New York Daily News*, September 24, 1945.

Humes, Edward. "Ken Walsh: Ex-Flier Credits Decoration to Experience, Luck." *Orange County Register*, November 8, 1987.

Johnson, Vic, TSgt. "Captive." *The Flyer* (Langley AFB), March 5, 1993.

Johnston, George H. "When the Legion Retreated: A Dramatic but Tragic Story of the French Revolt against Japanese Domination in Indo-China This Year; Part I." *The Argus* (Melbourne, Australia), July 28, 1945.

———. "When the Legion Retreated: A Dramatic but Tragic Story of the French Revolt against Japanese Domination in Indo-China This Year; Part II." *The Argus* (Melbourne, Australia), August 4, 1945.

O'Neill, Bill, Sgt. "He Quadruples in 'Brass': Marine Reserve Flier Holds Many Positions." *Oregon Journal*, October 6, 1957.

Rice, Theron J., S/Sgt. "Wounded Corsair Pilot, Son of Employe [*sic*], Made 'Miracle Landing.'" *Marine Corps Chevron*, 1945.

Trumbull, Robert. "Zamperini, Olympic Miler, Is Safe after Epic Survival." *New York Times*, September 9, 1945.

"Unaware of Airstrip, Crash-Lands Plane." *St. Louis Globe-Democrat*, July 30, 1945.

United Press. "US Flier Blasts His 25th Jap Plane, Nears Record." *Salt Lake Tribune*, December 29, 1943.

"Vicksburg Flier Sensed Fate of Flame-Swept Bunker Hill." *Commercial Appeal*, June 28, 1945.

Magazines

Gallico, Paul. "The Pilot Who Kept on Fighting." *Esquire*, December 1943.

"Grampaw Pettibone: He Robbed Himself." *Naval Aviation News*, September 1, 1945.

Guttman, Jon. "Ace in a Day." *Aviation History*, July 2007.

"In & around the Trade." *Radio Service Dealer*, February 1946.

Jacob, Jan, and Barrett Tillman. "The Wolf Gang: A History of CVG 84." *The Hook*, August 1990.

Mickelsen, Martin L. "A Mission of Vengeance: Vichy French in Indochina in World War II." *Air Power History*, Fall 2008.

"'Pappy' Boyington Comes Home." *Life*, October 1, 1945.

Scott, J. Davis. "Jap Bait." *Flying*, July 1948.

Scott, J. Davis, Cmdr. "No Hiding Place—off Okinawa." *Proceedings* 83, no. 11 (November 1957).

Syrkin, Mark W., Major, USMCR (Ret.) "Marine Fighter Squadron 422 Is Missing." *Air Classics Magazine*, August 1976.

Woolard, Annette. "A Soldier's Story: Edmund Carpenter II, Air-Ground Aid Section, 14th Air Force." *Delaware History*, Spring–Summer 1994.

Articles

Fukubayashi, Toru. "POW Camps in Japan Proper." Japan, December 2004.

Takeuchi, Shigeru. "A Study of POW Camps in Niigata Prefecture." Niigata, Japan: Niigata University of International and Information Studies, 2005.

———. "Chance Vought/LTV History." Special Collections, Library of the University of Texas at Dallas. www.utdallas.edu/libary/specialcollections/has/vought/history.pdf (accessed September 5, 2019).

Unpublished Works and Private Collections

Blackstock, John A., 1Lt. "VMF-218 Memories." 1945.

Brewer, George. "Hanson's Last Flight." June 8, 1994.

Chapman, John, Ens. "Personal History." Memoirs, March 2004.

Coumbe, Vernon T., Lt. Cmdr., USNR. Untitled collection containing the subject's personal papers.

De Mott, Richard W., Lt. "Diary of Lt. jg. Richard W. De Mott." 1945.

Dixon, James Cass, Lt. j.g., USNR. "The Personal Papers of Lt. jg. James Cass Dixon." Untitled collection of the subject's photos, personal correspondence, and service-related records, ca. 1942–1946.

Dixon, William, 2Lt. Personal memoirs, chapter 5. www.mansell.com/pow_resources/camplists/tokyo/omori/omori.html (accessed January 23, 2019).

Enders, Robert A., 2nd Lt. "Personal Statement of 2nd Lt. Robert A. Enders." 1944.

Langston, Earl W., Maj., USMCR (Ret.). "A Time for Miracles."

Lynch, Joseph O., Maj., USMC (Ret.). Untitled collection of the subject's photos, personal correspondence, and service-related records, ca. 1943–1963. Courtesy of the Lynch family.

Maitland, Alan, S/LT, RN. "Diary of 1841 Squadron: From 1 Mar 44 to 23 Jul 45." 1945.

Mickelsen, Martin. Unpublished Manuscript. Undated.

Moranville, H. Blake, Lt. Cmdr., USN (Ret.). "My Indochina Odyssey."

Oliver, Almon P., Cmdr., USN (Ret.). The Almon Oliver Collection of the Battleship *North Carolina*.

Overbeck, Ann Styles. "Recollections of War: Aboard the USS *Sea Devil* SS 400."

Sagers, Harold M., 2Lt. Unpublished account of being lost at sea. Undated.

Wallace, Glen. "Wally's War: Glen Wallace's War Diary 2, Kilroy Was Here; Remembering the War Years. 2010. Archived website, retrieved from the Library of Congress. los.gov/item/00096726/.

Wilson, Bob, and Sunny Wilson. "Memoirs of Sunny and Bob Wilson." 1988.

Recorded Interviews/Transcripts

Jean Balch, interview by William J. Alexander, National Museum of the Pacific War: Admiral Nimitz Museum and University of North Texas Oral History Collection, October 12, 1996.

Vice Adm. Gerald F. Bogan, "The Reminiscences of Vice Adm. Gerald F. Bogan, USN (Ret.)," interview by Cmdr. Etta-Belle Kitchen, USN (Ret.), US Naval Institute Press, 1970.

Henry "Hank" Bourgeois, "Becoming a Marine Aviator and Deployment to Guadalcanal," oral history, National World War II Museum, 2015. https://ww2online.org/view/henry-hank/bourgeois#becoming-a-marine-aviator-and-deployment-to-guadalcanal (accessed February 18, 2018).

Edmund N. Carpenter II, "Edmund N. Carpenter II," interview by Brandon Bies, Fort Hunt Oral History Project, May 8, 2008. https://nps.gov/museum/FOHU_oral_history/Edmund_Carpenter.html (accessed February 23, 2020).

Lt. Donald T. Chute, "Oral History," interview by Conrad Wood, Imperial War Museum, April 27, 1990. http://iwm.org.uk/collections/item/object/80011050 (accessed November 9, 2018).

Robert Gallup, "P. O. Box 1142," interview by David Lassman and Vincent Santucci, Fort Hunt Oral History, September 27, 2010.

Col. Rolland Rinabarger, "Capt. Rolland Rinabarger," interview by Col. Frank E. Walton, Collection of Frank Walton, VMF-214, National Naval Aviation Museum, April 16, 1982.

Captain Ralph E. Styles, "Oral History," interview by Lucian L. Vestal and Vice Adm. Earl Fowler, USN, Naval Historical Foundation, September 25–October 30, 2001.

Wesley S. Todd, USMC, "Oral History," interview by Mark Van Ells, Wisconsin Veterans Museum Research Center, 1996.

Rear Adm. Joseph C. Wylie Jr., "The Reminiscences of Rear Adm. Joseph C. Wylie Jr., USN (Ret.)," interview by Paul Stillwell, US Naval Institute Press, 2003.

Multimedia

Davies, John. *Heroes on Deck: World War II on Lake Michigan*. DVD. Chicago: Brian Kallies Productions, 2016.

Dodge, Terry. *Blue Devils: Marine Aviation Squadron VMF-451*, DVD. Berrien Springs, MI: TLD Productions, 2008.

Sykes, James T. *Overseas with a Marine Corsair, 1944*. YouTube video, 2012. https://youtube/wHh16f8nVY.

Blogs

RNZAF Proboard.

Sakaida, Henry. "Handsome Harry Sasaki: Japanese Interrogator of 'Pappy' Boyington." *A War to Be Won*, posted October 24, 2016.

Sakaida, Henry. "Unknown American Pilot Now Identified." *A War to Be Won*, posted February 7, 2018.

Wellerstein, Alex. "Neglected Niigata." *The Nuclear Secrecy Blog*, posted October 9, 2015.

Websites

118th Tactical Reconnaissance Squadron. "Hell of Ofuna—Max L. Parnell with Wayne G. Johnson." www.118trs.com/squadron-roster/max-parnell/hell-of-ofuna.com (accessed January 25, 2018).

14 USAAF 27 Troop Carrier Squadron. "Rescued in Enemy Territory to Fly Again." www.14usaaf27tcs.4mg.com/Rescuedtofly.htm (accessed May 2, 2017).

Aviation Archaeology. www.aviationarchaeology.com.

The Center for Research: Allied POWs under the Japanese. www.mansell.com.

Connecticut Air & Space Center. www.ctairandspace.org.

Connecticut Corsair. www.connecticutcorsair.com.

Daninthecbi.com: A Tribute to Frederic N. Hernandez. "From the Collection of 2nd Lt. Frank D. Padgett, Co-Pilot, 373rd Bomb Squad." www.daninthecbi.com/padgett.html (accessed January 28, 2018).

Flying Leatherneck Aviation Museum. www.flyingleatherneck.org.

Fold3. www.fold3.com.

Imperial Japanese Navy Page. www.combinedfleet.com.

Naval War in Pacific 1941–1945. www.pacific.walka.cz.

Navsource Naval History: Photographic History of the US Navy. www.navsource.org.

Newspapers.com. www.newspapers.com.

Pacifc Wrecks. www.pacificwrecks.com.

Saigoneer: Icons of Old Saigon; The Maison Centrale de Saigon. www.saigoneer.com.

USS Bennington CV-20/CVA-20/CVS-20: Her History and Her Crew, February 26, 1944—December 7, 1994. "Chronological Narrative and History of Marine Fighting Squadron VMF-123 (1942-1945): Air Groups." www.uss-bennington.org (accessed February 29, 2016).

USS Yorktown. "Yorktown Aviator: My Experience as Prisoner of War by the Imperial Japanese (Jean Balch)." www.yorktownsailor.com/yorktown/pow.htm (accessed March 21, 2012).

VBF-85. www.bf-85.com.

VMF-213. www.vmf-213.com.

VMF-216. www.vmf216.com.

VMF-222. www.thefortynineteens.com.

The Warbird's Forum. "The Unlucky Prisoners of Rabaul." www.warbirdfoum.com (accessed June 26, 2019).

Wiki. www.wikipedia.org.

World War II—Dogfights, Bombers and Warbirds. www.facebook.com/Air.War.Timeline.

INDEX

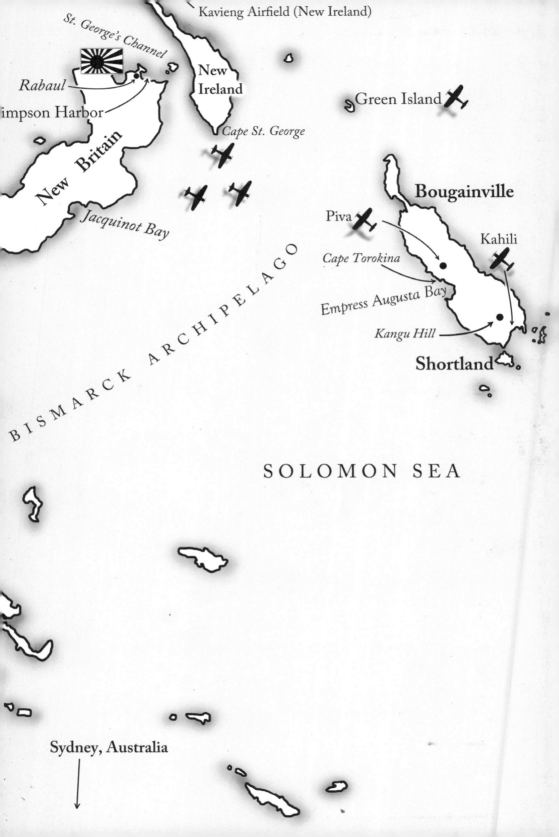

Kavieng Airfield (New Ireland)

St. George's Channel

Rabaul

impson Harbor

New Britain

Jacquinot Bay

New Ireland

Cape St. George

BISMARCK ARCHIPELAGO

SOLOMON SEA

Sydney, Australia

Green Island

Bougainville

Piva

Kahili

Cape Torokina

Empress Augusta Bay

Kangu Hill

Shortland